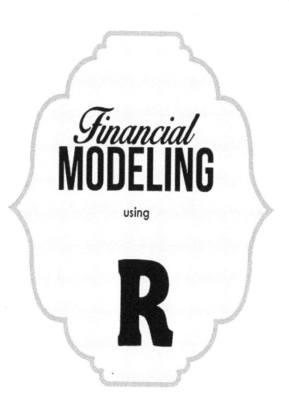

Financial
MODELING

using

R

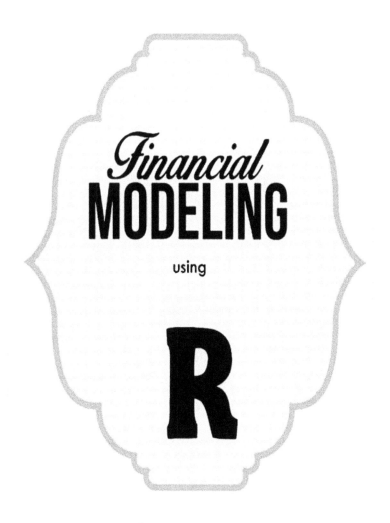

Financial
MODELING
using

R

YUXING YAN

LEGAIA
BOOKS

Legaia Books™
555 Fayetteville Street
Suite 201 Raleigh, NC 27601
www.legaiabooks.com
info@legaiabooks.com
Phone: (704) 216-4194

Financial Modeling using R
Yuxing Yan

Published by Legaia Books & Yuxing Yan 7/10/2017

ISBN: 978-1-946946-45-4 (sc)

To my parents

ACKNOWLEDGMENTS

I would like to thank Ben Amoako-Adu, Brian Smith (who taught me the first two finance courses and offered unstinting support for many years after my graduation), George Athanassakos (one of his assignments "forced" me to learn C), Jin-Chun Duan, Wei-Hung Mao, Jerome Detemple, Bill Sealey, Chris Jacobs, Mo Chaudhury (my former professors at McGill), and Lawrence Kryzanowski (his wonderful teaching inspired me to concentrate on empirical finance).

There is no doubt that my experience at Wharton has shaped my thinking and enhanced my skill sets. I thank Chris Schull and Michael Boldin for offering me the job; Mark Keintz, Dong Xu, Steven Crispi, and Dave Robinson who helped me greatly during my first two years at Wharton; and Eric Zhu, Paul Ratnaraj, Premal Vora, Shuguang Zhang, Michelle Duan, Nicholle Mcniece, Russ Ney, Robin Nussbaum- Gold, and Mireia Gine for all their help.

In addition, I'd like to thank Shaobo Ji, Tong Yu, Shaoming Huang, Xing Zhang, Changwen Miao, Karyl Leggio, Lisa Fairchild, K. G. Viswanathan, Na Wang, Mark Lennon, Daniel Folkinshteyn, and Qiyu Zhang for helping me in many ways. I also want to thank Shaojun Zhang and Qian Sun, my former colleagues and coauthors on several papers, for their valuable input and discussions. Particularly, I'd like to thank Yan, Yuming (my brother) and Wang, Yan (my sister-in-law) for helping and supporting our parents in China.

In terms of this book, I really want to thank my students, especially students at Loyola University Maryland when I introduced R to several financial-modeling courses the very first time. The inputs from students at Loyola University Maryland, University at Buffalo, and Canisius College have improved the quality of this book greatly. I thank Jeffery Gao for reviewing several chapters of the first draft of the book, James Yan for helping me generate several high-resolution images, and R Foundation for giving me the permission to use the R logo.

Finally and most importantly, I thank my wife, Xiaoning Jin, for her strong support; my daughter, Jing Yan; and son, James Yan—for the understanding and love they have showered me over the years.

CONTENTS

TABLES

Preface

After eight years working as a consultant at Wharton School, I returned to teaching in 2010.[1] One of my first teaching assignments was financial modeling to MSF students. I had taught this course many times at Nanyang Technical University in Singapore. Like most instructors, the computational tool I adopted was Excel. However, this time, I decided to teach R instead. The major reason is rooted in my firm belief that an ambitious finance-major student should grasp at least one computer language. Among many good candidates, R is one of the best. After that course, I taught several slightly different courses by using R— four more times at Loyola, once at Canisius College, and twice at University at Buffalo. This book is based on my lecture notes for those courses.

Vision. This book will be an ideal textbook for many quantitative courses such as (next generation) financial modeling, portfolio theory, empirical research in finance, computational finance, and risk management. The book discusses three unique characteristics of R: 1) it is free software, 2) it has the ability to download and process big data, and 3) it uses publicly available financial information.

Free software. R is free and powerful. It is a perfect match between R and financial modeling. Another added advantage of using R is that after learning R, it becomes trivial to understand S-plus, a popular language used extensively in Wall Street. R is way too powerful than Excel, which is used almost exclusively by virtually all current textbooks designed for financial-modeling courses.

Big data. When using Excel, it is difficult to imagine downloading and processing historical daily trading data for twenty stocks, let alone one hundred or more. Using R, we could easily download and process data for any number of stocks. Emerson and Kane (2012) demonstrate that R could process data as big as 250G.

Public data. In an information era, it would be a shame for our instructors not to use rich public information such as Yahoo!Finance, Google Finance, Professor French's data library, Federal Reserve Bank's data library, and the United States Census Bureau for our teaching and research. In this book, I offer several hundred simple/small programs to download and process public data. For example, using Beta("IBM", 1990), we estimate a beta for IBM in 1990. By issuing getIncomeStatement("DELL"), we download and save the latest several years' income statements for DELL.

To-the-point approach. Unlike most textbooks that use a systematic approach to teach programming, this book applies a to-the-point approach. For example, when I discuss the Black-Scholes-Merton option model in chapter 3, within thirty minutes of reading the first page, students can learn how to write R codes to price a standard European call option.

---

[1] I thank Karyl Leggion for offering me a teaching position at Loyola University Maryland.

Audience. This book can cater to 1) graduate students from financial-engineering programs, 2) MBA/MSF (master of science in finance) students, 3) senior undergraduates majoring in finance, 4) practitioners in Wall Street.

No need for prior knowledge related to R. This book doesn't require a learner to have any prior knowledge related to R. However, readers at different levels should adopt different approaches. If a student has taken two finance courses already, he/she could skip subsections related to basic finance concepts and theory and go directly to subsections related to R.

Basic finance knowledge. Readers have ideally taken at least one finance course such as corporate finance or financial management or have worked in the finance industry for a minimum of two years. Ideal readers are those who have taken both corporate finance and portfolio theory.

Small programs. Another feature of the book is that it offers hundreds of small programs with just one or a few lines. For example, we use a one-line R program to download daily trading data for IBM from 1962 to today from Yahoo!Finance. To download the last three years' balance sheets for DELL, the program has two lines. By offering so many small programs, I could hopefully take intimidation out of programming.

Fun. When programming becomes less intimidating because of so many one-line or two-line programs, a beginner would start to enjoy programming. When teaching the DuPont identity, which decomposes ROE (Return on Equity) into three different ratios, for financial statement analysis, I asked my students how long they could calculate the DuPont identity after I offered them a ticker symbol such as IBM or WMT. I really impressed them when I showed them that I could do it in two seconds.

Reference book. Learners could use this book as a reference. For example, after a person has studied this book, he/she could put all his/her programs into just one text file. He/she could call related programs or codes quickly using just one line of R codes.

Thirty minutes or less. The first page of each chapter plays a big role to attempt to inspire a potential learner. A typical learner is expected to take less than thrity minutes to grasp basic concepts. Here is a typical example. After reading the first page of chapter 3 (options theory), a reader who has no clue about option theory should be able to write five-line codes to price a European call option.

A job interview. Let me use a hypothetical scenario to conclude. One of my students went to a job interview with a major investment bank in Wall Street. She was given one hour with an empty Internetconnected computer. Within one hour, she installed R, uploaded one text file, checked some of her 120 programs included in that text file, and downloaded and processed trading and accounting information for a hundred stocks. After that, she answered all types of questions: What is the IBM's beta in 2009? If holding 100 shares of IBM, 200 shares of DELL, plus 300 shares of Walmart, what is VaR today if the confidence level is 99% with a ten-day holding period? How is the annual volatility from daily price data calculated? What is the annual volatility for DELL last year? For a given 10 stocks, how do you construct a set of optimal portfolios? What is the related efficient frontier?

Technical support. Despite many advantages of using R compared with other more expensive languages, one of its shortcomings is its lack of technical support.

It is understandable since we really cannot be too picky when we are offered a free lunch. In this regard, I will try my best to offer my support to my readers or those who apply R to finance. Over the past five years, I have answered several hundred questions related to applying R to finance from my students in Loyola University, Buffalo University, and Canisius College. In addition, I have answered about a hundred questions related to Python (after I published my book titled *Python for Finance* in 2014). From 2003 to 2010, working at Wharton School, I had answered over a thousand questions related to SAS, MATLAB, and occasionally, Fortran and C. My email address is yuxing. yan@canisius.edu.

For this book, I generated a web page that includes many useful materials such as the table of contents page of this book, cover page, (future) errata, several free books, R conferences, and others: http://canisius.edu/~yany/R.shtml. Another idea is to form a small group with volunteers to help one another. If you are interested, please send me an e-mail.

ABOUT THE AUTHOR

Dr. Yuxing Yan graduated from McGill University with a PhD in finance. Since then, he has been teaching various finance courses at eight universities: McGill University, Wilfrid Laurier University (both in Canada), Nanyang Technical University (in Singapore), Loyola University Maryland, Hofstra University, Univeristy of Maryland University College, University at Buffalo, and Canisius College (all five in the United States). He is active in doing research with twenty publications. Some papers are coauthored. His research has been published in the *Journal of Accounting and Finance, Journal of Banking and Finance, Journal of Empirical Finance, The Real Estate Review, Pacific-Basin Finance Journal, Applied Financial Economics, and Annals of Operations Research.* He is good at several computer languages such as SAS, C, MATLAB, R and Python. At Wharton Research Data Services (WRDS), he has debugged over several hundred programs for the WRDS' users. In 2014, he published a book titled *Python for Finance*, published by Packt Publishing. The second edition was published in 2017. In addition, the Chinese version (based on the first edition) and Korean version (based on the second edition) were published in 2017 as well.

Currently, they (his co-author and he) are writing a new book titled "Hands-on Data Science with Anaconda" which is expected to be published in late 2018. There are three 80 percents and 20 percents: 80 percent for teaching schools, 20 percent for research schools; 80 percent based on public data, 20 percent based on expensive financial databases and 80 percent for the beginners and 20 percent for the experienced programmers. The definition of *teaching school* is very simple: no SAS (computer language) nor CRSP (famous financial database). Thus, my school, Canisius College, is a teaching school while the Wharton School is a research school.

CHAPTER 1

R Basics and Finance 101

In this chapter, we offer a brief introduction to R such as how to install the software, how to launch and quit R, whether R is case sensitive, and how to assign a value to a variable. In a sense, we assume that the reader, especially finance-major students, knows nothing about the wonderful software. In addition, we go through the basic formulae when a student takes corporate finance or Finance 101.

1.1. How to Download and Install R

To install R, we have to do the following five steps:

1. Go to http://www.r-project.org
2. Click **CRAN** under **Download** (left-hand side).
3. Choose a mirror address.
4. Choose appropriate PC software (Mac or Windows).
5. Click **base**.

After you have finished installation, an R icon will appear on your desktop.

1.2. How to Launch R and Quit R

To start R, double click the R icon on your desktop.

To quit, just type **q()** from the R prompt >. Anything after symbol # is a comment.

```
> q() # first way to quit
# this is a comment line
# > is the R prompt
```

When quitting, the program will ask you whether to "Save the workspace image," which means to keep all your variables or functions for future usage. At this stage, just answer no.

See below for another way to quit.

```
# [click] "file" on the menu bar - - > "exit"
```

To quit R without saving, we use **q("no")** command.

```
> q("no") # quit R without saving variables and functions
> q("yes") # quit R and keep variables and functions
```

1.3. R Basic Concepts and Functions

To assign a value to a variable, we use <-, =, or ->.

```
> x<-10 # assign 10 to x
> y=20 # assign 20 to y
> 30 ->z # assign 30 to z
> title<-"Hello" # title is a character (string) variable
```

To show the value of a variable, simply type its name.

```
> x
[1] 10
```

In R, we don't need to define a variable before using it.

```
# a variable is not formally defined before its assignment
> fv<-100
```

R is case sensitive, which means that capital X and lowercase x are different variables.

```
> x<-10
> X
Error: object 'X' not found
```

To put several R commands on one line, semicolons are used.

```
# semi-colon (;) can be used to separate different lines
> fv<-10; pv<-100; n<-10; rate<-0.05
```

To assign values to a vector, we use the c() function, where c means "column."

```
# assign values to a vector
> x<-c(1,2.5,3.4,6.2)
```

If the increment value is 1, we could use n1:n2.

```
> y<-1:50 # assign 1, 2, 3, . . ., 50 to y (y is a vector)
```

We could reverse the order.

```
> z<-10:1 # assign 10,9, 8, . . ., 1 to z (z is a vector)
```

Try the following codes and print x to see the result.

```
> x<-1.5 :10
```

1.4. List Function and Remove Function

Sometimes we need to check all existing variables (objects). For this reason, we use the **ls()** function.

```
> ls()
```

When a variable is no longer needed, we could remove it from the memory.

```
> rm(x) # remove variable called x
```

To remove several variables (objects) simultaneously, we use a comma to separate them.

```
> rm(x,y,pv) # remove x, y and pv
```

To remove all variables (objects), we have the codes below.

```
>rm(list=ls()) # remove all variables (objects)
```

The second way to remove all objects (variables) is given below.

```
# [click] "Misc" - - > "Remove all objects…"
```

To print a character variable (a string) on the screen, we could use the cat() or the print() functions. Remember to put our sentences in double or single quotation marks.

```
> cat("hello, world!\n\n\n") #\n is for a new line
hello, world!
>
```

The **print()** function could be used instead.

```
> print('hello R!')
[1] "hello R!"
```

Note that **\n** is not a working equivalent for the **print()** function.

```
> print('hello world\n')
[1] "hello world\n"
```

We could also print a defined variable.

```
> x<-'this is great'
> print(x)
[1] "this is great"
```

1.5. Next-Line Symbol (+) and Go Back to the R Prompt

When one command occupies multiple lines, the symbol + will appear. Assume that we intend to assign 1 to 10 to x.

```
> x<-1:10 # assign 1,2,… 10 to x
```

For some reasons, we hit the **Enter** key before we finish the whole command, as shown below. In other words, we use several lines to finish the command.

```
> x<-1: # we accidently hit the enter key
+ 10 # continue typing the rest of your command
>
```

Often, especially for a beginner, we type a few wrong keys, such as a double or single quotation mark without its pair. Sometimes we simply don't want to figure out where the issue is since it might be too time-consuming. Instead we just want to go back to the R prompt and retype the command. In those cases, we hit the **Esc** key at top left of our keyboard to return to the R prompt (>).

```
> x<-'9" (999asdfklj
+ > # use 'Esc' to come back to the R prompt
```

1.6. Finding Help

There exist several ways to find information for a specific R function. If we are interested in the mean function, we can issue **?mean, help(mean)**, or **example(mean)**.

```
>?mean # find information related to the function
```

The command **help(mean)** achieves the same goal as **?mean**.

```
> help(mean) # same as ?mean
```

To get examples for a specific function, we use the **example()** function.

```
> example(mean) # get examples related to the function
```

We can also use the **Help** on the menu bar.

```
# [click] "Help" - -> "FAQ on R"
```

The following picture shows all the entries after clicking **Help** on the menu bar.

```
Help
       Console
       FAQ on R
       FAQ on R for Windows
       Manuals (in PDF)
       R functions (text) ...
       Html help
       Search help ...
       search.r-project.org...
       Apropos...
       R Project home page
       CRAN home page
       About
```

When unsure of the spelling of the function in question, we use the apropos() function.

```
> apropos("mean")
[1] ".colMeans" ".rowMeans" "colMeans" "kmeans"
[5] "mean" "mean.Date" "mean.default" "mean.difftime"
[9] "mean.POSIXct" "mean.POSIXlt" "rowMeans" "weighted.mean"
```

To start (end) with a phrase, we use ^ ($), such as apropos("^col") and apropos("col$"). In addition, to show all functions with a length of 3, we issue apropos("^.{3}$").

1.7. Using R as a Calculator

R can be used as a calculator since it is straightforward to call various embedded R functions. For example, the **mean()** function is for average.

```
> x<-1:50
> mean(x)
[1] 25.5
```

You can try other functions as well, such as **max()**, **min()**, **median()**, **sd()**, and **var()**.

```
> x<-1:50
> max(x)
[1] 50
> min(x)
[1] 1
> median(x)
[1] 25.5
> sd(x)
[1] 14.57738
```

1.8. Using Arrow Keys to Recall the Previous Commands

To recall the previous command and modify it, we use up arrow key.

```
> x<-1:500
> y<-10:510
```

After a set of commands lines have been issued, we can use both the up and down arrow keys to move back and forth to recall and correct the old commands. This is extremely convenient for checking and modifying our codes since we can recall the previous command with a new input or a minor modification.

```
# use upper or down arrow keys to recall previous commands
```

1.9. A General Formula for Finance 101

Let's look at the following summation (S). The first value is 1/2. The next value is the half of the previous one.

$$S = \frac{1}{2} + \frac{1}{4} + \frac{1}{8} + \frac{1}{16} + \cdots$$

If you draw a square and shade half then shade a quarter then one-eighth and so on, eventually you will fill the entire square (i.e., the final shaded area will be 1). For such a summation, we have a simple formula.

Equation 1

$$\begin{cases} S = a_1 + a_1 q + q_1 q^2 + a_1 q^3 + \dots \\ S = \dfrac{a_1}{1-q} \qquad where\ q < 1 \end{cases}$$

For the above case, we could double check our original guess:

$$\frac{\frac{1}{2}}{1 - \frac{1}{2}} = \frac{0.5}{0.5} = 1$$

Equation 1 could be used to derive and explain the present-value formulae for perpetuity, where the same cash flows occur at the same interval forever and, for annuity, where the same cash flows happen for n periods.

1.10. Time Value of Money

It is common knowledge that $100 today is more valuable than $100 in two years since we could deposit this $100 in a bank for two years to earn extra money. The difference between what we will receive in two years and today's $100 is the interest we earn. In this chapter, we focus on three important concepts: equivalency, benchmark of present value, and discount rate.

Equivalency. If you expect a check of $100 in one year, how much are you willing to accept today? The amount you choose will be your equivalent value today. Assume that you will be glad to receive $90 today. This implies that $90 today is equivalent to $100 in a year. When looking at cash flows happening at different points in time, we try to apply this concept of equivalency to compare them.

Benchmark of present value. Obviously we could have many equivalent amounts at different points in time. For instance, we have two future cash flows of $100 in one year and $125 in two years. Which cash flow is more valuable for us? According to the concept of equivalency, we could find the equivalent amount of $125 in one year and compare it with $100. Because of equivalency, the verdict will be the same even if we choose a different benchmark. Nevertheless, we usually choose present value as our benchmark (find today's values of those two future values and compare them).

Discount rate. For a given future cash flow, we apply a discount rate to estimate its equivalent present value. At the moment, we treat the discount rate and the interest rate as equivalents. A more advanced definition of *discount rate* is it should be "the summation of the risk-free interest rate plus a risk premium associated with the risk level of a project under consideration." For different discount rates (e.g., 10% and 8%), we have different equivalent PVs, as shown below.

```
> 100/(1+0.1)^2
 [1] 82.64463
> 100/(1+0.08)^2
 [1] 85.73388
```

1.11. Review of Basic Finance Formulae

Time value of money means that the same cash flow happening at different points in time would have different present values.

Equation 2

$$PV = \frac{FV}{(1+R)^n} \quad ,$$

where
PV is present value,
FV is future value,
R is the cost of capital (discount rate),
and *n* is the number of periods.

Later we will show that it is a good idea to interpret R as an effective period rate. For example, we are supposed to receive a $5 payment in two years. Assume that the interest rate (discount rate) is 10% per year. What is the present value? By using equation 2, we have

$$\frac{5}{(1 + 0.1)^2} = 4.13$$

This means that the equivalent amount today is $4.13. Based on the concept of equivalency, from equation 2, we could easily derive the expression for a future value:

Equation 3

$$FV = PV \, (1 + R)^n$$

Perpetuity

If we will receive a fixed amount at the end of each period forever and the first cash inflow occurs at the end of the first period, it is called perpetuity. The timeline is given below.

```
  c          c            c            c          c              c              c
|-----------|-------------|-------------|  ..... |---------------|  ... .......
T 0        T 1          T 2          T 3       T n          T n+1              T ∞
```

The present value of perpetuity will be the summation of all the discounted future cash flows.

$$PV(perpetuity) = \frac{c}{(1+R)^1} + \frac{c}{(1+R)^2} + \frac{c}{(1+R)^3} + \cdots.$$

Actually, the above pattern is the same as the following standard form with

$$a_1 = c / (1+R) \text{ and } q = 1 / (1+R)$$

$$S = a_1 + a_1 q + q_1 q^2 + a_1 q^3 + \ldots$$

Since we know that **R>0, q=1/(1+R)** must be less than 1. According to equation 1, we have the following:

$$S = \frac{a_1}{1-q} = \frac{\frac{c}{1+R}}{1 - \frac{1}{1+R}} = c/R$$

Thus, the present value of perpetuity is

Equation 4

$$PV(perpetuity) = \frac{c}{R},$$

where c is the cash flow at the end of each period with the first cash flow occurring at the end of the first period.

Perpetuity Due

If the first cash flow occurs today instead of at the end of the first period (see its cash-flows blow), the perpetuity is called perpetuity due.

```
     c          c          c          c        c        c
   |----------|----------|----------|......|....... ..
  T 0        T 1        T 2        T 3     T n      T ∞
```

Equation 5

$$PV(perpetuity\ due) = \frac{c}{R}(1+R)$$

For equation 5, the first way to derive it from equation 4 is shown below.

```
 c            c            c            c            c            c            c
|----\--------|----\--------|------------|  .....  |------------|  . . . . . .
T₀    \      T₁    \       T₂           T₃          Tₙ           Tₙ₊₁          T∞
       \            \
        c            c            c            c            c            c
|--------------|--------------|------------|  .....  |------------|  . . . . . .
T₀            T₁             T₂           T₃          Tₙ           Tₙ₊₁          T∞
```

We can compare the first pair of cash flows: c versus c/(1+R). Thus, the present value of the first cash flow of perpetuity due is (1+r) multiplied by the first cash flow of perpetuity. This is also true for the second pair: c/(1+R) versus c/(1+R)2. Actually, this is true for all pairs of cash flows. Summing all cash flows, we would conclude that the present value of perpetuity due is the present value of a perpetuity multiplied by (1+R). The second derivation is simpler. A perpetuity due is the summation of one cash flow today plus the present value of a normal perpetuity—that is, c+c/R, which is c/R × (1+R).

When the future cash flows grow at a constant growth rate (g), we call it a growing perpetuity. See the following timeline.

```
        c        c(1+g)¹                  c(1+g)ⁿ⁻¹      c(1+g)ⁿ
|------------|------------|------------|  .....  |------------|  . . . . . .
T₀          T₁           T₂           T₃          Tₙ           Tₙ₊₁
```

The present value of a growing perpetuity is given in equation 6.

Equation 6
$$PV(growing\ perpetuity) = \frac{c}{R-g} \quad ,$$

where g (grow rate) should be less than R (discount rate).

An *annuity* is defined as "a set of equivalent n cash flows occurring in the future." If the first cash flow occurs at the end of the first period, the present value of an annuity is

```
     c        c        c        c        c        c
|--------|--------|--------|..........|..........
T₀      T₁       T₂       T₃          Tₙ          T∞
```

where C is a recursive payment,
R is discount rate,
and n is the number of periods.

Equation 7 is more complex than equation 5. However, with a little imagination, we could combine equation 4 and the PV of one cash flow $PV = \frac{1}{(1+R)n}$ to "derive" the above equation. This can be done by decomposing an annuity into two perpetuities.

$$PV(annuity) = \frac{C}{R}[1 - \frac{1}{(1+R)^n}]$$

The first cash flow for perpetuity A occurs at the end of the first period while the first cash flow for perpetuity B occurs at the end of period n+1. Summation of those two perpetuities (A and B), c and −c, are cancelled out after period n. Because of this, the present values of scenario 1 and scenario 2 are the same.

From the second scenario, we have:

$$PV(perpetuity\ A) + PV(perpetuity\ B) = \frac{c}{R} - PV\left(\frac{c}{R}\right) = \frac{c}{R} - \frac{1}{(1+R)^n}\frac{c}{R}$$

The future value of an annuity will be given by equation 8.

Equation 8

$$FV(annuity) = \frac{PMT}{R}[(1+R)^n - 1]$$

Next we discuss how to estimate the price (present value) of a coupon bond. By holding a coupon bond, we will receive regular coupon payments plus the principal at maturity. Based on the definition, we could treat the price of a bond as a summation of PV (coupons) and PV (principal).

Equation 9

$$PV(bond) = \frac{C}{r}\left[1 - \frac{1}{(1+r)^n}\right] + \frac{Face\ value}{(1+r)^n},$$

where C is the coupon amount (coupon rate × face value / number of payments per year),
r is the discount rate (APR divided by the number of compounding periods per year),
Face value is the principal,
and n is the number of (payment) periods.

Assume that the face value is 100 with 15 years until maturity and the annual coupon rate is 8% with semiannual coupon payments. Then the value of each coupon payment is 100 × 0.08/2 = $4. If the annual interest rate is 9.2% compounded semiannually, we have an effective semiannual rate of 4.6% (0.092/2). Plug in those values together with n=30 (15×2) and c=4 (0.08×100/2), and we can obtain the price of the coupon bond.

Conversion of Effective Rates

If the annual interest rate is 10% compounded semiannually, what is the corresponding effective annual rate? Here is our two-step approach:

1. Determine which effective rate is given.
2. Convert one effective rate to another (apply the future-value formula twice).

Since the APR is 10% compounding semiannually, we are given an effective semiannual rate of 5% (10%/2). This is also true for other compounding frequencies. For example, if the compounding frequency is quarterly instead of semiannually, we are given an effective quarterly rate of 2.5% (0.1/4).

Assume that we deposit $1 today. We should receive the same amount of money in one year regardless of whether we apply an effective annual rate or an effective semiannual rate.

Equation 10

$$FV = 1(1+0.05)^2$$
$$FV = 1*(1+R)^1$$

In other words, we have $1 \left(1 + R_{effectiveannual}\right) = \$1 \left(1 + R_{effective\_semi}\right)^2$

Hence, we have $R_{annual} = (1 + 0.05)^2 - 1 = 0.1025$

Two generalized formulae are given below, where Rm is the annual nominal rate compounded m times a year.

Equation 11

$$\begin{cases} \left(1 + R_{effective_{annual}}\right) = (1 + \frac{R_m}{m})^m \\ e^{R_{continuously}} = (1 + \frac{R_m}{m})^m \end{cases}$$

We have the similar formulae when Rc is the continuously compounded rate.

Equation 12

$$\begin{cases} R_{effective_{annual}} = \left(1 + \frac{R_m}{m}\right)^m - 1 \\ R_c = m * \ln\left(1 + \frac{R_m}{m}\right) \\ R_m = m * \left(e^{\frac{R_c}{m}} - 1\right) \end{cases}$$

1.12. NPV Rule

NPV (net present value) is defined as "the summation of the present values of all cash flows (present plus future cash flows)." Alternatively, we could define *NPV* as "the difference between the present value of the benefits (cash inflows) and the present value of the costs (cash outflows)." Here is a simple example.

A project has a useful life of 5 years. At the end of the first year, we have a $100 cash inflow. This annual cash inflow increases to $200 for the next 4 years. The initial investment is $400. What is the NPV if the discount rate is 10%? Applying the NPV definition, we have the following formula.

$$PV(project) = -400 + {}^{100}/_{1.1} + {}^{200}/_{1.1^2} + {}^{200}/_{1.1^3} + {}^{200}/_{1.1^4} + {}^{200}/_{1.1^5} = 267.25$$

The NPV for this project is $267.25.

To accept or reject a stand-alone project, we apply the following NPV rule:

$$\begin{cases} \text{if } NPV > 0, \text{ accept} \\ \text{if } NPV < 0, \text{ reject} \end{cases}$$

Since the net present value of our project is $267.25, we accept the project. For two exclusive projects, where choosing A would mean rejecting B and vice versa, we have the following decision rule. If both projects have negative NPV, we reject both. Otherwise, we choose the project with a higher NPV.

1.13. IRR Rule

IRR stands for the internal rate of return. It is the discount rate at which the NPV equal zero. For example, if we invest $100 today and receive $110 in one year, then NPV can be expressed by the following equation.

$$NPV = -100 + \frac{110}{(1+IRR)}$$

Since a discount rate of 10% will make the above NPV equals zero, IRR is 10% in this case. If we have multiple future cash flows—$90, $50, and $30—at the end of each year for the next three years, we have

$$NPV = -100 + \frac{90}{(1+IRR)} + \frac{50}{(1+IRR)^2} + \frac{30}{(1+IRR)^3}$$

The solution yields 41%. Later in this chapter, we will show how to use Excel to estimate IRR. When evaluating a stand-alone project and the cost of capital is given, the IRR rule is given below.

$$\begin{cases} \text{if } IRR > R_c, \text{ accept} \\ \text{if } IRR < R_c, \text{ reject} \end{cases}$$

where Rc is the cost of capital.

For a normal project, where cash outflows occur before any cash inflows, the NPV rule and the IRR rule would offer the same conclusions most of the time. For abnormal projects, where some cash inflows are followed by cash outflows, the NPV and the IRR rule might offer conflicting conclusions. When the future cash flows change signs n times, we might end up with n different IRR estimates.

There are several reasons why the NPV rule is preferred to the IRR rule. First, there might be no IRR that makes the NPV equal to zero . Second, there might be multiple IRRs. This is true when the future cash flows change signs more than once. In other words, we might find two IRRs, such as 9% and 14%. If our cost of capital is 10%, we would not be able to apply the IRR rule to decide whether to choose or reject the project. Third, the assumption of the reinvestment rate underlying the IRR rule is not realistic. For those cases, the NPV rule dominates IRR rule.

1.14. Payback Rule

Payback period is defined as "the number of years we need to recover our initial investment." If our initial investment is $350 and our annual cash inflow is $120, occurring at the end of each year for the foreseeable future, our payback period is 2.9 years (2 + (350-2*120)/120). The payback rule is based on the following principle.

$$\begin{cases} T < T_C, & accept \\ T > T_C, & reject, \end{cases}$$

where T is an estimated payback period
and T_C is an acceptable minimum payback period.

For the above case, if the company's cutoff point is higher than 2.9 years, we reject the project. Otherwise, we accept the project. The advantage of the payback rule is its simplicity. However, this rule has many shortcomings. First, it ignores the time value of money: $100 today has the same value as $100 in two years. The first problem could be overcome by using the so-called present-value payback rule, where we apply the present value of all future cash flows instead of their face values. Second, it ignores the future cash flows after the payback period. Third, there is no theory on how to choose a cutoff period.

1.15. Incremental Cash-Flow Method

Assume that we have two mutually exclusive projects A and B. To rank them, we could estimate the NPV for each of them, NPV_A and NPV_B. The decision rule is that if both NPVs are negative, we reject both. Otherwise, we choose the project with a higher NPV.

If many of the future cash flows of those two projects are the same, we could use the incremental cash-flow method to simplify our calculations. In this case, we have a new project called C=A-B. The cash flows of this new project will be the cash flows from A minus the cash flows from B. The decision rule will be different. If $NPV_{A-B} > 0$, we accept project A and reject project B. Conversely, if $NPV_{A-B} < 0$, we reject project A and accept project B. Note that if we apply the incremental cash-flow method, we have only two outcomes instead of three.

Exercises

1.1. What is the present value of $156 received in 4 years with an annual discount rate of 3.5%?

1.2. If the annual payment is $35 with 25 years remaining, what is the present value if the annual discountrate is 9.41%?

1.3. What is the future value of perpetuity with a periodic annual payment of $4 and a 3.4% annual discount rate?

1.4. What is the present value of perpetuity with an annual payment of $4 paid every 6 months (twice per year) and a 3.4% annual rate compounding annually?

1.5. If a firm's earnings per share grows from $1 to $2 over an eight-year period (the total growth is 100%), what is its annual growth rate?

1.6. A project contributes cash inflows of $5,000 and $8,000 at the end of the first and second years. The initial cost is $3,000. The appropriate discount rates are 10% and 12% for the first and the second years respectively. What is the NPV of the project?

1.7. Universal Data Corp. has just paid a dividend of $6. These dividends are expected to grow at a rate of 6% in the foreseeable future. The risk of this company suggests that future cash flows should be discounted at a rate of 10%. What is its stock price?

1.8. Firm A will issue new bonds with annual coupon payment of $80 and a face value of $1000. Interest payments are made semiannually, and the bond matures in 2 years. The spot interest rate for the first year is 10%. At the end of the first year, the one-year spot rate is expected to be 12%.

a) What is the present value of the bond?

b) What is the lump sum you are willing to accept at the end of the second year?

1.9. Richard's rich aunt has promised him a payment of $5,000 if he completes college in four years. Richard has just finished a very difficult sophomore (second) year, including taking several finance courses. Richard would very much like to take a long vacation. The appropriate discount rate is 10% compounded semiannually. What is value that Richard would be giving up today if he took his vacation?

1.10. Four years ago, Boosters Inc. paid a dividend of $0.80 per share. Today it paid a dividend of $1.66. The firm expects to enjoy the same dividend growing rate for the next 5 years. Thereafter, the growth rate will level off at 2% per year.

If the required return of this stock remains at 19%, what is the current stock price?

1.11. What are the advantages and barriers of using R?

1.12. What is the difference between function 1s() and rm()?

1.13. Generate a vector from 2 to 15 then from 20 to 40. Estimate its mean, standard deviation, and median.

1.14. What might be the disadvantages of using R?

1.15. How do you assign a value to a new variable?

1.16. Is R case sensitive, and how do you get help for a specific function?

1.17. How do you add a comment using R, and will the R compiler compile it?

1.18. Does an empty space play a role in R?

1.19. How do you download manuals related to R?

1.20. Do we have to define a variable, such as an integer, or character before we use it?

CHAPTER 2

Writing a Function in R

The simplest function takes just one line. Below, a function called **dd** is generated, which doubles any input value.

```
> dd<-function(x)x*2
```

To call it, just treat it as any embedded R function, such as **min()** or **max()**.

```
> dd(2.45)
[1] 4.9
> dd(2.14)
[1] 4.28
```

The structure of a user-defined function is a function name (such as **dd** in the above case) followed by **<-function()**. We insert our input values in the parentheses. The last part will be the body of our function.

2.1. Introduction

Most of the computations carried out in R involve evaluation of various functions, supplied by R via various packages (We devote two chapters to discuss R packages—see chapters 16 and 31) or written by individual users. In this chapter, we focus on how to write simple functions. After familiar ourselves with the basic structure—how to input values, how to add comments—we will use R as a financial calculator. In other words, we could write most finance-associated functions in R according to their formulae presented in chapter 1. It is straightforward to call them. For example, calling **pv_f(100,0.1,2)**, we calculate the present value of $100 received in 2 years with a 10% annual interest rate. In the next several chapters, we will explore this further by analyzing nonstandard and more complex functions, such as the Black-Sholes- Merton option model.

2.2. Writing a Simple One-Line Function in R

Below, a present-value function is generated with just one line.

```
> pv_f<-function(fv,r,n)  fv(1+r)^n
```

We could write a function without any input. For instance, type **q()** to quit R. If you type **exit()**, you will get an error message.

```
> exit()
Error: could not find function "exit"
```

Thus, we could write a function called **exit()**, which is equivalent to **q()**.

```
> exit<-function() q()
```

2.3. Input Values: Positional Arguments, Keyword Arguments, and Mixed Ones

To call a function, we have three methods to input values: positional, keyword, or mixed.

Positional Arguments

The meaning of an input variable depends on its position. What is the present value of $100 occurring in one year with a discount rate of 8%? According to the structure of the **pv_f()**, the order of inputs is a future value, an effective period rate, and the number of periods.

```
> pv_f(100,0.08,1)
[1] 92.59259
```

If we have the following order of inputs, **pv_f(1,100,0.08)**, then the first input value of the future value will be $1, the interest rate is 10,000%, and the number of periods is 0.08. The final result will be $0.69 instead of $92.59. Thus, we have to be careful with the order of our input variables.

```
> pv_f(1,100,0.08)
[1] 0.6912805
> 1/(1+100)^0.08
[1] 0.6912805
```

Keyword Approach

Specify a keyword in front of each argument such as **fv=100**.

```
> pv_f(fv=100,n=1,r=0.08)
[1] 92.5926
```

The advantage of the keyword approach is that the order of input variables no longer plays a role. See the following three equivalent ways of inputting data.

```
> pv_f(fv=100,n=2,r=0.1)
[1] 82.64463
> pv_f(n=2,fv=100,r=0.1)
[1] 82.64463
> pv_f(r=0.1,fv=100,n=2)
[1] 82.64463
```

To view all *user-defined* functions, type **ls()**.

```
> ls()
[1] "dd" "pv_f"
```

To know the structure of a specific function, simply type its name, such as **pv_f**.

```
> pv_f
function(fv,r,n)fv/(1+r)^n
```

Mixed Approach

The knowledge about the above two methods should suffice. However, for the completeness, we introduce this method, which has the following procedure.

- Rule 1. Exact match: Match keywords from your input variables that are the exactly same as the keywords specified by the function.
- Rule 2. Partial match: After rule 1, partially match keywords.
- Rule 3. Positional match: After rules 1 and 2, anything left will be matched according to the position of each input variable.

Assume that we have a function with the following form.

```
>my_f<-function(x,y,aa,aabb){
cat("x=",x, "\n")
}
```

Case 1 is given below.

```
# case 1
> my_f(aa=1,2,3,4) # according to rule 1: aa=1
# according to rule 3: x=2, y=3, aabb=4
```

Here is the case 2.

```
# case 2
> my_f(aabb=1,a=2,3,4) # according to rule 1: aabb=1
# according to rule 2: aa=2
# according to rule 3: x=3, y=4
```

We can check our results with the following codes.

```
# use this function to check
function(x,y,aa,aabb) {
cat("x=",x, "\n")
cat("y=",y,"\n")
cat("aa=",aa,"\n")
cat("aabb=",aabb,"\n")
}
```

2.4. Programs with Multiple Lines

For a multiple-line function, a pair of curly braces, { and }, is used to embrace those lines.

```
my_function<-function(x,y,z){
# line 1
# line 2
# line 3
# more
}
```

For those simplest one-line functions, we still can add a pair of curly braces to circle the main function body.

```
pv_f<-function(fv,r,n) {
fv*(1+r)^(-n)
}
```

To make our functions self-explanatory, the best strategy is to add a few comments such as the objective of the program, definitions of input variables, plus one or two examples on how to apply the function.

```
pv_perpetuity<-function(c,r){
"Objective: estimate the present value of perpetuity
c : cash flow (1st at the end of 1st period
r : effective period rate
e.g.,
> pv_perpetuity(10,0.08)
[1] 125
"
return(c/r)
}
```

In the above program, the last line before the second curly brace, we use **return()**. This is a standard command of returning our final result. Adding **return()** makes our programs clearer; even its omission causes no error. In R, there are two ways to add a comment. The number sign (#) indicates that the rest of the line will be a comment. The only exception is when # is a part of a string, such as **x<-"the # of observations is 100"**.

The R complier will ignore comments when it compiles the program. For a multipleline comment, it is cumbersome to apply many number signs since we have to add one in front of each comment line. In those cases, a pair of double quotation marks is used to encircle all those comment lines (see the above example).

2.5. Well-Indented Codes Are More Readable

The following two programs are essentially the same except indentation. Obviously the first one is easier to read.

```
pv_perpetuity_due<-function(c,r){
    "Objective: estimate the present value of a perpetuity
            c : cash flow (1st at the end of 1st period
            r : effective period discount rate
             e.g.,
          > pv_perpetuity(10,0.08)
               [1] 125
       "
    return(c/r*(1+r))
}
```

The second program below has the same codes.

```
pv_perpetuity_due<-function(c,r){
"Objective: estimate the present value of a perpetuity
c : cash flow (1st at the end of 1st period
r : effective period discount rate
e.g.,
 > pv_perpetuity(10,0.08)
[1] 125
"
return(c/r*(1+r))
}
```

For a simple function such as the example above, the effectiveness of a good indentation is less obvious. However, when we have a more complex program, such as multiple loops and blocks, a proper indentation will be more critical.

2.6. Using Notepad as a Text Editor

There are several ways to initiate Notepad.

1. Click **Start** then **Notepad**.
2. Click **Start** then enter *notepad*.

Another way to make our lives a bit easier is to put Notepad on our desktops. Alternatively we can use the editor included in R to generate a new program or modify our existing programs.

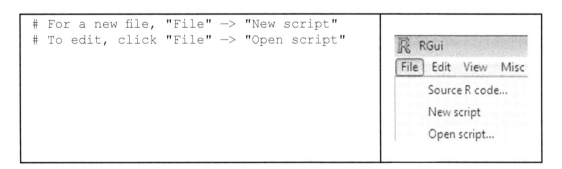

```
# For a new file, "File" -> "New script"
# To edit, click "File" -> "Open script"
```

In addition, we can use WordPad, MS Word, or other word editors to write or edit our programs. Just remember to apply a text format when saving our programs.

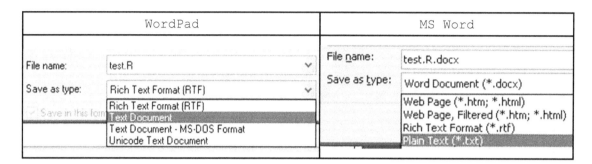

2.7. Extensions of R Programs Are Not Critical

When writing an R program, its extension is not important. For example, we could name it **test. txt**, **test.R**, or just **test** (i.e., completely ignoring the extension). The advantage of a **.txt** extension is that our computers will automatically launch Notepad to open the program when we click it. Similarly, if we intend to use the R editor to open our programs, it is a good idea to adopt a **.R** extension. Another advantage of using **.R** as an extension is it distinguishes our programs with other files such as input, output, or data files with a **.txt** extension.

2.8. How to Run an R Program

Assume that our program has the following three lines for three functions.

```
pv_f<-function(fv,r,n)fv/(1+r)^n
fv_f<-function(pv,r,n) pv*(1+r)^n
pv_perpetuity<-function(c,r)c/r
```

Method 1: Copy and Paste

First, we use Notepad to generate those three lines then highlight them and paste them to the R console. A careful reader would find that this procedure is equivalent to typing those three lines on the R console. For a short program, this method is quite convenient. This method could be used to debug our or others' R programs. We will discuss it further in chapter 3: "Black-Scholes-Merton Option Model."

Method 2: Using the source() Function

After we generated the above three lines using an editor such as Notepad and saved it (e.g., **c:/ my_project/test.R**), now we can run the program using the function of **source()**.

```
> source("c:/my_project/test.R")
```

To view whether all three functions are available, we use the **ls()** function.

```
> ls()
[1] "fv_f" "pv_f" "pv_perpetuity"
```

The second way to use the **source()** function is to click **File** on the R menu bar. Go to **Source R codes…**, then locate your program. How about generating the following multiple-line program and saving it to a file called **c:/my_project/test02.R**?

```
pv_f<-function(fv,r,n) {
"Objective: estimate present value
fv : future value
r : discount rate
n : number of periods
e.g.,
> pv_f(100,0.1,1)
[1] 90.90909
";return(fv*(1+r)^(-n))
}
```

Below is the general procedure to call a prewritten R program.

```
# 2-step to run a R program
# [click] "file" ->"change dir…" -> [choose working directory]
# [click] "file" ->"Source R code"-> [choose your R program]
```

If we don't want to change our working directory, then we can simply include a path in our codes (i.e., using so-called absolute-path method).

```
> source("c/yan/w1_03.R") # 2nd way to run an R program
> source("c:/my_project/test_02.R") # 3rd way to run an R program
```

To view each step when executing, we add **echo=T**.

```
> source("c:/my_project/test_02.R") # echo=T: print each step
```

2.9. Using Meaningful Variable Names and Using the Tab Key Magically

For programming clarity, it is always a good idea to generate meaningful variables, such as pv for present value, fv for future value, pv_f for present value function, pv_annuity_f for present value function for annuity. By using those good names, we and other users would understand programs more easily. In addition, we can reduce unnecessary comments dramatically. Below is an example of using meaningful variables names.

```
data Mid3;
    set Mid3;
    DollarRealizedSpread_LR_SW=waDollarRealizedSpread_LR_SW/sumsize;
    DollarRealizedSpread_LR_DW=waDollarRealizedSpread_LR_DW/sumdollar;
    PercentRealizedSpread_LR_SW=waPercentRealizedSpread_LR_SW/sumsize;
    PercentRealizedSpread_LR_DW=waPercentRealizedSpread_LR_DW/sumdollar;
    DollarPriceImpact_LR_SW=waDollarPriceImpact_LR_SW/sumsize;
    DollarPriceImpact_LR_DW=waDollarPriceImpact_LR_DW/sumdollar;
    PercentPriceImpact_LR_SW=waPercentPriceImpact_LR_SW/sumsize;
    PercentPriceImpact_LR_DW=waPercentPriceImpact_LR_DW/sumdollar;
    DollarRealizedSpread_EOH_SW=waDollarRealizedSpread_EOH_SW/sumsize;
    DollarRealizedSpread_EOH_DW=waDollarRealizedSpread_EOH_DW/sumdollar;
    PercentRealizedSpread_EOH_SW=waPercentRealizedSpread_EOH_SW/sumsize;
    PercentRealizedSpread_EOH_DW=waPercentRealizedSpread_EOH_DW/sumdollar;
    DollarPriceImpact_EOH_SW=waDollarPriceImpact_EOH_SW/sumsize;
    DollarPriceImpact_EOH_DW=waDollarPriceImpact_EOH_DW/sumdollar;
    PercentPriceImpact_EOH_SW=waPercentPriceImpact_EOH_SW/sumsize;
    PercentPriceImpact_EOH_DW=waPercentPriceImpact_EOH_DW/sumdollar;
      DollarRealizedSpread_CLNV_SW=waDollarRealizedSpread_CLNV_SW/sumsize;
    DollarRealizedSpread_CLNV_DW=waDollarRealizedSpread_CLNV_DW/sumdollar;
    PercentRealizedSpread_CLNV_SW=waPercentRealizedSpread_CLNV_SW/sumsize;
    PercentRealizedSpread_CLNV_DW=waPercentRealizedSpread_CLNV_DW/sumdollar;
    DollarPriceImpact_CLNV_SW=waDollarPriceImpact_CLNV_SW/sumsize;
    DollarPriceImpact_CLNV_DW=waDollarPriceImpact_CLNV_DW/sumdollar;
    PercentPriceImpact_CLNV_SW=waPercentPriceImpact_CLNV_SW/sumsize;
    PercentPriceImpact_CLNV_DW=waPercentPriceImpact_CLNV_DW/sumdollar;
run;
```

The above codes are SAS codes. The complete codes could be downloaded at http://canisius.edu/~yany/longVariableNames.pdf. The name of the paper is "Liquidity Measurement Problems in Fast, Competitive Markets: Expensive and Cheap Solutions" by Holden and Jacobsen, a *Journal of Finance* paper.

Magic Use of the Tab Key

Assume that we have defined several meaningful names (see below). In chapter 1, we know that we could type a variable name to show its value. For instance, if we type pvAnnuity, we will get 100.

```
> pvAnnuity<-100
> pvPerpetuity<-200
> fvAnnuityDue=300
> pvAnnuity
[1] 100
```

Obviously, typing those long names is prone to error. Try the following:

```
> pvA # now we hit tab key to see the magic!
```

After hitting the **Tab** key, the complete name of **pvAnnuity** would pop up. The rule is that we just need to type enough letters to distinguish this variable from others; then we hit the **Tab** key. This is true when we type the **source()** command. Assume that we have a **pv_f.R** program located under **c:/yan/teaching/04_MGF690/pv_f.R** (# location c:/yan/teaching/04_MGF690/pv_f.R).

We can hit the **Tab** key several times to save time and effort or impress others.

```
> source("c:/yan/te # hit the tab key now
> source("c:/yan/teaching/ # we will see this one
> source("c:/yan/teaching/04 # type 2 integers, hit tab key
> source("c:/yan/teaching/04_MGF690/# see this
```

2.10. Changing Our Working Directory

To find out the current working directory, we use the getwd() function.

```
> getwd()
[1] "C:/Users/yyan/Documents"
```

It is always a good idea to generate a directory that contains all our data, programs, and other related materials for one specific project. After launching R, usually we want our working directory associated with the directory. The first way to change our working directory is to use the menu bar.

```
#[click] "File" - -> "Change dir…"
```

Alternatively we can use the **setwd()** function to change our current working directory. After it is done, we use **getwd()** to confirm.

```
> setwd("c:/temp") # change our current working directory
> getwd() # find out our current working directory
[1] "c:/temp"
```

2.11. Listing Files Under the Current Working Directory

The **dir()** function is used to list all programs, data sets, and other files under our current working directory.

```
> dir() # show all programs in the current working directory
```

Sometimes we want to pick up just a few files. In those cases, we specify a pattern by using **pattern='my_pattern'**.

```
> dir(pattern="ratio") # list files with "ratio" in their names
```

If we intend to check the files under another directory, add path="…". Again, this is called absolutepath method.

```
> dir(path="c:/temp/",pattern='test.R')
```

2.12. Default Value for an Input Argument

We can have default values for some or all of our input arguments.

```
> pv_f<-function(fv=100,r=0.05,n=1) fv*(1+r)^(-n)
```

Below shows how to call this function.

```
> pv_f() # use all default values
[1] 95.2381
> pv_f(fv=150) # use two default values
[1] 142.8571
```

With no default specified and we call the **pv_f** function without giving an appropriate input set, we would get an error message.

```
> pv_f<-function(fv,r,n) fv*(1+r)^(-n)
> pv_f()
Error in fv * (1 + r)^(-n) : 'fv' is missing
```

2.13. Comparison Between Two Listing Functions

We should not be confused between **dir()** and **ls()**. The former, **dir()**, lists files under our current working directory (or another directory if using the absolute-path method) while the **ls()** function lists all objects in our current working space (memory).

```
> ls() # list all objects
```

R objects include variables, lists, data frames, vectors, metrics, arrays, and functions. Don't worry if you have no clue about the meaning of *lists, data frames, metrics,* or *arrays.* We will discuss those in the later chapters.

```
> ls(pat='test') # show all objects contain 'test'
```

Another way to show all objectives is to use the function of **objects()**.

```
> objects() # 2nd way to show all objects
```

We can use the rm() function to remove unnecessary variables (objects) from our memory.

```
> rm(x) # remove x only
> rm(x,y) # remove both x and y
```

There are several ways to remove all objects.

```
# rm(list=ls((all=TRUE)) # remove all objects (method 1)
# rm(list=ls()) # a simpler version to remove all
# 2nd way to remove all objects
# [click] "Misc" -> "Remove all objects"
```

On the other hand, if we want to remove a file from our working directory, we have to delete it manually or issue the following command from the R prompt.

```
> file.remove('test.R') # relative path
> file.remove('c:/temp/test2.R') # absolute path
```

2.14. Grouping Many Small Functions into One File

When we have many small functions around a topic, it is a good idea to put them into a program. Then we issue one-line R codes to "activate" those functions.

There are several issues here. First, each individual program should be bug free. It is really time-consuming to debug multiple programs simultaneously. Second, add enough comments to each program. Third, arrange those programs in a logical order. Last but not least, we could add a nice header explaining the purpose of our set of programs.

```
"fin_101.R
Objective : a set of 50 programs related to Finance 101
Author : John Doe
Date : 10/2/2013
Modified : 7/3/2014
A list of all functions
1)     pv_f()
2)     fv_f()
3)     IRR()
4)     Bond_price()
5)     pv_annuity()
6)     pv_perpeturity()
"
# program one
# program two
# program three
```

If you are taking a financial-modeling course and using this book, it is a good idea to have a text file, such as **mgf690.R** or another name, for the whole course. There are several advantages for keeping such a text file. First, after you figure out a simple program, you can include it in this file. Second, since the file is in a text format, it is very easy to open, view, and modify. Third, many codes in the early chapters are quite useful for the later chapters. Thus, you can simply copy and paste relevant programs as your starting program. Fourth, it is quite easy to upload/activate your most used programs. Last but not least, by the end of the course, you should have a file that contains eighty R programs related to various functions. Those functions could be useful in the future.

2.15 Using R as a Financial Calculator

We could put all our finance functions written in R into a simple program and call it **fin_101.txt**. Then we can activate it by using **source("path/fin_101.txt")**, where *path* will be your specific path. Users could generate their own functions as well by following these steps.

Table 2.1. Steps to run **fin_101.txt**

Step	Description
1	Put all programs (functions) into a text file (e.g., **fin_101.txt**) and save the file to a specific location (e.g., **c:\temp\fin_101.txt**).
2	Launch R.
3	From R, click **File** then **Change dir** then **c:\temp**
4	Click **File** then **Source R codes**… then **fin_101.txt**

Now you are ready to call those functions included in **fin_101.txt** and use R as a financial calculator. Remember to use the **ls()** function to list all functions and type **pv_f** to view its usage. For step 4, the equivalent command is

```
> source('fin_101.txt')
```

If you don't want to change your working directory, you could combine steps 3 and 4 by issuing the following command:

```
> source('c:\\test_R\\fin_101.txt')
```

Or

```
> source("c:/test_R/fin_101.txt")
```

Table 2.2 below lists the advantages and barriers of using R in our introductory finance courses. Its flexibility means that users could adopt their own favorite function names. For instance, a user could rename **pv_f** as pv_function or **my_PV_function**. When an undergraduate student pursues a masters degree, the knowledge of R will give her/him a comparative advantage. The knowledge and skills of using R add certain weight when a graduate tries to land a Wall Street job since many financial institutions are using S-PLUS, a cousin of R. If you want to keep the original function, you can add another name instead.
See an example below.

```
> my_PV_function(fv,r,n) pv_f(fv,r,n)
```

In the above program, the new function of **my_PF_function()** is the same as our original **pv_f()** function.

Table 2.2. Advantages and barriers of using R in Finance 101

Advantages of Using R	
1	No cost (free downloading)
2	No black box (transparent in terms of formulae and logic)
3	More flexible than a financial calculator or Excel (For example, a user could generate their own functions by renaming the existing functions.)
4	Users could view examples for each function.
5	Could estimate market risk, total risk, liquidity measure, CAPM
6	Could download data from the Internet such as Yahoo Finance
7	Way more powerful than financial calculators and Excel
8	Extensible for many extrafunctionalities
9	Very useful for doing research
10	Good for a person's curriculum vitae
11	Used intensively in the financial industry
12	Many researchers around the world continue to develop R. More R packages would come.
13	More than three dozen packages are related to finance.
Disadvantages of Using R	
1	Most instructors don't know R.
2	It is easy to design a closed-book exam with a financial calculator.
3	Finance textbooks (in Finance 101) don't include R.
4	The current authors of finance textbooks might be reluctant to change their textbooks to incorporate R. If a textbook depends on both financial calculators and Excel, it is difficult for a student to learn another tool such as R. If a finance textbook is written with R as the primary tool of calculation, it will be well received by students.
5	The current publishers might be reluctant to change.
6	Resistance from the manufacturers of financial calculators
7	Mentality

2.16. Error Handling

Assume that we don't allow a negative interest rate (which means that you deposit your money in a bank and pay the bank the interest instead of the bank paying you).

```
> pv_f(fv=100,r=0.1,n=1)
[1] 90.90909
> pv_f(fv=100,r=-0.1,n=1) # accidently input a negative interest rate
[1] 111.1111
```

In these cases, we can use the **if-stop** function. See the following codes:

```
pv_f<-function(fv,r,n){
if(r<0)stop("r should be positive")
return(fv/(1+r)^n)
}
```

2.17. Changing Your Starting Working Directory

You can start your R every time from a predetermined directory or subdirectory that contains all our files, data, and/or programs.

```
# [right click] R icon
# [click] properties at the bottom
# From 'Start in' choose to start your directory
```

For example, if we intend to make R start from our working directory called **c:\yan**, we can modify the **Start In** accordingly. See below:

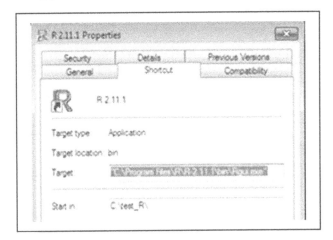

Exercises

2.1. What are the key components of an R function?

2.2. Write a new R function called std(), which is the same as the embedded R function called sd(). By the way, the sd() function estimates the standard deviation of an input variable (a vector or matrix).

2.3. Explain the following function.

```
> echo<-function(x) print(x)
```

2.4. Write an R function to estimate the present value of a perpetuity where c is the cash flows and r is the discount rate. The first cash flow happens at the end of nth period.

2.5. Writing an R program to estimate IRR (Internal Rate of Return) for a given set of cash flows. You can assume the first cash flow occurs today.

2.6. A project contributes a cash inflow of $5,000 at the end of the first year and a cash inflow of $8,000 at the end of the second year. The initial cost is $3,000. The appropriate discount rates are 10% and 12% for the first and the second year respectively. What is the present value of the project?

2.7. Write an R function to estimate the following sum:

$$S = a_1 + a_1q + a_1q^2 + a_1q^3 + \ldots + a_1q^n + a_1q^{n+1} + \cdots$$
$$S = \frac{a_1}{1-q} \qquad q < 1$$

2.8. Modify your codes related to 2.7 to disallow situations where .

2.9. Write an R program to price the present value of a growing perpetuity.

2.10. Modify the above program to price a growing perpetuity due.

2.11. What is the effective annual rate for a 10% annual rate compounding semiannually?

2.12. Write an R function to estimate the effective annual rate for a given APR (annual percentage rate) compounding m times per year:

$$R_{annual} = \left(1 + \frac{R_m}{m}\right)^m - 1.$$

2.13. You have just noticed in the financial pages of the local newspaper that you can buy a bond for $750. If the coupon rate is 10%, coupon payments are semiannual, and there are 10 years to maturity, should you make the purchase if your required return on investments of this type is 13%? The face value is $1,000.

2.14. Write an R function call pv_bond() to estimate the price of a bond given c (coupon payment), R (discount rate), P (principal), and n (the number of periods).

2.15. If a firm's earnings per share grow from $1 to $2 over 7 years, what is the annual growth rate?

2.16. If the annual rate is 9.5%, compounded quarterly, what is the equivalent continuously compounded rate?

2.17. Write an R program to estimate a continuously compounded rate from another rate,

$$R_{cont} = m * \ln\left(1 + \frac{R_m}{m}\right),$$ where m is the number of compounding periods per year.

2.18. The continuously compounded rate is 8.34%. What is the corresponding annual rate compounded semiannually?

2.19. Write an R program to estimate Rm (annual rate compounded m times per year) for a given rate compounded continuously (R_c). $R_m = m(e^{\frac{R_c}{m}} - 1)$

2.20. Combine at least ten basic finance-related functions such as pv_f and fv_f to generate a file called fin_101.txt.

2.21. Write an R function to calculate BMI (body mass index), which is defined as weight in kilograms divided by height (in meters) squared. $BMI = \frac{W}{H^2} = \frac{kg}{m^2}$

There are two types of inputs: 1) Input *kilogram* and *meter* directly. 2) Input *foot* (or *inch*) and *pound*. Modify the program further to include the following information below. After offering BMI value, show the following text based on their corresponding ranges:

Description	BMI
Underweight	`<18.5`
Normal	`18.5 to 25`
Overweight	`25 to 30`
Obese	`>30`

2.22. Write a financial calculator with as many functions as possible (open-ended question).

CHAPTER 3

Black-Scholes-Merton Option Model

For a stock, a call-option buyer has a right to pay x dollars to purchase the stock worth **sT** dollars. Obviously, only when **sT** is larger than x would the option buyer exercise her right. A call-option buyer's payoff is given below, where **sT** is the stock price at the maturity date **T**, **x** is exercise price, and **abs()** is the absolute value function.

```
> payoff_call<-function(sT,x)(sT-x+abs(sT-x))/2
```

It seems that we can have a simpler payoff function (see below).

```
> payoff_call<-function(sT,x) max(sT-x,0)
```

Unfortunately it works only for scalar input variables. We will come back to this again later in the chapter. When the exercise price is 5 and the price is 6.5, the payoffs will be 1.5. On the other hand, if the stock price is $3, the payoff will be zero since the call-option buyer would not pay $5 to buy a $3 stock.

```
> payoff_call(6.5,5)
[1] 1.5
> payoff_call(3,5)
[1] 0
```

A European option can be exercised only at maturity while an American option can be exercised any time before or at its maturity. For a European call, our R program for the famous Black-Scholes-Merton model has five lines, where s is today's price, **T** is maturity in years, **r** is a continuously compounded riskfree rate, **sigma** is the volatility of the stock, **log()** is natural log, and **pnorm()** represents the cumulative standard normal distribution.

```
call_f<-function(s,x,T,r,sigma){
   d1 = (log(s/x)+(r+sigma*sigma/2.)*T)/(sigma*sqrt(T))
   d2 = d1-sigma*sqrt(T)
   s*pnorm(d1)-x*exp(-r*T)*pnorm(d2)
}
```

With a set of input values, we can call this function easily.

```
> call_f(40,42,0.5,0.1,0.2)
[1] 2.277780 # value of this European call option is $2.28
```

3.1. Introduction

An option gives its buyer a right to buy (call option) or sell (put option) something in the future to the option seller at a predetermined price (exercise price). For example, if we buy a European call option to acquire the underlying stock for $30 at the end of 3 months, its payoff on maturity day will be:

Equation 1

$$payoff\ (call) = Max\ (S_T - 30, 0),$$

where S_T is the stock price at the maturity date (T), and T is *0.25* ($^3/_{12}$) years. Assume that 3 months later, the stock price is $25. We would not exercise our call option to pay $30 in exchange for the stock since we could buy the same stock with $25 in the open market. On the other hand, if the stock price is $40, we will exercise our right to reap a payoff of $10 (i.e., buy the stock at $30 and sell it at $40).

```
payoff_call<-function(sT,x){
t<-(sT-x)
return((t+abs(t))/2)
}
```

Calling the payoff function is straightforward.

```
> payoff_call(25,30)
[1] 0
> payoff_call(40,30)
[1] 10
```

Preferably we can add more explanations, plus one or two examples.

```
payoff_call<-function(sT,x){
  "Objective: payoff function of a European call option
  sT: stock price at maturity day T
  x: exercise price
  e.g., > payoff_call(45,30)
  [1] 15
  "
  tt<-(sT-x)
  return((tt+abs(tt))/2)
}
```

The payoff for a call-option seller is the opposite of its buyer. It is important to remember that this is a zero-sum game: you win, I lose; or I win, you lose. For example, an investor sold 3 call options with an exercise price of $10. When the stock price is $15, the investor's payoff is shown below.

```
> payoff_call<-function(sT,x) return((sT-x+abs(sT-x))/2)
> sT <-15
> 3*(-payoff_call(sT,10))
[1] -15
```

Since the stock price is $15, larger than $10 (exercise price), the buyer gains $5 for each option. Thus, the total loss to the option writer will be 3×5=15. In the real world, each option contract contains 100 stocks.

3.2. One Input Argument Could Be a Vector

For the pv_f() function, if all inputs are scalars, our output will be a scalar as well.

```
> pv_f<-function(fv,r,n)  fv/(1+r)^n
> pv_f(100,0.1,1)
[1]  90.90909
```

However, when one input variable is a vector (multiple values instead of just one value), the output will be a vector as well.

```
> fv<-c(100,200,150)
> pv_f(fv,0.1,1)
[1]  90.90909 181.81818 136.36364
```

On the other hand, if we have one future value, one maturity date, but five different discount rates, then the code yields five different present values. Try to input two vectors, such **as fv<-c(100,200)** and **r<-c(0.1,0.05,0.08)**, to see the result.

```
> pv_f<-function(fv,r,n)  fv/(1+r)^n
> r<-c(0.1,0.09,0.085,0.075,0.065)
> pv_f(100,1,r)
[1]  93.30330 93.95227 94.27845 94.93421 95.59453
```

3.3. A Simple Graph

R is a powerful tool for graphing (see a simple example below). To graph, we will devote a whole chapter for it, chapter 29: "Simple Graphs in R."

```
> x<-seq(-5,5,by=0.2)
> y<-5+x^2
> plot(x,y)
```

3.4. Payoff Function with a Graphical Presentation

Below, the R codes and the graph refer to the payoff function for a long call position. The vertical axis is for payoff while the horizontal one is for stock price at maturity day.

```
sT<-seq(10,50,by=5)# stock prices
x<-30 # exercise price
payoff<-payoff_call(sT,x)
plot(sT,payoff,type="l")
# "l" is lower case letter of L
```

The following codes will achieve the same result.

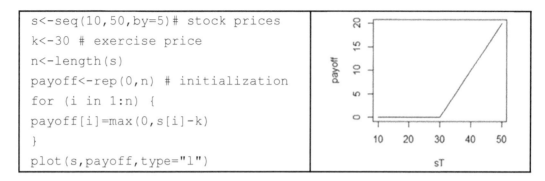

```
s<-seq(10,50,by=5)# stock prices
k<-30 # exercise price
n<-length(s)
payoff<-rep(0,n) # initialization
for (i in 1:n) {
payoff[i]=max(0,s[i]-k)
}
plot(s,payoff,type="l")
```

A European option can be exercised only on maturity day while an American option can be exercised any time before or on its maturity day. Since an American option can be held until it matures, its price (option premium) should be higher than or equal to its European counterpart.

Equation 2

$$\begin{cases} C_{American} \geq C_{European} \\ P_{American} \geq P_{European} \end{cases}$$

where P is the price of a put option that gives its buyer a right to sell something to the option writer (seller) at a predetermined price (exercise price). An option buyer has to pay to acquire a right to buy or sell at an agreed exercise price while an option writer (seller) receives an upfront premium to bear an obligation. Table 3.1 summarizes the major features of various options.

Table 3.1. Long/short, call/put, European/American options and directions of initial cash flows

	Buyer (long position)	Seller (short position)	European options	American options
Call	A right to buy a security (commodity) at a fixed price	An obligation to sell a security (commodity) at a fixed price	Exercised on maturity day only	Exercised any time before or on maturity day
Put	A right to sell a security with a prefixed price	An obligation to buy a security (commodity) at a fixed price		
Cash flow	Upfront cash outflow	Upfront cash inflow		

3.5. Profit/Loss Functions

If the call premium (option price) is c, the profit/loss function for a call-option buyer is the difference between her payoff and her initial investment (c). Obviously, the timing of cash flows of paying an option premium upfront and its payoff at maturity day is different. Here we ignore the time value of money since maturities are usually quite short.

Equation 3

$$Profit/loss(call) = Max\ (S_T - X,\ 0) - c$$

The following R codes show the graph of a profit/loss function.

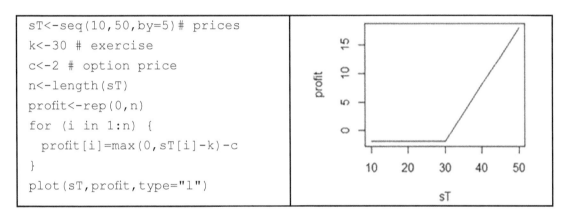

```
sT<-seq(10,50,by=5)# prices
k<-30 # exercise
c<-2 # option price
n<-length(sT)
profit<-rep(0,n)
for (i in 1:n) {
  profit[i]=max(0,sT[i]-k)-c
}
plot(sT,profit,type="l")
```

A put option gives its buyer a right to sell a security (commodity) to the put-option buyer in the future at a predetermined price X. Here is its payoff function.

$$Payoff\ (put) = Max\ (X - S_T,\ 0),$$

where S_T is the stock price at maturity, T is maturity in years, and X is the strike price (exercise price). Similarly we can write an R program to generate a payoff vector for a set of stock prices—$\mathbf{S_T}$ is a vector.

See the R codes and the corresponding graph below.

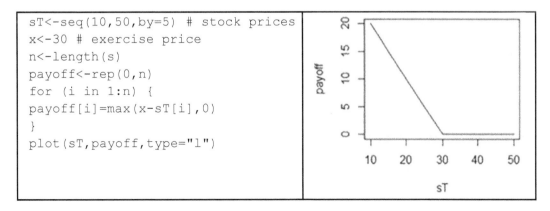

```
sT<-seq(10,50,by=5) # stock prices
x<-30 # exercise price
n<-length(s)
payoff<-rep(0,n)
for (i in 1:n) {
payoff[i]=max(x-sT[i],0)
}
plot(sT,payoff,type="l")
```

Similarly we have the following profit/loss function for a put-option buyer.

Equation 5

$$Profit/loss\ (put) = Max(X - S_T, 0) - p$$

where p is the put premium (price).

3.6. Black-Scholes-Merton Option Model on Nondividend-Paying Stocks

The Black-Scholes-Merton option model is a closed-form solution to price a European option on a stock that does not pay any dividends before its maturity date. If we use S_0 for the price today, X for the exercise price, r for the continuously compounded risk-free rate, T for the maturity in years, $\sigma\sigma$ for the volatility of the underlying security, the closed-form formulae for a European call (c) and put (p) are:

$$\begin{cases} c = S_0 N(d_1) - X e^{-rT} N(d_2) \\ p = X e^{-rT} N(-d_2) - S_0 N(-d_1) \\ d_1 = \dfrac{\ln\left(\frac{S_0}{X}\right) + (r + \frac{1}{2}\sigma^2)T}{\sigma\sqrt{T}} \\ d_2 = \dfrac{\ln\left(\frac{S_0}{X}\right) + (r - \frac{1}{2}\sigma^2)T}{\sigma\sqrt{T}} = d_1 - \sigma\sqrt{T} \end{cases}$$

where the N() function is the cumulative standard normal distribution.

The following R codes represent the above equations to evaluate a European call. Almost all input variables are self-explanatory, except the function called **pnorm()**, which is the cumulative normal distribution, **N()** in the above equations. In the next section, we will explain this function in more detail.

```
# Black-Scholes-Merton option model
bs_call<-function(S,X,T,r,sigma){
"Objective : calculate call price
S : stock price today
X : exercise price
r : risk-free rate
sigma : volatility of the stock
e.g., bs_call(40,42,0.5,0.1,0.2) # [1] 2.277780
"
d1 = (log(S/X)+(r+sigma*sigma/2.)*T)/(sigma*sqrt(T))
d2 = d1-sigma*sqrt(T)
return(S*pnorm(d1)-X*exp(-r*T)*pnorm(d2))
}
```

The current stock price is $40, the strike price is $42, the time to maturity is 6 months, the risk-free rate is 10% compounded continuously, and the volatility of the underlying stock is 20% (compounded continuously)—then the European call is worth $2.28.

```
> bs_call(40,42,0.5,0.1,0.2) # T=1/12=0.5
[1] 2.277780
```

3.7. Finding Option Values Using the Cumulative Normal Distribution Table

Before we discuss how to use the R function to retrieve values from a cumulative normal distribution, we'll first show how to use such a table (see the table below). It is the **N()** function in the Black-Scholes-Merton model. For example, **N(0.0)=0.5, N(0.21)= 0.5832**. When **x=-0.1, N(-0.1)=1-N(0.1) = 1- 0.5398= 0.4602.**

Table 3.2. N(x), cumulative normal distribution when $X \geq 0$ $X \geq 0$.
When x<0, we use - N(|x|).

X	0.00	0.01	0.02	0.03	0.04	0.05	0.06	0.07	0.08	0.09
0.0	0.5000	0.5040	0.5080	0.5120	0.5160	0.5199	0.5239	0.5279	0.5319	0.5359
0.1	0.5398	0.5438	0.5478	0.5517	0.5557	0.5596	0.5636	0.5675	0.5714	0.5753
0.2	0.5793	0.5832	0.5871	0.5910	0.5948	0.5987	0.6026	0.6064	0.6103	0.6141
0.3	0.6179	0.6217	0.6255	0.6293	0.6331	0.6368	0.6406	0.6443	0.6480	0.6517
0.4	0.6554	0.6591	0.6628	0.6664	0.6700	0.6736	0.6772	0.6808	0.6844	0.6879
0.5	0.6915	0.6950	0.6985	0.7019	0.7054	0.7088	0.7123	0.7157	0.7190	0.7224
0.6	0.7257	0.7291	0.7324	0.7357	0.7389	0.7422	0.7454	0.7486	0.7517	0.7549
0.7	0.7580	0.7611	0.7642	0.7673	0.7704	0.7734	0.7764	0.7794	0.7823	0.7852
0.8	0.7881	0.7910	0.7939	0.7967	0.7995	0.8023	0.8051	0.8078	0.8106	0.8133
0.9	0.8159	0.8186	0.8212	0.8238	0.8264	0.8289	0.8315	0.8340	0.8365	0.8389
1.0	0.8413	0.8438	0.8461	0.8485	0.8508	0.8531	0.8554	0.8577	0.8599	0.8621
1.1	0.8643	0.8665	0.8686	0.8708	0.8729	0.8749	0.8770	0.8790	0.8810	0.8830
1.2	0.8849	0.8869	0.8888	0.8907	0.8925	0.8944	0.8962	0.8980	0.8997	0.9015
1.3	0.9032	0.9049	0.9066	0.9082	0.9099	0.9115	0.9131	0.9147	0.9162	0.9177
1.4	0.9192	0.9207	0.9222	0.9236	0.9251	0.9265	0.9279	0.9292	0.9306	0.9319
1.5	0.9332	0.9345	0.9357	0.9370	0.9382	0.9394	0.9406	0.9418	0.9429	0.9441

1.6	0.9452	0.9463	0.9474	0.9484	0.9495	0.9505	0.9515	0.9525	0.9535	0.9545
1.7	0.9554	0.9564	0.9573	0.9582	0.9591	0.9599	0.9608	0.9616	0.9625	0.9633
1.8	0.9641	0.9649	0.9656	0.9664	0.9671	0.9678	0.9686	0.9693	0.9699	0.9706
1.9	0.9713	0.9719	0.9726	0.9732	0.9671	0.9744	0.9750	0.9756	0.9761	0.9767
2.0	0.9772	0.9778	0.9783	0.9788	0.9793	0.9798	0.9803	0.9808	0.9812	0.9817
2.1	0.9821	0.9826	0.9830	0.9834	0.9838	0.9842	0.9846	0.9850	0.9854	0.9857
2.2	0.9861	0.9864	0.9868	0.9871	0.9875	0.9878	0.9881	0.9884	0.9887	0.9890
2.3	0.9893	0.9896	0.9898	0.9901	0.9904	0.9906	0.9909	0.9911	0.9913	0.9916
2.4	0.9918	0.9920	0.9922	0.9925	0.9927	0.9929	0.9931	0.9932	0.9934	0.9936
2.5	0.9938	0.9940	0.9941	0.9943	0.9945	0.9946	0.9948	0.9949	0.9951	0.9952
2.6	0.9953	0.9955	0.9956	0.9957	0.9959	0.9960	0.9961	0.9962	0.9963	0.9964
2.7	0.9965	0.9966	0.9967	0.9968	0.9969	0.9970	0.9971	0.9972	0.9973	0.9974
2.8	0.9974	0.9975	0.9976	0.9977	0.9977	0.9978	0.9979	0.9979	0.9980	0.9981
2.9	0.9981	0.9982	0.9982	0.9983	0.9984	0.9984	0.9985	0.9985	0.9986	0.9986
3.0	0.9987	0.9987	0.9987	0.9988	0.9988	0.9989	0.9989	0.9989	0.9990	0.9990
3.1	0.9990	0.9991	0.9991	0.9991	0.9992	0.9992	0.9992	0.9992	0.9993	0.9993
3.2	0.9993	0.9993	0.9994	0.9994	0.9994	0.9994	0.9994	0.9995	0.9995	0.9995
3.3	0.9995	0.9995	0.9995	0.9996	0.9996	0.9996	0.9996	0.9996	0.9996	0.9997
3.4	0.9997	0.9997	0.9997	0.9997	0.9997	0.9997	0.9997	0.9997	0.9997	0.9998
3.5	0.9998	0.9998	0.9998	0.9998	0.9998	0.9998	0.9998	0.9998	0.9998	0.9998
3.6	0.9998	0.9998	0.9999	0.9999	0.9999	0.9999	0.9999	0.9999	0.9999	0.9999
3.7	0.9999	0.9999	0.9999	0.9999	0.9999	0.9999	0.9999	0.9999	0.9999	0.9999
3.8	0.9999	0.9999	0.9999	0.9999	0.9999	0.9999	0.9999	0.9999	0.9999	0.9999
3.9	1.0000	1.0000	1.0000	1.0000	1.0000	1.0000	1.0000	1.0000	1.0000	1.0000
4.0	1.0000	1.0000	1.0000	1.0000	1.0000	1.0000	1.0000	1.0000	1.0000	1.0000

Assume that we have **S=40, X=42, T=0.5, r=0.1**, and **sigma=0.2**. Applying the formulae for d_1 and d_2, we have $d_1=0.07926551$ and $d_2=-0.06215585$.

```
> d1 = (log(40/42)+(0.1+0.2*0.2/2.)*0.5)/(0.2*sqrt(0.5))
> d1
[1] 0.07926551
> d2<-d1-0.2*sqrt(0.5)
> d2
[1] -0.06215585
```

To find out the value of N(d1) and N(d2) for a given value of d1 and d2, we use the cumulative standard normal distribution table.

```
> 0.5279+(0.07-0.079)/(0.08-0.07)*(0.5319-0.5279)
> [1] 0.5243 # for N(d1) N(d2)= 1- 0.5329
```

Putting them together, we have the premium for this call option, which is slightly different from 2.28.

```
> 40*0.5243-42*exp(-0.1*0.5)*(1-0.5329)
[1] 2.310591
```

3.8. R function for the Cumulative Normal Distribution

First, the density function for the standard normal distribution is given below.

Equation 7

$$f(x) = \frac{1}{\sqrt{2\pi}} e^{-\frac{x^2}{2}}$$

In R, the density function corresponding to equation 7 is **dnorm**. For example, we could use **dnorm(0)** to get its density value at zero.

```
> dnorm(0)
[1] 0.3989423
```

Manually we could check its value using equation 7.

```
> 1/sqrt(2*pi)
[1] 0.3989423
```

The corresponding cumulative standard normal function in R is **pnorm()**. Since a standard normal distribution is symmetric centered on zero, **pnorm(0)** should be 0.5.

```
> pnorm(0)
[1] 0.5
```

3.9. Hedge, Speculation, and Arbitrage

Assume that a US importer will pay ten million pounds in three months to import certain equipment from Great Britain. He or she is concerned with a potential depreciation of the US dollar against the pound. There are several ways to hedge such a risk: buy pounds now, enter a futures contract to buy ten million pounds in three months with a fixed exchange rate, or buy call options with a fixed exchange rate as its exercise price. The first two choices would eliminate any uncertainty. However, when the pound depreciates, we would regret our action. On the other hand, entering a call option would guarantee a maximum exchange rate today. At the same time, if the pound depreciates, the importer will reap the benefits. Such activities are called hedging since we take the opposite position of our risks.

Speculation means betting on the direction of a market, individual securities, or exchange rates. For example, if an investor expects that the stock price of IBM would increase, he or she could buy the underlying stocks, long its future contracts, or buy call options. Buying the underlying stocks would entail certain risk, but taking a long position in futures is much riskier than buying underlying securities. If investors expect the market as a whole might fall in the short term, they could buy index put options. The key is that the speculator takes a position based on his/her belief.

Arbitrage occurs when an investor (arbitrageur) observes a mispricing where he or she could profit from that opportunity without bearing any risk. For example, if an investor finds that the same security has two different prices traded on two stock exchanges, he or she could buy low and sell high simultaneously to profit from the discrepancy.

3.10. Various Trading Strategies

Let's look at the simplest scenario. A firm faces a great uncertainty in the near future because of its forthcoming restructuring. However, we are not sure how the market would take such an event (i.e., if it would react positively or negatively). To take the advantage of such an opportunity, we could buy a call and buy a put with the same exercise prices. Assume that the exercise price is $30. The payoff of our position is given below.

```
payoff_call<-function(sT,x)(sT-x+abs(sT-x))/2
payoff_put<-function(sT,x)(x-sT+abs(x-sT))/2
sT<-seq(0,50,by=5)
y<-payoff_call(sT,30)+payoff_put(sT,30)
plot(sT,y,'l')

# the last parameter of plot() is a lower case
of L
```

The graph in the right panel above shows that whichever way the stock goes, we would profit. When would we lose? Obviously when the stock does not change much (i.e., our expectations fail to materialize).

In general, we can adopt various trading strategies, using underlying securities such as stocks, call options, put options, futures, and/or bonds to satisfy our needs.

Spread refers to using the same type of options such as all calls (or puts). For example, we could use calls to form a bull spread.

Bull Spread with Calls

Buy a call option on a stock with an exercise price of X_1 and sell a call option with the exact same features except for exercise price (X_2) with $X_1 < X_2$. Since $X_1 < X_2$ and the call with a lower exercise price is more valuable, the call purchased is more expensive than the call sold.

The bull spread with calls involves an initial investment. Below is the R program for a bull spread with calls. The expectation of the investors who adopt such a strategy is that the stock price will rise (bull view)

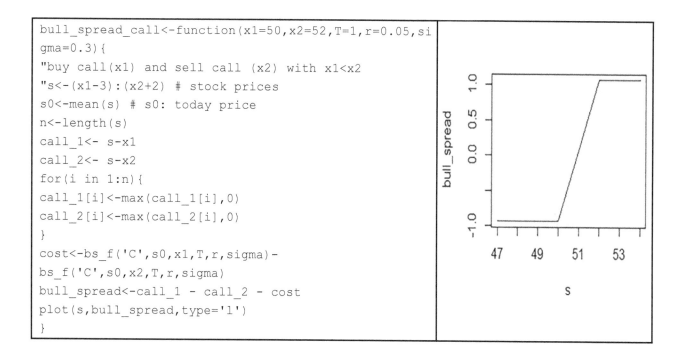

```
bull_spread_call<-function(x1=50,x2=52,T=1,r=0.05,si
gma=0.3){
"buy call(x1) and sell call (x2) with x1<x2
"s<-(x1-3):(x2+2) # stock prices
s0<-mean(s) # s0: today price
n<-length(s)
call_1<- s-x1
call_2<- s-x2
for(i in 1:n){
call_1[i]<-max(call_1[i],0)
call_2[i]<-max(call_2[i],0)
}
cost<-bs_f('C',s0,x1,T,r,sigma)-
bs_f('C',s0,x2,T,r,sigma)
bull_spread<-call_1 - call_2 - cost
plot(s,bull_spread,type='l')
}
```

Similarly a bull spread can be formed by using put options (see the exercise at the end of the chapter). Below, the frequently used spreads and combinations are listed with the related features.

Table 3.3. Various trading strategies and their properties

Names	Description	Direction of initial cash flow	Expectation of future price movement
Bull spread with calls	Buy a call (x_1) sell a call (x_2) [$x_1 < x_2$]	Outflow	Rise
Bull spread with puts	Buy a put (x_1), sell a put (x_2) [$x_1 < x_2$]	Inflow	Rise
Bear spread with puts	Buy a put (x_2), sell a put (x_1) [$x_1 < x_2$]	Outflow	Fall
Bear spread with calls	Buy a call (x_2), sell a call (x_1) [$x_1 < x_2$]	Inflow	Fall
Straddle	Buy a call & a put with the same x	Outflow	Rise or fall
Strip	Buy two puts and a call (with the same x)	Outflow	Prob (fall) > prob (rise)

Strap	Buy two calls and one put (with the same x)	Outflow	prob (rise)> prob(fall)
Strangle	Buy a call (x2) and buy a put (x1) [x1 < x2]	Outflow	Rise or fall
Butterfly with calls	Buy two calls (k1,k3) and sell two calls (x2) $x2=(x1+x3)/2$	Outflow	Stay around x_2
Butterfly with puts	Buy two puts (x1,x3) and sell two puts (x2) $x2=(x1+x3)/2$	Outflow	Stay around x_2
Calendar spread	Sell a call (T_1) and buy a call (T_2) with the same strike price and $T_1 < T_2$	Outflow	Stay around x_2

3.11. Greeks

Delta (Δ) is defined as "the derivative of the option to its underlying security price." Thus, the *delta of a call* is defined as

Equation 8

$$\Delta = \frac{\partial C}{\partial S}$$

The delta of a European call on a nondividend-paying stock is

Equation 9

$$\Delta_{call} = N\,(d_1)$$

The delta for a European put on a nondividend-paying stock is

Equation 10

$$\Delta_{put} = N\,(d_1) - 1$$

If we sell a European call, we could hold Δ shares of the same stock to hedge our position. This is named a delta hedge. Since the delta (Δ) is a function of the underlying stock (S), to maintain an effective hedge, we have to rebalance our holding constantly. This is called dynamic hedging. The delta of a portfolio is the weighted deltas of individual securities in the portfolio. Note that when we short a security, its weight will be negative.

Equation 11

$$\Delta_{port} = \sum_{i=1}^{n} w_i \Delta_i$$

3.12. Put-Call Parity

Let's look at a call with an exercise price of $20, a maturity of 3 months, and a risk-free rate of 5%. The present value of this future $20 is given below.

```
> 20*exp(-0.05*3/12)
[1] 19.75156
```

In three months, what will be the wealth of our portfolio, which consists of a call on the same stock plus $19.75 cash, today?

If the stock price is below $20, we don't exercise the call and keep the cash. If the stock price is above $20, we use our cash—$20 in three months—to exercise our call option to own the stock. Thus, our portfolio value will be the maximum of those two values: stock price in 3 months or $20—that is, **max(s,20)**.

```
# C + PV(K) = C+ 19.75
# wealth at T is max(s,20) for holding a call plus cash of pv(x)
```

On the other hand, how about a portfolio with a stock plus a put option with an exercise price of $20?

If the stock price falls below $20, we exercise the put option and get $20. If the stock price is above $20, we simply keep the stock. Thus, our portfolio value will be the maximum of those two values: stock price in 3 months or $20—that is, **max(s,20)**.

```
# S+P
# wealth at T is max(s,20)for holding a put plus underlying stock
```

Thus, for both portfolios, we have the same terminal wealth of **max(s,20)**. Based on the no-arbitrage principle, for European calls and puts, we have the following equality (i.e., put-call parity).

Equation 12

$$C + Xe^{-rfT} = P + S_0$$

When the stock has known dividend payments before its maturity date, we have the following equality.

Equation 13

$$C + PV(D) + Xe^{-rfT} = P + S_0,$$

where *PV(D)* is the present value of all dividends before the maturity date (*T*).

3.13. Using Excel to Get the Result from the Black-Scholes-Merton Model

The following image shows how to use Excel to price a European call option. Again, the key is the cumulative (standard) normal distribution (see the Excel NORMSDIST() function).

	A	B	C	D	E	F
1	S=	42				
2	x=	40				
3	T=	0.5				
4	R=	0.1				
5	sigma=	0.2				
6						
7	d1=	0.6278		" =(LN(B1/B2)+(B4-0.5*B5*B5)*B3)/(B5*SQRT(B3))		
8	d2=	0.4864		"=B7-B5*SQRT(B3)"		
9	black-scholes=	4.7407		"=B1*NORMSDIST(B7)-B2*EXP(-B4*B3)*NORMSDIST(B8)		

3.14. Retrieving Publicly Available Options Data

To get option data from Yahoo Finance or MarketWatch, we have the following structure. The **library()** function loads an R package called XML. To install it, issue the following codes:

```
> library(XML)
> x<-readHTMLTable(" ")
```

If you receive an error message when loading the package, it means that XML is not preinstalled.

```
>install.packages('XML')
```

To find out what kind of link (Web page) we can use, we have the following steps:

1. Go to http://finance.yahoo.com.
2. Type "IBM" in the search box (top left-hand side).
3. Click **Options** on the left-hand side.

After we have the Web link, we use it as the input variable for the readHTMLTable() function.

```
> x<-readHTMLTable("http://finance.yahoo.com/q/op?s=IBM+Options")
> y<-as.matrix(x[[3]])
> y2<-subset(y,substr(y[,2],1,3)=="IBM")
> colnames(y2)<-y[6,]
```
```
> head(y2)
152.50 IBM150605P00152500   0.37  0.00   0.06  0.00   0.00%   27  51   50.00%
[1,] "144.00" "IBM150605P00144000" "0.19" "0.00" "0.06" "0.00" "0.00%" "10" "10" "66.02%"
[2,] "145.00" "IBM150605P00145000" "0.10" "0.00" "0.06" "0.00" "0.00%" "7" "7" "63.67%"
[3,] "148.00" "IBM150605P00148000" "0.19" "0.00" "0.05" "0.00" "0.00%" "18" "18" "55.08%"
[4,] "149.00" "IBM150605P00149000" "0.21" "0.00" "0.05" "0.00" "0.00%" "18" "18" "52.73%"
[5,] "150.00" "IBM150605P00150000" "0.20" "0.00" "0.06" "0.00" "0.00%" "7" "31" "51.56%"
[6,] "152.50" "IBM150605P00152500" "0.37" "0.00" "0.06" "0.00" "0.00%" "27" "51" "50.00%"
```

For the second column (variable) under Symbol, we could see the letter *C* (e.g., IBM120218C00100000), which indicate it is a call option. Using the **tail()** function, we can find data related to put options.

```
> tail(y2)
      152.50    IBM150605P00152500    0.37    0.00    0.06    0.00    0.00%  27 51 50.00%

[12,] "167.50" "IBM150605P00167500" "0.55" "0.51" "0.54" "0.13" "30.95%" "407" "830" "20.51%"
[13,] "170.00" "IBM150605P00170000" "1.43" "1.39" "1.44" "0.20" "16.26%" "577" "850" "19.87%"
[14,] "172.50" "IBM150605P00172500" "2.26" "2.87" "4.30" "0.00" "0.00%"  "71"  "535" "39.70%"
[15,] "175.00" "IBM150605P00175000" "4.62" "5.05" "6.70" "0.00" "0.00%"  "2"   "336" "50.29%"
[16,] "177.50" "IBM150605P00177500" "7.55" "7.60" "7.75" "0.55"  "7.86%" "2"   "55"  "29.40%"
[17,] "180.00" "IBM150605P00180000" "8.00" "9.25" "12.00" "0.00" "0.00%"  "5"   "15"  "76.51%"
```

It is not convenient to just type those command lines. Based on chapter 2, we know that we can write our own function to download the option data for a given ticker symbol (see exercise 3.41).

3.15. Using R Package of quantmod to Retrieve Option Data

It is not quite efficient to use the procedure discussed in the last section. Fortunately we have an R package named **quantmod** by which we can retrieve option data more efficiently

```
> require(quantmod)
> x<-getOptionChain("IBM")
> x # just show a few lines for calls and puts
$calls
  Strike Last Chg Bid Ask Vol OI
IBM120818C00105000 105 92.30 0.00 89.45 91.75 NA 1
IBM120818C00150000 150 36.00 0.00 45.85 46.75 1 1
IBM120818C00160000 160 26.20 0.00 34.55 36.75 5 9
IBM120818C00165000 165 23.00 0.00 30.35 31.60 8 4
IBM120803C00170000 170 25.25 0.00 26.25 26.45 7 7
IBM120818C00170000 170 25.25 0.00 26.10 26.65 25 119

$puts
  Strike Last Chg Bid Ask Vol OI
IBM120818P00110000 110 0.05 0.00 NA 0.03 10 20
IBM120818P00115000 115 0.06 0.00 NA 0.03 10 10
IBM120818P00120000 120 0.03 0.00 NA 0.03 1 21
IBM120818P00125000 125 0.04 0.00 NA 0.03 27 30
IBM120818P00130000 130 0.03 0.00 NA 0.03 6 8
IBM120818P00140000 140 0.04 0.00 NA 0.05 26 45
IBM120818P00145000 145 0.02 0.00 NA 0.06 76 185
```

3.16. Implied Volatility

In one of the previous sections, we showed that for a given set of input value of **s=40, x=42, T=0.5, r=0.1**, and **sigma=0.2**, we can find that the call price is $2.28.

```
> call_f(40,42,0.5,0.1,0.2)
[1] 2.277780 # value of this European call option is $2.28
```

The last input variable of sigma is the volatility of the underlying security. Usually we use historical return data to estimate its value. Here our assumption is that the future's volatility will be the same as the past. Since we can observe call or put prices, we can find the implied volatility. An implied volatility means that when we inert its values in the Black-Scholes-Merton formula, it will give us the same call price we observed. There are two ways to estimate an implied volatility.

Method 1

Generate a set of volatilities, estimate their corresponding calls, and choose the volatility that minimizes the difference between its call and the observed call. Below are the steps.

Assume that we are given a call price such as c0 with all related variables: **s0, T, k**, and the Black-Scholes-Merton call option model is available, **bs_call**.

1. Generate a vector of volatility (i.e., sigma).
2. Run a loop for all such volatilities.
3. Estimate call value based on one given sigma.
4. Calculate **abs(c-c0)**. If its value is smaller than the previous one, **implied_vol=sigma**.
5. Report the final **implied_vol**.

Method 2

Use binary search. Here is the logic: assume that c(observed) is our observed call price.

1. Choose two extreme volatilities, **low_vol** and **high_vol**. Their corresponding call prices will be **call(low_vol)** and **call(high_vol)**. The first check is that **call(low_vol)< call(observed)<call(high_ vol)**.
2. Estimate the midpoint of two volatilities: **mid_vol=(low_vol+high_vol)/2**. Estimate the **call value: call(mid_vol)**.
3. Conduct the following tests: If **call(obs) > call(mid_vol)**, then **low_vol = mid_vol** and go to step 2. If **call(obs) < call(mid_vol)l** , then **high_vol= mid_vol** and go to step 2.

Note: For step 3, literally, we move half of the available area. In the process, we could set up a conversion criteria. For example, the difference between our calculated call price and observed call price is less than 0.01.

Exercises

3.1. What is the difference between an American call and a European call?

3.2. What is the definition of T in the Black-Scholes-Merton model?

3.3. Can we apply the Black-Scholes-Merton model to price an American put?

3.4. What is the unit of rf in the Black-Scholes-Merton model?

3.5. If the annual rate is 3.4%, compounded semiannually, what is the value of rf that we should use for the Black-Scholes-Merton model?

3.6. How do you use options to hedge?

3.7. What are the differences between hedging, speculation, and arbitrage?

3.8. How do you treat predetermined cash dividends to price a European call?

3.9. Why is an American call worth more than a corresponding European call?

3.10. Assume you are a mutual manager and your portfolio's β is strongly correlated with the market. You are worried about the short-term fall of the market. What could you do to protect your portfolio?

3.11. The current price of stock A is $38.5; the strike prices for a call and a put are both $37. If the continuously compounded risk-free rate is 3.2%, maturity is 3 months, and the volatility of stock A is 0.25, what are the prices for a European call and put?

3.12. Use the put-call parity to verify the above solutions.

3.13. When the strike prices for call and put in 3.11 are different, can we apply the put-call parity?

3.14. For a set of input values, such as s=40, x=40, t=3/12=0.25, r=0.05, and sigma=0.20 using the Black-Scholes-Merton model, we can estimate the value of the call. Now keep all parameters constant except S (current price of stocks). Show the relationship (a graph is better) between calls and S.

3.15. Using the Black-Scholes-Merton model, show the relationship between a call and X (exercise price).

3.16. Using the Black-Scholes-Merton model, show the relationship between a call and R_f.

3.17. Using the Black-Scholes-Merton model, show the relationship between a call and T (maturity date).

3.18. Using the Black-Scholes-Merton model, show the relationship between a call and .

3.19. Repeating 3.14 to 3.18 for a put option, use the Black-Scholes-Merton model.

3.20. Here is my portfolio: long an underlying stock, long a call option. Write an R program showing the payoff function of this portfolio. Assume that the current stock price is $40 and the strike price of the European call is $45.

3.21. Bull spread with puts. Buy a put on a stock with K_1 and sell a put with a strike price of K_2 ($K_1 < K_2$). Since $K_1 < K_2$, the put purchased is less valuable than the put sold. The bull spread with puts involves upfront cash inflow. Write an R program for payoff and profit/loss functions. Draw a graph.

3.22. Bear spread with puts. Investors expect the stock price is going to fall. Buy a put with K_2 and sell a put with K_1 ($K_1 < K_2$). Since $K_1 < K_2$, the put purchased is more valuable than the put sold. The bear spread with puts involves initial cash outflow. Write an R program for payoff and profit/loss functions then graph.

3.23. Butterfly spread. Buy two calls with K_1 and K_3. Sell two calls with K_2 ($K_2 = 0.5 \ (K_1 + K_3)$).

a) Show that this strategy involves an initial investment. In other words, prove that $C_1 + C_2 \geq 2 C_2$. You form a portfolio of long C_1, C_3, and short $2 \ C_2$.

b) Write an R program to show its profit function.

3.24. Write an R program to estimate the implied volatility for the following set of parameters: Call price is $5, European call. Maturity date is 6 months. Strike price is $42, and the current price is $40. The volatility of the underlying stock is 25%, and the continuously compounded risk-free rate is 5%.

3.25. We form a trading strategy called *straddle* by buying a call and a put with the same exercise price. The expectation of adopting such a strategy is that the stock will be very volatile, but we are not sure about the direction of the movement.

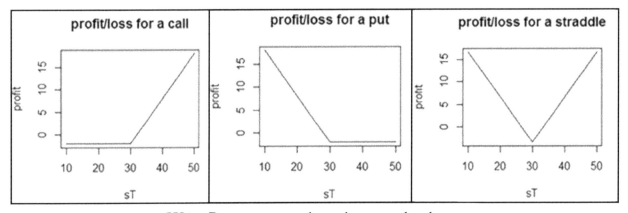

Write R programs to show three graphs above.

3.26. You have the following portfolio: long 100 shares, short 77 calls on the same stocks, and long 88 puts on the same stocks. Assume that the current stock price is $40, the strike price for the call is $45, and the strike price of the put is $38.

a) Write the payoff function for you portfolio

b) What is the profit /loss function? Assume that the call and put premiums are $3 and $4 respectively.

c) Write an R program for the above two tasks.

3.27. Draw a graph for the portfolio presented in 3.25.

3.28. If we buy two puts and one call with the same exercise price, the strategy is called *strips* (see below).

profit/loss for a strips

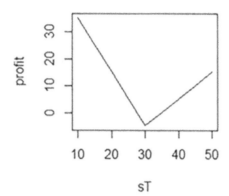

What is the expectation of such a strategy? Write a program to show the above graph.

3.29. If we buy one put and two calls with the same exercise price, the strategy is called strap (see the graph below).

profit/loss for a straps

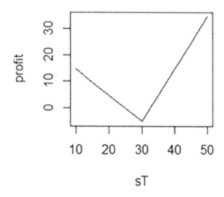

What is the expectation of such a strategy?
Write an R program to show above graph.

3.30. Write an R program to draw a graph showing the relation of delta (Δ) of a European call on nondividend stock with its underlying stock price (x axis).

3.31. Write an R program to draw a graph showing the relation of delta (Δ) of a European put on nondividend stock with its underlying stock price (x axis).

3.32. Write an R program to show the relation between delta (Δ) of a European call on nondividend stock with its time to maturity for three categories: in the money, at the money, and out the money.

3.33. Assume that call and put options are both Europeans. Use put-call parity to show that the butterfly formed by calls will be the same as the butterfly formed by puts.

3.34. Explain the implied volatility from this Web page: http://optionstrategist.com/free/analysis/data/index.html

3.35. Check the following codes:

```
x<-10
if(x>0)
print("x>0")
else
print("x<=0")
```

3.36. The current stock price is $30. The exercise price is $30. The risk-free interest rate is 6% per annum, compounding semiannually. The volatility is 25% per annum. The time to maturity is four months, and the underlying stock will pay $1 dividends at the end of the first month and fifth months respectively.

What are the prices of a European call and a European put?

CHAPTER 4

Financial-Statement Analysis

To find the latest financial statements for IBM from MarketWatch, we have three steps:

1. Go to http://www.marketwatch.com.
2. Type "IBM" in the search box (top right hand).
3. Click **Financial**.

Thus, we have the following link, which is used in the **readHTMLTable()** function. The related Web page is http://www.marketwatch.com/investing/stock/ibm/financials. To retrieve the IBM's financial statement, we upload XML and apply the **readHTMLTable()** function. Note that when XML is not installed, **issue >intall.packages('XML')**.

```
>library(XML)
>x<-readHTMLTable("http://www.marketwatch.com/investing/stock/IBM/financials")
> x[[1]] # show the contents of first part.
Fiscal year Jan-Dec.USD millions. 2007 2008 2009 2010 2011 5-yeartrend
 Sales/Revenue $98.79B $103.63B $95.76B $99.87B $108.02B
 Sales Growth - 4.90% -7.60% 4.29% 8.16%
Cost of Goods Sold (COGS)incl. D&A 57.69B 58.6B 52.56B 54.42B 56.78B
COGS excluding D&A 52.49B 53.15B 47.56B 49.59B 56.78B
Depreciation & Amortization Expense 5.2B 5.45B 4.99B 4.83B -
Depreciation 4.04B 4.14B 3.77B 3.66B -
Amortization of Intangibles 1.16B 1.31B 1.22B 1.17B -
 COGS Growth - 1.57% -10.31% 3.54% 4.34%
 Gross Income 41.1B 45.03B 43.2B 45.45B 51.25B
 Gross Income Growth - 9.58% -4.06% 5.21% 12.74%
 Gross Profit Margin - - - - 47.44% NA
```

4.1. Introduction

Financial-statement analysis plays a central role in financial analysis. The objective of financial statements is to offer reliable information related to a firm's short-term and long-term performance, risk level, ownership structure, insider trading, material changes, and other important issues to shareholders, regulators, lending institutions, financial analysts, internal managers, and other stakeholders. In the United States, these financial statements are prepared based on GAAP (generally accepted accounting principles).
See http://cpaclass.com/gaap/gaap-us-01a.htm. Internationally the standard is IFRS (International

Financial Reporting Standards). See http://www.ifrsclass.com/index.htm. At the end of each fiscal year, fiscal quarters, and when necessary, companies file annual/quarterly/interim financial statements with the SEC (US Securities and Exchange Commission).

4.2. Where to Get Data Related to Financial Statements

Yahoo Finance, Google Finance, and SEC filings are free to access. However, a potential user has to spend time and effort downloading and processing data. Compustat is a user-friendly product with a much longer historical time series, but it is very expensive. Fortunately, for teaching purposes, free data sources are more than enough. The table below lists the related information.

Table 4.1. Data sources for financial statement analysis

Time frame	Description	Web links
Short-term (3–4 years)	Yahoo Finance	http://finance.yahoo.com
	Google Finance	http://www.google.com/finance
	MarketWatch	http://www.marketwatch.com
	SEC filings	http://www.sec.gov/edgar.shtml
Medium-term (from 1994 onward)	SEC filings	http://www.sec.gov/edgar.shtml
	Capital IQ-Compustat	http://www.compustat.com/myproducts.aspx
Long-term (back to 1950)	Capital IQ-Compustat	http://www.compustat.com/myproducts.aspx

Actually, we will see that these free data is much more adaptable than most expensive financial databases. For instance, it is not possible to write a two-line program to access a firm's annual financial statements using the Compustat database. For these reasons, we will discuss only publicly available data. Yahoo Finance and Google Finance will be the focus of this chapter.

4.3. An Example of Current Ratio

To retrieve the lat several years' annual balance sheet for DELL, we have two-line R codes. To install **quantmod**, click **Packages…** on the menu bar. Click **Install Packages…**, choose a location, then install the package. For more details, please consult chapter 40: "Introduction to R Packages."

```
> library(quantmod)
> x<-viewFin(getFin("DELL",auto.assign=FALSE),"BS","A")
```

In the codes, **BS** is for balance sheet while **A** is for annual statement. To view the first several data items, we could use the **head()** function.

```
> head(x)
2011-01-28 2010-01-29 2009-01-30 2008-02-01
Cash & Equivalents 13913 10635 8352 7764
Short Term Investments 452 373 740 208
Cash and Short Term Investments 14365 11008 9092 7972
Accounts Receivable - Trade, Net 6493 5837 4731 5961
Receivables - Other NA NA NA NA
Total Receivables, Net 10136 8543 6443 7693
```

Companies need cash or its equivalents to deal with their daily operations such as paying account payables. To measure such ability, a current ratio can be used.

Equation 1

$$Current\ ratio = \frac{Total\ Current\ Assets}{Total\ Current\ Liabilities}$$

To get those to data items, we use the following codes.

```
> x[grep('Total Current',rownames(x)),]
2011-01-28 2010-01-29 2009-01-30 2008-02-01
Total Current Assets 29021 24245 20151 19880
Total Current Liabilities 19483 18960 14859 18526
```

In the above codes, **x[condition,]** will extract the rows from x when the condition is satisfied. The function of **grep("keyword", phrase)** will be true if the keyword is contained in the given phrase. The **rownames()** function will extract all row names that contain the data items. For example, the first row is named Revenue. Since the total current assets and the total current liabilities for DELL in 2011 are 29,021 and 19,483, its corresponding current ratio is 1.45.

4.4. Income Statement

An income statement (**IS**) is a summary of a company's activities over a period, usually over one (fiscal) year or a (fiscal) quarter. The basic format is shown below:

Basic format	Example
Revenue - Cost - Interest payment	Revenue = 100 - Cost = - 50 - Interest payment = - 10
EBT - Tax	EBT = 40 Tax rate is 0.34 -13.6
Net Income	Net Income = 26.4

Note that EBT is "earnings before tax." Yahoo Finance is an excellent source for retrieving financial statements from the last several years. Using DELL as an example, we have the following steps.

1. Go to http://finance.yahoo.com. 2. Enter "DELL" in the Get Quote box. 3. Click **Income Statement** at the left-bottom part	**FINANCIALS** Income Statement Balance Sheet Cash Flow

Alternatively we can use the following link:

```
http://finance.yahoo.com/q/is?s=DELL+Income+Statement&annual
```

For DELL's quarterly income statements, see the following link:

```
http://finance.yahoo.com/q/is?s=DELL # quarterly Income Statement
```

4.5. Balance Sheet

Unlike income statements that cover certain periods, a balance sheet (BS) is a snapshot at time T, such as at the end of a fiscal year. For example, if the total assets of a company are $1m, the balance sheet will show: 1) what type of assets (tangible or intangible) contribute to this final value of $1m and 2) who has a claim on such an amount. Potential claimers could be banks, other debt holders, preferred equity holders, common stockholders.

Example	
Cash = 0.2m	Short-term debt = 0.1m
Equipment = 0.5m	Long-term debt = 0.3m
Other values = 0.3m	Equity =: 0.6m
Total assets= 1.0m	Total assets = 1.0m

To retrieve a balance sheet for DELL using Yahoo Finance, we have three steps.

1. Go to http://finance.yahoo.com. 2. Enter "DELL" in the Get Quote box. 3. Click **Balance Sheet** at the left-bottom part	**FINANCIALS** Income Statement Balance Sheet Cash Flow

Alternatively we can use the following links for annual (or quarterly) balance sheets for DELL.

- http://finance.yahoo.com/q/bs?s=DELL+Balance+Sheet&annual
- http://finance.yahoo.com/q/bs?s=DELL

4.6. Cash-Flow Statements

In addition to the income statement and balance sheet, the third type of financial statement is the cashflow statement (CFS), which has been a part of a company's SEC filings since 1987. A cash-flow statement records the amount of cash and cash equivalents entering and leaving a company. A CFS helps investors and other stakeholders understand how a company's operations are running in terms of cash flows (i.e., where its money is coming from and how it is being spent). To find the cash-flow statement for DELL manually, we have the following three-step approach:

1. Go to http://finance.yahoo.com.
2. Enter "DELL" in the Get Quotes box.
3. Click **Cash Flow Statements** (left-bottom part of the screen).

Alternatively we can use the following Web page:
http://finance.yahoo.com/q/cf?s=DELL+Cash+Flow&annual.

4.7. Common-Size Financial Statements

To compare the performance of a firm over several years or compare its performance with other firms in the same industry, we use so-called common-size financial statements. For example, last year's cash and equivalents was $1m, and this year's corresponding value is $1.1m. With those two values alone, it is difficult to figure out what the impact is of this specific data item. If we know further that the ratio of this data item over total sales is a constant over two years, then it is easier to interpret our results.

A common-size financial statement is defined as below:

Equation 2

$$New\ Data\ Item = \frac{Original\ Data\ Item}{Reference\ Data\ Item}$$

For income statements, usually we use total sales as our reference data item. For example, for cost of goods sold, we would have

Equation 3

$$Cost\ of\ goods\ sold\ (common\ size) = \frac{Cost\ of\ goods\ sold}{Total\ sales}$$

For balance sheets, usually we use the total assets as our reference data item.
Equation 4

$$Cash\ (common\ size) = \frac{Cash}{Total\ Assets}$$

4.8. The Definitions of Key Ratios

The profitability ratios include gross margin, operating margin, EBIT margin and net-profit margin, ROE (return on equity), and ROA (return on assets). For example, ROE is a measure of the equity owner's profitability. Several ratios with *margin* in their names use sales as their denominator. Operating margin is used to measure the efficiency of the underlying operation since it is free from the impact of a firm's capital structure.

Equation 5

$$\begin{cases} Gross\ Margin = \dfrac{Gross\ profit}{Sales} = \dfrac{Sales - Cost\ of\ sales}{Sales} \\[2ex] Operating\ Margin = \dfrac{Operating\ Income}{Sales} \\[2ex] Net\ Profit\ Margin = \dfrac{Net\ Income}{Total\ sales} \end{cases}$$

The two most widely used measures of profitability are ROE and ROA.
Equation 6

$$\begin{cases} ROE\ (return\ on\ equity) = \dfrac{Net\ income}{Book\ value\ of\ equity} \\[2ex] ROA\ (return\ on\ assets) = \dfrac{Net\ income}{Total\ Assets} \end{cases}$$

ROE measures how profitable a firm is to its (common) shareholders while ROA measures the firm's profitability to its debt and equity holders jointly. Depending on objectives, we might prefer one over another. For example, when we intend to compare the performance of two companies, it is better to use ROA instead of ROE since the latter includes the impact of capital structure. On the other hand, when ranking two firms to prepare our investments, we prefer ROE.

In computing ratios, we often use average total assets, the average of this year and last year's total assets, as our denominator.

$$ROA\ (return\ on\ assets) = \frac{Net\ Income}{Average\ Total\ Assets}$$

Two often used ratios are market-to-book and EPS ratios.

Equation 7

$$Market\ to\ book = \frac{Market\ value\ of\ equity}{Book\ value\ of\ equity}$$

Equation 8

$$EPAS = \frac{Net\ Income}{shares\ outstanding}$$

One way to measure the size of a firm is to use the *market capitalization*, which is defined as the stock price times the shares outstanding. P/E (price-earnings) ratio is one of the most used measures to classify stocks into different categories.

PEG ratio is a forward-looking ratio defined below:

Equation 9

$$PEG\ ratio = \frac{P/E}{5\text{-}year\ expected\ growth\ rate}$$

The DuPont identity can be decomposed into three components, which could then be analyzed separately.

Equation 10

$$ROE = \underbrace{\frac{Net\ Income}{Sales}}_{Net\ profit\ margin} * \underbrace{\frac{Sales}{Total\ assets}}_{Assit\ turnover} * \underbrace{\frac{Total\ assets}{Book\ value\ of\ equity}}_{Equity\ Multiplier}$$

When a firm has a higher ROE this year than last year, we could apply the DuPont identity to find out which area(s) the firm did better. To measure a firm's financial leverage, we use the debt-equity ratio:

Equation 11

$$Debt\ Equity\ Ratio = \frac{Long\ term\ debt}{Book\ Value\ of\ Equity}$$

Alternatively we can use long-term-debt-over-total-assets ratio.

Equation 12

$$Debt\ over\ Total\ Assets = \frac{Long\ term\ debt}{Total\ Assets}$$

4.9. Key Statistics from Yahoo Finance

Since financial statements have many data items (lines), investors and other users usually choose certain important data items (numbers) and several ratios to grasp the key aspects of those statements. For example, market capitalization, stock price times number of shares outstanding, reflects the size of a firm. From Yahoo finance, we have the following three steps to locate the key statistics for DELL (see http://finance.yahoo.com/q/ks?s=dell+Key+Statistics).

1. Go to http://finnance.yahoo.com.
2. Enter "DELL" in the Get Quotes box.
3. Click **Key Statistics** under Company on the left-hand side.

The key statistics are shown below:

Key Statistics

Data provided by Capital IQ, except where noted.

Valuation Measures	
Market Cap (intraday)[5]:	27.43B
Enterprise Value (Mar 18, 2011)[3]:	19.91B
Trailing P/E (ttm, intraday):	10.55
Forward P/E (fye Jan 28, 2013)[1]:	8.00
PEG Ratio (5 yr expected)[1]:	1.96
Price/Sales (ttm):	0.44
Price/Book (mrq):	3.50
Enterprise Value/Revenue (ttm)[3]:	0.32
Enterprise Value/EBITDA (ttm)[3]:	4.46

Based on the above information, we know that the size of the firm is $27.43 billion. The enterprise value of a firm is defined as total assets - debt - cash, which could be viewed as how much a potential buyer has to pay to buy DELL. The other notations are given in the following table:

Table 4.2. The notations for the key statistics from Yahoo Finance

Notation	Meanings	Unit	Meanings
Mrq	Most recent quarter	K	Thousands
ttm	Trailing twelve months	M	Millions
yoy	Year over year	B	Billions
lfy	Last fiscal year		
fye	Fiscal year ending		

For instance, if we intend to collect ROA and ROE (see the information below) to find the definitions of those terms, consult Yahoo Help (see http://help.yahoo.com/l/us/yahoo/finance/tools/fitakeystats.html).

Income Statement	
Revenue (ttm):	61.49B
Revenue Per Share (ttm):	31.63
Qtrly Revenue Growth (yoy):	5.30%
Gross Profit (ttm):	9.26B
EBITDA (ttm):	4.46B
Net Income Avl to Common (ttm):	2.64B
Diluted EPS (ttm):	1.35
Qtrly Earnings Growth (yoy):	177.50%
Balance Sheet	
Total Cash (mrq):	14.36B
Total Cash Per Share (mrq):	7.47
Total Debt (mrq):	6.00B
Total Debt/Equity (mrq):	77.22
Current Ratio (mrq):	1.49
Book Value Per Share (mrq):	4.04
Cash Flow Statement	
Operating Cash Flow (ttm):	3.97B
Levered Free Cash Flow (ttm):	1.53B

Financial Highlights	
Fiscal Year	
Fiscal Year Ends:	Jan 28
Most Recent Quarter (mrq):	Jan 28, 2011
Profitability	
Profit Margin (ttm):	4.29%
Operating Margin (ttm):	5.68%
Management Effectiveness	
Return on Assets (ttm):	6.04%
Return on Equity (ttm):	39.31%

4.10. Using R to Download Income Statements

We are going to use a package called quantmod (quantitative financial modeling framework). To install it, issue > **install.packages("quantmod")**. For Apple's financial info, we have the following two-line codes.

```
> library(quantmod)
> getFinancials("AAPL")
  [1] "AAPL.f"
```

After issuing the two commands above, we download all financial statements—including annual financial statements, quarterly income statements, balance sheets, and cash-flow statements—related to Apple. The saved variable is called **AAPL.f**. If issue **ls()**, we will find it.

```
> ls()
[1] "AAPL.f"
```

Again, just type the variable's name, and we can get more information.

```
> AAPL.f
Financial Statement for AAPL
Retrieved from google at 2011-06-13 09:54:13
Use "viewFinancials" or "viewFin" to view
```

According to the above information, we can use both **viewFinancials()** or **viewFin()** functions to retrieve (view) a specific financial statement. For example, to retrieve the annual income statements, we have the following one-line command (where **Q** is for quarterly, **BS** for the balance sheet, and **CF** for the cash-flow statements).

```
>x<-viewFin(AAPL.f,"IS","A") # IS: Income statement
> dim(x) # A for Annual
[1] 49 4
```

There are forty-nine data items with four fiscal years' data (four columns). See a few lines below: [using 4four at the same time???]

```
> head(x)
2010-09-25 2009-09-26 2008-09-27 2007-09-29
Revenue 65225 42905 37491 24578
Other Revenue, Total NA NA NA NA
Total Revenue 65225 42905 37491 24578
Cost of Revenue, Total 39541 25683 24294 16426
Gross Profit 25684 17222 13197 8152
Selling/General/Admin. Expenses, Total 5517 4149 3761 2963
```

The column names are for fiscal years while row names are for accounting entries.

```
> colnames(x)
[1] "2010-09-25" "2009-09-26" "2008-09-27" "2007-09-29"
```

To show the row names, we use the **rownames()** function.

```
> rownames(x)
[1]  "Revenue"
[2]  "Other Revenue, Total"
[3]  "Total Revenue"
[4]  "Cost of Revenue, Total"
[5]  "Gross Profit"
[6]  "Selling/General/Admin. Expenses, Total"
[7]  "Research & Development"
[8]  "Depreciation/Amortization"
[9]  "Interest Expense(Income)-Net Operating"
[10] "Unusual Expense (Income)"
[11] "Other Operating Expenses, Total"
[12] "Total Operating Expense"
[13] "Operating Income"
[14] "Interest Income(Expense), Net Non-Operating"
[15] "Gain (Loss) on Sale of Assets"
[16] "Other, Net"
[17] "Income Before Tax"
[18] "Income After Tax"
[19] "Minority Interest"
[20] "Equity In Affiliates"
[21] "Net Income Before Extra. Items"
[22] "Accounting Change"
[23] "Discontinued Operations"
[24] "Extraordinary Item"
[25] "Net Income"
[26] "Preferred Dividends"
[27] "Income Available to Common Excl. Extra Items"
[28] "Income Available to Common Incl. Extra Items"
[29] "Basic Weighted Average Shares"
[30] "Basic EPS Excluding Extraordinary Items"
[31] "Basic EPS Including Extraordinary Items"
[32] "Dilution Adjustment"
[33] "Diluted Weighted Average Shares"
[34] "Diluted EPS Excluding Extraordinary Items"
[35] "Diluted EPS Including Extraordinary Items"
[36] "Dividends per Share-Common Stock Primary Issue"
[37] "Gross Dividends-Common Stock"
[38] "Net Income after Stock Based Comp. Expense"
[39] "Basic EPS after Stock Based Comp. Expense"
[40] "Diluted EPS after Stock Based Comp. Expense"
[41] "Depreciation, Supplemental"
[42] "Total Special Items"
[43] "Normalized Income Before Taxes"
[44] "Effect of Special Items on Income Taxes"
[45] "Income Taxes Ex. Impact of Special Items"
[46] "Normalized Income After Taxes"
[47] "Normalized Income Avail to Common"
[48] "Basic Normalized EPS"
[49] "Diluted Normalized EPS"
```

To retrieve the net income, you use the **grep()** function. See the related codes below:

```
> x[grep('Net Income',rownames(x)),]
  2010-09-25 2009-09-26 2008-09-27 2007-09-29
Net Income Before Extra. Items 14013 8235 6119 3495
Net Income 14013 8235 6119 3495
Net Income after Stock Based Comp. Expense NA NA NA NA
```

4.11. Using R to Download Balance Sheets

To get the last several years' balance sheets (BS), we use the following codes:

```
> library(quantmod)
> getFinancials("AAPL")
 [1] "AAPL.f"
> y<-viewFin(AAPL.f,"BS","A") # BS:Balance Sheet, A=Annual
> dim(y)
 [1] 42 4
```

```
> rownames(y)
 [1] "Cash & Equivalents"
 [2] "Short Term Investments"
 [3] "Cash and Short Term Investments"
 [4] "Accounts Receivable-Trade, Net"
 [5] "Receivables-Other"
 [6] "Total Receivables, Net"
 [7] "Total Inventory"
 [8] "Prepaid Expenses"
 [9] "Other Current Assets, Total"
[10] "Total Current Assets"
[11] "Property/Plant/Equipment, Total-Gross"
[12] "Accumulated Depreciation, Total"
[13] "Goodwill, Net"
[14] "Intangibles, Net"
[15] "Long Term Investments"
[16] "Other Long Term Assets, Total"
[17] "Total Assets"
[18] "Accounts Payable"
[19] "Accrued Expenses"
[20] "Notes Payable/Short Term Debt"
[21] "Current Port. of LT Debt/Capital Leases"
[22] "Other Current liabilities, Total"
[23] "Total Current Liabilities"
[24] "Long Term Debt"
[25] "Capital Lease Obligations"
[26] "Total Long Term Debt"
[27] "Total Debt"
[28] "Deferred Income Tax"
[29] "Minority Interest"
[30] "Other Liabilities, Total"
```

```
[31] "Total Liabilities"
[32] "Redeemable Preferred Stock, Total"
[33] "Preferred Stock-Non Redeemable, Net"
[34] "Common Stock, Total"
[35] "Additional Paid-In Capital"
[36] "Retained Earnings (Accumulated Deficit)"
[37] "Treasury Stock-Common"
[38] "Other Equity, Total"
[39] "Total Equity"
[40] "Total Liabilities & Shareholders&#39; Equity"
[41] "Shares Outs-Common Stock Primary Issue"
[42] "Total Common Shares Outstanding"
```

To estimate a current ratio, retrieve the current assets and current liability.

```
> library(quantmod)
> getFinancials("IBM")
> x<-viewFin(IBM.f,"BS","A")#IS:Income statement,A=Annual
Annual Balance Sheet for IBM
> x[grep('Total Current',rownames(x)),]
 2013-12-31 2012-12-31 2011-12-31 2010-12-31
Total Current Assets 51350 49433 50928 48116
Total Current Liabilities 40154 43625 42126 40562
```

For example, the current assets and the current liabilities in 2010 are $48,116,000 and $40,562,000. Thus, its current ratio is 1.186. Alternatively we can use the following codes to get the current assets:

```
> CA<-x[grep('Total Current Ass',rownames(x)),]
> CA
2013-12-31 2012-12-31 2011-12-31 2010-12-31
 51350 49433 50928 48116
> CL<-x[grep('Total Current Lia',rownames(x)),]
> CL
2013-12-31 2012-12-31 2011-12-31 2010-12-31
 40154 43625 42126 40562
> CA/CL
2013-12-31 2012-12-31 2011-12-31 2010-12-31
 1.278827 1.133135 1.208945 1.186233
```

4.12. Using R to Retrieve Cash-Flow Statements

To get the last several years' cash-flow statements for DELL (see the codes below).

```
> library(quantmod) # CF: Cash Flow Statement, A: Annual
> cf<-viewFin(getFin("DELL",auto.assign=FALSE),"CF","A")
```

To construct a cash-flow statement, we start with net income. Then we add back non-cash-flow "expenses," such as the depreciation and amortization. We deduct the cash expenses. The cash-flow statements for DELL are shown below.

```
> cf
```

	2013-02-01	2012-02-03	2011-01-28	2010-01-29
Net Income/Starting Line	2372	3492	2635	1433
Depreciation/Depletion	1144	936	970	852
Amortization	NA	NA	NA	NA
Deferred Taxes	-428	19	-45	-52
Non-Cash Items	642	612	736	902
Changes in Working Capital	-447	468	-327	771
Cash from Operating Activities	3283	5527	3969	3906
Capital Expenditures	-513	-675	-444	-367
Other Investing Cash Flow Items, Total	-2803	-5491	-721	-3442
Cash from Investing Activities	-3316	-6166	-1165	-3809
Financing Cash Flow Items	8	4	2	-2
Total Cash Dividends Paid	-278	NA	NA	NA
Issuance (Retirement) of Stock, Net	-672	-2677	-788	2
Issuance (Retirement) of Debt, Net	-268	3250	1263	2012
Cash from Financing Activities	-1210	577	477	2012
Foreign Exchange Effects	-40	1	-3	174
Net Change in Cash	-1283	-61	3278	2283
Cash Interest Paid, Supplemental	279	267	188	151
Cash Taxes Paid, Supplemental	283	408	435	434

```
attr(,"col desc")
[1] "52 weeks ending 2013-02-01" "52 weeks ending 2012-02-03" "52 weeks ending 2011-01-28"
[4] "52 weeks ending 2010-01-29"
>
```

4.13. Using R to Construct a Common-Size Financial Statement

In R, to get a common-size balance sheet is easy. Find out the total assets and divide all data items by it.

```
>x<-viewFin(getFin("IBM",auto.assign=FALSE),"BS","A")
>y<-x[grep('Total Assets',rownames(x)),]
> k<-matrix(1,nrow(x),ncol(x))
> for(i in 1:ncol(k)) k[,i]<-y[i]
> z<-x/k
```

To double check the result, just show a couple of data items.

```
> x[1:3,]
  2010-12-31 2009-12-31 2008-12-31 2007-12-31
Cash & Equivalents 10661 12183 12741 14991
Short Term Investments 990 1791 166 1155
Cash and Short Term Investments 11651 13974 12907 16146
> y
2010-12-31 2009-12-31 2008-12-31 2007-12-31
  113450 109022 109524 120432
> z[1:3,]
  2010-12-31 2009-12-31 2008-12-31 2007-12-31
Cash & Equivalents 0.093970912 0.11174809 0.116330667 0.124476883
Short Term Investments 0.008726311 0.01642788 0.001515650 0.009590474
Cash and Short Term Investments 0.102697223 0.12817596 0.117846317 0.134067358
```

The common-size cash and equivalents is 0.09397 (10661/113450), and the common-size short-term investment is 0.00872 (990/113450). To make the above output more readable, we can use the **round()** function to reduce the number of decimals.

```
> z2<-round(z,digits=3)
> z2[1:3,]
  2010-12-31 2009-12-31 2008-12-31 2007-12-31
Cash & Equivalents 0.094 0.111 0.112 0.137
Short Term Investments 0.009 0.015 0.002 0.010
Cash and Short Term Investments 0.106 0.123 0.118 0.142
```

4.14. Using R to Download/Save Financial Statements (for Excel)

It is tedious and time-consuming to download financial statements manually. Fortunately we can do so by using R.

```
> library(quantmod)
>y<-viewFin(getFin("IBM",auto.assign=FALSE),"IS","A")
>rownames(y)<-gsub(",",";",rownames(y))
>write.csv(y,file='ibm_is.csv',quote=F)
```

4.15. Using R to Download Key Statistics from Yahoo

In the following codes, we upload an R library called XML.

```
> library(XML)
> x<-readHTMLTable("http://finance.yahoo.com/q/ks?s=dell+Key+Statistics")
> x[[10]]
```

```
  V1 V2
1 Market Cap (intraday)5: 27.47B
2 Enterprise Value (Mar 18, 2011)3: 19.91B
3 Trailing P/E (ttm, intraday): 10.58
4 Forward P/E (fye Jan 28, 2013)1: 8.02
5 PEG Ratio (5 yr expected)1: 1.96
6 Price/Sales (ttm): 0.44
7 Price/Book (mrq): 3.50
8 Enterprise Value/Revenue (ttm)3: 0.32
9 Enterprise Value/EBITDA (ttm)3: 4.46
> library(XML)
> x<-readHTMLTable("http://finance.yahoo.com/q/ks?s=ibm+Key+Statistics")
> x[[16]]
  V1 V2
1 Return on Assets (ttm): 10.27%
2 Return on Equity (ttm): 107.73%
> dim(x[[16]])
[1] 2 2
> x[[16]][2,2]
[1] 107.73%
Levels: 10.27% 107.73%
```

4.16. Three R Data Sets: is50, bs50, and cf50

To download **is50.RData** data set, just issue **http://canisius.edu/~yany/is50.RData**. The **is** is for income statement, **bs** is for balance sheet, and **cf** is for cash flow. For example, **is50** data set contains more than fifty firms' income statements of the last three to four years. Below, we briefly explain how to construct the R data set called **is50.RData**. The other two data sets are generated similarly.

Step 1

The dimension of income statements is forty-nine by four (i.e., forty-nine data items plus four years).

```
> library(quantmod)
> x<-viewFin(getFin("AAPL",auto.assign=FALSE),"IS","A")
> dim(x)
[1] 49 4
> x[1:3,]
  2010-09-25 2009-09-26 2008-09-27 2007-09-29
Revenue 65225 42905 37491 24578
Other Revenue, Total NA NA NA NA
Total Revenue 65225 42905 37491 24578
```

Step 2

Transpose. To facilitate an easy estimation, we put many firms' income statements over several years into one data set. Literally we transpose the above format: four columns become four rows, and forty-nine rows become forty-nine columns. To distinguish different firm years, we add ticker and date. Thus, we end up with fifty-one columns (see below).

```
> dim(is50)
[1] 252 51
```

Since there are fifty-one columns now, it is difficult to use the head() function to show the first several lines. However, we can pick up a few rows with a couple of columns.

```
> is50[1:10,1:4]
  ticker date Revenue Other Revenue, Total
16 AAPL 2007-09-29 24578 NA
15 AAPL 2008-09-27 37491 NA
14 AAPL 2009-09-26 42905 NA
13 AAPL 2010-09-25 65225 NA
20 ABX 2007-12-31 6014 NA
19 ABX 2008-12-31 7613 NA
18 ABX 2009-12-31 8136 NA
17 ABX 2010-12-31 10924 NA
24 ADM 2007-06-30 44018 NA
23 ADM 2008-06-30 69816 NA
```

Now, the question is, If we are interested in getting the total revenue and total sales, how do we retrieve those two columns? Below is a two-step approach.

1. Find the number of columns of your interest.
2. Retrieve the relevant data.

To find the corresponding columns, we can generate an output file.

```
> x<-colnames(is50)
> write.table(x,file="is_names.txt")
```

Below is the output:

```
"x"
"1" "ticker"
"2" "date"
"3" "Revenue"
"4" "Other Revenue, Total"
"5" "Total Revenue"
"6" "Cost of Revenue, Total"
"7" "Gross Profit"
"8" "Selling/General/Admin. Expenses, Total"
"9" "Research & Development"
"10" "Depreciation/Amortization"
"11" "Interest Expense(Income)-Net Operating"
"12" "Unusual Expense (Income)"
"13" "Other Operating Expenses, Total"
"14" "Total Operating Expense"
"15" "Operating Income"
"16" "Interest Income(Expense), Net Non-Operating"
"17" "Gain (Loss) on Sale of Assets"
"18" "Other, Net"
"19" "Income Before Tax"
"20" "Income After Tax"
"21" "Minority Interest"
"22" "Equity In Affiliates"
"23" "Net Income Before Extra. Items"
"24" "Accounting Change"
"25" "Discontinued Operations"
"26" "Extraordinary Item"
"27" "Net Income"
"28" "Preferred Dividends"
"29" "Income Available to Common Excl. Extra Items"
"30" "Income Available to Common Incl. Extra Items"
"31" "Basic Weighted Average Shares"
"32" "Basic EPS Excluding Extraordinary Items"
"33" "Basic EPS Including Extraordinary Items"
"34" "Dilution Adjustment"
"35" "Diluted Weighted Average Shares"
"36" "Diluted EPS Excluding Extraordinary Items"
"37" "Diluted EPS Including Extraordinary Items"
"38" "Dividends per Share-Common Stock Primary Issue"
"39" "Gross Dividends-Common Stock"
```

```
"40" "Net Income after Stock Based Comp. Expense"
"41" "Basic EPS after Stock Based Comp. Expense"
"42" "Diluted EPS after Stock Based Comp. Expense"
"43" "Depreciation, Supplemental"
"44" "Total Special Items"
"45" "Normalized Income Before Taxes"
"46" "Effect of Special Items on Income Taxes"
"47" "Income Taxes Ex. Impact of Special Items"
"48" "Normalized Income After Taxes"
"49" "Normalized Income Avail to Common"
"50" "Basic Normalized EPS"
"51" "Diluted Normalized EPS"
```

Since the column of revenue is 3 and net income is 27, we can use the following codes to retrieve those two columns. Note that the first two columns are needed to distinguish between firms and fiscal years.

```
> a<-c(1:3, 27)
> k<-is50[,a]
> k[1:10,]
   ticker date Revenue Net Income
16 AAPL 2007-09-29 24578 3495
15 AAPL 2008-09-27 37491 6119
14 AAPL 2009-09-26 42905 8235
13 AAPL 2010-09-25 65225 14013
20 ABX 2007-12-31 6014 1119
19 ABX 2008-12-31 7613 785
18 ABX 2009-12-31 8136 -4274
17 ABX 2010-12-31 10924 3274
24 ADM 2007-06-30 44018 2162
23 ADM 2008-06-30 69816 1780
```

Instead of manually searching a column's number, we use the **substr()** function. There an issue with this approach (see the exercise of 9.24).

```
> load("is50.RData")
> x<-is50
> n1<-x[substr(colnames(x),1,7)=="Revenue"]
> final<-data.frame(x[1,2],n1)
```

4.17. A Quick Introduction to R Package of quantmod

The package is about the "quantitative financial modeling and trading framework for R." It makes modeling easier by constructing some useful functions. In this chapter, we will use the **getFin()** function extensively—the short form of getFinancials(), which retrieves balance sheets, income statements, or cash-flow statements for both quarterly or annual frequencies from Google Finance. There are many additional useful functions as well. For example, if we want to know the current quotations for a specific stock, we could use **getQuote()**.

```
> library(quantmod)
> getQuote("IBM")
  Trade Time Last Change % Change Open High Low Volume
IBM 2011-06-03 04:00:00 165.05 -1.04 -0.63% 164.43 165.89 164.13 5230500
```

To retrieve the current quotation for several stocks, see the codes below.

```
> getQuote("IBM;DELL;SPY")
  Trade Time Last Change % Change Open High Low Volume
IBM 2011-06-03 04:00:00 165.05 -1.040 -0.63% 164.43 165.890 164.13 5230500
DELL 2011-06-03 03:48:00 15.62 -0.145 -0.92% 15.55 15.815 15.52 17427186
SPY 2011-06-03 04:00:00 130.42 -1.310 -0.99% 130.15 131.420 130.08 234690128
```

To retrieve the historical stock splits for a specific stock, we have one-line codes.

```
> getSplits("DELL")
  DELL.spl
1992-04-10 0.6666667
1995-10-30 0.5000000
1996-12-09 0.5000000
```

Finally the following table offers the definitions of most used ratios based on various financial statements.

Table 4.3. List of financial ratios and their definitions

Short-term liquidity	Current ratio= $\dfrac{current\ assets}{current\ liability}$	Quick Ratio= $\dfrac{current\ assets\ -inventory}{current\ liability}$
	Cash ratio= $\dfrac{cash}{current\ liability}$	
Leverage	Debt equity ratio= $\dfrac{Long\ term\ Debt}{Book\ Value\ of\ Equity}$	Debt over total assets= $\dfrac{Total\ Assets}{Book\ Value\ of\ Equity}$
	Long-term debt over total assets	$=\dfrac{Long\text{-}term\ Debt}{Total\ Assets}$
Margin	Gross margin	$=\dfrac{Gross\ profit}{Sales}=\dfrac{Sales\ -\ Cost\ of\ sales}{Sales}$
	Operating margin= $\dfrac{Operating\ Income}{Sales}$	Net profit margin= $\dfrac{Net\ Income}{Total\ Sales}$
Profitability	ROA (return on assets)	$=\dfrac{Net\ Income}{Total\ Sales}\ or\ =\dfrac{Net\ Income}{Average\ Total\ Assets}$
	ROE (return on equity)= $\dfrac{Net\ Income}{Equity}$	
DuPont identity	ROE= $\underbrace{\dfrac{Net\ Income}{Total\ Sales}}_{Net\ profit\ margin}*\underbrace{\dfrac{Sales}{Total\ assets}}_{Assit\ turnover}*\underbrace{\dfrac{Total\ assets}{Book\ value\ of\ equity}}_{Equity\ Multiplier}$	
	EPS= $\dfrac{Net\ Income}{shares\ outstanding}$	Market to book ratio= $\dfrac{Market\ value\ of\ equity}{Book\ value\ of\ equity}$
	P/E ratio	$=\dfrac{Market\ capitalization}{Net\ income}$

Exercises

4.1. What are the major differences between a balance sheet and an income statement?

4.2. From where do we retrieve the financial statements for IBM in the past three years?

4.3. From where do we retrieve the past ten years' financial statements for DELL?

4.4. From which databases can we retrieve all historical financial statements from Apple Ltd.?

4.5. In terms of use, what is the difference between an ROA and an ROE?

4.6. What is the use of financial statements?

4.7. Who uses the information contained in financial statements?

4.8. How does a firm compile its financial statements?

4.9. Is it true that all firms should file annual financial statements before December 31each year?

4.10. What is use of SEC?

4.11. Does a private firm have to file financial statements with SEC?

4.12. Do all public firms have trading data, such as daily stock closing prices?

4.13. What is the latest ROA and ROE for IBM, DELL, and MSFT?

4.14. Write an R program to retrieve the ROA and ROE for DELL, IBM, C, APPL, and WMT.

4.15. Write an R program to estimate the quick ratio
   = (*Current Assets – Inventory) / (Current Liabilities*)) for DELL.

4.16. Extend the R program related to the quick ratio to analyze the same ratios for one hundred firms.

4.17. Both the current ratio and the quick ratio measure the short-term liquidity. A more conservative ratio is call-cash ratio *(cash Ratio =* $\frac{cash + Marketable\ Securities}{current\ Liabilities}$ *)*. Write an R program to collect such a ratio for IBM.

4.18. Write an R program to collect the shares outstanding for MSFT and IBM.

4.19. Write an R program to collect several firms' market capitalizations, defined as "the share price multiplied by the shares outstanding."

4.20. Write an R program to collect analyst estimates for several stocks.

4.21. Write an R program to monitor a specific stock and report any change.

4.22. For IBM in 2010, its ROA and ROE are 6.04% and 39.31 %. What is its implied debt-equity ratio?

4.23. Verify the above result by searching IBM's Web page and explain the difference.

4.24. Write an R program to retrieve fiscal-year-ending dates for twenty tickers.

4.25. Try the following codes to identify the issue. Find a way to solve it.

```
> load("is50.RData")
> x<-is50
> n1<-x[substr(colnames(x),1,7)=="Revenue"]
> n2<-x[substr(colnames(x),1,10)=="Net Income"]
> final<-data.frame(x[1,2],n1,n2)
```

4.26. Download the balance sheets (BS), income statements (IS), and cash-flow statements (CF) for IBM and study the relationship of its CF with the other two's. Write an R program to replicate CF from BS and IS.

```
> library(quantmod)
>x<-viewFin(getFin("IBM",auto.assign=FALSE),"BS","A")
>y<-viewFin(getFin("IBM",auto.assign=FALSE),"IS","A")
>z<-viewFin(getFin("IBM",auto.assign=FALSE),"CF","A")
```

4.27. Are the tax rates different for IBM and DELL in 2010? (Hint: use before tax income and after tax income data items.)

4.28. Generate a function called **save1()**, which takes three input variables: ticker, type, and out file name.

Type takes three values: IS, BS, and CF. Below are examples:

>save1('ibm','bs','c:/temp/ibm_bs.csv')

>save1('ibm','is','ibm_bs.txt')

(Hint: start from the following two lines.)

```
>library(XML)
>x<-readHTMLTable("http://www.marketwatch.com/investing/stock/IBM/financials")
```

4.29. Write an R program to estimate ROA for a given ticker.

4.30. Write an R program to estimate ROE for a given ticker.

CHAPTER 5

Open Data

We can use a one-line R command to download the historical daily price data for IBM.

```
x<-read.csv("http://canisius.edu/~yany/data/ibm.csv")
```

To view the first two records, use **x[1:2,]** or **head(x,2)**.

```
> head(x,2)
  Date Open High Low Close Volume Adj.Close
1 2014-09-10 190.12 192.15 190.10 191.54 2764000 191.54
2 2014-09-09 190.34 190.74 189.78 189.99 2390400 189.99
```

Open is the open price. **High (low)** is the highest (lowest) price reached during the day. **Close** is the daily closing price. **Volume** is the daily trading volume, and **Adj.Close** is the closing price adjusted by stock splits and other distributions. To view the last two lines, we use the **tail()** function.

```
> tail(x,2)
      Date Open High Low Close Volume Adj.Close
12461 1962-01-03 572.0 577.0 572 577 288000 2.62
12462 1962-01-02 578.5 578.5 572 572 387200 2.59
```

We can download and save the data as a text file (DELL in this case). Try the codes without **quote=F** and **row.names=F** to see the difference.

```
x<-read.csv("http://canisius.edu/~yany/data/ibm.csv")
> write.table(x,file='dell.txt',quote=F,row.names=F)
```

In the last command, the relative path method is used (i.e., **dell.txt** is saved under the current working directory). To find out the exact path of our current working directory, we apply the **getwd()** function.

Note that readers would get a different location.

```
> getwd()
[1] "C:/Users/yyan/Documents"
```

5.1. Introduction

In the Internet era, we are constantly overwhelmed with data. However, few finance students know how to estimate β, the Sharpe ratio, and various other metrics for Fortune 500 stocks in 2014. It would be a shame if we do not apply the publicly available financial data to teaching, research, and/or investment. In this chapter, the focus will be on how to retrieve such data.

For example, Yahoo Finance offers rich information, such as historical trading price, current price, and option and bond data. Such publicly available data could be used to estimate β (market risk), volatility (total risk), Sharpe ratio, Jensen's alpha, Treynor ratio, liquidity, transaction costs and to conduct financialstatement analysis (ratio analysis) and performance evaluation. Some public data sources are listed in the following table.

Table 5.1. A list of open data sources

Name	Web page	Data types	Related topics
Yahoo Finance	http://finance.yahoo.com	Current and historical pricing, analyst forecast, options, balance sheet, income statement	CAPM, portfolio theory, liquidity measure, momentum strategy, VaR, options
Google Finance	http://www.google.com/finance	Current or historical trading prices	Stock-trading data
Federal Reserve	http://www.federalreserve.gov/releases/h15/data.htm	interest rates, rates for AAA, AA-rated bonds	Fixed income, bond, term structure
MarketWatch	http://www.marketwatch.com	Financial statements	Corporate finance, investment
SEC filing	http://www.sec.gov/edgar.shtml	Balance sheet, income statement, holdings	Ratio analysis, fundamental analysis
Oanda	http://www.oanda.com	Foreign-exchange rates, price for precious metals	International finance, commodity trading
Prof. French's data library	http://mba.tuck.dartmouth.edu/pages/faculty/ken.french/data_library.html	Fama-French factors, market index, risk-free rate, industry classification	Factor models, CAPM
Census Bureau	http://www.census.gov/ http://www.census.gov/compendia/statab/hist_stats.html	Census data	Real income, trading strategy
US Department of the Treasury	http://www.treas.gov	US treasure yield	Fixed income
FINRA	http://cxa.marketwatch.com/finra/BondCenter/Default.aspx	Bond price and yield	Fixed income
Bureau of Labor Statistics	http://www.bls.gov/ http://download.bls.gov/	Inflation, employment, unemployment, payand benefits	Macroeconomics
Bureau of Economic Analysis	http://www.bea.gov/	GDP and the like	Macroeconomics
National Bureau of Economic Research	http://www.nber.org/	Business cycles, vital statistics, report of presidents	Macroeconomics, financial stability

Note that FINRA (Financial Industry Regulatory Authority) is the largest independent regulator for all securities firms doing business in the United States. In R, it is convenient to use R data sets that usually have an extension of **.RData**. The major reason for using R data sets is efficiency as it is much faster to apply R data sets than other formats. In this book, we will use many types of R data sets. The following table offers some R data sets we can use in this book.

Table 5.2 A list of RData related to finance

(The extension of each data set is **.RData** [e.g., the complete name for **retDIBM** is **retDIBM. RData**], which will be included in the accompanying CD.)

Name	Description	Location /package
BondsData	Economic and financial data	fEcofin
CIAFactbook	Economic and financial data sets	fEcofin
Performance Analytics Data	Economic and financial data sets	fEcofin
PortfolioData	Economic and financial data sets	fEcofin
Time Series Data	Economic and financial data sets	fEcofin
WFE Statistics	Economic and financial data sets	fEcofin
	Rmetrics—extreme financial market data	fExtremes
ret DIBM	Daily return, Rf, and market returns from S&P 500	http://canisius.edu/~yany/RData
prc DIBM	Daily open, high, low, trading volume, close and adjusted close	http://canisius.edu/~yany/RData
ret D50	Fifty stocks' return data	http://canisius.edu/~yany/RData
prc 50	Fifty stocks, daily open, high, low, close, volume, adjusted close	http://canisius.edu/~yany/RData
ret M	Monthly return data	http://canisius.edu/~yany/RData
euro_Dollar	Eurodollar deposit rate	http://canisius.edu/~yany/RData
is50	Fifty firms' annual income statements	http://canisius.edu/~yany/RData
bs50	Fifty firms' annual balance sheets	http://canisius.edu/~yany/RData
cf50	Fifty firms' annual cashflow statements	http://canisius.edu/~yany/RData

5.2. Introduction to Yahoo Finance

Yahoo Finance (http://finance.yahoo.com) offers historical market data, recent years' financial statements, current quotes, analyst recommendations, options data, and more. The historical quote data includes daily, weekly, monthly data and dividends. The historical data includes open, high, low, trading volume, close prices (which are not adjusted for splits and dividends), and adjusted close prices. Historical quotes typically do not go back further than 1970.

5.3. Introduction to Google Finance

Like Yahoo Finance, Google Finance, http://www.google.com/finance, offers a significant amount of public information, such as News, Option Chains, Related Companies (good for competitor and industry analysis, see Chapter 10), Historical Prices, and Financials (Income Statement, Balance Sheet, and Cash Flow Statements).

5.4. Getting Help with Yahoo Finance

We could use the following Web site to find help:

http://help.yahoo.com/l/us/yahoo/finance/definitions/

5.5. Manually Downloading Historical Stock Data from Yahoo Finance

Below, we show how to manually retrieve the monthly data for DELL.

Step	Action
1	Go to http://finance.yahoo.com/.
2	Enter "DELL" in the Get Quotes box.
3	Click on **Historical Prices** on the left-hand side.
4	Choose the appropriate data range and click **Monthly** then click **Get Prices**.
5	Move to the bottom of the screen and click **Download to Spreadsheet**.

5.6. Estimating Returns from a CSV File Downloaded from Yahoo Finance

Assume that we have the following daily historical data from Yahoo Finance for IBM and that the file name is **ibm.csv** (as seen a couple of lines below).

Date,Open,High,Low,Close,Volume,Adj Close
2011-02-08,164.82,166.25,164.32,166.05,5612600,166.05
2011-02-07,164.08,164.99,164.02,164.82,4928100,164.17
2011-02-04,163.48,164.14,163.22,164.00,3755200,163.35

The following R codes are used to retrieve the data saved on our local computer. The **ibm.csv** is the name of our input file, and **sep=','** tells the program to use a comma as a separator. Since the first line isour header, which gives the names of variables with the same structure, we use **header=T**. The headline contains the names of the columns. Try to omit **header=T** to see the effect.

```
x <-read.table('ibm.csv',sep=',',header=T) # relative path
> x[1:2,]
  Date Open   High   Low    Close  Volume   Adj.    Close
1 2011-02-08 164.82 166.25 164.32 166.05 5612600 166.05
2 2011-02-07 164.08 164.99 164.02 164.82 4928100 164.17
```

Alternatively we can define a variable called **infile**. In the following case, we use the absolute-path method (i.e., access a file under any directory or subdirectory). For the relative path, we access a file under the current working directory.

```
>infile <-'c:/temp/ibm.csv' # absolute path
>x<-read.table(infile,sep=',',header=T)
```

5.7. Generating a Variable called Date

There are many ways to construct a date variable. In this chapter, we will discuss it the best way: **as.Date()**.

For other methods, please consult chapter 36: "Date."

```
> x<-as.Date("1990-01-31","%Y-%m-%d")
> x+1
[1] "1990-02-01"
```

If the input string variable has another format, we modify our codes accordingly.

```
> x<-as.Date("1990/01/31","%Y/%m/%d")
> y<-as.Date("01/31/1990","%m/%d/%Y")
```

When the input variables have a standard format, we can omit the second part.

```
> as.Date("1990-01-31")+1
[1] "1990-02-01"
> as.Date("1990/01/31")+2
[1] "1990-02-02"
```

For a nonstandard format, the omission of the format will cause an error.

```
> x<-as.Date("1990\01\31")
Error in charToDate(x):
character string is not in a standard unambiguous format
```

Below, we combine our new date variable with a closing price.

```
> x<-read.table('ibm.csv',sep=',',header=T)
> d<-data.frame(as.Date(x[,1],format="%Y%m%d"),x[,7])
> d<-d[order(d[,1]),] # Sort by date (ascending)
> ibm<-data.frame(d[,1],d[,2])
> colnames(ibm)<-c('date','adj_price')
> head(x)
  Date Open High Low Close Volume Adj.Close
1 2011-07-15 175.08 175.94 174.07 175.54 5347100 175.54
2 2011-07-14 174.40 176.10 173.84 174.23 4613100 174.23
3 2011-07-13 174.90 176.32 174.00 174.32 4074800 174.32
4 2011-07-12 174.93 175.37 173.89 174.05 5036800 174.05
5 2011-07-11 174.90 176.15 174.61 174.99 4766500 174.99
6 2011-07-08 175.49 176.49 175.01 176.49 4399900 176.49
```

5.8. Using R to Retrieve Data from Yahoo Finance Directly

The following one-line command is typical in retrieving the historical daily price data for IBM from Yahoo Finance.

```
x<-read.csv("http://canisius.edu/~yany/data/ibm.csv")
```

Usually we can use the **head()** and **tail()** functions to view the first and last several lines. The function **str()** shows the structure of a data set.

```
> str(x)
'data.frame': 13442 obs. of 7 variables:
$ Date : Factor w/ 13442 levels "1962-01-02","1962-01-03",..: 13442 13441
13440 13439 13438 13437 13436 13435 13434 13433 ...
$ Open : num 171 172 173 173 173 ...
$ High : num 172 172 173 174 174 ...
$ Low : num 170 169 172 173 172 ...
$ Close : num 172 170 172 173 174 ...
$ Volume : int 2749100 3840000 2704700 2293600 2300300 2519600 1923600 2913700
   2435700 2411500 ...
$ Adj.Close: num 172 170 172 173 174 ...
```

5.9. Estimating Returns

Let's check the date, the latest first then go back to more remote dates.

```
x<-read.csv("http://canisius.edu/~yany/data/ibm.csv")
> head(x)
Date Open High Low Close Volume Adj.Close
1 2011-06-07 165.11 165.24 163.61 163.69 4187000 163.69
2 2011-06-06 164.76 165.58 164.27 164.75 3619700 164.75
3 2011-06-03 164.30 165.89 164.13 165.05 5230500 165.05
4 2011-06-02 166.44 167.10 165.71 166.09 3854100 166.09
5 2011-06-01 168.90 169.58 166.50 166.56 5134600 166.56
6 2011-05-31 168.44 169.89 167.82 168.93 9123400 168.93
```

We could use a loop to estimate returns. Obviously, for the first observation, return will be **(163.69-164.75)/164.75 or (x[1,7]-x[2,7])/x[2,7]**.

```
x<-read.csv("http://canisius.edu/~yany/data/ibm.csv")
> n<-nrow(x)
> ret2<-NA
> for (i in 1:(n-1))
+ ret2[i]<-(x[i,7]-x[i+1,7])/x[i+1,7]
```

Actually, a better way is to use the following codes to estimate returns:

```
x<-read.csv("http://canisius.edu/~yany/data/ibm.csv")
n<-nrow(x)
ret<-(x[1:(n-1),7]-x[2:n,7])/x[2:n,7])
```

Most of the time, we put date, price, and return together. Below, we sort the data by date then estimate returns. The final output will be date, adjusted price, and returns.

```
x<-read.csv("http://canisius.edu/~yany/data/ibm.csv")
> d<-data.frame(format(as.Date(x[,1]),"%Y%m%d"),x[,7])
>d<-d[order(d[,1]),] # Sort by date (ascending)
>n<-nrow(d)
>ibm<-data.frame(d[2:n,1],d[2:n,2],(d[2:n,2]-d[1:n-1,2])/d[1:n-1,2])
> colnames(ibm)<-c('date','adj_price','ret')
```

The following codes are related to the function of **order()**.

```
> x
[1] 1 2 4 -1
> y<-x[order(x)] # from the smallest to the highest
> y
[1] -1 1 2 4
> y2<-x[order(x,decreasing=T)]
> y2
[1] 4 2 1 -1
```

5.10. Adding a New Variable Called ticker

To make our output more meaningful, we could add ticker as our first variable.

```
x<-read.csv("http://canisius.edu/~yany/data/dell.csv")
> d<-cbind("DELL",x)
> a<-colnames(d)
> a[1]<-"ticker"
> colnames(d)<-a
> d[1:2,]
  ticker Date Open High Low Close Volume Adj.Close
1 DELL 2011-02-08 13.95 14.17 13.83 13.87 17274200 13.87
2 DELL 2011-02-07 13.94 14.10 13.92 13.99 12081000 13.99
```

5.11. Saving our Data to a Text File

The following two lines are used to download historical daily data for Yahoo (YHOO) and save it to an external text file.

```
x<-read.csv("http://canisius.edu/~yany/data/yahoo.csv",header=T)
> write.table(x,file='yahoo.txt',quote=F,row.names=F)
```

A few lines of the above output, **yahoo.txt**, are given below.

```
Date Open High Low Close Volume Adj.Close
2011-02-04 16.74 16.91 16.45 16.79 18987400 16.79
2011-02-03 16.48 16.91 16.4 16.69 32918400 16.69
2011-02-02 16.25 16.66 16.25 16.57 20811600 16.57
```

If we omit **quote=F, row.names=F**, the output format is given below.

```
"Date" "Open" "High" "Low" "Close" "Volume" "Adj.Close"
"1" "2011-02-07" 16.81 17 16.77 16.8 16022400 16.8
"2" "2011-02-04" 16.74 16.91 16.45 16.79 18987400 16.79
"3" "2011-02-03" 16.48 16.91 16.4 16.69 32918400 16.69
```

To save to a CSV file, we have two methods.

```
> write.table(x,file='c.csv',sep=',',quote=F,row.names=F)
```

Alternatively we can use the **write.csv()** function.

```
> write.csv(x,file='c.csv',quote=F,row.names=F)
```

5.12. Saving an R Data Set

To save a data set called x with an R data set format, we use the save() function.

```
> x<-read.csv("http://canisius.edu/data/ibm.csv",header=T)
> save(x,file='ibm.RData')
```

5.13. Retrieving Market Index Data from Yahoo Finance

The codes are the same as retrieving individual stock data except the tickers. For example, S&P 500 has a ticker of **^GSPC**.

```
> x<-read.csv("http://canisius.edu/~yany/data/^GSPC.csv",header=T)
> x[1:2,]
      Date Open High  Low Close Adj.Close  Volume
1 1950-01-01 16.66 17.09 16.65 17.05    17.05 42570000
2 1950-02-01 17.05 17.35 16.99 17.22    17.22 33430000
> n<-nrow(x)
> x[(n-1):n,]
       Date   Open   High   Low  Close Adj.Close   Volume
813 2017-09-01 2474.42 2519.44 2446.55 2519.36  2519.36 63046220000
814 2017-10-01 2521.20 2575.44 2520.40 2575.21  2575.21 45115760000
```

The following table lists the most widely used market indices.

Table 5.3. Yahoo ticker symbols for several widely used market indices

Ticker	Description	Category
^DJI	Dow Jones Industrial Average	DJI
^GSPC	S&P 500 INDEX.RTH	SNP
^NSEI	S&P CNX Nifty	NSE
^NYA	NYSE Composite Index (new method)	NYSE
^VIX	Volatility S&P 500	Chicago Board Options Exchange
^TNX	CBOE Interest Rate 10-year T-Note	Chicago Board Options Exchange
^FTSE	FTSE 100	London
^JKSE	Composite Index	Jakarta
^HSI	Hang Seng Index	Hong Kong
^N225	Nikkei 225	Osaka Securities Exchange
^STI	Straits Times Index	Singapore

5.14. Downloading Monthly Data from Yahoo Finance

The following codes can be used to retrieve monthly historical price data from Yahoo finance for IBM.

```
> k1<-'http://ichart.finance.yahoo.com/table.csv?s=IBM&'
> k2<-'a=01&b=01&c=2010&d=31&e=12&'
> k3<-'f=2010&g=m&ignore=.csv'
> k<-paste(k1,k2,k3,sep='')
> x<-read.csv(file=k,header=T)
```

In the above program, we use **'a='**, **'b='**, and the like. Their meanings are given below.

Table 5.4. Description of '=i', where i=a,b,c,d,e,f, and g

Letter	Description
a	Beginning day
b	Beginning month
c	Beginning year
d	Ending day
e	Ending month
f	Ending year
g	Frequency—**d** for daily **m** for monthly

A better strategy is to download monthly historical price data as long as possible. Then cut the time seriously according to your need.

5.15. Introduction to the Federal Reserve Data Library

The related link is http://www.federalreserve.gov/econresdata/default.htm. The Federal Reserve has a lot of data. For instance, they have data related to interest rates, such as Eurodollar deposit rates. There are two ways to retrieve such interest-rate data. First, we can use their Data Download Program, as seen in the following steps.

Go to http://www.federalreserve.gov/econresdata/default.htm.
Click **Data Download Program** (i.e., http://www.federalreserve.gov/datadownload/).
Select the data you intend to access and click **Go to download**.

Alternatively we can simply download a text file from the following Web page:
http://www.federalreserve.gov/releases/h15/data.htm

For example, we choose Eurodollar deposit one-month rate (business daily) and save the data as **H15_ED_1m.txt**.

The first couple of lines are given below.

```
"Series Description","U.S. -- SHORT-TERM INTEREST
RATES: DAILY 1-MONTH EURO-DOLLAR DEPOSIT RATE "
"Unit:","Percent:_Per_Year"
"Multiplier:","1"
"Currency:","NA"
"Unique Identifier: ","H15/H15/RILSPDEPM01_N.B"
"Time Period","RILSPDEPM01_N.B"
1971-01-04,6.38
1971-01-05,6.31
```

To skip the first six lines of header, we use **skip=6**.

```
>> x<-read.csv("h15_ED_m1.csv",skip=5)
> x[1:2,]
Time.Period RILSPDEPM01_N.B
1 1971-01-04        6.38
2 1971-01-05        6.31
```

There are some nonnumeric values in the second column, as seen below.

```
> y<-subset(x,x[,2]=='ND')
> y[1:3,]
DATE EDM1
24 02/04/1971 ND
30 02/12/1971 ND
31 02/15/1971 ND
```

To delete the observations with **ND** in the second column, use the **subset()** function. In the following example, we choose a subset when the values of the second column are bigger than 4.

```
> t1<-c(1,2,3) # 1st column
> t2<-c(2,4,5) # 2nd column
> t3<-cbind(t1,t2) # combine them
> t3
t1 t2
[1,] 1 2
[2,] 2 4
[3,] 3 5
> t3<-subset(t3,t3[,2]>4) # select a subset with a condition
> t3
t1 t2
[1,] 3 5
```

We intend to select the records where the second column does not equal ND. We can use the code >x2<-subset(x,x[,2]!='ND'), see the unequal number of observations before and after the command.

```
> dim(x)
 [1] 11582    2
>x2<-subset(x,x[,2]!='ND')
> dim(x2)
 [1] 11301    2
```

Here are the complete codes:

```
>x<-read.csv("h15_ED_m1.csv",skip=5)
>x2<-subset(x,x[,2]!='ND')           # choose a subset
>t1<-as.Date(x2[,1],"%Y-%m-%d")
>t2<-as.numeric(as.character(x2[,2]))/100 # percent to decimal
>EDM1<-data.frame(t1,t2)             # combine 2 columns
>colnames(EDM1)<-c("date","EDM1") # add column names
```

The first and last several lines are given below:

```
> head(EDM1)              > tail(EDM1)
  date EDM1                 date EDM1
[1,] 19710401 0.0638     [10184,] 20113101 0.0032
[2,] 19710501 0.0631     [10185,] 20110102 0.0032
[3,] 19710601 0.0613     [10186,] 20110202 0.0032
[4,] 19710701 0.0619     [10187,] 20110302 0.0032
[5,] 19710801 0.0606     [10188,] 20110402 0.0032
[6,] 19711101 0.0594     [10189,] 20110702 0.0032
```

5.16. Professor French's Data Library (Fama-French Factors and Others)

The web page is given below.

http://mba.tuck.dartmouth.edu/pages/faculty/ken.french/data_library.html

Professor French has a data library that contains the daily, weekly, and monthly Fama-French factors and other useful data sets. After clicking **Fama-French Factors**, we can download a zip file called **F-F_Research_Data_Factors.zip**. Unzip it, and we will have a text file called **F_F_Research_Data_Factors.txt**, which includes both monthly and annual Fama-French factors. The first several lines are given below. For more details, see chapter 7: "Multifactor Model, Sharpe Ratio, Treynor Ratio, and Jensen's α."

```
This file was created by CMPT_ME_BEME_RETS using the 201012 CRSP database.
The 1-month TBill return is from Ibbotson and Associates, Inc.
  Mkt-RF SMB HML RF
192607 2.62 -2.16 -2.92 0.22
192608 2.56 -1.49 4.88 0.25
192609 0.36 -1.38 -0.01 0.23
192610 -3.43 0.04 0.71 0.32
192611 2.44 -0.24 -0.31 0.31
```

5.17. SEC Filings

According to law in the USA, all public companies have to file their financial statements with the SEC (US Securities and Exchange Commission). Its main Web page is http://www.sec.gov/. SEC uses a service called EDGAR (Electronic Data Gathering, Analysis, and Retrieval) to collect its filings. The related Web page is http://www.sec.gov/edgar.shtml. Since SEC filings include so much useful information, we will allocate a whole chapter to that subject (see chapter 12).

5.18. Retrieving Data for Multiple Stocks from Yahoo Finance

The following loop will print the ticker in the variable called **tickers**.

```
> stocks<-c("IBM","DELL")
> for(stock in stocks) print(stock)
```

The following codes will retrieve the historical daily price data for each ticker from Yahoo Finance and print its first two observations.

```
tickers<-c("ibm","dell")
for(stock in tickers){
    print(stock)
    k<-'http://canisius.edu/~yany/data/$V' # variable $V
    k1<-sub("$V",stock,k,fixed=T) # sub() for substitution
    k2<-paste(k1,".csv",sep='')
    x<-read.csv(k2)
    print(x[1:2,])
}
```

After running the above codes, the following lines will appear on the screen.

```
[1] "ibm"
         Date   Open   High    Low  Close  Volume Adj.Close
1 2016-11-03 152.51 153.74 151.80 152.37 2843600    152.37
2 2016-11-02 152.48 153.35 151.67 151.95 3074400    151.95
[1] "dell"
         Date  Open  High   Low Close   Volume Adj.Close
1 2013-10-04 13.84 13.84 13.83 13.84  9115200     13.84
2 2013-10-03 13.83 13.85 13.83 13.83 12388500     13.83
```

Below are the codes:

```
stocks<-c("IBM","DELL")
for(stock in stocks) {
print(stock)
k<-'http://ichart.finance.yahoo.com/table.csv?s=$V&amp;a=00&amp;b=
2&amp;c=2010&amp;d=05&amp;e=2&amp;f=2010&amp;g=d&amp;ignore=.csv'
k1<-sub("$V",stock,k,fixed=T)
x<-read.csv(k1)
print(head(x))
}
```

5.19. Fine-Tuning

If we don't want to keep too many decimal places, we use the **round()** function.

```
ibm[,3]=round(ibm[,3],digits=6) # six decimal places
```

To save the data set to an external text file, add the following line:

```
write.table(ibm,file="ibm_ret",quote=F,row.names=F)
```

To save the data set as an R data set, use the following codes.

```
save(ibm,file="ibm.RData")
```

The program below is used to retrieve monthly data for any given stock (ticker).

```
stock<-'DELL'
k<-'http://ichart.finance.yahoo.com/table.csv?s=$V&amp;a=00&amp;b=
2&amp;c=1962&amp;d=05&amp;e=2&amp;f=2010&amp;g=d&amp;ignore=.csv'
k1<-sub("$V",stock,k,fixed=T)
x<-read.csv(k1)
```

From the above discussion, we know that there are many sources for publicly available financial data. To write R programs to access those data is not a trivial exercise since the structures of those data vary. One possible solution is to put all the open data on a dedicated server. Thus, we can use the same codes to access the different files from various locations.

```
d<-read.csv("c:/temp/dell.csv",header=T)
> head(d)
  Date Open High Low Close Volume Adj.Close
1 2010-12-03 13.56 13.71 13.49 13.69 15884500 13.69
2 2010-12-02 13.46 13.68 13.35 13.65 37856000 13.65
3 2010-12-01 13.47 13.59 13.39 13.41 19556300 13.41
4 2010-11-30 13.40 13.40 13.12 13.22 20717100 13.22
5 2010-11-29 13.53 13.66 13.33 13.57 18183700 13.57
6 2010-11-26 13.72 13.84 13.62 13.65 5387200  13.65
```

5.20. Using Monthly Returns or Daily Returns

Many research topics request specific data frequencies. For example, to check the short-term impact of certain events, such as the resignation of a CEO or the release of quarterly financial statements, we have to use daily data. For other topics, however, it seems that we can apply both monthly and daily data. Nevertheless, many researchers prefer to use monthly data. A major reason for this is the so-called microstructure effect, which has a more severe impact on the estimation of daily returns than on monthly returns. Two of such microstructure effects are bid-ask bounce and nonsynchronous trading.

When a stock has no trading on a specific day, usually we use the average of the last bid and ask as the closing price. For consecutive days without trading, the closing prices estimated this way would be bounced between bid and ask, which, in turn, will produce a negative autocorrelation for stock returns.

Assume both stocks A and B have trading today. To estimate today's returns, we use the closing price today and yesterday. Assume further that stock A is a small stock and its last trade ends at 11:30 a.m. Stock B is a heavily-traded stock whose last trade occurs close to market closing time (e.g., 4:00 p.m.). This phenomenon is called nonsynchronous trading. If we are not aware of this, we might find some superficial correlation.

For example, when the market is volatile, we might find that we could use stock B's return to predict stock A's next-day return. The logic of such a superficial link stems from nonsynchronous trading. Before stock B's trading ends late in the day, it contains the market-wide information up to 4:00 p.m. while the closing price for stock A contains the market information only up to the time of its last trade (in the morning). This explains why we can use stock B's return to predict stock A's return.

5.21. Converting Daily Returns to Monthly or Annual Ones

When daily returns are defined as percentage, the following formula is used.

Equation 6

$$R_m = \prod_{i=1}^{n}(1 + R_{daily,i}) - 1,$$

where is Rm the monthly return,
n is the number of trading days within the month,
$R_{daily,i}$ is the daily return on trading day i and

$$\prod_{i=1}^{n} X_i = X_1 * X_2 * ... * X_{n-1}X_n$$

If the daily returns are in a log-return format (see equation 3), the following formula is used instead. Obviously equation 5 is much simpler than equation 4. The monthly log return is the summation of the daily log returns.

Equation 7

$$R_m = \sum_{i=1}^{n} R_i$$

This is a very important property of log returns. Later in the book, we will use it intensively. The second way is to use the last trading price at the end of each month to calculate monthly returns.

Equation 8

$$R_m = \log\left(\frac{P_t}{P_{t-1}}\right)$$

For example, for the monthly return in February, we have

Equation 9

$$R_{Feb} = \frac{P_{last\_day(February)} - P_{Last\_day(January)}}{P_{last\_day(January)}}$$

Again, the log return is defined below:

Equation 10

$$R_m = \log\left(\frac{P_t}{P_{t-1}}\right)$$

The objective of the following codes is to retrieve the last day of each month.

```
beg<-as.Date("2000-02-01")
end<-as.Date("2000-05-31")
x<-seq(beg,end,by=1) # generate 365 calendar days
n<-length(x)
y<-as.Date("2000-02-01")
j=1
for(i in 1:(n-1)){
today_month <-format(x[i], "%m")
  tomorrow_month <-format(x[i+1],"%m")
  if(today_month != tomorrow_month){
  y[j]<-x[i]
  j<-j+1
  }
}
if(format(y[j-1],"%m") !=format(x[n],"%m"))
  y[j]<-x[n]
```

The output is shown below:

```
>y
[1] "2000-02-29" "2000-03-31" "2000-04-30" "2000-05-31"
```

A simpler version is shown below:

```
x<-seq(as.Date("2000-02-01"),as.Date("2000-05-31"),"days")
n<-length(x)
y<-subset(x,format(x[1:(n-1)],"%m")!=format(x[2:n],"%m"))
n2<-length(y)
if(format(y[n2],"%m") !=format(x[n],"%m"))
y[n2+1]<-x[n]
```

We can define a function called **month_()** (see below).

```
month_<-function(x) as.integer(format(x,"%m"))
x<-seq(as.Date("2000-02-01"),as.Date("2000-05-31"),by=1)
n<-length(x)
y<-subset(x,month_(x[1:(n-1)])!=month_(x[2:n]))
n2<-length(y)
if(format(y[n2],"%m") !=format(x[n],"%m"))
y[n2+1]<-x[n]
```

Converting log daily returns to monthly returns is easier than converting percentage daily returns to monthly returns.

5.22. A List of Functions from Various R Packages

In this chapter, we didn't discuss how to use various functions included in many R packages for the following reasons: First, we have covered enough information already, and any more would be too much. Second, we need some basic knowledge about R packages, which will be discussed in chapter 41: "Introduction to R Packages."

Table 5.5. Functions that can be used to retrieve publicly available data

Package	Function	Description
fImport	fredSeriess	Import market data from the FRED
	oandaSeries	Import FX market data from OANDA
	yahooSeries	Import data from chart.yahoo.com
	providerListings	Provider listing of symbols and descriptions
	yahooBriefing	Import briefings from Yahoo
	yahooKeystats	Import key statistics data from Yahoo
Quantmod	getDividends	Load financial dividend data
	getFX	Download exchange rates
	getFinancials	Download and view financial statements
	getMetals	Download daily metals prices
	getOptionChain	Download option chains
	getQuote	Download current stock quote
	getSplits	Load financial split data
	getSymbols	Load and manage data from multiple sources
	getSymbols.FRED	Download Federal Reserve Economic Data—FRED (R)
	getSymbols.MySQL	Retrieve data from MySQL database
	getSymbols.SQLite	Retrieve data from SQLite database
	getSymbols.csv	Load data from CSV file
	getSymbols.google	Download OHLC data From Google Finance
	getSymbols.oanda	Download currency and metals data from Oanda.com
	getSymbols.rda	Load Data from R Binary File
	getSymbols.yahoo	Download OHLC Data From Yahoo Finance
XML	readHTMLTable	Read data from one or more HTML tables

5.23. An R Data Set Called FIN690webs.RData

It is extremely frustrating to have typos when typing a long Web page such as **http://ichart.finance. yahoo.com/table.csv?s=$V&a=$01&b=$01&c=$1925&d=$12&e=31&f=2011&g=m&ignore=.csv.**

Thus, it is a good idea that we generate an R data set including those Web pages. The **FIN690webs. RData** can be downloaded from the another's Web page. Assume the location is **c:/temp/**.

```
> load("c:/temp/MGF690webs.RData")
```

A few lines from the data set called webs are shown below.

```
> head(webs)
[1] "http://canisius.edu/~yany/MGR690web.RData"
[2] "http://chart.yahoo.com/table.csv?s=IBM"
[3] "http://chart.yahoo.com/table.csv?s=$V"
[4] "http://ichart.finance.yahoo.com/table.csv?s=$V&amp;a=$01&amp;b=$01"
[5] "&amp;c=$1925&amp;d=$12&amp;e=31&amp;f=2011&amp;g=m&amp;ignore=.csv"
[6] "http://finance.yahoo.com/q/ks?s=dell+Key+Statistics"
```

Below, we show how to assign the second observation to a variable. Then we use it as our input to retrieve the historical daily price data for IBM.

```
> w<-webs[2]
> w
[1] "http://chart.yahoo.com/table.csv?s=IBM"
> x<-read.csv(w,header=T)
> head(x,2)
 Date Open High Low Close Volume Adj.Close
1 2011-12-13 193.46 194.3 190.64 191.15 5008400 191.15
2 2011-12-12 193.64 193.9 191.22 192.18 3796100 192.18
```

To get another ticker, use the **sub()** function, which conduces a substitution option.

```
> w<-webs[2]
> w
[1] "http://chart.yahoo.com/table.csv?s=IBM"
>w2<-sub("IBM","DELL",w) # replace IBM with DELL
> w2
[1] "http://chart.yahoo.com/table.csv?s=DELL"
```

Exercises

5.1. From where can we get daily stock-price data?

5.2. Manually download monthly and daily price data for Citigroup.

5.3. Convert daily price data for the Citigroup to daily returns.

5.4. Convert monthly price to monthly returns and convert daily returns to monthly returns. Are they the same?

5.5. What are the advantages and disadvantages of using public stock data versus private stock data (e.g., from some financial databases)?

5.6. Finding the annual cost of subscribing Compustat, related to accounting information and CRSP, related to trading data.

5.7. Download the IBM monthly data from Yahoo Finance and estimate its standard deviation and Sharpe ratio from January 2000 to December 2004.

5.8. What is the annual beta for IBM, DELL, and MSFT from 2001 to 2010?

5.9. What is the correlation between IBM and DELL from 2006 to 2010?

5.10. Estimate the mean weekday returns for IBM. Do you observe a weekday effect?

5.11. Has the volatility declined over the years? For example, you can select IBM, DELL, and MSFT to investigate this hypothesis.

5.12. What is the correlation between S&P 500 and DJI (Dow Jones Industrial Average)? (Note: S&P 500 Index ticker in Yahoo Finance is ^GSPC; for DJI, ^DJI.)

5.13. How do you download data for n given tickers?

5.14. Write an R program to input n tickers from an input file.

5.15. Explain this statement: If don't sort data, the following codes should be used to calculate returns.

```
> ibm<-data.frame(d[1:(n-1),1],d[1:(n-1),2],
(d[1:(n-1),2]-d[2:n,2])/d[2:n,2])
```

5.16. What is the correlation coefficient between the US stock market (S&P 500) and Hong Kong (HangSeng Index)?

5.17. Is it true that the Singaporean equity market is more strongly correlated with the Japanese equity market than the American equity market?

5.18. How do you download daily price data for fifty stocks and save it to just one text file?

5.19. If your input file of tickers include invalid tickers, write an R program to skip them.

IBM

DELL

ZZZ

C

5.20. Can we download returns data directly?

CHAPTER 6

CAPM (Capital Asset Pricing Model)

To estimate in CAPM, we run a linear regression of $y = \alpha + \beta x$. The following codes create x and y. The function of **rnorm(n)** produces n normally distributed random numbers. The function **set.seed(123)** guarantees that every call to **rnorm()** offers the same values. The **set.seed()** and **rnorm()** functions will be discussed further in the chapter related to the Monte Carlo simulation. The variable x will take values of 1.0, 1.2, 1.4,...up to 10.0 with an incremental value of 0.2 while y will take a value of $2+3x$ plus a random number.

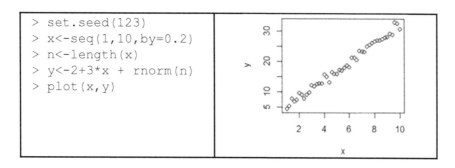

```
> set.seed(123)
> x<-seq(1,10,by=0.2)
> n<-length(x)
> y<-2+3*x + rnorm(n)
> plot(x,y)
```

To run a linear regression, we issue **lm(y~x)**, where *lm* stands for "linear model." The result shows that α is 2.066 (close to 2) while is 2.995 (close to 3). To find more information, we issue summary (lm(y~x)).

```
> lm(y~x)
Call: # output starts here
lm(formula = y ~ x)
Coefficients:
(Intercept) x
  2.066 2.995
```

6.1. Introduction

The CAPM (capital asset pricing model) theory was developed in the 1960s. It is quite popular among academics and practitioners due to its simplicity and usefulness. CAPM can be viewed as a one-factor model. Multiple-factor models will be discussed in the next chapter. Within this model, beta ( ) reflects the market risk of an underlying security while its volatility (standard deviation of returns) reflects the total risk.

6.2. Formula for CAPM

CAPM can be used to estimate the cost of equity, the cost a firm must pay if it issues equity as its source of capital. The basic logic behind CAPM is that individual stock returns (R_i R_i) are linearly correlated with a single risk factor (i.e., a stock-market index). The basic CAPM formula has the following form:

Equation 1

$$R_{i,t} - R_{f,t} = \alpha + \beta(R_{m,t} - R_{f,t}) + \varepsilon_t,$$

where $R_{i,t}$ is the return on stock i at time t,
$R_{f,t}$ is the risk-free rate at time t,
and $R_{m,t}$ is the market return (such as the S&P 500) at time t.

Usually we run the above linear regression to estimate beta. Alternatively we have the following formula to calculate beta:

Equation 2

$$\beta_i = \frac{cov(R_i, R_m)}{var(R_m)} = \frac{p(R_i, R_m) * \sigma_i}{\sigma_m},$$

where $cov(R_i, R_m)$ is the covariance between an individual stock's returns and the market returns,
$p(R_i, R_m)$ is the corresponding correlation,
σ_i is the standard deviation of stock's returns,
and σ_m is the standard deviation of market returns.

It is important to note that in equation 2, if the correlation and the market risk σ_m are held constant, a stock's beta σ_i will be positively correlated with its own total risk σ_i. Following the above example, we could estimate beta by applying equation 2.

```
> cov(x,y)/var(x)
[1] 2.995392
> cor(x,y)*sd(y)/sd(x)
[1] 2.995392
```

6.3. How to Retrieve Rstock, Rrisk-free, and Rmarket for CAPM

From chapter 5, we know that monthly, weekly, and daily price information is available from Yahoo Finance. We can convert price into return. To get a risk-free rate, we have several sources. Most practitioners use Eurodollar rates since they are the true interest rates paid when they borrow. To download the daily Eurodollar one-month rate manually, see three steps below.

1. Go to http://www.federalreserve.gov/releases/h15/data.htm.
2. Choose **Eurodollar Deposit Rate**. Click **Business Day**.

3. Save the data to a file with a text format.

Another way is to download the zip file (**h15.zip**) from the Federal Reserve Data Library then use a file called **H15_ED_M1.txt** (see chapter 5 for more details). The header and first several lines are shown below.

```
"Series Description","U.S. -- SHORT-TERM INTEREST
RATES: DAILY 1-MONTH EURO-DOLLAR DEPOSIT RATE "
"Unit:","Percent:_Per_Year"
"Multiplier:","1"
"Currency:","NA"
"Unique Identifier: ","H15/H15/RILSPDEPM01_N.B"
"Time Period","RILSPDEPM01_N.B"
1971-01-04,6.38
1971-01-05,6.31
1971-01-06,6.13
1971-01-07,6.19
```

Alternatively we can use the DDR (Data Download Program), which involves eight steps.

1. Go to http://www.federalreserve.gov/releases/h15/data.htm.
2. Click on **DDP** on the top-right corner.
3. Click on **Build package**.
4. Choose Selected Interest Rates and click **Continue**.
5. Choose other items accordingly then click **Add to package**.
6. Click on **Format package**.
7. Choose desired dates then click on **Go to download**.
8. Click on **Download file**.

Another way to obtain a risk-free rate is to use the T-Bill rate downloaded from Professor French's data library. The risk-free rates are included in his daily and monthly factor time series. Here are the steps:

1. Go to http://mba.tuck.dartmouth.edu/pages/faculty/ken.french/data_library.html.
2. Click **Fama/French Factors** for monthly (daily) factors.
3. Save it to your local computer and unzip it.

The first several lines (Fama-French monthly factors) are given below. For a more detailed description, please consult chapter 5: "Open Data."

```
This file was created by CMPT_ME_BEME_RETS using the 201006 CRSP database.
The 1-month TBill return is from Ibbotson and Associates, Inc.
  Mkt-RF SMB HML RF
192607 2.62 -2.16 -2.92 0.22
192608 2.56 -1.49 4.88 0.25
192609 0.36 -1.38 -0.01 0.23
192610 -3.43 0.04 0.71 0.32
```

6.4. retDIBM, prcDIBM, and Other R Data Sets

Four major R data sets are generated from the Yahoo Finance and Federal Reserve data libraries. They are called **retDIBM**, **prcDIBM**, **retD50**, and **retM50**—where *prc* is for price, *ret* for return, *D* for daily, and *M* for monthly. The **retDIBM** is a subset of **prcDIBM** by including only three variables (columns): ticker, date, and return. The **retDIBM** is a daily return data set for IBM, plus S&P 500 and Eurodollar rate. The same follows for other stock tickers. The **retD50** is a data set for fifty stocks.

http://canisius.edu/~yany/RData/ibm.RData
http://canisius.edu/~yany/RData/dell.RData
http://canisius.edu/~yany/RData/SP500.RData
http://canisius.edu/~yany/RData/daily100.RData
After saving **retDIBM.RData** to your local drive, you can use the **load()** function to upload it.

```
# assume the data set is located under the current directory
> load("retDIBM.RData") # relative path
```

Below is the command for the absolute path.

```
> load("c:/temp/retDIBM.RData") # absolute path
```

Using the **ls()** function, we can find three data sets included in **retDIBM.RData**.

```
> load("c:/temp/retDIBM.RData")
> ls()
[1] "EDM1" "ibm" "sp500"
```

We can load an R data set directly from the Web site instead of saving it to our local computer (see the R codes below).

```
> con<-url("http://canisius.edu/~yany/RData/retDIBM.RData")
> load(file=con)
> close(con)
```

We can also use the **head()**, **tail()**, **unique(yahoo_daily[,1]**, or **str()** functions to investigate the properties of these data sets further.

6.5. Percentage Returns vs. Log Returns

A percentage return, which is relatively easier to understand than a log return, is defined below.
Equation 3

$$R_t = \frac{P_t + D_t - P_{t-1}}{P_{t-1}} = \frac{P_t^{adj} - P_{t-1}^{adj}}{P_{t-1}^{adj}},$$

where P_t is the price at time t,
D_t is the dividend distributed between $t-1$ and, t

and P_t^{adj} is the adjusted prices (adjusted for stock splits, dividends, and other distributions) at time t.

In the following program, we generate a price vector and estimate the returns. We assume that the timing of price is sorted as $t-4$, $t-3$, $t-2$, $t-1$, and t.

```
> p<-c(10.0,10.02,9.90,10.30)
> n<-length(p)
> ret<-(p[2:n]-p[1:(n-1)])/p[1:(n-1)]
> ret
[1]  0.00200000 -0.01197605  0.04040404
```

A log return is defined as:
Equation 4

$$R_{t,log} = \log \left(\frac{P_t^{adj}}{P_{t-1}^{adj}} \right)$$

When returns are small, as is the case with daily returns, the difference between a percentage return and a log return is relatively negligible. For example, the percentage and log returns for Dell on February 11, 2011 are 0.866% and 0.863%, respectively.

```
Date,Open,High,Low,Close,Volume,Adj Close
2011-02-11,13.79,13.98,13.76,13.97,15354900,13.97
2011-02-10,13.82,13.97,13.70,13.85,13139000,13.85
2011-02-09,13.83,14.00,13.75,13.91,13175600,13.91
```

We have two ways to estimate returns: percentage and log return.

```
> (13.97-13.85)/13.85
[1]  0.00866426
> log(13.97/13.85)
[1]  0.00862694
```

6.6. Using R to Run CAPM

Based on two R data sets, **yahoo_daily.Rdata** and **ff_daily_factors.Rdata**, we can estimate stock's easily. Below, we estimate the for Citigroup in 2010. Please read chapter 5, "Open Data," to find out how to generate those two R data sets: **yahoo_daily.RData** and **ff_daily_factors.RData**.

```
# without using Rf in the regression
load("retD50.RData")
r<-retD50 # simplify the notation
ibm<-subset(r,r[,1]=="IBM" &format(r[,2],"%Y")=="2010")
ind<-subset(sp500,format(sp500[,1],"%Y")=="2010")
a<-data.frame(ibm[,2],ibm[,3])
colnames(a)<-c("date","Ri")
k<-merge(a,ind,by="date") # merge by date
y<-k$Ri # get dependent variable
x<-k$mkt # get independent variable
lm(y~x) # lm() for linear model
```

The corresponding output is shown below.

```
> lm(y~x)
Call:
lm(formula = y ~ x)
Coefficients:
(Intercept) x
  0.0001731 0.7719033
```

6.7. A Few R Programs to Run CAPM

The following program is used to estimate the market risk (beta) with four inputs: ticker, beginning year, ending year, and **d_or_m**, where the last input selects whether daily data or monthly data is used.

```
beta<-function(ticker,beg_year,end_yer,d_or_m){
  d<-yahoo_price(ticker,beg_year,end_yer,d_or_m)
  stock<-data.frame(d[,2],d[,9])
  colnames(stock)<-c('date','return')
  d2<-yahoo_price("^GSPC",beg_year,end_yer,d_or_m)
  index<-data.frame(d2[,2],d2[,9])
  colnames(index)<-c('date','mkt_ret')
  z<-merge(stock,index,by="date")
  print(lm(z$return~z$mkt_ret))
  print(' beta will be z$mkt_ret')
}
```

6.8. σannual, σmonthly, and σdaily

When we say IBM volatility is 20%, it means that the annualized standard deviation of its returns is 20%. Since usually monthly or daily data are used to estimate volatility, we have to convert a daily or monthly volatility into an annual one. See the following formulae:

Equation 5

$$\begin{cases} \sigma^2_{annual} = 252\sigma^2_{daily} \\ \sigma^2_{annual} = 12\sigma^2_{monthly} \end{cases}$$

Equation 5B

$$\begin{cases} \sigma_{annual} = \sqrt{252}\sigma_{daily} \\ \sigma_{annual} = \sqrt{12}\sigma_{monthly} \end{cases}$$

A more general formula to calculate the variance for an n-day variance from a daily variance is given below.

Equation 6

$$\begin{cases} \sigma^2_{n\_day} = n\sigma^2_{daily} \\ \sigma_{n\_day} = \sqrt{n}\sigma_{daily} \end{cases}$$

6.9. Moving (Rolling) Beta

Sometimes researchers need to generate a beta time series based on, for example, a three-year moving window. In such cases, we can write double loops. Let's look at a simple case, estimating the annual volatility for IBM over several years.

```
> load("retDIBM.RData")
> IBM[1:2,]
  Ticker  Date      Open    High    Low    Close  Volume  Adj_Close  Return
1 IBM 2013-10-08 181.89 181.99 178.71 178.72 5578300 178.72 0.018409
2 IBM 2013-10-07 181.85 183.31 181.85 182.01 3966400 182.01 0.011483
> >x<-IBM
> years<-unique(as.integer(format(x[,2],"%Y")))
> years[1:5]
[1] 2013 2012 2011 2010 2009
for(i in years[1:5]){
  y<-subset(x,format(x[,2],"%Y")==i)
var_daily<-var(y[,9])
var_annual<-nrow(y)*var_daily
cat("year=", i, var_annual, "\n")
}
```

Below is the output from the above program.

```
year= 1962 0.1100914
year= 1963 0.0244941
year= 1964 0.02601989
year= 1965 0.01968273
year= 1966 0.04826221
```

The following codes are used to calculate the annual betas for IBM.

```
load("retDIBM.Rdata")
stock<-data.frame(IBM$Date,IBM$Return)
colnames(stock)<-c("Date","Ret")
ind<-data.frame(sp500$Date,sp500$Return)
colnames(ind)<-c("Date","mkt")
x<-merge(stock,ind)
final<-merge(x,EDM1,x1="Date",x2="date")
years<-unique(as.integer(format(final[,1],"%Y")))
for(i in years[1:5]){ # for the first 5 years
  t<-subset(final,format(final[,1],"%Y")==i)
  a<-t$ret-t$EDM1
  y<-a$ret-a$EDM1
  cat("year=",i, "beta=",coef((lm(y~x)))[2], "\n")
}
```

The five annual betas are shown below.

```
year= 1971 beta= 1.090608
year= 1972 beta= 1.087801
year= 1973 beta= 1.129551
year= 1974 beta= 1.043098
year= 1975 beta= 1.169066
```

6.10. Estimating Beta for Any Number of Stocks

To estimate a few stocks, we can manually input the tickers of those stocks. Then we write a loop to estimate beta for each of them.

```
stocks<-c("IBM","DELL","C","MSFT")
for(stock in stocks) {
# your codes here
print(stock)
}
```

To estimate betas for a larger number of stocks, it is a good idea to create an input file first.

```
stocks<-read.table("tickers.txt")
for(stock in stocks) {
  # your codes here
  print(stock)
}
```

Another possibility is that we want to estimate beta for all stocks included in an R data set. In this case, we find the unique ticker symbols first.

```
load("retM.RData")
stocks<-unique(retD[,1])
for(stock in stocks) {
  # your codes here
  print(stock)
}
```

6.11. Issues in Forecasting β

Since beta tends to regress to 1, we can apply the following formula to adjust the beta estimate from CAPM.

Equation 7

$$\beta_{adj} = \frac{2}{3}\beta + \frac{1}{3}1.0$$

Table 6.1. Estimation methods used by several data providers

The estimation methodologies					
	Value Line	Reuters	Bloomberg	Yahoo	Capital IQ
Return frequency	Weekly	Monthly	Weekly	Monthly	Weekly, monthly (5 years)
Horizon (years)	5	5	2	3	1, 2, 5
Market index	NYSE Composite	S&P 500	S&P 500	S&P 500	S&P 500 and SSCI
Adjusted	Yes	No	Both	No	No

6.12. Scholes and Williams (1977) Adjustment for Beta

Many researchers find that would have an upward bias for frequently traded stocks and a downward bias for infrequently traded stocks. To overcome this, Scholes and Williams recommend the following adjustment.

Equation 8A

$$\beta = \frac{\beta^{-1} + \beta^0 + \beta^{+1}}{1 + \rho m}$$

where these three betas are from the following three regressions:

Equation 8B

$$\begin{cases} R_t = \alpha + \beta^{-1} R_{m,t-1} + \varepsilon_t \\ R_t = \alpha + \beta^0 R_{m,t} + \varepsilon_t \\ R_t = \alpha + \beta^{+1} R_{m,t+1} + \varepsilon_t \end{cases}$$

6.13. Dimson (1979) Adjustment for Beta

Along the same line, Dimson (1979) suggests the following method:

Equation 9A

$$\begin{cases} R_t = \alpha + \sum_{i=-k}^{k} \beta_i R_{m,t+i} + \epsilon_t \\ \beta = \sum_{i=-k}^{k} \beta_i \end{cases}$$

The most frequency used k value is 1. Thus, we have the next equation.

Equation 9B

$$\begin{cases} R_t = \alpha + \beta^{-1} R_{m,t-1} + \beta^0 R_{m,t} + \beta^{+1} R_{m,t+1} + \varepsilon_t \\ \beta = \beta^{-1} + \beta^0 + \beta^{+1} \end{cases}$$

6.14. Portfolio β

The β of a portfolio is the weighted average of the βs of individual stocks in that portfolio. The weight is the percentage of the portfolio value invested for each individual stock.

Equation 10

$$\beta_{port} = \sum_{i=1}^{n} w_i \beta_i$$

Equation 11

$$w_i = \frac{v_i}{\sum_i^n v_i}$$

where v_i is the value of stock i
and n is the number of stocks within the portfolio.

On December 31, 2002, a portfolio has 8000 shares of IBM, 5000 shares of Microsoft, and 2000 shares of Dell. What is the value of the portfolio? The following codes will show the observations of those three stocks on that day.

```
load("c:/yahoo_daily/prcM50.RData")
a<-prcM50 # make using the data set simpler
s<-c("IBM","MSFT","DELL") # three stocks
for(i in s){
  k<-subset(a,a[,1]==i & a[,2]=="2002-12-31")
  print(k)
}
```

We could calculate a portfolio beta that includes 10, 5, and 2 shares for those stocks.

```
load("c:/yahoo_daily/prcM50.RData")
a<-prcM50
s<-c("IBM","MSFT","DELL")
shares<-c(10,5,2)
value_port<-0
j<-1
value_port<-0
for(i in s){
  k<-subset(a,a[,1]==i & a[,2]=="2002-12-31")
  print(k)
  value_port<-value_port+shares[j]*k[,6]
  j<-j+1
}
value_port
```

Exercises

6.1. What is the definition of beta?

6.2. What type of risk does a beta try to measure?

6.3. What is the definition of market risk?

6.4. What is the opposite of market risk?

6.5. How do you measure market risk?

6.6. For a firm (or stock), is the total risk always larger than the market risk?

6.7. If stock A has a higher total risk than stock B, does it mean that A has a higher market risk as well?

6.8. How to measure risk?

6.9. Why do we care about the trade-off between risk and return?

6.10. What are the key assumptions underlying the CAPM?

6.11. What are the uses of the CAPM?

6.12. How do you predict the cost of equity of a firm?

6.13. How do you estimate WACC (weighted average cost of capital)?

6.14. Why do some firms adjust the beta by applying the following formula?

$$\beta_{adj} = \frac{2}{3}\beta + \frac{1}{3}1.0$$

6.15. Construct a portfolio with the following five stocks (IBM, C, GE, GOOG, and DELL). Estimate their equal-weighted monthly portfolio returns from 2001 to 2010.

6.16. Do the following:

a) Find the beta of IBM from Yahoo Finance. Go to Yahoo Finance then IBM then click Key Statistics on the left-had side (http://finance.yahoo.com/q/ks?s=IBM+Key+Statistics).

b) Download IBM's historical price data and estimate its beta.

c) Compare and comment on those two betas.

6.17. What is the total risk and market risk for DELL, IBM, GOOG, and C if we are using five-year monthly data?

6.18. Use Excel to estimate and for the following ten stocks. The time period covered should be the last five years (November 2005 to October 2010) by using monthly data from the Yahoo Finance and the Federal Reserve Web site (for risk-free rate).

	Company name	Ticker	Industry
1	Family Dollar stores	FDO	Retail
2	Wal-Mart Stores	WMT	Superstore
3	McDonald's	MCD	Restaurants
4	Dell company	DELL	Computer hardware
5	International Business Machine	IBM	Computer
6	Microsoft	MSFT	Software
7	General Electric	GE	Conglomerates
8	Google	GOOG	Internet services
9	Apple	AAPL	Computer hardware
10	eBay	EBAY	Internet services

6.19. Write an R program to repeat 6.18.

6.20. Download price data, as long as possible, from Yahoo Finance for a few stocks such as DELL, IBM, and MSFT. Then calculate their volatilities over several decades. For example, estimate volatilities for IBM over the following periods: 1962–1971, 1972–1982, 1982–1991, 1992–2001, 2002–2011. What is the trend of the volatility?

6.21. What is the correlation between (among) market indices? For example, you can download price data for S&P 500 (its Yahoo ticker is (^GSPC) and Dow Jones Industrial Average (^DJI) over the last ten years. Then estimate their returns and calculate the corresponding correlation. Comment on your result.

6.22. What is the correlation between IBM stock returns and DELL's from 2006 to 2010?

6.23. Which five stocks are most strongly correlated with IBM from 2006 to 2010?

6.24. On January 2 2000, your portfolio consists of 1,000 shares of IBM, 500 shares of Citigroup, and 400 shares of DELL. What is the portfolio's beta? You can use the past five-year monthly data to run CAPM.

CHAPTER 7

Fama-French Model, Sharpe Ratio, Treynor Ratio, Jensen's α

With the following three-factor model, we will estimate its intercept (α) and three coefficients (β_1, β_2, and β_3).

Equation 1

$$y = a + \beta_{1x1} + \beta_{2x2} + \beta_{3x3} + \varepsilon_t$$

The R codes to generate three input variables and run the above model are in the left panel below. The result, in the right panel, indicates that the intercept is 4.900 and three coefficients are 3.027, -1.281, and 5.005 respectively.

```
> set.seed(123)                        Call:
> x1<-seq(1,10,by=0.2)                 lm(formula = y ~ x)
> n<-length(x1)                        Coefficients:
> x2<-10 + runif(n)                    (Intercept) xx1 xx2 xx3
> x3<-runif(n)                           4.900 3.027 -1.281 5.005
> x<-cbind(x1,x2,x3)
> y<-2+3*x1-x2+5*(x3)+rnorm(n)
> lm(y~x)
```

The logic behind the so-called 52-week high-and-low trading strategy is that if today's price is close to 50-week high (low), there is a higher chance that the price will go higher (lower). To view the 52-week's range for IBM, see below.

```
>   x<-read.csv("http://canisius.edu/~yany/ibm.csv",header=T)
>   x[1,]
     Date    Open    High     Low  Close Adj.Close   Volume
1 1962-01-01 7.71333 7.71333 7.00333 7.22667  2.077532 8760000
```

Since today's price is the 52-week's high (174.54 versus 174.54), we should purchase IBM's stock (i.e., we should hold it). Actually we could use just one-line R codes to get a 52-week's range.

```
> range(read.csv("http://canisius.edu/~yany/data/ibm.csv",header=T)[1:252,5])
[1] 117.85 163.53
```

7.1. Fama-French Three-Factor Model

The famous Fama-French three-factor model is formulated below.

Equation 2

$$R_i = R_f + \beta_{mkt} (R_m - R_f) + \beta_{SMB} * SMB + \beta_{HML} * HML$$

where *SMB* (small minus big) is defined as "the returns of the small portfolios minus returns of the big portfolios," and *HML* (high minus low) is "the difference of returns of high book-to-market portfolios minus the returns of low book-to-market portfolios." (See Ken French's data library at http://mba.tuck.dartmouth.edu/pages/faculty/ken.french/data_library.html for more detailed definitions).

7.2. SMB (Small Minus Big)

Since small stocks are more risky, investors would demand high returns for bearing extra risks for holding them compared with big stocks that are usually stocks for more mature companies. Fama and French (1992, 1993) constructed a risk factor called SML (small minus big—http://mba.tuck.dartmouth.edu/pages/faculty/ken.french/data_library.html), which is the average return on three small-stock portfolios minus the average return on three big-stock portfolios,

Equation 3

$$SMB = \frac{1}{3}(SH + SM + SL) - \frac{1}{3}(BH + BM + BL),$$

where *S* stands for small,
B for big,
H for high,
M for median,
and *L* for low.

Those six portfolios are constructed in the following way: First, at the end of each year, the market capitalizations (stock price times shares outstanding) for the stocks listed on NYSE are ranked. We calculate a median. A stock is classified as small if its market capitalization is below this median; otherwise, it is a big stock. Second, the ratio of book value of equity over its market values (BE/ME) is estimated for each stock. Third, all stocks are broken into three book-to-market equity groups based on the breakpoints for the bottom 30% (low), middle 40% (median), and top 30% (high) of the ranked values of BE/ME for the NYSE listed stocks.

They define *book value of equity* (BE) as the "Compustat book value of stockholders equity plus balance sheet deferred taxed and investment tax credit minus the book value of preferred stocks." If a stock is small and belongs to a high book-to-market group, it will be in the portfolio of SH. Other stocks will be classified accordingly. Eventually each stock will be classified into one of those six portfolios: SH, SM, SL, BH, BM and BL. To estimate the returns of those six portfolios, the value-weighted method is applied. The weight of individual stocks is its market capitalization over the total market capitalization at the end of the previous year.

7.3. HML (High Minus Low)

HML is the difference in portfolio returns between the portfolio with high book-to-market values and the portfolio with low book-to-market values.

Equation 4

$$HML = \frac{1}{2}(SH + BH) - \frac{1}{2}(SL + BL),$$

7.4. Generating R Data Sets for Fama-French Factors

The related Web page is http://mba.tuck.dartmouth.edu/pages/faculty/ken.french/data_library. html. The above Web page contains both daily and monthly Fama-French factors, two of the most widely used frequencies. For the monthly factors, click **Fama-French Factors** to download a zip file called **F-F_Research_Data_Factors_TXT.zip**. After unzipping it, we will have monthly and annual Fama-French factors. A few top lines are shown below.

```
This file was created by CMPT_ME_BEME_RETS using the 201012 CRSP database.
The 1-month TBill return is from Ibbotson and Associates, Inc.
Mkt-RF SMB HML RF

192607 2.62 -2.16 -2.92 0.22
192608 2.56 -1.49 4.88 0.25
192609 0.36 -1.38 -0.01 0.23
192610 -3.43 0.04 0.71 0.32
192611 2.44 -0.24 -0.31 0.31
```

We can use following R codes to check the first several records. We can use **skip=4** to skip the first four lines (i.e., the header). The **nrow=10** imports ten lines.

```
>x<-read.table("F-F_Research_Data_factors.txt",skip=4,nrow=10)
>colnames(x)<-c("yyyymm","mkt_rf","SMB","HML","Rf")
> x
   yyyymm mkt_rf SMB HML Rf
1 192607 2.62 -2.16 -2.92 0.22
2 192608 2.56 -1.49 4.88 0.25
3 192609 0.36 -1.38 -0.01 0.23
4 192610 -3.43 0.04 0.71 0.32
5 192611 2.44 -0.24 -0.31 0.31
6 192612 2.77 -0.01 -0.10 0.28
7 192701 -0.11 -0.30 4.79 0.25
8 192702 4.32 -0.24 3.35 0.26
9 192703 0.32 -1.87 -2.58 0.30
10 192704 0.41 0.29 0.95 0.25
```

Through a trial and error, we can use **nrow=1014** to get all monthly factors. If we omit **nrow=1014**, we can find an error message.

The reason is that the original text file contains both monthly and annual factors. We can manually remove the annual factors. Then we don't have to specify the number of rows we would import.

```
> x<-read.table("F-F_Research_Data_factors.txt",skip=4,nrow=1014)
> tail(x)
   V1 V2 V3 V4 V5
1009 201007 7.24 -0.08 0.13 0.01
1010 201008 -4.40 -2.92 -1.71 0.01
1011 201009 9.24 3.97 -3.14 0.01
1012 201010 3.89 0.91 -2.14 0.01
1013 201011 0.58 3.72 -0.61 0.01
1014 201012 6.77 0.81 3.55 0.01
```

Below are the complete codes. Please note that the last four columns are divided by 100.

```
> x<-read.table("F-F_Research_Data_factors.txt",skip=4,nrow=1014)
> colnames(x)<-c("date","mkt_rf","SMB","HML","Rf")
> x[,2:5]<-x[,2:5]/100 # from percent to decimal
> ff_monthly_factors<-x # use a better name
> save(ff_monthly_factors,file="ff_monthly_factors.RData")
```

7.5. R Codes for the Fama-French Three-Factor Model

Based on two R data sets—**yahoo_daily.Rdata** and **ff_daily_factors.Rdata**—we can estimate the stock's β easily. Below, we estimate the for Citigroup in 2010. (Read chapter 4 to see how to generate those two R data sets: **yahoo_daily.RData** and **ff_daily_factors.RData**.)

```
load("retD50.RData")
load("ff_daily_factors.RData")
stock<-"C" # C for Citigroup
year<-2010 # year we are interested
y<-yahoo_daily # simplify the notation
f<-ff_daily_factors # simplify the notation
a<-subset(y,y[,1]==stock & as.integer(y[,2]/10000)==year)
b<-subset(f,as.integer(f[,1]/10000)==year)
a2<-cbind(a[,2],a[,9]) # only choose date and return
colnames(a2)<-c("date","return")# assign column names
k<-merge(a2,b,by="date") # merge by date
y<-k$return-k$Rf # dependent variable
x<-cbind(k$mkt_rf,k$SMB,k$HML) # independent variables
lm(y~x) # lm() for linear model
```

The result is shown below:

```
> lm(y~x)
Call:
lm(formula = y ~ x)
Coefficients:
(Intercept) x1 x2 x3
0.001214 0.900756 -0.161982 1.705548
```

We can compare the coefficient of the market risk for both CAPM (one-factor model) with those based on the Fama-French three-factor model.

```
> source("http://canisius.edu/~yany/Beta.R")
> Beta("C",2010)
[1] "Beta for C in 2010 = 1.4444"
```

7.6. Momentum Strategy

Momentum is defined as "a stock moving in the same direction for consecutive periods of time." Accordingly a trading strategy, called *buy winners and sell losers*, can be designed. Jegadeesh and Titman (1993) tested this strategy. For example, they use six months as an evaluation period to classify winners and losers and the next six months as a holding period. First they rank all stocks into ten portfolios (deciles) based on their past six months' total returns. The highest return decile is called winner while the bottom decile is called loser. The trading strategy is to take a long position with winners and a short position with losers (i.e., long the first portfolio and short the tenth portfolio). For each month, they reclassify both winners and losers and rebalance their long-short portfolio. They find that this strategy is indeed a profitable trading strategy. Note that Jegadeesh and Titman (1993) do not consider transaction costs.

7.7. Downloading the Momentum Factors

If we add the momentum factor, we can have a four-fatcor model. To download the momentum factor, go to Professor Ken French's data library: http://mba.tuck.dartmouth.edu/pages/faculty/ken.french/data_library.html.

```
Momentum Factor (Mom) Details
Momentum Factor (Mom) [Daily] Details
```

Below is the Fama-French-Carhart's four-factor model.

Equation 5
$$R_i = R_f + \beta_{mkt}(R_m - R_f) + \beta_{SMB} * SMB + \beta_{HML} * HML + \beta_{Mom} * MOM$$

To download those four factors (market, SMB, HML, and momentum), we go to Professor Ken French's data library to download two zipped files for those four factors.

7.8. Sharpe Ratio

The Sharpe ratio measures a trade-off between risk and return. It is defined as "a ratio of benefits over cost (risk)."

Equation 6
$$Sharpe = \frac{R-R_f}{\sigma} = \frac{\overline{R-R_f}}{\sqrt{var(R-R_f)}}$$

When two projects have the same returns, we prefer the project with a lower risk. When two projects have the same risk, we choose the project with a higher return. However, usually returns and risks are positively correlated. Which project should we choose if project X has both a higher return and a higher risk than project Y? In such a case, we could rank projects based on their Sharpe ratios.

In the following codes, assume we can access an R data set called **retDIBM.RData**, which contains three data sets: daily return for IBM, daily return for S&P 500 (not used in the Sharpe-ratio calculation), and **Rf** (Eurodollar one-month deposit rate).

```
load("retDIBM.RData")
rf_daily<-(1+EDM1[,2])^(1/30)-1
rf<-data.frame(EDM1[,1],rf_daily)
colnames(rf)<-c("date","rf") # try if omit this line
a<-merge(ibm,sp500,by="date") # merge 3 data sets
x<-merge(a,rf,by="date")
t<-x$ret-x$rf
mean(t)/sd(t) # Sharpe ratio
```

7.9. Treynor Ratio

As we discussed in the previous chapters, investors care about the market risk (β) instead of the total risk (σ). The reason behind such a statement is that a rational investor could diversify away firm-specific risk by investing in several stocks. Thus, they are compensated for bearing systematic risk and will not be compensated for bearing firm-specific risk. Based on this conclusion, if we have stocks A and B with ($\sigma_A > \sigma_B$ and $\beta_A < \beta_B$), we should observe a higher expected rate of returns for B than for A (i.e., $R_A < R_B$).

Treynor ratio is similar to the Sharpe ratio. The only difference is that Treynor ratio applies the market risk (β) instead of the total risk (σ) in the denominator.

Equation 7
$$Treynor\ Ratio = \frac{R - R_f}{\beta}$$

7.10. retMIBM, prcMIDM, retM50, prcM50 R Data Sets

Again **ret** is for return, **prc** is for price, and **M** for monthly. The **retM** is a subset of **prcM** by including only ticker, date, and return, and 50 is for fifty stocks.

- ○ http://canisius.edu/~yany/RData/retMIBM.RData
- ○ http://canisius.edu/~yany/RData/prcMIBM.RData
- ○ http://canisius.edu/~yany/RData/retM50.RData.
- ○ http://canisius.edu/~yany/RData/rcM50.RData.

To load the data set related to Yahoo Daily, just issue the following commands.

```
> load("retMIBM.RData") # relative path
> load("c:/temp/retMIBM.RData") # absolute path
```

Alternatively we can load an R data set directly.

```
> con<-url("http://canisius.edu/~yany/RData/retMIBM.RData")
> load(file=con)
> close(con)
```

The first line defines a linking location. The second line loads the data set. The last line disconnects the linking. This command can be omitted. Including such a line (command) is a practice of good programming. Then we can use the **head()**, **tail()**, **unique(yahoo_daily[,1])**, and **str()** functions to "look" at the data sets. For example, we want to know how many stocks (ticker symbols) are available from this data set. The command used is **unique()**.

```
> length(unique(retM50[,1]))
[1] 50
```

7.11. The 52-Week's High

Here is one related Web page: http://www.ehow.com/way_5509556_week-high-stock-trading-strategy.html. In finance, we have a trading strategy based on the last 52-week's range. It states that investors compare the current stock price with the 52-week's high and low. If the current price is close to the 52-week high, it means that the stock migh be on an upswing—or that a sharp drop might be looming. . The opposite is also true: if the current price is close to its 52-week's low, then the stock is a loser —or a good buy. . Below is a related example program for Citigroup (ticker is C) on February 13, 2015 from the Yahoo Finance.

```
> x<-read.csv("http://finance.google.com/finance/historical?q=C&startdate=Jan+01,
+2007&enddate=Feb+12,+2015&output=csv")
  > x[1,]
         Date  Open  High   Low Close    Volume
  1 12-Feb-15 49.94 51.09 49.77 50.89 28926844
  > range(x[1:252,5])
  [1] 45.68 56.37
```

To verify, go to http://finance.yahoo.com. Enter a ticker of C in the Get Quotes box. The following codes are used to get the past three day's high. First, we need a program to generate the terminal stock price. The R codes for a sock path are given below. We will discuss this function in more detail in chapter 9: "Monte Carlo Simulation."

```
Stock_price<-function(S,r,T,n,sigma){
  delta_T<-T/n
  ST<-seq(1:n)*0
  ST[1]<-S
  for (i in 2:n)
  ST[i]<-ST[i-1]*exp((r-0.5*sigma*sigma)*delta_T+sigma*rnorm(1)*sqrt(delta_T))
  return(ST)
}
```

It is a good idea to generate our own prices and use a much smaller window, such as three days or four days, to test our program since we can manually check each step. Below, we generate date and prices first.

```
# - Generate date and prices --- #
n<-100 # number of stock prices
date<-1:n
T<-1 # maturity date in years
rf<-0.03 # risk-free rate
S<-20 # stock price at time 0
sigma<-0.1 # volatility of the underlying security
set.seed(12345)
```

```
price<-Stock_price(S,rf,T,n,sigma)
x<-cbind(date,price)
> head(x)
date price
[1,] 1 20.00000
[2,] 2 20.12248
[3,] 3 20.27082
[4,] 4 20.25373
[5,] 5 20.16713
[6,] 6 20.29477
```

Assume that we are interested in 3 days instead of 252 days. We estimate its 3-day highs. The y variable defined below contains three columns: date (t), price at t, and 3 days' high (from $t-3$ to $t-1$).

```
# -- estimate 3-day high --- #
y<-matrix(0,n-3,3)
for(i in 4:n){
j<-i-3
y[j,1]<-x[i,1] # date variable
y[j,2]<-max(x[i,2]) # price at t
y[j,3]<-max(x[(i-3):(i-1),2]) # high over the last 3 days
}
```

We print the first several lines for both x and y variables. Since the window is 3 days, the first day for the y variable should start from day 4. This is true that the first variable in **y[1,]** is 4. From the first three prices in x, we know that the maximum is 20.27082. This is true for the maximum in the first y (i.e., **y[1,3]**).

```
> head(x)
date price
[1,] 1 20.00000
[2,] 2 20.12248
[3,] 3 20.27082
[4,] 4 20.25373-
[5,] 5 20.16713
[6,] 6 20.29477
```

```
> head(y)
     [,1] [,2]     [,3]
[1,]  4 20.25373 20.27082
[2,]  5 20.16713 20.27082
[3,]  6 20.29477 20.27082
[4,]  7 19.93413 20.29477
[5,]  8 20.06515 20.29477
[6,]  9 20.01481 20.29477
```

Again, the major reason to use a very short window such as three days is that we could easily check and debug our program. After being sure about the accuracy of our codes, we adjust the length of our window according to our need.

7.12. Jensen's α, Rolling Beta, and Scholes and William's β

7.12.1. Jensen's α

Jensen's *alpha* is defined as "the difference between a portfolio return and the return predicted by the CAPM." This measure is developed by Michael C. Jensen in 1960s. When CAPM holds, we expect α α is zero in equation 1 (i.e., $R_i - R_f = \alpha + \beta (R_m - R_f)$). Based on CAPM, we can estimate beta and predict the future returns based on the excess market returns.

Equation 8

$$\alpha_p = \overline{R}_p - \overline{R}_{predicted} = \overline{R}_p - [\overline{R}_p + \hat{\beta}_p (\overline{R}_m - \overline{R}_f)],$$

where α_p is the Jensen's α,
$\overline{R}_p$ is the mean portfolio return,
$\overline{R}_f$ is the mean return of the risk-free rate,
$\overline{R}_m - \overline{R}_f$ is the mean excess return of a market index,
and $\hat{\beta}_p$ is the estimated portfolio beta.

We can have many different ways to estimate alpha. Assume that we have ten-year data for a portfolio. We can choose use a three-year window to estimate beta. Thus, we use the first three-year data to estimate the beta of the portfolio then estimate the alpha for the fourth year. Use the data from year two to year four to update our beta estimate. Then calculate alpha in year five. For this case, we end up with seven betas and seven alphas.

If a capital assets pricing model is good, the mean alpha should be close to zero. Thus, we could use mean alpha to rank the quality of different assets pricing model. The CAPM is a one-factor model while Fama-French is a three-factor model. Since the Fama-French model is developed in the '90s, we expect its mean alpha to be way below the value from the CAPM.

If we use the same assets pricing model, we can rank the performance of mutual funds by Jensen's alpha. The higher the alpha is, the better the performance of a mutual fund's performance.

7.12.2. Rolling Beta

Assume that we want to estimate the annual beta for a stock from 1970 to 2010. Since we know the program to estimate one year's beta, we can write a loop to call this program repeatedly (see the codes below).

```
ticker<-"IBM"
final<-NA
for(i in 1970:2010) {
final[i-1970+1]<-Beta(ticker,i)
}
```

In chapter 6: "CAPM," we discussed the rolling beta already. Although the above program is much simpler and easier to understand, it is not efficient. The major reason is that if we estimate thirty annual betas for one firm, we download its price time series thirty times. It is a good idea to download the time series just once.

7.12.3. Scholes and William's β

Scholes and William (1977) suggest another way to estimate beta. Their methodology includes the following steps:

1. Convert percentage return to log return for stocks: **log_ret=log(ret+1)**. Do the same thing for the market: **log_ret_m=log(ret+1)**.

   a. Conditions
      i Use one-year daily returns and minimum trading dates >126 (half year).
      ii Use trade-only observations.
      iii Use trade-only value-weighted market index of NYSE/AMEX.
2. Get the three-day moving average for market return: **ret3m(t)=[log_ret_m(t-1)+log_ret_m(t)+log_ret_m(t+1)]**.
3. Use instrumental variable instead of formula on page 185 of the CRSP manual.

Exercises

7.1. What is the Fama-French three-factor model?

7.2. What is the definition of SMB?

7.3. What is the definition of HML?

7.4. What is momentum strategy?

7.5. From where can we download Fama-French monthly factors?

7.6. From where can we download Fama-French daily factors?

7.7. Is the SMB factor a portfolio?

7.8. If holding SMB portfolio (based on the Fama-French SMB factor) from January 1, 2000 to December 31, 2010, what is the total return? Estimate total returns based on both daily and monthly SMB.

7.9. Why did you get different results in 7.8?

7.10. Try the same thing (same as questions 7.8 and 7.9) for HML.

7.11. Try the same thing (same as questions 7.8 and 7.9) for **mkt_rf**.

7.12. Estimate IBM's beta based on the Fama-French three-factor model by using the monthly data

from Yahoo Finance and from Professor French's data library.

7.13. What is the difference between the Sharpe ratio and the Treynor ratio?

7.14. Can we use just one period to estimate Jensen's alpha?

7.15. What is the Sharpe ratio for IBM based on the last five years' monthly data?

7.16. Based on the Sharpe ratio and the past three years' daily data, which stock should you choose, IBM or Google?

7.17. Will your decision on the previous question change if you apply Treynor ratio instead of Sharpe ratio?

7.18. Construct a portfolio of five stocks—such as IBM, C, GE, GOOG, and WMT—and estimate their monthly portfolio returns from 2001 to 2010. What is their portfolio's beta?

7.19. What is the alpha of the above portfolio if we use the first five years to estimate the beta of the portfolio?

7.20. Write a program to estimate 52-week's high and low for DELL.

7.21. Download **F-F_Research_Data_Factors_TXT.zip** from French's data library. Unzip it, and access the text file **F-F_Research_Data_Factors.txt**. Write an R program to process annual Fama-French factors and save your final output to an R data set.

7.21. Download the monthly Fama-French 5 factors time series from Prof. French's Data Library. Write an R program to generate a data set called ffMonthly5.RData.

7.22. Run the Fama-French 5-factor model for IBM and Walmart based on the latest 5-year monthly data. Compare its performance with the Fama-French 3-factor model and CAPM.

CHAPTER 8

T-Test, F-Test, Durbin-Watson, Normality and Granger Causality Tests, Event Study

Hypothesis: IBM's mean daily return is zero. First, let us generate IBM's return vector.

```
>y<-read.csv("http://finance.google.com/
finance/historical?q=IBM&startdate=Jan+01,+2007&enddate=Jan+12,+2017&output=csv")
> n<-nrow(y)
> ret<-(y[1:(n-1),7]-y[2:n,7])/y[2:n,7]
```

Next, we conduct a t-test to confirm or reject the above hypothesis.

```
> t.test(ret,mu=0)
  One Sample t-test
data: ret
t = 3.242, df = 12481, p-value = 0.00119
alternative hypothesis: true mean is not equal to 0
95 percent confidence interval:
  0.0001860478 0.0007550279
sample estimates:
  mean of x
0.0004705379
```

In the above codes, the mean is assumed to be zero (**mu=0**). Since the t value is 3.2 and p value is 0.001, we reject the null hypothesis. In other words, our result concludes that the IBM's mean return is not zero.

8.1. Introduction

In finance, we have many hypotheses, such as whether a stock's mean return is 0.02%, the volatility of a portfolio is a constant, the mean return of IBM is the same as the mean return of Apple, the mean returns on Mondays is the same as the mean returns on other weekdays, the variance of returns on Mondays (a three-calendar-day return) is three times the variance of returns on other weekdays (a true one-day return), and variance of stock returns is constant.

To accept and reject those hypotheses, we need to conduct certain statistical tests. For example, to test the January effect (returns in January is lower than returns in other months), we apply a t-test. In this chapter, we will discuss several widely used tests such as t-test, f-test, Durbin-Watson autocorrelation test, Granger causality test, normality test, and Wilcoxon signed-rank test.

8.2. Rule of Thumb for a T-Test

Usually, we compare our t value, an output from our test, with a critical value that depends on the degreeof freedom (number of observation) and our chosen confidence level. However, the following general rules apply.

1. With a high t value, we tend to reject the null hypothesis.
2. With a lower p value, we tend to reject the null hypothesis.
3. When the value falls outside our confidence interval, reject the null hypothesis.

For a 5% confidence level, we have the following similar rules. Here we assume a moderate number of observations, such as larger than 25.

1. When t value > 2, we reject.
2. When p value < 5%, we reject.
3. When the tested value falls outside our 95% confidence interval, we reject.

8.3. T-Test for a One-Time Series

A t-test can be used to test whether the mean return is a fixed number. In the following test, since t=3.21 and p=0.001, we reject the null hypothesis that the mean returns is zero (**mu=0**).

```
y<-read.csv("http://finance.google.com/finance/
historical?q=AAPL&startdate=Jan+01,+2007&enddate=Jan+12,+2017&output=csv")
n<-nrow(y)
ret<-(y[1:(n-1),7]-y[2:n,7])/y[2:n,7]
t.test(ret,mu=0) # Ho : mean return is zero (mu=0)
One Sample t-test
data: ret
```
```
t = 3.4427, df = 8616, p-value = 0.0005786
alternative hypothesis: true mean is not equal to 0
95 percent confidence interval:
 0.000487034 0.001774993
sample estimates:
  mean of x
0.001131013
```

The t-test assumes that the test statistic follows a Student's t distribution if the null hypothesis is supported. When the number of a sample size increases, the underlying distribution would approach a normal distribution. When deciding whether to reject or accept the underlying hypothesis, we can look at the t value, p value, and/or the 95% confidence interval.

- Check t value. We choose a confidence level such as 5%; then we find out what the corresponding critical value is (http://www.ruf.rice.edu/~bioslabs/tools/stats/ttable.html).

For example, for a degree of freedom of 8616, the critical value is close to a normal distribution (i.e., $T_{critical}=1.96$). When our value is higher than 1.96, we reject the underlying hypothesis. Otherwise, we accept the hypothesis. Since the t value is 3.44 and larger than 1.96, we reject the underlying hypothesis. A rule of thumb: if the t value is larger than 2, we reject. The higher the t value, the more probable we are of rejecting the underlying hypothesis.

- The p value is the probability of the underlying hypothesis being true. Since the p value is 0.06%, which is much smaller than 5%, we reject the underlying hypothesis. The rule of thumb: the lower the p value, the higher the chance to reject.
- If the mean value falls in the confidence interval, we accept the hypothesis. If it is outside the range, we reject. Since 0 is outside the rage (0.000487034 0.001774993), we reject the hypothesis.

From the above result, we know that the mean is close to 0.00113. Thus, we could test it with the following codes.

```
> t.test(ret,mu=0.000113)
 One Sample t-test
data: ret
t = 3.0988, df = 8616, p-value = 0.001949
alternative hypothesis: true mean is not equal to 0.000113
95 percent confidence interval:
 0.000487034 0.001774993
sample estimates:
 mean of x
0.001131013
```

8.4. Tests for Equal Means

First, let us look at a simple example with just two lines. The data set used is called sleep (see the first line below). A few records are shown in the right panel below. Are the two group means of extra equal? If our confidence level is 5%, then the result shows that we cannot reject the null hypothesis (i.e., the result confirms that the two means are equal).

```
> data(sleep)
> oneway.test(extra ~ group, data = sleep)
One-way analysis of means (not assuming equal
variances)
data: extra and group
F = 3.4626, num df = 1.000, denom df = 17.776,
p-value = 0.07939
```

```
> head(sleep,5)
 extra group ID
1 0.7 1 1
2 -1.6 1 2
3 -0.2 1 3
4 -1.2 1 4
5 -0.1 1 5
> tail(sleep,5)
 extra group ID
16 4.4 2 6
17 5.5 2 7
18 1.6 2 8
19 4.6 2 9
20 3.4 2 10
```

To test whether the mean returns for IBM and Apple are equal, we use the **t.test()** function.

```
x<-read.csv("http://canisius.edu/~yany/ibm.csv",header=T)
n<-nrow(x)
ret<-data.frame(as.Date(x[1:(n-1),1]),x[2:n,6]/x[1:(n-1),6]-1)
colnames(ret)<-c("DATE","IBMret")

y<-read.csv("http://canisius.edu/~yany/aapl.csv",header=T)
n2<-nrow(y)
ret2<-data.frame(as.Date(y[1:(n-1),1]),y[2:n,6]/y[1:(n-1),6]-1)
colnames(ret2)<-c("DATE","APPLret")
final<-merge(ret,ret2)
t.test(final$IBMret,final$AAPLret)
```

The output is shown below. The null hypothesis is that they have equal means. Since the t statistic is 2.72, we reject the null hypothesis. In other words, those two stocks have different mean returns. We can double check this by looking at the p value which is 0.006. When our significant levels are 1% or 5%, we reject the null hypothesis that their means are equal.

```
        One Sample t-test
data:   final$IBMret
t = 2.7424, df = 441, p-value = 0.006347
alternative hypothesis: true mean is not equal to 0
95 percent confidence interval:
 0.002700752 0.016362390
sample estimates:
  mean of x
0.009531571
```

8.5. Introduction to F-Test

F-test can be used to test whether two populations have equal variances. The null hypothesis is that two variances are equal (i.e., $S_1^2 / S_2^2 = 1$). Let's test some time series with known mean and variances.

```
x <- rnorm(500, mean = 0, sd =0.5)
y <- rnorm(1000,mean = 0.5,sd =0.2)
var.test(x,y)
```

From the result below, the **num df** is "numerator degree of freedom," and **denom df** is the "denominator degree of freedom." From an F-distribution table of **http://www.medcalc.org/manual/f-table.php**, we can find the critical value is 1.11 with a numerator DF of 499 and a denominator DF of 999. Since our f value of 7.73 is higher than 1.11, we reject the underlying hypothesis that those two variances are equal. At the same time, since the p value is very small, we reject the hull hypothesis as well. When the variances are equal, their ratio will be 1. Since 1 is outside the 95% confident interval, which ranges from 6.65 to 9.02, we reject.

```
F test to compare two variances
data: x and y
F = 7.7295, num df = 499, denom df = 999, p-value < 2.2e-16
alternative hypothesis: true ratio of variances is not equal to 1
95 percent confidence interval:
6.651996 9.016787
sample estimates:
ratio of variances
7.729519
```

To test if IBM's returns have the same variances, we have the following codes. Based on the p value, we reject the null hypothesis (i.e., we confirm that IBM's variance is not a constant).

```
a<-read.csv("http://canisius.edu/~yany/ibm.csv",header=T)
n<-nrow(a)
ret<-a[2:n,6]/a[1:(n-1),6]-1
x<-ret[1:as.integer(length(ret)/2)]
y<-ret[as.integer(length(ret)/2):length(ret)]
var.test(x,y)


      F test to compare two variances
data:  x and y
F = 0.6147, num df = 333, denom df = 335, p-value = 9.848e-06
alternative hypothesis: true ratio of variances is not equal to 1
95 percent confidence interval:
 0.4958724 0.7620647
sample estimates:
ratio of variances
     0.6147035
```

The following codes show us that the variances for IBM and AAPL over the last three years (252*3=756) are 0.0297% and 0.0798% respectively. Are they statistically different?

```
>d <- read.csv("http://finance.google.com/finance/
historical?q=AAPL&startdate=Jan+01,+2007&enddate=Jan+12,+2017&output=csv")
> n<-nrow(d)
> ret_IBM<-(d[1:(n-1),7]-d[2:n,7])/d[2:n,7]
> d2<->read.csv("http://chart.yahoo.com/table.csv?s=AAPL",header=T)
> n<-nrow(d2)
> ret_AAPL<-(d2[1:(n-1),7]-d2[2:n,7])/d2[2:n,7]
> var(ret_IBM[1:756])
[1] 0.00012579
>var(ret_AAPL[1:756])
[1] 0.0002880371
```

To test whether IBM has the same variances as AAPL over the last three years, we have the following codes. The null hypothesis is that they are the same. Based on the p value, we reject the null hypothesis.

```
> var.test(ret_IBM[1:756],ret_AAPL[1:756])
F test to compare two variances
data: ret_IBM[1:756] and ret_AAPL[1:756]
F = 0.4367, num df = 755, denom df = 755, p-value < 2.2e-16
alternative hypothesis: true ratio of variances is not equal to 1
95 percent confidence interval:
0.3786117 0.5037340
sample estimates:
ratio of variances
0.4367145
```

If we know the ratio of the two variances, we can test this one as well. The ratio is 5.96, and it is located within the 97% confidence interval of [5.08, 6.90]. Thus, we accept the null hypothesis that they are equal.

```
> x <- rnorm(500,mean = 0, sd = 0.5)
> y <- rnorm(1000,mean = 0.5,sd =0.2)
> var.test(x,y,ratio=0.5^2/0.2^2)
F test to compare two variances
data: x and y
F = 0.9461, num df = 499, denom df = 999, p-value = 0.4821
alternative hypothesis: true ratio of variances is not equal to 6.25
95 percent confidence interval:
5.089073 6.898244
sample estimates:
ratio of variances
5.913427
```

8.6. Durbin-Watson Autocorrelation Test

The Durbin-Watson test is used to test the existence of an autocorrelation, which is defined as "the correlation between a return and its lag." Most of the time, we use one-step lag—that is, $corr(R_t, R_{t-1})$.

Table 8.1. The range of D-W statistic (0–4)

D-W statistic	Autocorrelation
≈ 2	No autocorrelation
> 2	Negative autocorrelation
< 2	Positive autocorrelation

The range of D-W statistic is from 0 to 4. When the D-W statistic is close to 2, it indicates no autocorrelation, a value toward 0 for a positive autocorrelation, while a value close to 4 for a negative one.

Below, the **cor()** function shows that the returns are negatively autocorrelated for IBM. Note that the result is based on the data collected on February 15, 2015.

```
>d<-read.csv("http://finance.google.com/finance/
historical?q=AAPL&startdate=Jan+01,+2007&enddate=Jan+12,+2017&output=csv")>
n<-nrow(d)
> ret<-(d[1:(n-1),7]-d[2:n,7])/d[2:n,7]
> cor(ret[2:(n-1)],ret[1:(n-2)])
[1] -0.01585543
```

Based on the output for a Durbin-Watson autocorrelation test, we accept the null hypothesis that the IBM's daily returns have a negative autocorrelation. Note that the alternative hypothesis—the autocorrelation of IBM's return—is positive. To install **lmtest** package, click **Packages…** then **Install Packages…** For more details, please consult chapter 32: "Introduction to R Packages."

```
> library(lmtest)
>y<-read.csv("http://finance.google.com/
finance/historical?q=AAPL&startdate=Jan+01,+2007&enddate=Jan+12,+2017&output=csv")
> n<-nrow(y)
> ret<-(y[1:(n-1),7]-y[2:n,7])/y[2:n,7]
> m<-as.integer(length(ret)/2)
> x<-rep(c(-1,1),m)
> dwtest(ret[1:(2*m)]~x)

  Durbin-Watson test

data: ret[1:(2 * m)] ~ x
DW = 2.0314, p-value = 0.9658
alternative hypothesis: true autocorrelation is greater than 0
```

Below, we generate a time series that is negatively correlated. First, we generate AR(1) error term with parameter **rho=0**.

```
>library(lmtest)
>ma<- rnorm(100)  # rho=0 (white noise)
>x <- rep(c(-1,1), 50)
> head(x,10)
  [1] -1 1 -1 1 -1 1 -1 1 -1 1
>y1<- 1 + x + ma
>dwtest(y1 ~ x)

  Durbin-Watson test

data: y1 ~ x
DW = 1.7672, p-value = 0.1411
alternative hypothesis: true autocorrelation is greater than 0
```

To generate a time series with rho=0.4 and -0.3, we have the following codes.

```
>set.seed(123)
>ma<- rnorm(100)  # rho=0 (white noise)
>x <- rep(c(-1,1), 50)
>rho<- 0.4
>ma2 <- filter(ma, rho, method="recursive")
>y2 <- 1 + x + ma2
>dwtest(y2 ~ x)  # DW = 1.2856, p-value = 0.0002256
rho<- -0.3
ma2 <- filter(ma, rho, method="recursive")
y2 <- 1 + x + ma2
dwtest(y2 ~ x)  # DW = 2.5345, p-value = 0.9975
```

8.7. Granger Causality Test

The Granger causality test is used to determine whether a one-time series is a factor or offers useful information in forecasting another. Usually we ask which comes first, chick or eggs? This is the common sense of causality (i.e., which one causes the next one). We have a data set called **ChickEgg**, which has two columns: number of chicks and number of eggs. We want to know whether the lag values of the number of chicks can be used to predict the number of eggs. If this is true, we say that the number of chicks Granger-causes the number of eggs. If this is not true, we say that the number of chicks does not Granger-cause the number of eggs.

```
>library(lmtest)
>data(ChickEgg)
>dim(ChickEgg) # [1] 54 2
>ChickEgg[1:10,]
  chicken egg
 [1,]  468491 3581
 [2,]  449743 3532
 [3,]  436815 3327
 [4,]  444523 3255
 [5,]  433937 3156
```

The following two tests show us which came first: the chicken or the egg. First, we test whether the chicken Granger-causes the egg (see codes below).

```
> grangertest(egg ~ chicken, order = 3, data = ChickEgg)
Granger causality test
Model 1: egg ~ Lags(egg, 1:3) + Lags(chicken, 1:3)
Model 2: egg ~ Lags(egg, 1:3)
  Res.Df Df F Pr(>F)
1 44
2 47 -3 0.5916 0.6238
```

Based on the result that the p value is 0.62, we cannot reject the null hypothesis. Thus, we conclude that the chick variable does not Granger-causes the eggs (i.e., the chick variable has no explaining power to predict the future value of the egg).

On the other hand, the next one is used to test whether the egg Granger-causes the chicken. Since the p value is 0.002966, we can reject the null hypothesis if our confidence level is 1%. Two stars (**) indicates that the result is significant at 0.01 level. Thus, we conclude that the egg Granger-causes the chicken.

```
> grangertest(chicken ~ egg, order = 3, data = ChickEgg)
Granger causality test
Model 1: chicken ~ Lags(chicken, 1:3) + Lags(egg, 1:3)
Model 2: chicken ~ Lags(chicken, 1:3)
Res.Df Df F Pr(>F)
1 44
2 47 -3 5.405 0.002966 **
--
```

```
Signif. codes: 0 '***' 0.001 '**' 0.01 '*' 0.05 '.' 0.1 ' ' 1
>grangertest(egg ~ chicken, order = 3, data = ChickEgg
```

Next, let's use real stock-market data. In chapter 6: "CAPM," we know that the market return is the only factor in the CAPM. Thus, it is natural for us to argue that the lags of market returns would help predict individual stocks' future returns in addition to its own lags. In a sense, Model 1 is better than Model 2 in the following equation.

Equation 1

$$\begin{cases} Model\ 1: R_{i,t} = lag\ (R_{i,t\text{-}1}) + lag(R_{m,t\text{-}1}) \\ Model\ 2: R_{i,t} = lag\ (R_{i,t\text{-}1}) \end{cases}$$

The following program uses the S&P 500 as the market index (ticker symbol is ^GSPC) and tests whether we could use S&P 500 to predict IBM's future returns.

```
>d<-read.csv("http://canisius.edu/~yany/data/ibm.csv")[,7]
>n<-length(d)
>ret<-(d[1:(n-1)]-d[2:n])/d[2:n]
>rm(d,n)
>d2<-read.csv("http://chart.yahoo.com/table.csv?s=^GSPC",header=T)[,7]
>n2<-length(d2)
>mkt<-(d2[1:(n2-1)]-d2[2:n2])/d2[2:n2]
>ret_mkt<-data.frame(cbind(ret[1:500],mkt[1:500]))
>colnames(ret_mkt)<-c("ret","mkt")
```

```
> grangertest(ret ~ mkt, order = 1, data = ret_mkt)
Granger causality test
Model 1: ret ~ Lags(ret, 1:1) + Lags(mkt, 1:1)
Model 2: ret ~ Lags(ret, 1:1)
  Res.Df Df F Pr(>F)
1 496
2 497 -1 13.053 0.0003337 ***
--
Signif. codes: 0 '***' 0.001 '**' 0.01 '*' 0.05 '.' 0.1 ' ' 1
```

Our result shows that, yes, we can use the S&P 500 returns to explain practically IBM's future returns. Note that we use one lag, and the result is run on February 15, 2015.

8.8. Wilcoxon Signed-Rank Test

Sometimes we want to confirm whether two matched data samples come from the same distribution. The Wilcoxon signed-tank test, **wilcox.test()**, achieves this *without* assuming that the samples follow a normal distribution.

```
> x <- c(1.83, 0.50, 1.62, 2.48, 1.68, 1.88, 1.55, 3.06, 1.30)
> y <- c(0.878, 0.647, 0.598, 2.05, 1.06, 1.29, 1.06, 3.14, 1.29)
> wilcox.test(x, y, paired = TRUE, alternative = "greater")
 Wilcoxon signed rank test
data: x and y
V = 40, p-value = 0.01953
alternative hypothesis: true location shift is greater than 0
```

At 5% significance level, we conclude that those two time series are from identical populations. For IBM's and DELL's returns, we confirm that they come from the same distribution: p=0.95.

```
> wilcox.test(ret_IBM[1:504],ret_DELL[1:504],paired=TRUE)
  Wilcoxon signed rank test with continuity correction
data: ret_IBM[1:504] and ret_DELL[1:504]
V = 63430, p-value = 0.9514
alternative hypothesis: true location shift is not equal to 0
```

8.9. Pearson's Correlation and Spearman's Rank Correlation

The concept related to correlation up to now is called Pearson's correlation, and it is defined below.

Equation 2

$$\begin{cases} \rho_{xy} = \dfrac{\mathbf{cov(x, y)}}{\sigma_x \sigma_y} \\ cov(x, y) = \dfrac{\sum_{i=1}^{n}(x_i - \bar{x})(y_i - \bar{y})}{n - 1} \end{cases}$$

We use very simple numbers.

i	x	y
1	$x_1 = 1$	$y_i = 1$
2	$x_2 = 2$	$y_2 = 2$
3	$x_3 = 3$	$y_3 = 3$

To use R codes to estimate Spearman's correlation, we have the following codes. It should not surprise us when we get a perfect negative correlation (see above values).

```
> cor(x,y,method='spearman')
[1] -1
```

Note that the default setting for the **cor(x,y)** function is "pearson."

```
> x<-c(2.6,2.7,7.8)
> y<-c(10.4,3.5,0.6)
> cor(x,y,method="pearson")
[1] -0.7396709
```

8.10. Normality Test

The Shapiro-Wilk test tests the null hypothesis that a sample **x1, .., xn** came from a normally distributed population. In this test, we call the **shapiro.test()** function. The null hypothesis is that the input sequence is normally distributed. Below, we generate a set of random numbers from a standard normal distribution.

```
>set.seed(12345)
>x<-rnorm(1000)
> mean(x)
[1]  0.04619816
> sd(x)
[1]  0.9987476
```

Since we draw those values from a normal distribution, we are supposed to accept the null. The value of 0.19 indicates that we accept the null hypothesis.

```
> shapiro.test(x)
Shapiro-Wilk normality test
data: x
W = 0.9978, p-value = 0.1988
```

We know that a uniform distribution is not normal. The tiny p value confirms that we should reject the null hypothesis.

```
x<-runif(1000)
shapiro.test(x)
Shapiro-Wilk normality test
data: x
W = 0.9569, p-value < 2.2e-16
```

8.11. Event Study

Event study is one of the most applied techniques used in financial research. The logic goes this way: We observe a set of similar events. Our related question is what the impact is of those same or similar events. For example, we observe stock splits, quarterly-earning announcements, announcements that firms would finance a profitable project by issuing new equity or new debt, and the like. Theoretically speaking, a stock split should have no impact on the value of the firms. However, based on the clientele theory, some investors prefer the stocks in certain ranges such as between $5 and $50. Thus, when a high-priced stock, such as $70, going through a two-for-one split, we should expect that those investors might consider it. The R package, related to the event study, is called **eventstudies**. To install and load the package, we have the following commands.

```
>install.packages("eventstudites")
>library(eventstudies)
```

There are two data sets included in the package called **StockPriceReturns** and **SplitDates**.

```
>data(StockPriceReturns)
>data(SplitDates)
> dim(StockPriceReturns)
[1] 3246 30
> head(StockPriceReturns,1)
Bajaj.Auto BHEL Bharti.Airtel Cipla Coal.India Dr.Reddy GAIL
2000-04-03 NA 4.917104 NA 6.810041 NA -3.254165 7.617895
HDFC.Bank Hero.Motocorp Hindalco.Industries Hindustan.Unilever HDFC
```

```
2000-04-03 -5.2116 3.065919 -3.056759 7.692309 7.693191
ICICI ITC Infosys Jindal.Steel Larsen.&.Toubro
2000-04-03 -4.725288 6.823068 -8.337262 1.283715 4.255961
Mahindra.&.Mahindra Maruti.Suzuki NTPC ONGC Reliance.Industries
2000-04-03 -8.338161 NA NA -0.4876977 3.560651
SBI Sterlite.Industries Sun.Pharmaceutical TCS Tata.Motors
2000-04-03 5.186233 -8.340269 -8.134564 NA 1.888274
Tata.Power Tata.Steel Wipro
2000-04-03 2.643326 2.601679 -7.338846
> head(SplitDates)
unit when
5 BHEL 2011-10-03
6 Bharti.Airtel 2009-07-24
8 Cipla 2004-05-11
9 Coal.India 2010-02-16
10 Dr.Reddy 2001-10-10
11 HDFC.Bank 2011-07-14
```

Based on the menu, we have the following codes to run an event study.

```
>data(StockPriceReturns)
>data(SplitDates)
>es.results <- phys2eventtime(z=StockPriceReturns,events=SplitDates,width=5)
>es.w <- window(es.results$z.e, start=-5, end=+5)
>eventtime <- remap.cumsum(es.w, is.pc=FALSE, base=0)
inference.Ecar(z.e=eventtime, to.plot=FALSE)
```

The related output is shown below:

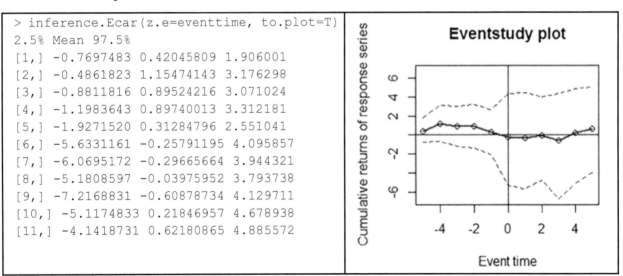

```
> inference.Ecar(z.e=eventtime, to.plot=T)
2.5% Mean 97.5%
[1,] -0.7697483 0.42045809 1.906001
[2,] -0.4861823 1.15474143 3.176298
[3,] -0.8811816 0.89524216 3.071024
[4,] -1.1983643 0.89740013 3.312181
[5,] -1.9271520 0.31284796 2.551041
[6,] -5.6331161 -0.25791195 4.095857
[7,] -6.0695172 -0.29665664 3.944321
[8,] -5.1808597 -0.03975952 3.793738
[9,] -7.2168831 -0.60878734 4.129711
[10,] -5.1174833 0.21846957 4.678938
[11,] -4.1418731 0.62180865 4.885572
```

Exercises

8.1. What is the difference between a t-test and an f-test?

8.2. Where can we apply a t-test?

8.3. Where can we apply an f-test?

8.4. Is the volatility of IBM's returns over the last ten years a constant?

8.5. Based on IBM, MSFT, DELL, and C (Citigroup) data, are returns on Monday different from other weekdays?

8.6. For Walmart, is its mean daily return 0.002%?

8.7. Are the mean daily returns for IBM and WMT equal?

8.8. For IBM, estimate volatility based on monthly and daily return. Does the following equation hold?

$$\sigma^2_{monthly} = 21\sigma^2_{daily}$$

8.9. Use more stocks to test the above equation. Pay attention to different stocks in terms of sizes (i.e., small stocks versus big stocks).

8.10. What is the average of mean volatility for individual stocks over the past ten years?

8.11. Is the market volatility constant over the years? (Hint: you can use S&P 500 as the market portfolio.)

8.12. Is it true that the volatility of individual stocks has been decreasing over the years? Use hard evidence to support or reject it.

8.13. Do the market returns Granger-cause Apple's returns?

8.14. What are the correlations between IBM and its competitors?

8.15. What might be the causes of the bias when we estimate an annualized volatility by using daily returns compared with using monthly returns?

8.16. Write an R program to test equality of their volatilities for given tickers and the number of observations (from now back to history). The format is given below.

```
> equal_vol2stoks("IBM","MSFT",500)
```

8.17. Download a few market indices—such as United States, England, Japan, and China—to conduct Granger causality tests.

8.18. Download the monthly factors (MKT, SMB, and HML) from Professor French's data library (http://mba.tuck.dartmouth.edu/pages/faculty/ken.french/data_library.html) and conduct Granger causality tests among those factors. Comment on your results.

8.19. Go to Yahoo Finance to find the beta for IBM, DELL, and MSFT then try to replicate those betas.

8.20. Use the annual beta to test the following formula, which is used to adjust beta.

$$\beta_{adj} = \frac{2}{3}\beta + \frac{1}{3}1.0$$

(Hint: choose a few stocks, estimate their annual beta, then estimate their autocorrelations.)

8.21. What is the impact in terms of beta by omitting the risk-free rate? In other words, you can try the following two formulae to see if the betas of IBM in 2010 are different.

$$R_i = R_f + \beta \ (R_m - R_f),$$
$$R_i = a + \beta R_m$$

8.22. With the Web page http://www.enchantedlearning.com/history/us/pres/list.shtml, we can find which party a US president belongs to. Thus, we can generate the following table. The party and range variables are from the Web page. year2 is the second number of NGE minus 1.

Table 8.2. Parties and presidents since 1923

PARTY	RANGE	YEAR1	YEAR2
Republican	1923-1929	1923	1928
Republican	1929-1933	1929	1932
Democratic	1933-1945	1933	1944
Democratic	1945-1953	1945	1952
Republican	1953-1961	1953	1960
Democratic	1961-1963	1961	1962
Democratic	1963-1969	1963	1968
Republican	1969-1974	1969	1973
Republican	1974-1977	1974	1976
Democratic	1977-1981	1977	1980
Republican	1981-1989	1981	1988
Republican	1989-1993	1989	1992
Democratic	1993-2001	1993	2000
Republican	2001-2009	2001	2008
Democratic	2009-2012	2009	2011

Write an R program to answer the following question: Are the monthly mean returns under the two types of presidents (from Democratic and from Republican parties) equal?

i) Download S&P 500's historical monthly price from Yahoo Finance (^GSPC).
ii) Estimate monthly returns.
iii) Classify those returns into two groups.
iv) Test the hypothesis: the mean of the two groups are equal.

CHAPTER 9

Monte Carlo Simulation

To generate 100 normally distributed random numbers, use the following codes.

```
> x<- rnorm(100)
```

In order to generate the *same* random numbers every time we run the codes, we use the **set.seed()** function. For a comparison, you can run the first program without invoking the **set.seed()** function.

```
> set.seed(123)
> x<- rnorm(100)
> x[1:3]
[1] 1.2240818 0.3598138 0.4007715
```

To randomly select 10 stocks among 500, we can apply the **runif()** function. The second part of the program uses a data set called **SnP500List**, which is the constituents of S&P 500 in 2005. The data set is included in the R package called **PortRisk**. If you get an error message when uploading the package, then install it by using **install.packages("PortRisk")**.

```
>set.seed(729)
> x<-unique(as.integer(runif(20,1,500)))
> x2<-x[1:10]
> x2
  [1] 110 434 188 415 485 477 474 495 90 66
434 TEG Integrys Energy Group Inc.
188 FRX Forest Laboratories
415 SPG Simon Property Group Inc
485 WY Weyerhaeuser Corp.
477 WHR Whirlpool Corp.
474 WEC Wisconsin Energy Corporation
495 XYL Xylem Inc.
90 CHK Chesapeake Energy
66 BMS Bemis Company
```

To replicate the Black-Scholes-Merton option model by using Monte Carlo simulation, we have fourline R codes. The input values of s, x, T, r, sigma, and n are today's stock price, exercise price, maturity (in years), risk-free rate, volatility, and number of simulation. The default value of n is 100.

```
bsCallSimulation<-function(s,x,T,r,sigma,n=100){
  ST<-s*exp((r-sigma*sigma/2.0)*T + sigma*rnorm(n)*sqrt(T))
  mean(((ST-x) + abs(ST-x))/2)*exp(-r*T)
}
```

In the program, **ST** is the future stock price at **T**, and **((ST-x) + abs(ST-x))/2** is equivalent to **max(ST,x)**.

```
> bs_call(40,42,0.5,0.1,0.2)
[1] 2.27778
> set.seed(212)
> bsCallSimulation(40,42,0.5,0.1,0.2,5000)
[1] 2.268195
```

9.1. Simulation and Finance

In finance, there are many applications of the Monte Carlo–simulation technique. This method was first introduced to corporate finance by Hertz (1964). Later Boyle (1977) used the simulation to price various options. Below are a few examples.

Investment decision. Assume that several potential investment projects are available, and the NPV rule is applied to rank them. The issue is that there are too many uncertainties in the future, such as costs of ten raw materials, several labor costs, cost of short-term and long-term debts, cost of equity, just to name a few. In this case, simulation can be used to find the NPV based on various combinations of many input variables.

Scenario analysis. Many CEOs prefer to have all possible scenarios in the future, especially the best, worst, and most-likely ones. If there are many independent variables that might change in the evaluation, it would be difficult to manually handle all possibilities. Fortunately we can use simulation to generate those scenarios.

Price Asian options. The recent unrests in the Middle East make many crude-oil consumers (companies) nervous about the cost of the commodity. There exist many ways to hedge such a risk (e.g., buy a call on crude oil). Recall that the payoff of a European call is:

$$payoff\ (call) = max(S_T - X, 0),$$

where, S_T is the price of crude oil on the maturity date (*T*) and X is the exercise price. However, most companies consume crude oil on a daily frequency. Thus, they are about the average of daily prices than the terminal price. To hedge such a risk more effectively, an Asian option should be used (see its payoff function below).

$$payoff\ (Asian\ option,\ average\ price) = max\ (S_{average} - X, 0)$$

where $S_{average}$ is the average price from T_0 to T. Unlike the Black-Scholes-Merton option model, there is no closed-form solution for Asian options. Fortunately we can apply the Monte Carlo simulation to price those path-dependent options. European options are path-independent options.

In this chapter, we will discuss how to generate random numbers and paths followed by stock prices, replicate the Black-Scholes-Merton model, price Asian options and other financial applications. For example, if we want to generate 1,000 random numbers evenly distributed between 0 and 1, we use the following one-line codes.

```
x<-runif(1000)
```

After generating a set of random numbers, we can check their properties such as mean, min, max, and standard deviation. Later we will conduct a normality test as well.

```
>min(x)
[1] 0.008416585
>max(x)
[1] 0.9740309
>mean(x)
[1] 0.5166573
```

In table 9.1, several functions are given for the two most used distributions: uniform and normal.

Table 9.1. Distributions, cumulative distributions, random-number generator for two most used distributions (standard normal and uniform distribution between [0,1]), where n is an integer

Distribution	Random Distribution	Density	Cumulative distribution
Uniform [0,1]	runif(n)	dunif(n)	punif(n)
Standard normal	rnorm(n)	dnorm(n)	pnorm(n)

For a general normal distribution, we add mean and standard deviation to the related functions. For a uniform distribution, we can specify minimum and maximum as two additional inputs. The next table lists those extra input variables and how to input them.

Table 9.2. Distribution, cumulative distribution, random-number generator, where *n* is an integer and **[min,max]** is the range for a uniform distribution

Distribution	Random Distribution	Density	Cumulative distribution
Uniform [a, b]	runif(n, min, max)	dunif(x, min, max, log)	punif(q, min, max, lower.tail, log.p)
Normal distribution	rnorm(n, mean, sd)	rnorm(n, mean, sd)	pnorm(q, mean, sd, lower.tail, log.p)
Binomial	rbinom(n, size, prob)	dbinom(x, size, prob, log)	pbinom(q, size, prob, lower.tail, log.p)

9.2. A Normal Distribution

The major assumption underlying the famous Black-Scholes-Merton option model is that the prices of a stock follow a lognormal distribution while its returns follow a normal distribution. Thus, we should familiarize ourselves with normal distributions. The density function for a normal distribution is defined as

Equation 3

$$f(x) = \frac{1}{\sqrt{2\pi\sigma^2}} e^{-\frac{(x-\mu)^2}{2\sigma^2}},$$

where μ is the mean of the distribution and is the standard deviation of the distribution. For a normal distribution with a specified mean and standard deviation, we use the following codes:

```
>x<-rnorm(100, mean = 5, sd = 3)
>mean(x)
[1]  5.356629
>sd(x)
[1]  2.770360
```

Note that when you run the above codes, you will get a quite different set of values. To fix the value, see the next section.

The density function for a standard normal distribution is μ=0 and =1 in the above equation. Thus, equation 3 becomes

Equation 4

$$f(x) = \frac{1}{\sqrt{2\pi}} e^{-\frac{x^2}{2}}$$

For a standard normal distribution, we can use both formats below.

```
x<-rnorm(100, mean = 0, sd = 1)
x2<-rnorm(100)
```

9.3. Concept of Seed

If we regenerate ten random numbers a second time, the values of the second set will be quite different from the first set (see the output below).

```
> rnorm(10)
 [1] 1.10177950 0.75578151 -0.23823356 0.98744470 0.74139013 0.08934727
 [7] -0.95494386 -0.19515038 0.92552126 0.48297852
> rnorm(10)
 [1] -0.5963106 -2.1852868 -0.6748659 -2.1190612 -1.2651980 -0.3736616
 [7] -0.6875554 -0.8721588 -0.1017610 -0.2537805
>
```

This should have little impact on most research topics since the mean and standard deviation of the output are the same if we have a relatively large sample. However, sometimes we demand a fixed set of random numbers every time we run the codes. For example, when an instructor shows the codes on the blackboard, students prefer to have the exact same values on their own screens. For those cases, we use the **set.seed()** function.

```
> set.seed(10)
> rnorm(10)
  [1]  0.01874617 -0.18425254 -1.37133055 -0.59916772  0.29454513
  [6]  0.38979430 -1.20807618 -0.36367602 -1.62667268 -0.25647839
> rnorm(10)
  [1] -0.5963106 -2.1852868 -0.6748659 -2.1190612 -1.2651980
  [6] -0.3736616 -0.6875554 -0.8721588 -0.1017610 -0.2537805
> set.seed(10)
> rnorm(10)
  [1]  0.01874617 -0.18425254 -1.37133055 -0.59916772  0.29454513
  [6]  0.38979430 -1.20807618 -0.36367602 -1.62667268 -0.25647839
```

9.4. Q-Q Plot

A q-q plot will be a straight line if the underlying sequence matches the benchmark distribution. For the normal test, we use the **qqnorm()** function.

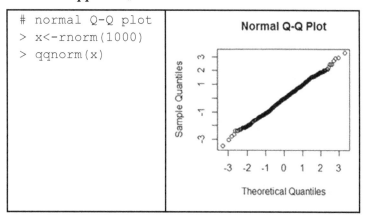

```
# normal Q-Q plot
> x<-rnorm(1000)
> qqnorm(x)
```

On the other hand, if we have random numbers from a non-normal distribution, such as from a uniform distribution, we will get a nonlinear line.

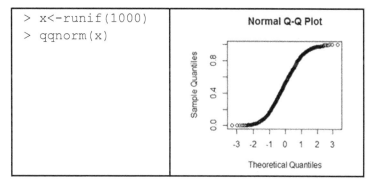

```
> x<-runif(1000)
> qqnorm(x)
```

Those q-q plots just show us a picture whether the data follow a specific distribution. However, q-q plots are not a formal test.

9.5. Monte Carlo Simulation

For a normal distribution, we can use **rnorm(n, mu, std)** to generate n random numbers (see the example below). The first letter *r* in **rnom()** stands for "random."

```
mu<-0.25
std<-0.3
n<-100
rnorm(n,mu,std)
```
```
[1]  0.281563545 -0.272513928 0.443574098 0.279131267 0.226979892
[6]  0.547585203 -0.007775228 0.165526094 0.869874181 0.066534107
[11] 0.344683847 0.448088013 -0.266660722 -0.390387815 0.270683679
[16] 0.510346523 -0.437013254 0.204942914 0.169365462 0.787399612
```

To generate random numbers from a lognormal function, we use the **rlnorm()** function.

```
log_normal_random<-function(n) return(rlnorm(n))
```

9.6. Simulating Stock Prices (Paths)

We assume that the stock price follows a lognormal distribution.
Equation 5

$$S_{t+1} = S_t + \hat{\mu}S_t\Delta t + \sigma S_t \epsilon \sqrt{\Delta t},$$

where S_{t+1} is the stock price at *t+1*,
$\hat{\mu}$ is the expected stock return $\Delta t = {}^T/n$
T is the maturity (in years),
n is the number of steps,
ϵ is a random number from a standard normal distribution,
and σ is the volatility.

The above equation will lead to the following equation, which will be used in our programs.
Equation 6

$$S_{t+1} = S_t \exp\left(\hat{\mu} - \frac{1}{2}\sigma^2\right)\Delta t + \sigma\epsilon\sqrt{\Delta t})$$

In a risk-neutral work, no investors require compensation for bearing risks. Thus, in such a world, the expected return on any security (investment) is the risk-free rate. Thus, the above equation becomes
Equation 7

$$S_{t+1} = S_t \exp\left(r - \frac{1}{2}\sigma^2\right)\Delta t + \sigma\epsilon\sqrt{\Delta t})$$

The R codes for the paths for a stock's prices are given below.

```
ST_path_f<-function(S,r,T,n,sigma){
  delta_T<-T/n
  ST<-seq(1:n)*0
  ST[1]<-S
  for (i in 2:n)
  ST[i]<-ST[i-1]*exp((r-0.5*sigma*sigma)*delta_T+sigma*rnorm(1)*sqrt(delta_T))
  return(ST)
}
```

The output is an n by 1 vector showing n prices along the path. For the terminal stock price, we have the following equation:

Equation 8

$$S_T = S_0 \exp\left(\left(\hat{\mu} - \frac{\sigma^2}{2}\right)T + \sigma\epsilon\sqrt{T}\right)$$

In a risk-neutral world, we have the equivalent equation.

Equation 9

$$S_T = S_0 \exp\left(\left(r - \frac{\sigma^2}{2}\right)T + \sigma\epsilon\sqrt{T}\right)$$

The following program gives the terminal stock price with a set of input values.

```
ST_f<-function(S,r,T,sigma){
S*exp((r-0.5*sigma*sigma)*T+sigma*rnorm(1)*sqrt(T))
}
```

We can apply the function easily by inputting a set of values.

```
> ST_f(40,0.1,1,0.2)
[1] 34.13524
```

9.7. Using Simulation to Replicate the Black-Scholes-Merton Model

From chapter 3: "Black-Scholes-Merton Option Model," we know that the price of a European call will be 4.76 (see R codes below to call a Black-Scholes function).

```
call_f<-function(s,x,T,r,sigma){
   d1 = (log(s/x)+(r+sigma*sigma/2.)*T)/(sigma*sqrt(T))
   d2 = d1-sigma*sqrt(T)
   s*pnorm(d1)-x*exp(-r*T)*pnorm(d2)
}
```

Assume that we have a stock with a current price of $42, the strike price is $40, the time to maturity is 6 months, the continuously compounded risk-free rate is 10%, and the volatility of the underlying stock is 20%.

```
bs_f('C',42,40,0.5,0.1,0.2) # usage: bs_f(flag,S,X,T,r,sigma)
[1] 4.759422
```

According to equation 9, we can write the following R codes to use the simulation to price a European call option.

```
bs_call_simulation<-function(s,x,r,T,sigma,n=100){
  ST<-s*exp((r-sigma*sigma/2.0)*T + sigma*rnorm(n)*sqrt(T))
  payoff<-((ST-x) + abs(ST-x))/2
  mean(payoff)*exp(-r*T)
}
> bs_simulation(42,40,0.1,0.5,0.2,5000)
[1] 4.691878
```

Note that if you run the above codes, you will get a different result (i.e., not 4.691878). Why?

9.8. Using the Monte Carlo Simulation to Price Asian Options

The payoffs associated with these options are determined by the path of the underlying asset's price, such as Asian, barrier, and lookback options. The payoff of an Asian average terminal price is given below:

Equation 10

$$payoff\ (Asian\ option,\ average\ price) = max\ (S_{average} - X, 0)$$

Assume that the path of a stock (**ST_f**) is available. We can use the following codes to price an Asian average price call.

```
asian_call_ave_price<-function(S,r,T,n_steps,sigma,x,n_trial){
  payoff<-payoff<-rep(0,time=n_trial) # initialization
  for(i in 1:n_trial){
    Saverage<- mean(ST_path_f(S,r,T,n_steps,sigma))
      payoff[i]<-max(Saverage-x,0)
  }
  return(mean(payoff)*exp(-r*T))
}
> asian_call_ave_price(50,0.1,1,1000,0.2,20,100)
[1] 30.07172
```

Another type of Asian options uses S_average as the exercise price.

Equation 11

$$payoff\ (Asian\ call,\ average\ strike\ price) = max\ (S_T - S_{average}, 0)$$

9.9. Correlated Random Sequences

Sometimes we need to generate two sequences of correlated random numbers. Let's assume that the correlation between those two-time series is ρ ρ. Below is the procedure to generate those two sequences.

1) Generate two sequences of uncorrelated normally distributed random numbers. Let's call them x1 and x2.
2) Generate y_1 and y_2 using the following formulae:

Equation 12

$$y_1 = x_1$$

Equation 13

$$y_2 = \rho x_1 + \sqrt{1 - \rho^2 x_2}$$

where y_1 and y_2 are the sequence we need. The corresponding codes are given below:

```
x1<-rnorm(1000)
x2<-rnorm(1000)
cor(x1,x2)
[1] -0.006533303 # correlation coefficient is almost zero
rho<-0.5 # assume a value
y1<-x1
y2<-x1*rho + sqrt(1-rho^2)*x2
cor(y1,y2)
[1] 0.522907 # test the correlation coefficient
```

9.10. Randomly Select m Stocks

We defined *m* as "the number of stocks."

```
set.seed(124)
m<-5 # number of stocks a choice variable
load("retM50.RData")
n_stock<-length(unique(retM50[,1]))
x<-unique(as.integer(runif(2200,0,n_stock))%%n_stock+1)
id<-matrix(x[1:m],m,1)
colnames(id)<-"ID"
y2<-unique(retM50[,1])
id2<-1:n_stock
stocks<-data.frame(y2,id2)
colnames(stocks)<-c("ticker","ID")
final<-merge(stocks,id,by="ID")
```

```
> final
ID ticker
1 5 A
2 12 AFL
3 20 AOL
4 21 AP
5 26 BA
```

9.11. Sobol Sequency

When generating a set of normal distributions, we don't have control in terms of which random numbers would pop up. When the number of random numbers is huge, it takes a while to get our final results. The Sobol sequence would be more evenly distributed than our original random numbers from a normal distribution. Thus, we can increase the efficiency when applying the Sobol sequence. The following codes, in the right panel below, show how to generate 100 random numbers from a Sobol sequence.

The two graphs are shown below:

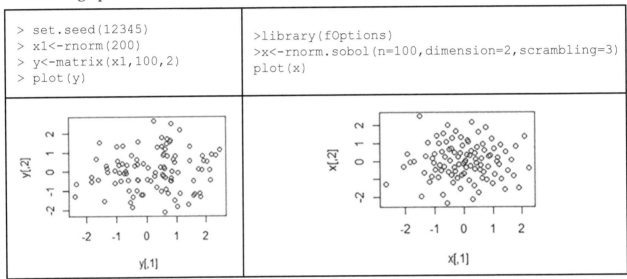

```
> set.seed(12345)
> x1<-rnorm(200)
> y<-matrix(x1,100,2)
> plot(y)
```

```
>library(fOptions)
>x<-rnorm.sobol(n=100,dimension=2,scrambling=3)
plot(x)
```

9.12. Shapiro-Wilk Normality Test

The Shapiro-Wilk test confirms whether a sample $x_1, .., x_n$ came from a normally distributed population. The null hypothesis test is that the sequence is normally distributed. In the following test, the p value is 0.693. If the chosen confidence level is 0.05, we cannot reject the null hypothesis. In other words, we confirm that the sequence follows a normal distribution.

```
>x<-rnorm(1000)
>mean(x)
[1] -0.02819767
>sd(x)
[1] 0.9951352
>shapiro.test(x)
   Shapiro-Wilk normality test
data: x
W = 0.9987, p-value = 0.693
```

Let's look at the obvious non-normal sequence:

```
x<-runif(1000)
shapiro.test(x)
  Shapiro-Wilk normality test
data: x
W = 0.9569, p-value < 2.2e-16
```

9.13. Time Used to Run a Simulation

Usually we are less concerned with the computer time when we estimate many of our simulation tasks. However, when our tasks become more complex, or when we use large numbers of random numbers, the time needed for our analysis might increase dramatically. Thus, we need a method to estimate our costs in terms of computer time. Below, we generate a set of random numbers and estimate their mean.

```
> set.seed(123)
> n<-100
> mean(rnorm(n))
[1] 0.0904059
```

Actually we can combine the last two lines into one, such as **mean(rnorm(100))**. Obviously, when n increases, we need more time to get our final result. Then how much time do we need?

```
> system.time(mean(rnorm(100000)))
user system elapsed
0.04 0.00 0.04
> system.time(mean(rnorm(10000000)))
user system elapsed
3.79 0.02 3.85
```

This process took a total of 3.81 seconds of CPU time (3.79+0.02=3.81), out of which, 3.79 seconds was spent in user space and the rest of 0.02 seconds in kernel mode on behalf of the process (system). Elapsed real time was 3.85 seconds.

Table 9.3. Three types of time for running a program

Names	User CPU time	System CPU time	Total time
R-name	User	System	Elapsed
Explanation	Time spent on the processor running your program's codes (or codes in libraries)	Time spent running codes in the operating system kernel on behalf of your program	Time needed for the process

9.14. What Is Your Chance to Win a Lottery?

First, let's look at a very simple case. There are three balls marked as 1, 2, and 3 in a bag. What is the chance that you randomly pick up two balls and they are balls 1 and 2? How many different combinations are there? In this case, we can manually count: (1,2), (2, 3) and (1, 3). Thus, we have 1/3 chance to pick up balls 1 and 2.

For n different balls, picking up r balls will have the following combinations.

$$\begin{bmatrix} n \\ r \end{bmatrix} = \frac{n!}{r!*(n-r)!},$$

where $n!$ is called factorial and n!=n*(n-1)*(n-2) .... (n-1). For example, 4!=4*3*2*1=24.
Using the above example, what is the chance to pick up (1,2)? Total combinations are:

$$\begin{bmatrix} 3 \\ 2 \end{bmatrix} = \frac{3!}{2!*(3-2)!} = \frac{3*2}{2*1*1} = 3$$

Since (1, 2) is one combination and we have three different combinations, the chance will be 1/3. How about in a Mega Millions game?

Game design: Choose five white balls out of fifty-six white balls, plus one red ball out of forty-six red balls. For example, on March 30, 2012, the winning numbers are 2, 4, 23, 38, 46 (white balls) and 23 (red ball). The total covmbinations of a Mega Millions game is $\begin{bmatrix} 56 \\ 5 \end{bmatrix} * 46 = \frac{56!}{5!*(56-5)!} * 46$. The related R function is called **factorial()**.

```
> factorial(4)
[1] 24
> factorial(56)/(factorial(5)*factorial(56-5))*46
[1] 175711536
```

The chance will be 1 out of 176 million. Alternatively we can write our own program to estimate a factorial.

```
fac<-function(n){
  if(n==1)
  return(1)
  else
  return(n*fac(n-1))
}
```

The third way to estimate a factorial is to use the **gamma** function.

```
factorial_f<-function(n) gamma(n+1)
> factorial_f(8)
[1] 40320
> factorial(8)
[1] 40320
```

In addition, we can write our own R program to estimate the number of unique combination for picking r ball from n different balls.

```
n_combinations<-function(n,r)gamma(n+1)/gamma(r+1)/gamma(n-r+1)
```

Exercises

9.1. Download the daily data for IBM for five years and estimate its returns. Is its q-q plot a straight line?

9.2. Do the same thing in 9.1 using monthly data instead of daily.

9.3. We can convert random numbers from a uniform distribution to a normal distribution by using the following formula: $norm = \sum_{i=1}^{12} \epsilon_i - 6$. Generate five thousand normally distributed random numbers, estimate their mean, standard deviation, and q-q plot.

9.4. Assume that the current stock price is $10.25, the mean value in the past 5 years is $9.35, and the standard deviation is 4.24. Write a program to generate 1,000 future prices.

9.5. Download a five-year (January 2, 2004 to December 31, 2008) IBM price data from Yahoo Finance. Test whether its daily returns follow a normal distribution.

9.6. Download the price data for ten stocks (see the following ticker symbols) over a five-year (January 2, 2007 to December 31, 2011) period from Yahoo Finance. Form an equal-weighted portfolio and conduct a Shapiro-Wilk test on its portfolio daily returns.

	Company name	Ticker	Industry
1	Family Dollar stores	FDO	Retail
2	Wal-Mart Stores	WMT	Superstore
3	McDonald's	MCD	Restaurants
4	Dell company	DELL	Computer hardware
5	International Business Machine	IBM	Computer
6	Microsoft	MSFT	Software
7	General Electric	GE	Conglomerates
8	Google	GOOG	Internet services
9	Apple	AAPL	Computer hardware
10	eBay	EBAY	Internet services

9.7. Go to Yahoo Finance to find out today's IBM price then download its historical-prices information to estimate its mean and standard deviation for the past five years. Generate predictions for one-year daily prices in the future.

9.8. The following simple program can be used to calculate π. Explain the logic.

```
n<-100
x<-runif(n)  # generate random numbers
y<-runif(n)  # generate random numbers
z<-0*(1:n)
for(i in 1:n){
if( (x[i]-0.5)^2 + (y[i]-0.5)^2<=0.5^2) z[i]=4;
}
print(mean(z))
```

9.9. For the Powerball games, we choose five white balls out of fifty-nine white balls numbered from 1 to 59 and one red ball out of thirty-nine red balls numbered from 1 to 39. Write an R program to choose those six balls randomly.

9.10. Verify the statistics based on figure 9.1.

9.11. For twenty tickers, download and save their daily price as twenty different CSV files. Write an R program to randomly select five stocks and estimate their equal-weighted portfolio returns and risk.

9.12. Repeat the above program but save it as one file instead of twenty separate CSV files. (Hint: generate an extravariable called ticker.)

9.13. There are fifteen students in the class. Write an R program to select seven of them randomly.

9.14. Test the time difference by retrieving prcD50.Rdata and prcD50.csv. Load prcD50Rdata first then save it as a CSV file.

9.15. Usually we observe the negative relationship between the portfolio's volatility and the number of stocks in the portfolio. Write an R program to show the relationship between variance (standard deviation) of a portfolio and the number of stock in it.

9.16. What is the probability for picking up 1, 2, 3, and 4 from ten balls marked from 1 to 10? Use two methods:

a. Use the formula.

b. Write an R program to generate a set of five random numbers. (Hint: use the runif() function.)

9.17. Write an R program to generate 176 million sets of combinations in terms of the Mega Millions game. What is the chance to win (1, 2, 3, 4, 5) and (1)?

9.18. Show that equation 5 and 6 are equivalent.

9.19. Retrieving seven stocks from twenty stocks, what is the probability of choosing the first seven stocks? Use simulation to prove your result.

9.20. Assume that we have five-hundred multiple-choice questions. We can have the following input file.

#	Question	A1	A2	A3	A4	correct
1	1+1=	3	4	2	2/5	A3
2	The present value formula is	FV/(1+R)	FV/(1+R)^n	PV*(1+R)^n	PV*(1+R)	A2
3	The highest risk portfolio is	Small-stock portfolio	Corporate bond portfolio	S&P 500	T-bills	A1
500	The risk and return are negatively correlated.	True	False			A2

Write an R program to input this file then randomize the answers for each multiple-choice question.

9.21. Based on 9.20, another input will save our one column if we always put our correct answer first. Below is the input text file with separated by a semicolon (;).

Question; correct; a2, a3 , a4

1+1=; 2 ; 3; 4; 2.5

The present value formula is FV/(1+R)^n ; FV/(1+R) ; PV*(1+R)^n ; PV*(1+R).

CHAPTER 10

Portfolio Theory

When given the volatilities of two stocks (σ_1, σ_2), their correlation (ρ), and one weight (w_1, or w_2), we can find the volatility of this two-stock portfolio.

```
vol2stocks<-function(sigma1,sigma2,rho,weight_1){
  x1<-weight_1
  x2<-1-x1
  var<-x1^2*sigma1^2 +x2^2*sigma2^2+2*x1*x2*rho*sigma1*sigma2
  return(sqrt(var))
}
```

The graph below shows the impact of correlation on a two-stock portfolio's volatility. The portfolio risk is smaller when stock returns are not perfectly positively correlated.

```
> vol2stocks(0.1,0.2,-0.3,0.1)
[1] 0.177257
> vol2stocks(0.1,0.2,0.3,0.1)
[1] 0.183248

> rho<-seq(-0.2,0.5,by=0.01)
> vol<-vol2stocks(0.3,0.2,rho,0.5)
> plot(rho,vol)
```

10.1. Introduction

Portfolio theory occupies a unique position in finance. Common sense tells us that we should not put all our eggs in one basket (i.e., it is a good idea to diversify our investment). In this chapter, we will discuss the various risk measures for individual stocks and portfolios, such as how to choose an efficient portfolio for a given set of stocks and how to construct an "efficient" portfolio frontier. Our focus will be on how to apply the portfolio theories to real-world situations.

For example, today we have $10 million cash, and we intend to buy just two stocks, such as IBM and Walmart. If we have 60% invested in IBM and 40% in Walmart, what is our total risk? What is the least risky portfolio we can form based on those two stocks? For a given risk level, what is the highest portfolio return we can achieve?

Having ten stocks available, how do we allocate our investment? How do we construct an efficient frontier based on fifty stocks? Do not put all your eggs in the same basket. What is the implied assumption for those different baskets?

10.2. Variance, Standard Deviation, and Correlation

In finance, it is a convention to use both variance and standard deviation to represent the risk since they describe uncertainty. Usually we use standard deviation of returns to represent the volatility for an individual stock (portfolio).

Equation 1

$$\begin{cases} var = \sigma^2 = \dfrac{\sum_{i=1}^{n}(R_i - \bar{R})^2}{n-1}, \\ \sigma = \sqrt{\sigma^2} \end{cases}$$

where R_i is the ith return,
$\bar{R}$ is the mean,
and n is the number of returns.

Covariance measures the comovement. A negative value indicates that the two securities move in opposite directions while a positive one indicates the same direction. Most stocks have positive covariance among them. In terms of comovement, correlation (ρ) is a much better measure since its value has a range of $[-1, 1]$.

For example, if we are given **cov(R_A,R_B)=0.4** and **cov(R_A,R_C)=1.3**, we cannot conclude which stock is more strongly associated with stock A. On the other hand, if we know that $\rho(R_A, R_B)=0.3$, and $\rho(R_A, R_C)=0.2$, then we can conclude that stock B is more strongly associated with stock A.

Equation 2

$$\begin{cases} \text{covariance } (\sigma_{A,B}) = \dfrac{\sum_{i=1}^{n}(R_{A,i}-\bar{R}_A)(R_{B,i}-\bar{R}_B)}{n-1} \\ \text{correlation } (R_A, R_B) = \rho(R_A, R_B) = \dfrac{\sigma_{A,B}}{\sigma_A * \sigma_B} \end{cases}$$

The R functions for variance and standard deviation are **var()** and **sd()**.

```
> var(1:10)
[1] 9.166667
> sd(1:10)
[1] 3.027650
```

The following R codes estimate a given stock's annualized volatility from date 1 to date 2 by retrieving daily prices from Yahoo Finance.

176

```
vol_stock<-function(ticker,date1,date2){
    t<-'http://canisius.edu/~yany/data/$VDaily.csv'
    x<-read.csv(sub("$V",ticker,t ,fixed=T))
    n<-nrow(x)
    ret<-x[2:n,6]/x[1:(n-1),6]-1
    d<-data.frame(as.Date(x[2:n,1]),ret)
    colnames(d)<-c("date","ret ")
    vol_daily<- sd(subset(d[,2],d[,1]>=date1 & d[,1]<=date2))
    return(vol_daily*sqrt(252))
}
```

When calling the function, pay attention to the format of **date1** and **date2**.

```
> date1<-as.Date("2003-01-01")
> date2<-as.Date("2003-12-31")
> vol_stock("ibm",date1,date2)
 [1] 0.2339628
```

10.3. Markowitz Mean-Variance Efficiency

The objective of portfolio theory is to allocate our assets optimally in terms of risk and return. Markowitz argues that we should consider only the first two moments of a security's return distribution: mean and variance. The third and fourth moments are skewness and kurtosis respectively. When discussing preferences between two stocks, we have an easy rule: 1) For a given risk, a rational investor prefers stock with a higher expected return. 2) For a given return, a rational investor prefers stock with a lower risk level.

In the following graph below in the left panel, stock A is better than stock B since it has a higher expected return but with the same risk. Stock C is better than stock D since the former has a lower risk but with the same expected returns.

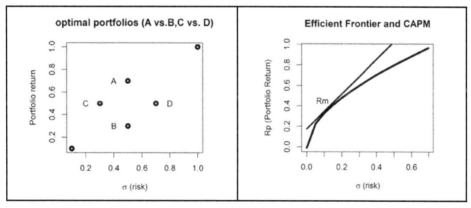

In the diagram in the right panel, the vertical axis is expected returns while the horizon axis is standard deviation. The shaded area represents feasible portfolios. The top envelope is the efficient portfolio frontier that contains those portfolios satisfying the above rule (i.e., for a given risk, the portfolio with the highest returns among all feasible portfolios is preferable; and for a given return, the portfolio with the lowest risk is preferable).

In his doctoral thesis, Markowitz (1955) proposed this mean-variance diagram. Sharpe (1956) adds a risk-free rate and a line liking this rate with the market portfolio. The line is tangent on the efficient portfolio frontier. This line represents an optimal investment strategy: focus on two investments: a risk-free asset and the market portfolio.

In the graph, P* represents the market portfolio. Harry Markowitz, William Sharpe, and Merton Miller shared 1990's Nobel Economics Prize. Markowitz was awarded the prize for having developed the theory of portfolio choice; Sharpe, for his contributions to the theory of price formation for financial assets (CAPM); and Miller, for his contributions to the theory of corporate finance.

10.4. Single-Period Portfolio Optimization

Sometimes we call single-period portfolio optimization as Markowitz portfolio optimization. Our input data sets include the expected returns, the standard deviations, and the correlation matrix between those assets. Our output will be an efficient frontier formed by those assets. In the rest of the chapter, we will use historical returns to represent expected returns and use the historical correlation in the place of expected correlation.

10.5. Return Matrix

The following program is used to estimate the monthly returns for a given ticker. The output has only two variables: date and return. When estimating return, we use the original sorting order, from the earliest to the latest. For more details about sorting, please consult chapter 5: "Open Data."

```
googleDailyRet<-function(ticker){
    today<-Sys.Date()
    today.y <- as.numeric(strsplit(as.character(today), "-", )[[1]][1])
    today.m <- as.numeric(strsplit(as.character(today), "-", )[[1]][2])
    today.d <- as.numeric(strsplit(as.character(today), "-", )[[1]][3])
    to.m<-month.abb[today.m]
    t1<-"http://finance.google.com/finance/historical?q="
    t2<-paste(t1,ticker,sep='')
    t3<-paste(t2, "&startdate=Jan+01,+1970&enddate=",to.m,sep='')
    t4<-paste(t3, "+",today.d,",+",today.y,"&output=csv",sep='')
    x<-read.csv(t4,header=T)
    n<-nrow(x)
    dd<-Sys.Date()
    for(i in 1:n){
        tt<-toString(x[i,1])
        dd[i]<-as.Date(tt,"%d-%b-%y")
    }
    p<-x[,5]
    ret<-(p[1:(n-1)]-p[2:n])/p[2:n]
    d<-data.frame(dd[1:(n-1)],x[1:(n-1),5],ret)
    colnames(d)<-c('Date','Price','Ret')
    return(d)
}
```

Below, we retrieve data for four stocks.

```
begdate<-as.Date("2006-01-01")
enddate<-as.Date("2010-12-01")
stocks<-c("IBM","C","MSFT","DELL")
d<-yahooMonthlyRet("^GSPC") # ^GSPC is S&P500
base<-subset(d,d[,1]>=begdate & d[,1]<=enddate)
rm(d)
for(i in 1:length(stocks)){
  d<-monthly_ret(stocks[i])
  base<-merge(base,d)
}
```

A few lines from the output are given below.

```
> head(base)
  date ^GSPC IBM C MSFT DELL
1 2006-01-03 0.025466839 -0.01093479 -0.04016808 0.0762389 -0.0213689
2 2006-02-01 0.000453097 -0.01051638 0.00613391 -0.0421094 -0.0105766
3 2006-03-01 0.011095841 0.02779670 0.01853536 0.0127362 0.0262069
4 2006-04-03 0.012155660 -0.00159088 0.06854440 -0.1127789 -0.1196237
5 2006-05-01 -0.030916901 -0.02615854 -0.01301019 -0.0580704 -0.0312977
6 2006-06-01 0.000086608 -0.03858740 -0.02128293 0.0286408 -0.0362490
```

By using the above codes, we expect sixty months (i.e., the number of rows is sixty). However, if one stock has only forty-five months' returns, we end up with only forty-five rows instead of sixty. The reason is that when **merge(x,y)** is used, by default the final output is the overlapping result. Sometimes we demand that our output have an intended dimension by adding **NA** for the shorter columns (see an example below).

```
> x<-c(1,2,3,4,5,6)            > x2
> y<-c(1,2.,3,4.6)              id value2
> x2<-matrix(x,3,2)            [1,] 1 4
> y2<-matrix(y,2,2)            [2,] 2 5
> colnames(x2)<-c("id","value1")  [3,] 3 6
> colnames(y2)<-c("id","value2")  > y2
> merge(x2,y2)                  id value2
  id value1 value2             [1,] 1 3.0
1 1 4 3.0                      [2,] 2 4.6
2 2 5 4.6
> merge(x2,y2,all.x=T)
  id value1 value2
1 1 4 3.0
2 2 5 4.6
3 3 6 NA
```

all.x is referred to the first variable in the **merge()** function.

10.6. Portfolio Returns

The portfolio return is the weighted individual stock returns.
Equation 3

$$R_{port} = \sum_{i=1}^{n} w_i R_i$$

where n is number of stocks, w_i and R_i is are weight and expected return for stock i.

For example, the following table gives the holding for the four stocks on January 1, 2010. What is the return and terminal value for this portfolio on December 31, 2010?

Stock	Number of shares	Stock	Number of shares
IBM	5,000	MSFT	10,000
DELL	6,000	WMAT	20,000

Assume that the stock prices on January 1, 2010 are $P^0_{IBM}, P^0_{IBM}, P^0_{IBM}$ and P^0_{IBM}. The portfolio value will be $P^0_{port} = \sum_{i=1}^{4} n_i P^0_i$. Similarly, on December 31, 2010, we have $P^1_{port} = \sum_{i=1}^{4} 4 \, n_i P^1_i$. The portfolio return will be $((P^1_{port} - P^0_{port})/P^0_{port})$.

10.7. Portfolio Volatility for a Two-Stock Portfolio

The variance of a two-stock portfolio is given below.
Equation 4

$$\sigma^2_{port} = x_1^2 \sigma_1^2 + x_2^2 \sigma_2^2 + 2x_1 x_2 \sigma_{1,2} = x_1^2 \sigma_1^2 + x_2^2 \sigma_2^2 + 2x_1 x_2 \rho \sigma_1 \sigma_2,$$

where x_1 (σ_1) and x_2 (σ_2) are weight (standard deviation) for stocks 1 and 2 respectively.

The R program corresponding to the above equation is given below. The return matrix is an n by 2 matrix (n rows of returns for two stock columns), and **weight_1** is the portfolio weight for the first stock.
Obviously the weight for the second stock is **1-weight_1**.

```
portfolio_vol_2stocks<-function(ret_matrix,weight_1){
 x1<-weight_1
 x2<-1-x1
 std1<-sd(ret_matrix[,1])
 std2<-sd(ret_matrix[,2])
 return(x1^2*std1^2 +x2^2*std2^2+2*x1*x2*cov(ret_matrix[,1],ret_matrix[,2]))
}
```

From equation 2, we can see if rho (ρ) is negative, it might be possible to form a risk-free portfolio by choosing appropriate weights (x_1 and x_2). Why use the word *possible* instead of *always*?

```
weights_zero_risk2stock_port<-function(sigma1,sigma2,rho){
 " > weights_zero_risk2stock_port(0.1,0.2,-1)
  x1 x2
  [1,] 1.651 -0.651
  [2,] 0.418 0.582
"
x<-matrix(NA,2,2)
 a<-sigma1^2 + sigma2^2 -2*rho*sigma1*sigma2^2
 b<-2*rho*sigma1*sigma2 - 2*sigma2^2
 c<-sigma2^2
 if(b^2<4*a*c) {
   stop("no solution")
 } else{
   x[1,1]<- (-b+sqrt(b^2-4*a*c))/(2*a)
   x[1,2]<-1-x[1,1]
   x[2,1]<- (-b -sqrt(b^2-4*a*c))/(2*a)
   x[2,2]<-1-x[2,1]
 }
 colnames(x)<-c("x1","x2")
 return(round(cbind(x),digits=3))
 }
```

We can call the above function with a set of input values.

```
> weight2stock_port_zero_risk(0.1,0.3,-0.4)
   weight1 weight2
[1,] 1.208 -0.208
[2,] 0.695 0.305
```

In the following program, for a given set of two tickers, we use the last two years' daily data from Yahoo Finance to estimate the standard deviations for those stocks and their correlation. Then we construct a portfolio with minimum risk.

```
min_vol_2stocks<-function(ticker1,ticker2){
   x<-get_ret(ticker1)
   y<-get_ret(ticker2)
   d<-merge(x,y)
   s1<-sd(d[,2])
   s2<-sd(d[,3])
   rho<-cor(d[,2],d[,3])
   w<-seq(0,1,by=0.01)
   vol<-port_vol2stocks(s1,s2,rho,w)
   k<-cbind(w,vol,s1,s2,rho)
   f<-round(matrix(k[k[,2]==min(vol),],1,5),digits=4)
   colnames(f)<-colnames(f)<-c(paste(ticker1,"_weight",sep=""),"port_vol",
   paste(ticker1,"_vol",sep=""),paste(ticker2, "_vol",sep=""),"rho")
   return(f)
}
get_ret<-function(ticker){
       x<-read.csv(sub("$V",ticker,'http://canisius.edu/~yany/data/$V.csv'
,fixed=T))
   n<-nrow(x)
   p<-x$Adj.Close
```

```
ret<-p[2:n]/p[1:(n-1)]-1
    d<-data.frame(as.Date(x[2:n,1]),ret)
    colnames(d)<-c("date",ticker)
    return(d)
}
port_vol2stocks<-function(s1,s2,rho,w1){
    x1<-w1;x2<-1-x1
    return(sqrt(x1^2*s1^2 +x2^2*s2^2+2*x1*x2*rho*s1*s2))
}
```

We call the program by inputting two tickers.

```
> min_vol_2stocks("ibm","c")
      ibm_weight port_vol ibm_vol  c_vol     rho
[1,]        0.96   0.0141  0.0146 0.0897 -0.1024
```

10.8. Portfolio Volatility for an n-Stock Portfolio

The variance of an n-stock portfolio is given below:

Equation 5

$$\sigma^2_{port} = \sum_{i=1}^{n} \sum_{j=1}^{n} x_i x_j \sigma_{i,j}$$

where, $\sigma_{i,i} = \sigma_i^2$

Based on the formula, the following R codes are used to estimate the volatility of an n- stock portfolio. Of course, a two-stock portfolio is just a special case. (See the exercise 10.17 to collapse equation 5 into equation 4 when n=2.)

```
portfolio_vol<-function(ret_matrix,weight){
    m<-ncol(ret_matrix)
    m2<-length(weight)
    if(m!=m2) stop(" dimensions are not matched!!!")
    COV<-cov(ret_matrix)
    sum<-0
    for(i in 1:m)
      for(j in 1:m)
          sum<-sum + weight[i]*weight[j]*COV[i,j]
    return(sqrt(sum))
}
```

Here is a simple call of the function.

```
set.seed(12345) # this guarantees the same result
ret<-matrix(rnorm(60),12,5)# 5 stocks with 12 monthly returns
w<-c(0.1,0.2,0.2,0.4,0.1) # weights of those 5 stocks
portfolio_vol(ret,w)
[1] 0.6781459
```

10.9. Variance-Covariance Matrix

If the first column of a data matrix is a date variable, we simply remove it before estimating a variance-covariance matrix.

```
 > n<-ncol(base)
> cov(data.frame(base[,2:n]))
  X.GSPC IBM C MSFT DELL
X.GSPC 0.00265409 0.00190412 0.00673323 0.00284733 0.00364046
IBM 0.00190412 0.00327740 0.00360486 0.00161514 0.00331785
C 0.00673323 0.00360486 0.03734504 0.00634977 0.00845029
MSFT 0.00284733 0.00161514 0.00634977 0.00642708 0.00522903
DELL 0.00364046 0.00331785 0.00845029 0.00522903 0.01138958
```

If we exclude the market index from our variance-covariance matrix, we can use the following codes to select stocks only.

```
> stocks<-c("IBM","C","MSFT","DELL") # repeat this for clarity
> stock_matrix<-base[,stocks]
> cov(data.frame(stock_matrix))
  IBM C MSFT DELL
IBM 0.00327740 0.00360486 0.00161514 0.00331785
C 0.00360486 0.03734504 0.00634977 0.00845029
MSFT 0.00161514 0.00634977 0.00642708 0.00522903
DELL 0.00331785 0.00845029 0.00522903 0.01138958
```

10.10. Correlation Matrix

We can use the **cor()** function to estimate a correlation matrix.

```
> cor(data.frame(base[,2:n]))
  X.GSPC IBM C MSFT DELL
X.GSPC 1.000000 0.645613 0.676316 0.689405 0.662133
IBM 0.645613 1.000000 0.325842 0.351916 0.543048
C 0.676316 0.325842 1.000000 0.409860 0.409733
MSFT 0.689405 0.351916 0.409860 1.000000 0.611168
DELL 0.662133 0.543048 0.409733 0.611168 1.000000
```

Based on the first row, we know that MSFT has the highest correlation with the S&P 500 market index (**^GSPC**) among all four stocks. If we don't want so many decimals, we can use the **round()** function to make our output more readable.

```
> round(cor(data.frame(base[,2:n])),digits=3)
  X.GSPC IBM C MSFT DELL
X.GSPC 1.000 0.646 0.676 0.689 0.662
IBM 0.646 1.000 0.326 0.352 0.543
C 0.676 0.326 1.000 0.410 0.410
MSFT 0.689 0.352 0.410 1.000 0.611
DELL 0.662 0.543 0.410 0.611 1.000
```

10.11. Example of a Minimum-Risk Portfolio for a Two-Stock Portfolio

Assume that we have two stocks with variances of 0.0036 and 0.0576. The two stocks are negatively, perfectly correlated. What is the weights (X_1, X_2) when the portfolio volatility is minimum? There exist at least three ways to get a solution.

Method 1

Plug in given values into equation 4 and set it equal to zero, where $x=x_1$ and $x_2=1-x$.

$$x_1^2\sigma_1^2 + x_2^2\sigma_2^2 + 2x_1x_2\sigma_{1,2} = x_1^2\sigma_1^2 + x_2^2\sigma_2^2 + 2x_1x_2\rho\sigma_1\sigma_2 = 0$$

$$x^2 * 0.0036 + (1-x)^2 * 0.0576 - 2x(1-x)\sqrt{0.0036}\sqrt{0.0576} = 0$$

For a general formula of, $ax^2 + bx + c = 0$ we have the following two solutions.
Equation 6

$$x = \frac{b \pm \sqrt{b^2 - 4ac}}{2a}$$

Based on a, b, and c, we have a solution of x=80%. In other words, when x1=0.80 and x2=0.2, our twostock portfolio will be risk free.

Method 2

We generate x_1 from 0 to 100% and $x_2=1-x_1$. Applying equation 4, we can generate a set of portfolio variances for a given correlation (-1 in this case). After that, we sort our portfolio variance from smallest to highest. The first observation will be our minimum-variance portfolio.

```
std1<-sqrt(0.0036)
std2<-sqrt(0.0576)
rho<- -1
x1<-seq(0,1,0.01)
x2<-1-x1
var_p<-x1^2*std1^2 + x2^2*std2^2 +2*x1*x2*rho*std1*std2
final<-cbind(x1,x2,var_p)
final2<-final[order(final[,3]),]
head(final2)
     x1   x2   var_p
[1,] 0.80 0.20 8.673617e-19
[2,] 0.79 0.21 9.000000e-06
[3,] 0.81 0.19 9.000000e-06
[4,] 0.78 0.22 3.600000e-05
[5,] 0.82 0.18 3.600000e-05
[6,] 0.77 0.23 8.100000e-05
```

Method 3

After we choose a pair of x_1 and x_2 (e.g., 0.1 and 0.90), we can estimate the corresponding two-stock portfolio variance. We choose five thousand pairs of x_1 and x_2 to estimate variances. Again, the smallestvariance portfolio will be our optional choice.

```
std1<-sqrt(0.0036)
std2<-sqrt(0.0576)
rho<- -1

x1<-runif(5000)
x2<-1-x1
var_p<-x1^2*std1^2 + x2^2*std2^2 +2*x1*x2*rho*std1*std2
final<-cbind(x1,x2,var_p)
final2<-final[order(final[,3]),]
head(final2)
  x1 x2 var_p
[1,]  0.7999653 0.2000347 1.081783e-10
[2,]  0.8000401 0.1999599 1.449664e-10
[3,]  0.8000787 0.1999213 5.568790e-10
[4,]  0.8001358 0.1998642 1.658932e-09
[5,]  0.8002285 0.1997715 4.698080e-09
[6,]  0.8003739 0.1996261 1.258483e-08
```

It seems that method 2 is better than method 3 while method 1 is better than method 2. The major reason is that our current case is quite simple. For a ten-stock portfolio, method 1 would fail. Designing a good loop is essential for method 2.

10.12. Minimization optim()

The R **optim()** function can be used to find a solution for a minimization problem. For example, we have the following objective function.

Equation 7

$$f = 3x^2 - 4x + 1$$

Since there is only one variable, we can solve it manually. Take the first-order derivative and set it to equal zero.

```
>f<-function(x)3*x^2-4*x+1
>optim(0.3,f)
>optim(0,f,method="Brent",lower = -100, upper = 100)
```

10.13. Quadratic Optimization

If the highest power is 1, then we call it a linear model. On the other hand, if the highest power is 2, we call it a quadratic function.

Equation 8

$$\begin{cases} linear\ equation: \quad S = 4L \\ quadratic\ equation: A = \pi r^2 \end{cases}$$

We have the following task to minimize certain values with a set of constraints.
Equation 9A

$$\begin{cases} minimize\ \ x_1^2 + 0.1x_2^2 + x_3^2 - x_1x_3 - x_2 \\ subject\ to: x_1 + x_2 + x_3 = 1 \\ x_1 \geq 0, x_2 \geq 0, x_3 \geq 0 \end{cases}$$

We can rewrite the above task by using the matrix format.
Equation 9B

$$\begin{cases} minimize\ \frac{1}{2}X^TQX + C^TX \\ AX = b \\ X \geq 0 \end{cases},$$

where $X = \begin{bmatrix} x_1 \\ x_2 \\ x_2 \end{bmatrix}$, $Q = \begin{bmatrix} 2 & 0 & -1 \\ 0 & 0.2 & 0 \\ -1 & 0 & 2 \end{bmatrix}$, $C = \begin{bmatrix} 0 \\ -1 \\ 0 \end{bmatrix}$, $A = \begin{bmatrix} 1 \\ 1 \\ 1 \end{bmatrix}$ and b=1.

It is a good exercise trying to expand equation 9B to see whether it is indeed the same as equation 9A.

10.14. A List of R Packages Related to Portfolio Theory

It is a good that we can use certain R packages related to portfolio theory to facilitate our operation. The following table offers a list of R packages associated with portfolio optimization, efficient frontier, and related issues.

Table 10.1. A list of R packages related to portfolio construction, optimization, and efficient frontier

Package	Description
portfolio	Equity-portfolio analysis
parma	Portfolio allocation and risk-management applications
PortRisk	Portfolio-risk analysis
MarkowitzR	Statistical significance of the Markowitz portfolio
pa	Performance attribution for equity portfolios
Crp.CSFP	Credit riskplus portfolio model
backtest	Portfolio-based conjectures about financial instruments
portfolioSim	Framework for simulating equity-portfolio strategies
FRAPO	Financial-risk modelling and portfolio optimization with R
stockPortfolio	Stock-model building and stock-portfolio analysis
Rportfolios	Random-portfolio generation
tawny	Portfolio-optimization strategies
Metafolio	Metapopulation simulations for conserving salmon through portfolio optimization

10.15. Finding Manuals Related to Those R Packages

There are several ways to find the manuals. Below, we use the portfolio package as an example.

Method 1. Locate the portfolio**doc** subdirectory on your machine first then the manual called **portfolio.pdf**.

```
> path.package('portfolio', quiet = FALSE)
[1] "C:/Users/yany/Documents/R/win-library/3.1/portfolio"
```

Method 2. Go to **r-project.org**, click **CRAN**, choose a mirror server, click **packages,** and search the list to find the PDF file.

10.16. Data Sets Included in Various R Packages

The following table gives the data sets included in various R packages that we can apply to test various portfolio theory and performance measures.

Table 10.2. Data sets included in those R packages designed for portfolio theory

Package	Name of data	Description
PortRisk	SnP500List	Constituents of S&P 500 in 2013
	SnP500Returns	Returns for 500 stocks in 2013 from January 2, 2013 to December 31, 2013
stockPortfolio	stock04	Data for 24 stocks and 1 index from 2004 to 2009
	stock94	Data for 24 stocks and 1 index from 1994 to 1999
	stock94Info	Ticker and industry information
	stock99	Data for 24 stocks and 1 index from 1999 to 2004
portfolio	dow.jan.2005	DJIA of January 2005
	global.2004	Large global companies in 2004
	assay	5000 largest global stocks as of December 31, 2004
parma	eftdata	Daily closing prices of 15 iShare ETFs for the period May 28, 2003 to June 1, 2012 (2272 periods)
pa	jan	A modified version of the data set based on MSCI Barra GEM2 data set in year 2010
	quarter	An edited version of the data set based on GEM2 data set in year 2010
	StockIndex	6 world indices: S&P 500, N225, FTSE100, CAC40, GDAX, and HSI from July 1991 to June 2011
	MultiAsset	Month-end price of stocks, bond indices, and gold from November 2004 to November 2011
	NASDAQ	Weekly price data of 2,196 NASDAQ constituents from March 3, 2003 to March 24, 2008
	FTSE100	Weekly price data of 79 FTSE 100 constituents from February 18, 2008 to March 24, 2008

FRAPO	INDTRCK1	Weekly price data of the Hang Seng Index and 31 constituents from March 1991 to September 1997
	INDTRCK2	Weekly price data of the DAX 100 and 85 constituents
	INDTRCK3	Weekly price data of the FTSE 100 index and 89 constituents from March 1991 to September 1997
	INDTRCK4	Weekly price data of S&P 100 index and 98 constituents from March 1991 to September 1997
	INDTRCK5	Weekly price data of Nikkei 225 index and 225 constituents from March 1991 to September 1997
	INDTRCK6	Weekly price data of S&P 500 index and 457 constituents from March 1991 to September 1997
backtest	starmine	StarMine rankings of some stocks in 1995 with corresponding returns and other data
portfolioSim	starmine.sim	StarMine rankings of 1995 and supplementary data
stockPortfolio	stock04	Monthly data for 24 stocks and S&P 500 from September 1, 2009 to October 1, 2004
	stock99	Monthly data for 24 stocks and S&P 500 from October 1, 1999 to September 1, 2004
	stock94Info	Information on which industry a stock belongs
tawny	sp500.subset	Daily returns for 75 stocks from May 5, 2008 to February 27, 2009

Below are several examples to retrieve data from various packages.

```
>library(portfolio)
>data(dow.jan.2005)
> dim(dow.jan.2005)
[1] 30 6
> data(SnP500List)
> head(SnP500List)
  Company
A Agilent Technologies Inc
AA Alcoa Inc
AAPL Apple Inc.
ABBV AbbVie
ABC AmerisourceBergen Corp
ABT Abbott Laboratories
> head(dow.jan.2005,2)
  symbol name price sector cap.bil month.ret
140  AA  ALCOA  INC  31.42  Materials  27.35045
-0.06078931
214 MO ALTRIA GROUP INC 61.10 Staples 125.41258
0.04468085
```

```
> data(SnP500Returns)
> dim(SnP500Returns)
[1] 252 500
```

10.17. Examples of Using Various Functions

In the following subsections, we discuss some functions included in various R packages listed in the above table.

10.17.1. Using the risk.attribution() Function

Assume that we want to estimate portfolio volatility (risk), individual stock's volatility, and their various contributions.

```
>library(PortRisk)
>data(SnP500Returns)
>stocks <- c("AAPL","IBM","INTC","MSFT")
>w <- c(10000,40000,20000,30000)
>begdate<-"2013-01-01"
>enddate<- "2013-01-31"
>risk.attribution(tickers=stocks,weights=w,start=begdate,
end =enddate,data=SnP500Returns)
```

The output is shown below, where **MCTR** is the marginal contribution to total risk in percentage, **CCTR** is the conditional contribution to total risk in percentage, and **CCTR(%)** is the percentage of the portfolio volatility contributed by the stock for the given weight.

```
      Weight MCTR CCTR CCTR(%) Volatility
AAPL 0.1 2.0614388 0.2061439 18.80638 3.505336
IBM 0.4 0.9297546 0.3719018 33.92837 1.169305
INTC 0.2 1.2062182 0.2412436 22.00851 1.948613
MSFT 0.3 0.9228293 0.2768488 25.25674 1.194353
Portfolio 1.0 NA 1.0961382 100.00000 1.096138
```

10.17.2. Setting a Target Return to Minimize Portfolio Risk

Four stocks are retrieved and used from a data set called **SMALL.RET**.

```
library(fPortfolio)
d<-SMALLCAP.RET
d2<-d[, c("BKE","GG","GYMB","KRON ")]
spec = portfolioSpec()
setSolver(spec) = "solveRquaprog"
setTargetReturn(spec) = mean(d2)
constraints = "LongOnly"
solution<-solveRquadprog(d2, spec, constraints)
```

The target return will be the grand mean of those four stocks.

```
> mean(d2)
[1] 0.02430841
> (mean(d2[,1])+mean(d2[,2])+mean(d2[,3])+mean(d2[,4]))/4
[1] 0.02430841
> solution[[4]][1:4]
[1] 0.2802874 0.3514335 0.1806685 0.1876105
```

In the above exercise, we fix an expected return (2.43%) to find the weights of those four stocks (i.e., an efficient four-stock portfolio). When we change the expected portfolio returns, we can find other efficient portfolios. Connecting those efficient portfolios leads to an efficient frontier.

10.17.3. Portfolio Optimization

The function **portfolio.optim()** is used to compute an efficient portfolio for a given return matrix in the mean-variance sense. The package used is **tseries**.

```
>require(fPortfolio)
>require(tseries)
>d<-SMALLCAP.RET[,c("BKE","GG","GYMB","KRON")]
>k<-portfolio.optim(d)
>k$pw
[1] 0.2802874 0.3514335 0.1806685 0.1876105
```

The complete format of the **portfolio.optim()** function is shown below:

```
# complete format
portfolio.optim(x, pm = mean(x), riskless = FALSE,shorts = FALSE,
rf = 0.0, reslow = NULL, reshigh = NULL,covmat = cov(x), ...)
```

Some notations are given in the following table:

Table 10.3. Descriptions of variables

Name	Description
X	Return matrix
pm	The desired mean portfolio return
riskless	A logic indicating whether there is a riskless lending and borrowing rate
shorts	A logic indicating whether short sales on the risky securities are allowed
rf	The risk-free rate
reslow	A vector specifying the (optional) lower bound on portfolio weights
reshigh	A vector specifying the (optional) upper bound on portfolio weights
covmat	The covariance matrix of asset returns

10.17.4. Efficient Portfolio of a Two-Stock Portfolio

The following codes are used to construct a two-stock efficient portfolio.

```
library(fPortfolio)
begdate<-as.Date("1978-01-01")
enddate<-as.Date("2009-12-01")
source("http://canisius.edu/~yany/R/yahooMonthlyRetTickerAsRet.R")
stock1<-yahooMonthlyRetTickerAsRet("IBM") # 1st stock
stock2<-yahooMonthlyRetTickerAsRet("DELL") # 2nd stock
sp500 <-yahooMonthlyRetTickerAsRet("^GSPC") # market index
d<-merge(stock1,stock2)
d2<-subset(d,d[,1]>=begdate & d[,1]<=enddate)
d3<-as.timeSeries(merge(d2,sp500))
```

```
data<-d3[,1:2]
factors<-d3[,3]
attr(data, "factors") <- factors
tailoredFrontierPlot(portfolioFrontier(data))#Long-only Markow M
```

The corresponding graph is shown below:

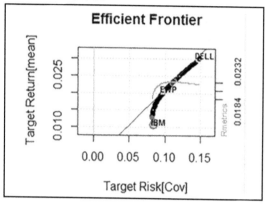

10.17.5. A Minimum-Variance Portfolio

The last line adds a point, which is the minimum-variance portfolio.

```
library(fPortfolio)
d<-SMALLCAP.RET
d2<-d[, c("BKE","GG","GYMB","KRON")]
f<-portfolioFrontier(data)
frontierPlot(f,pch=19,xlim=c(0,0.25),
ylim=c(0,0.035))
grid()
abline(h = 0, col = "grey")
abline(v = 0, col = "grey")
minvariancePoints(f,pch=19,col="red")
```

10.18. Portfolio Insurance (Hedging the Portfolio with a Target Beta)

Like options, we can hedge our risk by entering futures contracts. A futures contract is a contract where both sides (buyer and seller) decide to buy and sell an asset (or commodity) at a fixed price in the future.

For example, an importer expects to pay ten million pounds in three months. He/she can hedge this risk by entering futures contracts to fix the exchange rate today. For portfolio managers, they can enter index futures to protect their portfolio values. Assume that is their target portfolio beta, the current portfolio beta is , the current market value of the portfolio is $V_{portfolio}$, and the value of each index futures contract is $V_{futures}$. The following formula is used to estimate the number of futures contracts needed.

Equation 10

$$n = (\beta^* - \beta) \frac{V_{portfolio}}{V_{futures}} \; ,$$

where n is the number of futures contracts.

When n is negative (positive), it means a short (long) position. Here is an example. A company has a $36-million portfolio with a beta of 1.2. The futures price for a contract on the S&P 500 index is 1336.32 (February 16, 2011). A futures contract is $250 times the index level. How many contracts are needed to achieve the following three goals: eliminate all the systematic risk in the portfolio, reduce the beta to 0.9, or increase the beta to 1.8?

```
> (0-1.2)*36000000/(1336.32*250)
[1] -129.3103 # negative indicates a short position
```

S&P 500 INDEX, RTH (SNP: ^GSPC)	
Index Value:	1,336.32
Trade Time:	4:59PM EST
Change:	↑ 8.31 (0.63%)

The following function defines position of an index futures with target beta, beta of the current portfolio, the current value of the portfolio, and the index level.

```
n_index_futures<-function(beta_target,betaP,valueP,index){
  # objective: number of index futures contracts (sp500)
  return(beta_target-betaP)*valueP/(2500*index)
}
```

Exercises

10.1. In finance, how do we measure risk and benefit mathematically?

10.2. If stock A has a higher risk and a higher expected return than stock B, how do we rank them?

10.3. Is it true that variance and correlation of a pair of historical returns have the same sign?

10.4. What are the differences between covariance and correlation?

10.5. What is the impact of correlation on a portfolio's risk?

10.6. Why do we claim that correlation is a better measure than covariance when we evaluate the comovements between two stocks?

10.7. Based on the last five years' monthly data, what is the correlation between IBM and WMT?

10.8. Generate a variance-covariance matrix for eight stocks plus S&P 500 from Yahoo Finance. Their tickers are IBM, C, MSFT, WMT, AAPL, AF, AIG, AP, and ^GSPC.

10.9. Is the correlation constant between stocks over time? (Hint: you can pick up a couple of stocks then estimate correlations among them for several five-year periods, such as 1990–1994 and 1995–1999.)

10.10. Are larger stocks, measured by their market capitalization, more strongly correlated among themselves than the correlation of small stocks among themselves?

10.11. To form a portfolio, we have the following three stocks to choose from.

a. Is it possible to form a two-stock portfolio with zero portfolio risk?

b. What are the weights of those two stocks (to form a risk-free portfolio)?

Stock	Variance	Stock	Variance	Stock	Variance
A	0.0036	B	0.0576	C	0.0196

The corresponding correlation (coefficient) matrix is given below:

	A	B	C
A	1.0	-1.0	0.0
B	-1.0	1.0	0.7
C	0.0	0.7	1.0

10.12. Write an R program to estimate the expected portfolio return by using ten stocks. Use the last five years' data and assume your own weights.

10.13. Select the last three years' returns for fifty stocks. Estimate volatility for each stock. Their average will be $\overline{\sigma}_1$ and then form several equal-weighted two-stock portfolios and estimate their volatilities. Their average will be our $\overline{\sigma}_2$. Continue this way, and $\overline{\sigma}_n$ will be the average volatility for n-stock equal-weighted portfolios. Draw a graph with n (the number of n-stock portfolios) as the x axis and the volatility of the n-stock portfolio ($\overline{\sigma}_n$) as the y axis. Comment on it.

10.14. Choose five stocks from one industry and estimate their correlation matrix. Do the same thing for another industry. Comment on your results.

10.15. Write an R program to estimate the optimal portfolio construction by using three stocks of Citigroup, Microsoft, and Walmart.

10.16. Find the average of correlations for five industries, at least ten stocks in each industry.

10.17. To estimate the volatility of a portfolio, we have two formulae: for a two-stock portfolio and for an n-stock portfolio. Show that when n equals 2, we expand the formula to estimate the volatility of an n-stock portfolio. We end up with the same formula for a two-stock portfolio.

10.18. Is the following statement correct? Prove or disapprove it. Statement: Stock returns are uncorrelated.

10.19. Download IBM daily data for a year and estimate its Sharpe ratio by using two methods: 1) its definition and 2) the sharpe() function in the tseries package.

CHAPTER 11

VaR (Value at Risk)

For owning 100 shares of IBM's stocks, what is the market value today? Based on the following R codes, the market value of our holding is $16,040. Note that the value was estimated on February 17, 2015.

```
> x<-read.csv("http://finance.google.com/finance/historical?
q=IBM&startdate=Jan+01,+2015&enddate=Feb+17,+2015&output=csv")
> 100*x[1,5]
[1] 16096
```

Then what is the maximum loss in ten days with a 99% confidence level? The maximum possible loss is $1,816.28, which is our value at risk (VaR).

```
> n_shares<-100
> n_days<-10
> t1<-'http://finance.google.com/finance/historical?q=IBM&startdate=;'
> t2<-'Jan+01,+1970&enddate=Feb+17,+2017&output=csv'
> x<-read.csv(paste(t1,t2,sep=''))
> position<-n_shares*x[1,5]
> n<-nrow(x)
> ret<-(x[1:(n-1),5]-x[2:n,5])/x[2:n,5]
> mu<-(mean(ret)+1)^n_days-1
> VaR<-position*(mu-2.33*sd(ret)*sqrt(n_days))
> VaR
[1] - 1938.883
```

What is the maximum possible loss (VaR) if our holdings for IBM, Dell, and Walmart stocks are 100, 200, and 500 shares? After studying this chapter, readers should be able to answer this question.

11.1. Introduction to VaR

To evaluate the risk of a firm, a security, or a portfolio, various measures can be used, such as standard deviation, variance, beta, EPS, Sharpe ratio, or Treynor ratio. However, most CEOs prefer one simple number. One of the commonly used measures is VaR, which is defined as "the maximum loss with a confidence level over a predetermined period." Below are a few examples:

Today I own 200 shares of DELL stocks worth $2,942. The maximum loss tomorrow is $239 with a 99% confidence level.
Our mutual fund has a value of $10 million today. The maximum loss over the next three months is $0.5 million with 95% confidence.
The value of our bank is $150 million. The VaR of our bank is $10 million with a 99% confidence over the next six months.

The most commonly used parameters for VaR are 1% and 5% probabilities (99% and 95% confidence levels) and one-day and two-week (ten days) horizons. Based on the assumption of normality, we have the following general form:

Equation 1

$$VaR_{period} = position * (\mu_{period} - z * \sigma_{period}),$$

where *position* is the current market value of our portfolio,

μ_{period} is the expected period return,

z is the cutoff point depending on a confidence level,

and σ is the volatility.

For a normal distribution, z=2.33 for a 99% confident level and z=1.64 for a 95% confident level. When the time period is short, such as one day, we can ignore the impact of μ_{period}. Thus, we have the simplest form:

Equation 2

$$VaR = p * z * \sigma$$

What is the difference when we ignore the expected return in equation 2? The following codes show a tiny 1.23% based on a 99% confidence level for a one-day horizon.

```
> t1<-'http://finance.google.com/finance/historical?q=IBM&start'
>  t2<-'date=;Jan+01,1970&enddate=Feb+17,+2017&output=csv'
> x<-read.csv(paste(t1,t2,sep=''))
> n<-row(x)
> ret<-(x[1:(n-1),5]-x[2:n,5])/x[2:n,5]
> mean(ret)/(2.33*sd(ret))
[1]  0.007434063
```

11.2. A Normal Distribution and Its Graph Presentation

For a VaR's estimation, the parametric approach is based on the assumptions of the underlying distributions. Among them, a normal distribution is the most used because of its simplicity: the first two moments (mean and standard deviation) determine the whole distribution completely. Its density is defined below with a mean of μ and a standard deviation of σ.

Equation 3

$$f(x) = \frac{1}{\sqrt{2\pi\sigma^2}} e^{-\frac{(x-\mu)^2}{2\sigma^2}}$$

Setting μ to 0 and σ to 1, equation 3 collapses to a standard normal distribution.

Equation 4

$$f(x) = \frac{1}{\sqrt{2\pi}} e^{-\frac{x^2}{2}}$$

Four R functions associated with normal distributions are given in the next table.

Table 11.1. Summary of R functions related to normal distributions

Name	Function	Examples
Density	dnorm(n, mean, sd)	> dnorm(0) [1] 0.3989423
Random numbers	rnorm(n, mean, sd)	> x<-rnorm(5) > x[1:2] [1] -1.3010525 -0.9832462
Cumulative distribution	pnorm(q, mean, sd)	> pnorm(0) [1] 0.5
Anticumulative Function	qnorm(p, mean, sd)	> qnorm(0.01) [1] -2.326348 > qnorm(0.05) [1] -1.644854

For a standard normal distribution, we can easily verify the function **dnorm()** at zero (i.e., **dnorm(0)=0.3989423**) See the example below:

```
> 1/ sqrt(2*pi)  # from Equation (4)
[1] 0.3989423
```

The following codes show the distribution of a standard normal distribution.

```
> x<-seq(-4,4,length=500)
> y<-1/sqrt(2*pi)*exp(-x^2/2)
> plot(x,y,type="l",lwd=2,col="red")

# 'l' is the lower case letter of L
# lwd: line widths for the axis line
# and the tick marks
```
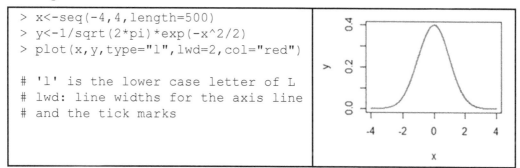

We know that the cutoff point on the left tail is 2.33 for a 99% confidence level (i.e., 1% of the left tail) for a standard normal distribution. The following codes can be used to show the 1% left tail of a standard normal distribution.

```
>x<-seq(-4,4,length=200)
>y<-dnorm(x,mean=0,sd=1)
>plot(x,y,type="l",lwd=2,col="red")
>x<-seq(-4,-2.33,length=200)
>y<-dnorm(x,mean=0,sd=1)
>polygon(c(-4,x,-2.33),c(0,y,0),col="gray")
```
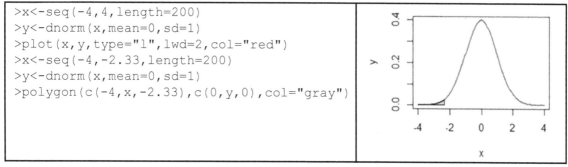

For our VaR estimation, the most relevant function is qnorm(), which gives the x value (cutoff point) for a given percentage of the left tail. For example, we know that a standard normal distribution is center at the y axis. Thus, qnorm(0.5) should give a zero.

```
> qnorm(0.5)
[1] 0
```

For a 99% confidence level (1% left tail), the x value for a standard normal distribution is given by calling the function—that is, **qnorm(0.01)**.

```
> qnorm(0.01) # i.e., qnorm(1-confident)
[1] -2.326348
```

The **pnorm()** and **qnorm()** functions are opposite of each other (a pair): **pnorm()** offers the cumulative value for a given x while the **qnorm()** function delivers an x value for a given cumulative value.

```
> pnorm(1.025)              > qnorm(0.8473184)
[1] 0.8473184              [1] 1.025
> pnorm(0)                  > qnorm(0.5)
[1] 0.5                    [1] 0
```

11.3. Confidence Level vs. Left Tail (Percentage Tail)

In this chapter, a 99% confident level is equivalent to a 1% left tail while a 95% confidence level is equivalent to a 5% left tail.

```
> confident<-0.99
> LeftTail<-1-confident
> qnorm(1-confident)
  [1] -2.326348
> qnorm(LeftTail)
  [1] -2.326348
```

For a confidence level of c, the corresponding left tail will be 1-c.

11.4. Estimating VaR Based on the Normality Assumption

If the underlying security follows a normal distribution, the VaR formula will be

Equation 5

$$VaR_{period} = position * [\mu_{period} + qnorm(1 - confident)\,\sigma_{period}],$$

For 99% and 95% confidence levels, equation 5 becomes the following formulae:

Confidence level	Formula
99%	$VaR_{period} = position\,(\mu_{period} - 2.33\sigma_{period})$
95%	$VaR_{period} = position\,(\mu_{period} - 1.64\sigma_{period})$

In R, we can use the **qnorm()** function to estimate the z value at 1% possibility (99% confidence) of the left tail. If the returns for DELL follow a normal distribution, then we can apply equation 5 to estimate its one-day VaR.

```
position<-1500 # dollar
x<-read.csv("http://canisius.edu/~yany/data/dell.csv",header=T)
n<-nrow(x)
p<-x$Adj.Close
ret<-p[2:n]/p[1:(n-1)]-1
VaR<-position*(mean(ret)-2.33*sd(ret))
VaR # [1] -118.3058
```

11.5. A Trivial Issue: Sign

When ignoring the impact of mean returns, we usually apply the following VaR formula for a 99% confident level: $VaR = 2.33 * P * \sigma_{daily}$. Since all three are positive, we end up with a positive VaR. However, if we consider the impact of mean returns, our formula will be $VaR = P * (R_{daily} - 2.33 \sigma_{daily})$. Since the daily mean is quite small (i.e., we could ignore it), the final value of VaR will be a negative value. Those two VaR values should be quite close except with opposite signs. Here is an example. Two equivalent statements are given below about the same initial investments: 1) Our initial investment is \$2 million. 2) Our initial cash flow is -\$2 million. A negative sign indicates a cash outflow while *investment* means cash outflow as well. We should remember a fundamental concept: when underlying security (portfolio) enjoys a positive mean return, its VaR values would be reduced (i.e., the risk would be reduced by a positive expected return). The opposite is true as well: a negative growth rate (mean return) would increase VaR.

11.6. One-Day VaR vs. n-Day VaR

All those transformations are based on the following equations between the variances of different frequencies.

Equation 6

$$\begin{cases} \sigma_{n\_day}^2 = n * \sigma_{daily}^2 \\ \sigma_{n\_day} = \sqrt{n} * \sigma_{daily} \end{cases}$$

For example, the annual volatility is equal to the daily volatility times the square root of 252 ($\sigma_{annual} = \sigma_{daily} \sqrt{252}$). Based on the daily return, we have the following general formula for VaR with a 99% or a 95% confidence level:

Equation 7A

$$\begin{cases} \mu_{n\_day} = (\mu_{daily} + 1)^n - 1 \\ \sigma_{n\_day} = \sigma_{daily}\sqrt{n} \\ VaR_{n\_day} = p * [\mu_{n\_day} + qnorm(1 - confident)\sigma_{n\_day}] \end{cases}$$

where μ_{daily} is the expected daily returns,

n is the number of days (investment horizon),

σ_{daily} is the daily volatility,

σ_{nday} is an *n*-day volatility,

confident is the confidence level (such as 99% or 95%),

and *p* is the position.

If we don't know the expected returns and we assume the expected mean return is the same as the realized mean return, then we have the following formulae instead:

Equation 7B

$$
\left\{
\begin{array}{l}
R_{n\_day} = (R_{daily} + 1)^n - 1 \\
\sigma_{n\_day} = \sigma_{daily}\sqrt{n} \\
VaR_{n\_day} = p * [\bar{R}_{n\_day} + qnorm(1 - confident)\sigma_{n\_day}]
\end{array}
\right.
$$

For the confidence levels of 99% and 95%, we have

Equation 7C

$$
\left\{
\begin{array}{l}
VaR_{n\_day} = p * [(\mu_{daily} + 1)^n - 1 - 2.33\sigma_{daily}\sqrt{n}] \\
VaR_{n\_day} = p * [(\mu_{daily} + 1)^n - 1 - 1.64\sigma_{daily}\sqrt{n}]
\end{array}
\right.
$$

11.7. VaR Based on Sorted Historical Returns

We know that stock returns do not necessarily follow a normal distribution. An alternative is to use sorted returns to evaluate VaR. Assume that we have a daily return vector called **ret**. We sort it from the smallest to the highest. Let's call the sorted return vector as **sorted_ret**. For a given confidence level, the one-period VaR is given below:

Equation 8

$$
\left\{
\begin{array}{l}
n = length(ret) \\
a = as.integer((1 - confident) * n), \\
VaR = position * sorted\_ret[a]
\end{array}
\right.
$$

where *position* is our wealth (value of our portfolio),

confident is the confidence level,

and *n* is the number of returns.

For example, if the length of the return vector is 200 and the confidence level is 99%, then the second value (200*0.01) of the sorted returns times our wealth will be our VaR. For owning 100 shares of IBM, the maximum loss—with a 99% confidence level and a one-day holding period—is #959. Usually, if we have a longer time series (i.e., more return observations), our final VaR would be more accurate.

```
> n_shares<-100
> confidence<-0.99
> ticker<-"IBM"
> t1<-'http://finance.google.com/finance/historical?q='
> t2<-paste(t1,ticker,'&startdate=Jun+02,+1970',sep='')
> x<-read.csv(paste(t2,'&enddate=Sep+10,+2014&output=csv',sep=''))
> position<-n_shares*x[1,5]
> n<-nrow(x)
> ret<-(x[1:(n-1),5]-x[2:n,5]/x[2:n,5]
> t<-as.interger(length(ret)*(1-confidence))
> ret2<-ret[order(ret)]
> VaR<-position*ret2[2]
> VaR
[1] -959.3576
```

Compared with the result based on the normality assumption, is it reasonable to assume that the VaR based on the sorted historical returns usually has a higher absolute value?

```
> n_shares<-100
> confidence<-0.99
> ticker<-"IBM"
> t1<-'http://finance.google.com/finance/historical?q='
> t2<-paste(t1,ticker,'&startdate=Jun+02,+1970',sep='')
> x<-read.csv(paste(t2,'&enddate=Sep+10,+2014&output=csv',sep=''))
> position<-n_shares*x[1,5]
> n<-nrow(x)
> ret<-(x[1:(n-1),5]-x[2:n,5]/x[2:n,5]
> t<-as.interger(length(ret)*(1-confidence))
> ret2<-ret[order(ret)]
> VaR<-position*ret2[2]
> VaR
[1] -959.3576
```

Question: how do we use historical return data to estimate *n* days' VaR?

11.8. Mean, Standard Deviation, Skewness, and Kurtosis

The following table offers the definitions of those four moments.

Table 11.2. First four moments of a distribution

Order	Definition	R function
First	Mean	> mean(x)
Second	Standard deviation	> sd(x)
Third	Skewness	> library(PerformanceAnalytics) > skewness(x)
		> source("c:/temp/FI725.txt") > skewness_f(x)
Fourth	Kurtosis	> library(PerformanceAnalytics) > skewness(x)
		> source("c:/temp/FI725.txt") > kurtosis_f(x)

Skewness measures symmetry while kurtosis tries to measure whether a distribution is peaked or flat relative to a normal distribution. In finance, usually we assume that stock/portfolio returns are meanvariance efficient (i.e., they follow a normal distribution. See chapter 10: "Portfolio Theory" for more details). For a standard normal distribution, the skewness is 0 and the kurtosis is 3. Some softwares define kurtosis as the excess kurtosis (see equation 9). In summary, the first two moments are enough to describe its whole distribution.

```
> library(PerformanceAnalytics)
> set.seed(100)
> x<-rnorm(50000)
> mean(x)
[1] 2.499166
> sd(x)
[1] 3.995863
> skewness(x)
[1] -0.005318185
> kurtosis(x)
[1] -0.01185601
```

The skewness and kurtosis are defined below:

Equation 9

$$\begin{cases} skewness(x) = \dfrac{\sum_{i=1}^{n}(x_i - \bar{x})^3}{(n-1)\sigma^3} \\[2mm] kurtosis(x) = \dfrac{\sum_{i=1}^{n}(x_i - \bar{x})^4}{(n-1)\sigma^4} \\[2mm] Excess\ kurtosis = \dfrac{\sum_{i=1}^{n}(x_i - \bar{x})^4}{(n-1)\sigma^4} - 3 \end{cases}$$

The **kurtosis()** function defined in the package called **Performance Analytics** is actually excess kurtosis (i.e., kurtosis minus 3). We can use data to demonstrate this. We know that a normal distribution has 0 for its skewness and 3 for its kurtosis.

```
> set.seed(12345)
> kurtosis(rnorm(500000))
[1] 0.002290026
```

11.9. Modified VaR (mVaR)

For a normal distribution, skewness and excess kurtosis are both zeros. However, skewness and excess kurtosis of many stock returns are not zero. The **mVaR** applies those four moments instead of two (see its definition in R below).

Equation 10

$$\begin{cases} z = pnorm(1 - confident) \\ S = skewness(ret) \\ K = excess\ kurtosis(ret) \\ a = z + \dfrac{1}{6}(z^2 - 1)S + \dfrac{1}{24}(z^3 - 3z)K - \dfrac{1}{36}(2z^3 - 5z)S^2 \\ mVaR = position * (\mu - a * \sigma) \end{cases}$$

where **z=abs(qnorm(1-confident)**, **skewness()**, and **kurtosis()** are from a package called **PerformanceAnalysics**.

Alternatively, readers can write their own R functions for skewness and kurtosis. Again, the **kurtosis()** function from the R package of **PerformanceAnalytics** offers excess kurtosis.

```
> library(PerformanceAnalytics)
> n_shares<-100
> confident<-0.99
> ticker<-"IBM"
> t1<-'http://finance.google.com/finance/historical?q='
> t2<-paste(t1,ticker,'&startdate=Jun+02,+1970',sep='')
> x<-read.csv(paste(t2,'&enddate=Sep+10,+2014&output=csv',sep=''))
> position<-n_shares*x[1,5]
> n<-nrow(x)
> ret<-(x[1:(n-1),5]-x[2:n,5])/x[2:n,5]
> S<-skewness(ret)  # [1] 0.1714269
> K<-kurtosis(ret)  # [1] 8.374797
```

11.10. VaR of a Portfolio

If our holding is 200 shares of IBM's stocks and 500 shares of DELL, what is our VaR with a 99% confidence level over a one-month horizon? The key is what the portfolio's volatility is. After we have the volatility, we can simply apply the related formulae to estimate the VaR of our portfolio. The variance for a two-stock portfolio is given below.

Equation 11

$$\left\{ \begin{array}{l} \sigma^2(R_p) = x_1^2\sigma_1^2 + x_2^2\sigma_2^2 + x_1x_2cov(R_1,R_2) \\ \sigma^2(R_p) = x_1^2\sigma_1^2 + x_2^2\sigma_2^2 + x_1x_2\rho_{1,2}\sigma_1\sigma_2 \end{array} \right. ,$$

where x_1 (x_2) is the weight of the first (second) stock,
σ_1 (σ_2) is the standard deviation of the first (second) stock,
$cov(R_1, R_2)$ is the covariance between the returns of those two stocks,
and ϱ is the correlation between them.

The following function delivers the portfolio risk (volatility) for a given return matrix (n by 2) and their weights.

```
portfolio_vol_2stocks<-function(ret_mat,weight_1){
 x1<-weight_1
 x2<-1-x1
 s1<-sd(ret_matrix[,1])
 s2<-sd(ret_matrix[,2])
 v<-x1^2*s1^2+x2^2*s2^2+2*x1*x2*cov(ret_mat[,1],ret_mat[,2])
 return(sqrt(v))
}
```

You can try the following codes to test the above function.

```
> set.seed(100)
> ret2<-matrix(rnorm(100),50,2)
> portfolio_vol_2stocks(ret2,0.4)
[1] 0.7869263
```

For an n-stock portfolio, we have the following formula:

Equation 12

$$\sigma^2\left(R_p\right) = \sum_{i=1}^{n} \sum_{j=1}^{n} x_i x_j \sigma_{i,j}^2 \,,$$

where σ_i^2, j is the covariance between stocks i and j when $i \neq j$ while $\sigma_i^2, j = \sigma_i^2$(variance of stock i) when $i = j$.

```
portfolio_vol<-function(ret_matrix,weight){
    m<-ncol(ret_matrix)
    m2<-length(weight)
if(m!=m2) stop(" not match!!!")
    COV<-cov(ret_matrix)
  sum<-0
  for(i in 1:m)
    for(j in 1:m)
      sum<-sum+ weight[i]*weight[j]*COV[i,j]
  return(sqrt(sum))
}
```

After having a portfolio's required rate of return and volatility, apply the same methodology to estimate VaR. For instance, based on the assumption of normality, we have

$$VaR_{period}^{port} = position_{port} * \left(\mu_{period}^{port} - z * \sigma_{period}^{port}\right).$$

where z has a positive value—that is, z=abs(qnorm(1-confident))—and the VaR period is a negative value.

11.11. Expected Shortfall

One of the major shortcomings of VaR is that it depends on the shape of the distribution of the underlying security (portfolio). If the assumption of normality holds or close to a hold, then VaR should be a good measure. Otherwise, we might underestimate the maximum loss (risk) if we observe a fat tail.

Another shortcoming is that we ignore the shape of the distribution after a VaR is hit. For example, if the left tail after the VaR is fatter than a normal distribution, then our VaR can underestimate the true risk. The opposite is true: if the left tail is thinner than the normal distribution, our VaR would overestimate the true risk. In those cases, we can apply a concept of *expected shortfall*.

Expected shortfall (ES) is the expected loss if VaR is hit. For example, our holding is 100 shares of IBM from our first example at the beginning of the chapter and our two-week VaR is $1,989. If this VaR is hit, what is our expected loss?

$$ES = (loss|z < -\alpha) = \frac{\int_{-\infty}^{-\alpha} xf(x)dx}{\int_{-\infty}^{-\alpha} f(x)dx} = \frac{-\emptyset(\alpha)}{F(\alpha)}$$

For our R presentation, we have the following form:
Equation 14

$$ES = (loss | z < -\alpha) = \frac{-dnorm(qnorm(1-divident),0.sigma)}{1-confident}$$

ES is also called conditional VaR (**CVaR**) or expected tail loss (**ETL**). The "expected shortfall at 5% level" is the expected return in the worst 5% cases.

```
> k<- -dnorm(qnorm(1-0.99),0,1)/0.01
> k
[1] -2.665214
> ES<-position*(mu+k*sd(ret)*sqrt(n_days))
> ES
[1] -2244.405
```

11.12. R Package PerformanceAnalytics

In the package, there is an R data set called **edhec**, which is EDHEC composite-hedge fund-style index returns. To upload and view the data set, see below. Issue **install.packages("PerformanceAnalytics")** to install the package.

```
> library(PerformanceAnalytics) # load the package
> data(edhec) # load the data set
> colnames(edhec)
 [1] "Convertible Arbitrage"    "CTA Global"
 [3] "Distressed Securities"    "Emerging Markets"
 [5] "Equity Market Neutral"    "Event Driven"
 [7] "Fixed Income Arbitrage"    "Global Macro"
 [9] "Long/Short Equity"    "Merger Arbitrage"
[11] "Relative Value"    "Short Selling"
[13] "Funds of Funds"
```

To view the first observation, we **use edhec[1,]** (see below).

```
> edhec[1,]
   Convertible Arbitrage CTA Global Distressed Securities
Emerging Markets Equity Market Neutral Event Driven
1997-01-30 0.0119 0.0393 0.0178 0.0791 0.0189 0.0213
   Fixed Income Arbitrage Global Macro Long/Short Equity
Merger Arbitrage Relative Value Short Selling
1997-01-30 0.0191 0.0573 0.0281 0.015 0.018 -0.0166
   Funds of Funds
1997-01-30 0.0317
```

The first way to call the VaR function is to use the "historical" method. From the result, and by issuing **colname(edhec)**, we know that the name of the first column is Convertible Arbitrage. To estimate its VaR, we specify the data source as **edhec[,1]**.

```
> VaR(edhec[,1], p=.95, method="historical")
   Convertible Arbitrage
VaR -0.01916
```

We can use the following codes to replicate VaR based on "historical."

```
> y<-data.frame(as.numeric(edhec[,1]))
> n<-as.integer(0.05*nrow(y)+0.5)
> y[order(y),1][n]
[1] -0.0196
```

The function includes several methods: **"modified"**, **"gaussian"**, **"historical"**, and **"kernel"**.

```
# method = c("modified","gaussian","historical","kernel"),
> VaR(edhec[,1],p=.95, method="historical")
 Convertible Arbitrage
VaR -0.01916
> VaR(edhec[,1], p=.95, method="gaussian")
 Convertible Arbitrage
VaR -0.02645782
> VaR(edhec[,1], p=.95, method="modified")
 Convertible Arbitrage
VaR -0.03247395
```

Now let's compare the results based on our own codes and by calling the **VaR** function embedded in the **PerformanceAnalytics** package. The codes show that two results are very close to each other.

```
> library(PerformanceAnalytics)
> n_shares<-100
> x<-read.csv("http://canisius.edu/~yany/data/ibm.csv",header=T)
> position<-n_shares*x$Close[n]
> n<-nrow(x)
> p<-x$Adj.Close
> ret<-p[2:n]/p[1:(n-1)]-1
> position*(mean(ret)-2.33*sd(ret))
[1] -384.0385
> VaR(ret, p=.99, method="gaussian")*position
          [,1]
VaR -383.4256
```

For various methods to estimate VaR, the following table summarizes several notations and their corresponding definitions.

Table 11.3. Several notations and their definitions

Method	Description
#Modified VaR >VaR(ret, p=.99, method="modified")	Uses Cornish-Fisher modified VaR
# Gaussian VaR >VaR(ret, p=.99, method="gaussian")	Uses traditional value at risk
# Historical VaR >VaR(ret, p=.99, method="historical")	Calculates traditional value at risk
# ModifiedES >ES(ret, p=.99, method="modified")	Uses Cornish-Fisher modified expected shortfall
# GaussianES >ES(ret, p=.99, method="gaussian")	Uses traditional expected shortfall
# HistoricalES > ES(ret, p=.99, method="historical")	Calculates historical expected shortfall

11.13. Basel Requirement on a Bank's Capital

To estimate a bank's VaR, the Basel Committee requires a 99% confidence level over ten business days with at least one-year historical data.

The bank's minimum capital requirement is 3*VaR (http://www.bis.org/bcbs/).

Exercises

11.1. Do DELL returns follow a normal distribution? Are their skewness and kurtosis 0 and 3 (excess kurtosis is zero)?

11.2. Write an R function to estimate mean, standard deviation, skewness, and kurtosis of a given ticker. For example, **moments4("ticker",begdate,enddate)**.

11.3. What are the values of skewness and kurtosis for a normal distribution? Generate n random numbers by using **rnorm()** to support your conclusion.

11.4. Assuming that we own 134 shares of Microsoft, what is the total value today? What is the maximum loss tomorrow with a 95% confidence level? What is the value if our holding period is one month instead of one day?

11.5. Repeat the last question (11.4) by using monthly return instead of daily return. Is the answer different from that in 11.4?

11.6. Write an R program to generate VaR using historical value. The structure of the function will be VaR_historical(ticker, confidence_level, n_days).

11.7. Our portfolio has 100 shares of IBM and 300 shares of Microsoft. What is the VaR with 99% confidence level for our one-day holding period?

11.8. To estimate a VaR for DELL over one month, we can convert daily VaR to monthly VaR or calculate the VaR from the monthly data directly. Are they different?

11.9. When estimating a VaR, we can use different time periods, such as the past one year or the past five years. Does this make a difference? Use a few tickers to explore and comment on your results.

11.10. Comment on the different VaR approaches such as those based on the normality assumption, historical returns, and the modified VaR.

11.11. If a fund has a 10% invested in IBM, 12% with Google, and the rest with Walmart, what is the volatility of the portfolio?

11.12. If the weights are 10% for IBM stocks, 12% for DELL, 20% for Walmart, and the rest of them for long-term, ten-year Treasury bond—what is the volatility of the portfolio?

11.13. Based on 11.11, if the portfolio value is $10 million, what is the VaR with 99% confidence level over the next six months?

11.14. Use a 99% confidence level and ten trading days as your holding period to estimate a VaR based on the historical returns method: 100 shares of IBM, 200 shares Citygroup, 200 shares Microsoft, and 400 shares Walmart.

11.15. Is it true that VaRs based on a normality assumption is usually less that the VaR based on historical returns? (Hint: you can use rolling window to a stock to show your result or answer. Alternatively you can use several stocks.)

11.16. Based on the codes for skewness, write an R function for kurtosis. Compare your function with the function of kurtosis() f rom PerformanceAnalytics.

11.17. Explain the following codes:

```
confident<-0.99
position<-1000000
x<-read.csv("http://canisius.edu/~yany/data/ibm.csv",header=T)
n<-nrow(x)
ret<-x$Adj.Close[2:n]/x$Adj.Close[1:(n-1)]-1
ret_sorted<-ret[order(ret)]
n2<-(1-confident)*n
VaR1<- ret_sorted[n2]*position
VaR2<-position*(mean(ret)-qnorm(1-confident)*sd(ret))
```

11.18. If our holding period is not one day, what is the format (formula) to estimate a VaR based on our historical returns?

11.19. If the holding period is two weeks (ten trading days), how do you estimate a VAR based on historical return data?

11.20. What is the maximum possible loss (VaR) if our holdings for IBM, DELL, and Walmart stocks are 100, 200, and 500 shares respectively? The confidence level is 99%, and the holding period is two weeks.

11.21. In this chapter, we showed the following codes and results.

```
> ret2<-matrix(rnorm(100),50,2)
> portfolio_vol_2stocks(ret2,0.4)
[1] 0.7869263
```

Repeat the above codes 100 times and estimate the mean-portfolio volatility. Why is this value different from 1.0?

CHAPTER 12

Credit Risk

Credit risk is the risk of failure to pay promised interest, principal, or other obligations. A credit rating reflects the credit worthiness of a firm or a bond. A firm's rating is different from a bond's rating since the latter depends on its maturity and certain features such as whether it is callable or puttable. To check the yields, a yield reflects the credit risk. The higher the yield, the higher its credit risk. For AAA-, AA-, and A-rated bonds,

```
> loc<-url(nhttp://canisius.edu/-yany/RData/AaaYieldMonthly.RData")
> load(loc)
> head(.AaaYieldMonthly,20)
    DATE YIELD
1  1919-01-01 0.0535
2  1919-02-01 0.0535
3  1919-03-01 0.0539
4  1919-04-01 0.0544
5  1919-05-01 0.0539
6  1919-06-01 0.0540
7  1919-07-01 0.0544
8  1919-08-01 0.0556
9  1919-09-01 0.0560
10 1919-10-01 0.0554
11 1919-11-01 0.0566
12 1919-12-01 0.0573
13 1920-01-01 0.0575
14 1920-02-01 0.0586
15 1920-03-01 0.0592
16 1920-04-01 0.0604
17 1920-05-01 0.0625
18 1920-06-01 0.0638
19 1920-07-01 0.0634
20 1920-08-01 0.0630
>
```

Usually for the same maturity, the higher the credit rating, the lower its required rate of return (yield, YTM [yield to maturity], or cost of borrowing). For the same credit rating, the longer its maturity, the higher the required yield.

12.1. Introduction

In this chapter, we discuss basic concepts related to credit risk, such as credit rating, credit spread, oneyear rating migration matrix, probability of default (PD), recovery rate, and loss given default (LGD). A credit spread, the difference between a firm's bond yield and a benchmark yield (risk-free rate), reflects its credit risk or default risk. For example, to estimate the present value of a coupon payment in two years for an AA-rated bond, the discount rate (yield) will be a risk-free yield (Treasury-note yield) plus the corresponding spread.

12.2. Basic Concepts of Default

Assume that the face value of a one-year bond is $100 with a coupon rate of 6% and a YTM (yield to maturity) of 7%. We have the following four cases.

Case 1. There is no default. The price today will be its discounted future cash flow, (6+100)/(1+0.07)— that is, $99.07.

Case 2. It is sure to default and recover nothing. Assume that we are 100% sure that the bond would default; and if it defaults, we get nothing. Of course, no one would purchase such a bond. Thus, its price would be zero.

Case 3. It might default; and if the firm defaults, we receive nothing. If it does not default, we receive the promised amount (6+100). If the default probability is P, the price of such a bond will be 99.07*(1-P). It is easy to see why this is the case: bond price = PV (all future cash flows) = (1-P)*PV (no default) + P*PV (default). Since the second item is zero, we end up with $99.07 * (1-P).

Case 4. It might default; and if the firm defaults, we recover something—that is, with a positive recovery rate ($R_{recovery}>0$). This is a general case, and all other three are special cases. All those cases are summarized in the following table.

Table 12.1. Four cases for different default probabilities and recovery rates
(P is default probability, face value is $100, annual coupon rate is 6% with an annual coupon payment, YTM is 7%, and $R_{recovery}$ is the recovery rate)

	Conditions	Default probability, recovery rate	Price
1	No default	P=0, Recovery rate (NA)	$99.07
2	Sure default; recover nothing	P=100%, $R_{recover}$=0	0
3	Certain chance to default; if default, recover nothing	0<P<100%, $R_{recovery}$=0	$99.07 *(1-P)
4	Certain chance to default; if default, recover something	0<P<100% , $R_{recovery}$>0	$99.07 *[1-P*(1-$R_{recovery}$)]

The price of a bond is the summation of all present values of its expected future cash flows. Equation 1

$$Price\ (bond) = PV\ (expected\ cash\ flows)$$

If **P** is default probability, we have the following expected future cash flow.

$$\begin{cases} expected\ FV = (1-P)FV + P * FV * R_{recovery} \\ \quad = FV - P * FV + P * FV * R_{recovery} \\ \quad = FV - FV * P(1 - R_{recovery}) \\ \quad = FV[1 - P * (1 - R_{recovery})] \end{cases}$$

Discounting all future cash flows would give us its price.

$$PV\ (bond\ with\ default) = PV(no\ default) * [1-P(1-R_{recovery})]$$

Assume that a bond has a 9.3% chance to default with a recovery rate of 65%. The price of this one-year bond will be $95.85, corresponding to a no default. The price is $99.07—(99.07*(1-0.093*(1-0.65))# [1] 95.84527)

12.3. Credit Spread (Default-Risk Premium)

For a given credit rating, we can find its credit spread by using historical data. Below is a typical table showing the relationship between credit-risk premium (spread) and the credit worthiness.

Table 12.2. Credit spread based on credit rating

Reuters Corporate Spreads for Industrials
03/28/2014

Rating	1 yr	2 yr	3 yr	5 yr	7 yr	10 yr	30 yr
Aaa/AAA	5	8	12	18	28	42	65
Aa1/AA+	10	18	25	34	42	54	77
Aa2/AA	14	29	38	50	57	65	89
Aa3/AA-	19	34	43	54	61	69	92
A1/A+	23	39	47	58	65	72	95
A2/A	24	39	49	61	69	77	103
A3/A-	32	49	59	72	80	89	117
Baa1/BBB+	38	61	75	92	103	115	151
Baa2/BBB	47	75	89	107	119	132	170
Baa3/BBB-	83	108	122	140	152	165	204
Ba1/BB+	157	182	198	217	232	248	286
Ba2/BB	231	256	274	295	312	330	367
Ba3/BB-	305	330	350	372	392	413	449
B1/B+	378	404	426	450	472	495	530
B2/B	452	478	502	527	552	578	612
B3/B-	526	552	578	604	632	660	693
Caa/CCC+	600	626	653	682	712	743	775
US Treasury Yield	0.13	0.45	0.93	1.74	2.31	2.73	3.55

The spreads in the table are in basis point. Each basis point is equal to 1/100th of 1 percent. Thus, for a BB rating, its spread for a two-year horizon is 256 basis points that are equal to 256*0.0001 (i.e., 0.0256). Note that the table above is for banks as of March 28, 2014. In total, there are five sections: industrials, utilities, transportation, banks, and finance (nonbanks). The source of the credit spread is http://www. bondsonline.com/Todays_Market/Corporate_Bond_Spreads.php.

After studying the above table carefully, we will find two monotone trends. First, the spread is a decreasing function of credit quality. The lower is a credit rating; the higher is its spread. Second, for the same credit rating, its spread increases with year. For example, for an AAA-rated bond, its spread in one year is 14 basis points while it is 40 in five years.

To estimate the price of a bond today, we list its future cash flows first then find out corresponding discount rates (yields) for all future cash flows. Those yields (discount rates) should be all different. The summation of the present values of those future cash flows will be our price. Here is an example.

One company plans to issue a $50-million (total face value) corporate bonds with a face value of $1,000 for each bond. The bonds would mature in ten years. The coupon rate is 8% with an annual coupon payment. How much could the firm raise today if its credit rating is BB+? See a similar exercise at the end of this chapter.

12.4. Getting Current Yield of T-Bill, T-Note, and T-Bond

From the above section, we know that a spread between a bond's yield and a treasure bond with the same maturity is the credit-risk premium. To find the treasure yields, see below. For example, with a five-year maturity, the yield for an average treasury bond is 1.96% per year.

```
> library(XML)
> readHTMLTable("http://finance.yahoo.com/bonds")[[2]][1:2]
  Maturity Yield
1 3 Month 0.01
2 6 Month 0.08
3 2 Year 0.60
4 3 Year 0.99
5 5 Year 1.96
6 10 Year 3.29
7 30 Year 4.40
```

12.5. Bond Yields for AAA- and AA-Rated Bonds

To retrieve the yields for AAA-and AA-bonds, we use the following codes:

```
>library(XML)
>x<-readHTMLTable("http://finance.yahoo.com/bonds/composite_bond_rates")
```

The above Web page offers three types of yields: US treasury bonds, municipal bonds, and corporate bonds.

```
> x[[3]][,1:2] # municipal bonds     > x[[4]][,1:2] #corporate bonds
  Maturity Yield                        Maturity Yield
1 2yr AA 0.65                         1 2yr AA 0.70
2 2yr AAA 0.45                        2 2yr A 1.14
3 2yr A 0.85                          3 5yr AAA 2.14
4 5yr AAA 0.97                        4 5yr AA 1.78
5 5yr AA 1.14                         5 5yr A 2.35
6 5yr A 1.40                          6 10yr AAA 3.91
7 10yr AAA 1.62                       7 10yr AA 3.11
8 10yr AA 2.08                        8 10yr A 3.17
9 10yr A 1.93                         9 20yr AAA 4.94
10 20yr AAA 3.08                      10 20yr AA 5.00
11 20yr AA 3.41                       11 20yr A 5.10
12 20yr A 3.52
```

12.6. Moody's Historical Yields for Corporate Bonds

From the Federal Research Bank data library, http://www.federalreserve.gov/releases/h15/data.htm., we can find the historical yields up to last month for corporate bonds with several credit ratings. We choose Aaa- or Baa-rated corporate bonds with four frequencies (daily, weekly, monthly, and annual). The header and the last several lines of historical yields for Moody's Aaa-rated bonds are shown below (monthly frequency). Moody's Aaa rates through December 6, 2001, are averages of Aaautility and A industrial bond rates. As of December 7, 2001, these rates are averages of Aaa industrial bonds only.

```
"Series Description","MOODY'S YIELD ON SEASONED CORPORATE BONDS-ALL
INDUSTRIES, AAA"
"Unit:","Percent:_Per_Year"
"Multiplier:","1"
"Currency:","NA"
"Unique Identifier: ","H15/H15/RIMLPAAAR_N.M"
"Time Period","RIMLPAAAR_N.M"
1919-01,5.35
1919-02,5.35
1919-03,5.39
2015-02,3.61
2015-03,3.64
2015-04,3.52
2015-05,3.98
```

Note that the values in the second column are in percentage and annualized. Thus, if we want to estimate a monthly yield (rate of return) in March 2012, the yield should be 0.003325 (3.99/100/12).

12.7. Credit Rating

Three major credit-ratings agencies in the United States are Moody's (http://www.moodys.com/), Standard & Poor's (http://www.standardandpoors.com/home/en/us), and Fitch (http://reports.fitchratings.com/). Although their ratings have different notations (letters), it is easy to translate one letter rating from a rating agency to another (see the following table).

Table 12.3. Equivalency of credit ratings among Moody's, S&P, and Fitch

	Moody's	S&P	Fitch		Moody's	S&P	Fitch
Investment grade	Aaa	AAA	AAA	**Speculative investment**	Ba1	BB+	BB+
	Aa1	AA+	AA+		Ba2	BB	BB
	Aa2	AA	AA		Ba3	BB-	BB-
	Aa3	AA-	AA-		B1	B+	B+
	A1	A+	A+		B2	B	B
	A2	A	A		B3	B-	B-
	A3	A-	A-		Caa1	CCC+	CCC
	Baa1	BBB+	BBB+		Caa2	CCC	
	Baa2	BBB	BBB		Caa3	CCC-	
	Baa3	BBB-	BBB-		Ca	CC	
						C	
					C	D	DDD

Any ratings equal to or above BBB are classified as investment grades. Many mutual funds, pension funds, are only allowed to buy bonds rated as investment grades.

12.8. Credit-Migration (Transition) Matrices

When a company has an AAA rating this year, what is its expected rating next year? What is its PD (default probability)? According to the following table, the probability that it keeps an AAA rating next year is 90.81%. Similarly the probability of an AAA-rated firm/bond becomes an AA-firm is 8.3%. The values along the main diagonal line (from northwest to southeast) are the probabilities of keeping the same rating next year. The values below the main diagonal line (left and bottom triangle) are the probabilities of an upgrading while the values above the diagonal line (up and right triangle) are the probabilities of a downgrading. The last column offers the default probabilities for various ratings. For example, an AAA-rated bond has 0.01% chance to default while a CCC-rated bond has 19.79%.

Table 12.4. One-year credit-rating-migration matrix

		Year T+1							
		AAA	AA	A	BBB	BB	B	CCC	Default
Year T	AAA	0.9081	0.0833	0.0068	0.0006	0.0008	0.0002	0.0001	0.0001
	AA	0.0070	0.9065	0.0779	0.0064	0.0006	0.0013	0.0002	0.0001
	A	0.0009	0.0227	0.9105	0.0552	0.0074	0.0026	0.0001	0.0006
	BBB	0.0002	0.0033	0.0595	0.8593	0.0530	0.0117	0.0112	0.0018
	BB	0.0003	0.0014	0.0067	0.0773	0.8053	0.0884	0.0100	0.0106
	B	0.0001	0.0011	0.0024	0.0043	0.0648	0.8346	0.0407	0.0520
	CCC	0.0021	0.0000	0.0022	0.0130	0.0238	0.1124	0.6486	0.1979
	Default	0.0000	0.0000	0.0000	0.0000	0.0000	0.0000	0.0000	0.0000

To retrieve the above table, use an R data set called **one_year_migration**.

```
> rm(list=ls())
> load("c:/temp/credit.RData")
> ls()
[1] "equivalent3rating"
[2] "moody5year_migration"
[3] "one_year_migration"
[4] "yield_AAA"
```

The following table gives the Moody's five-year-transition matrix. Please pay attention to the column under Default.

Table 12.5. Moody's average five-year rating-transition matrix (1920–1992)

		Year T+5								
		Aaa	Aa	A	Baa	Ba	B	Caa-C	Default	WR
Year T	Aaa	0.6078	0.1521	0.0433	0.0096	0.0049	0.0009	0.0003	0.0014	0.1796
	Aa	0.0343	0.5414	0.1593	0.0342	0.0116	0.0020	0.0002	0.0058	0.2112
	A	0.0020	0.0585	0.5574	0.1034	0.0258	0.0069	0.0008	0.0108	0.2343
	Baa	0.0009	0.0092	0.1001	0.4706	0.0803	0.0200	0.0032	0.0228	0.2928
	Ba	0.0004	0.0026	0.0192	0.1040	0.3648	0.0809	0.0129	0.0590	0.3562
	B	0.0002	0.0009	0.0048	0.0241	0.1025	0.3212	0.0353	0.1291	0.3819
	Caa-C	0.0000	0.0000	0.0002	0.0157	0.0403	0.0777	0.2960	0.2798	0.2904

Source: Moody's Investor Service, July 1997, "Moody's Rating Migration and the Credit Quality Correlation," **http://www.efalken.com/banking/html's/matrices.htm**. Note that WR (Withdraw Rating) indicates that Moody's has withdrawn their ratings.

12.9. Credit Rating and DP (Default Probability)

Rating and default are negatively correlated: the higher the rating, the lower its default probability. The cumulative historical default rates (in %) are given below.

Table 12.6. Relationship between the credit rating and the DP (default probability)

	Default rate (%)			
	Moody's		S&P	
Rating category	Muni	Corp	Muni	Corp
Aaa/AAA	0.00	0.52	0.00	0.60
Aa/AA	0.06	0.52	0.00	1.50
A/A	0.03	1.29	0.23	2.91
Baa/BBB	0.13	4.64	0.32	10.29
Ba/BB	2.65	19.12	1.74	29.93
B/B	11.86	43.34	8.48	53.72
Caa-C/CCC-C	16.58	69.18	44.81	69.19
Averages				
Investment grade	0.07	2.09	0.20	4.14
Noninvestment grade	4.29	31.37	7.37	42.35
All	0.10	9.70	0.29	12.98

Source: US Municipal Bond Fairness Act, 2008, http://monevator.com/2010/04/09/bond-default-rating-probability/.

For example, for an AAA-related corporate bond by Moody's, its default probability is 0.52%.

12.10. Recovery-Rate Given Default

The status (seniority) has a great impact on the recovery rates. According to Altman and Kishore (1997), we have the following table.

Table 12.7. Recovery rates based on the seniority

	Recovery rate (% of face value)
Senior-secured debt	58%
Senior-unsecured debt	48%
Senior-subordinate	35%
Subordinated	32%
Discounted and zero coupon	21%

A secured debt is a debt on which payment is guaranteed by an asset. *Senior* and *subordinated* refers to the priority structure.

Table 12.8. Recovery rates based on the industry

Industry	Average Recovery Rate	Number of observations
Public utilities	70.5%	56
Chemical, petroleum, rubber, and plastic products	62.7%	35
Machinery, instruments, and related products	48.7%	36
Services—business and personal	46.2%	14
Food and kindred products	45.3%	18
Wholesale and retail trade	44.0%	12
Diversified manufacturing	42.3%	20
Casino, hotel, and recreation	40.2%	21
Building materials, metals, and fabricated products	38.8%	68
Transportation and transportation equipment	38.4%	52
Communication, broadcasting, movie production	37.1%	65
Printing and publishing		
Financial institutions	35.7%	66
Construction and real estate	35.3%	35
General-merchandize stores	33.2%	89
Mining and petroleum drilling	33.0%	45
Textile and apparel products	31.7%	31
Wood, paper, and leather products	29.8%	11
Lodging, hospitals, and nursing facilities	26.5%	22
Total	41.0%	696

Source: http://www.riskworx.com/resources/Recovery%20Rates.pdf

12.11. Recovery Rate and LGD (Loss Given Default)

LGD (loss given default) is equal to 1 minus the recovery rate.

Equation 2

$$LGD = 1 - Recoverary\ rate$$

12.12. Altman's Z-Score

The so-called z-score is used to predict the possibility of a firm going bankrupt. This score is a weighted average of five ratios based on a firm's balance sheet and income statement. For public firms, Altman (1968) offers the following formula:

Equation 3

$$Z = 3.3X_1 + 0.99X_2 + 0.6X_3 + 1.2X_4 + 1.4X_5,$$

where the definitions of X_1, X_2, X_3, X_4, and X_5 are given in the following table:

Table 12.9. Definitions of variables in the estimation of Z-scores

Variable	Definition
X_1	EBIT/total assets
X_2	Net sales/total assets
X_3	Market value of equity/total liabilities
X_4	Working capital/total assets
X_5	Retained earnings/total assets

Based on the ranges of z-scores, we can classify public firms into the following four categories. Eidleman (1995) found that the z-score correctly predicted 72% of bankruptcies two years prior to the event.

Z-score range	Definition
> 3.0	Safe
2.7 to 2.99	On alert
1.8 to 2.7	Good chances of going bankrupt within two years
< 1.80	Probability of financial distress is very high

The following R codes can be used to estimate a firm's Z-score.

```
> library(quantmod)
> library(XML)
> source("c:/credit.txt")
> z_score("DELL")
2011-01-28 2010-01-29 2009-01-30 2008-02-01
  2.837700 2.641838 3.875225 3.620239
```

From the output shown in the last row, we know that the Z-scores for DELL is declining over the last four years, not a good sign. Altman's Z-score belongs to the categories called credit scoring (methods). On the other hand, more advanced models (e.g., KMV mode) are based on modern finance theories such as option theory.

12.13. Estimate Market Value and Its Volatility for KMV Model

KMV stands for Kealhofer, McQuown, and Vasicek, who found a company focusing on measuring default risk. KMV methodology is one of the most important methods to estimate the probability of default for a given company by using its balance-sheet information and the equity-market information (http://www.moodyskmv.com/). The objective of this section is to estimate the market value of total assets (A) and its corresponding volatility (σ_A). The result will be used later in the chapter. The basic idea is to treat the equity of a firm as a call option and the debt as its strike price. Let us look at the following simplest example.

If a firm has a debt of $80 and an equity of $20, then the total assets will be $100 (see the image below).

Assume that the assets jump to $110. The debt remains the same while the equity increases to $30. On the other hand, if the assets drop to $90, the equity will be only $10. Since the equity holders are the residual claimer, their value has the following expression:

Equation 4

$$E = \max\ (assets - debt,\ 0) = \max\ (A - D,\ 0)$$

Recalling for a call option, we have the following payoff function:

Equation 5

$$\text{Payoff (call)} = \max\ (S_T - K,\ 0)$$

This means that we can treat equity as a call option with debt as our exercise price. With appropriate notations, we will have the following formula for a firm's equity. KMV model is defined below.

Equation 6

$$\left\{ \begin{array}{l} E = A * N(d_1) - e^{-rT} N(d_2) \\ d_1 = \dfrac{\ln\left(\frac{A}{D}\right) + \left(r + \frac{1}{2}\sigma_A^2\right)T}{\sigma_A \sqrt{T}} \\ d_2 = d_1 - \sigma_A \sqrt{T} \end{array} \right.$$

We should pay attention to the estimated A (market value of total assets) from equation (7) since it is different from the summation of market value of assets plus the book value of the debt. The usages of those two derived values (A and) will be used in equations 10, 11, and 12.

12.14. R Codes for Estimating Total Assets and Its Volatility

The following R program is for estimating total assets (A) and its volatility (**sigmaA**) for a given equity (**E**), debt (**D**), maturity (**T**), risk-free rate (**r**), and the volatility of the equity (**sigmaE**). The basic logic of the program is that we input a large number of pairs of **A** and **sigmaE** then we estimate E and **sigmaE** based on equation 7. Since both E and sigmaE are known, we can estimate the differences: **diff_1=E – E** (known) and **diff_2 = sigmaE – sigmaE** (known). The pair of A and sigmaE, which minimizes the sum of those two absolute differences, will be our solution.

```
KMV<-function(E,D,T,r,sigmaE){
    n<-1000;m<-100
    for(i in 1:n){
        for(j in 1:m){
            A<-E+D/2+i*D/n
            sigmaA<-0.05+j*(0.5-0.05)/m
            d1 = (log(A/D)+(r+sigmaA*sigmaA/2.)*T)/(sigmaA*sqrt(T))
            d2 = d1-sigmaA*sqrt(T)
            diff1<- A*pnorm(d1)-D*exp(-r*T)*pnorm(d2)-E
            diff2<- A/E*pnorm(d1)*sigmaA-sigmaE
            if(i+j==2){
                diff<-abs(diff1) + abs(diff2)
                final<-c(A,sigmaA,diff)
            }else{
                if(abs(diff1)+abs(diff2)<diff){
                diff<-abs(diff1) +abs(diff2)
                final<-c(A,sigmaA,diff)
                }
            }
        }
    }
    return(final=round(final,digits=4))
}
```

Here is a KMV example: **E=110,688** (shares outstanding*price of stock), **D=64,062** (total debt), **R$_f$=0.07** (risk-free rate), **T=1** (1 year). Usually we use **T=1** in the KMV models. The result is A=170,558; σ_A=0.29. Based on the following codes, we have **A=170,393** and sigmaE=0.2615.

```
> KMV(D=64062,E=110688,T=1,r=0.07,sigmaE=0.4)
[1] 170393.7840 0.2615 0.0066
```

The output is A=170,393.78 and sigmaE=0.2615. To verify those two values, we can use the standard Black-Scholes-Merton option model.

```
> bs_f('c',170393,64062,1,0.07,0.2615)
[1] 110662.2
```

Please pay attention that the summation of the book value of debt and the market value of equity is 174,750 (≠170,558). Since the equity of a firm is the call option, we can use the Black-Scholes-Merton model to double check our result.

```
bs_f('C',170558,64062,1,0.07,0.29)
[1] 110828.0
```

12.15. Nonlinear Minimization

For the following quadratic equation, we know that the minimum value is 7, and this is achieved when x=0.

Equation 9

$$f(x) = 7 + x^2$$

We can use a function called **nlm()**, nonlinear minimization.

```
>f <- function(x) 7+x^2
>nlm(f, 10) # 10: starting value
$minimum
[1] 7
$estimate
[1] -2.49973e-12
$gradient
[1] 1.000089e-06
$code
[1] 1
$iterations
[1] 1
```

To make the output more readable, we use **transpose t()** (see the codes below).

```
>f <- function(x, a) 7+x^2
>t(nlm(f, 10))
  minimum estimate gradient code iterations
[1,] 7 -2.499626e-12 1.000089e-06 1 1
```

Sometimes we need to input a set of constant parameters, a.

Equation 10

$$f(x) = 7 + (x - a)^2$$

```
>f <- function(x, a) 7+(x-a)^2
>t(nlm(f, 10, a=10.5)) # 10 is an initial value
  minimum estimate gradient code iterations
[1,] 7 10.5 -4.229421e-13 1 2
```

For multiple-input variables plus parameters, we can use x, which has several variables. For example, we can use a vector of two.

```
>f <- function(x, a) 7+(x[1]-a)^2+ (x[2]-2*a)^2
>y<-nlm(f, x<-c(10,10), a=10.5)
>y$estimate
[1] 10.5 21.0
```

12.16. R Codes for a KMV Model with nlm()

First, we have a set of parameters of **E, D, T, rf**, and σ_E. For the following set of parameters, we have the correct results of **A=12.5** and σ_A=9.6%.

```
E=3;D=10;T=1;r=0.05;sigmaE=0.4;
a<-c(E,D,T,r,sigmaE)
KMV_f<-function(x,a){
  " nlm(f,x<-c(D,sigmaE),a) ->y
  y$estimate
  [1] 12.51195139 0.09608728 (correct)
  "
  A<-x[1]
  sigmaA<-x[2]
  E<- a[1]
  D<- a[2]
  T<- a[3]
  r<- a[4]
  sigmaE<-a[5]
  d1 = (log(A/D)+(r+sigmaA*sigmaA/2.)*T)/(sigmaA*sqrt(T))
  d2 = d1-sigmaA*sqrt(T)
  diff1<- A*pnorm(d1)-D*exp(-r*T)*pnorm(d2)-E
  diff2<- A/E*pnorm(d1)*sigmaA-sigmaE
  return(abs(diff1)/E + abs(diff2)/sigmaE)
}
```

Below we show the impact of using different initial values on the final results.

```
nlm(KMV_f,x<-c(E/2+D,sigmaE),a)$estimate
[1] 12.51162493 0.09609593
nlm(KMV_f,x<-c(E+D,sigmaE),a)$estimate
[1] 12.95429496 -0.05v366289
nlm(KMV_f,x<-c(D,sigmaE),a)$estimate
[1] 12.51195139 0.09608728
nlm(KMV_f,x<-c(D,0.7),a)$estimate
[1] 9.935777088 -0.004770128
nlm(KMV_f,x<-c(D,0.27),a)$estimate
[1] 12.51162747 0.09608916
```

12.17. Distance to Default

Distance to default (DD) is defined by the following formula, where A is the market value of the total assets and σ_A is its risk. The interpretation of this measure is clear: the higher the DD, the safer the firm.

Equation 11

$$DD = \frac{A - Default\ Point}{A * \sigma_A}$$

In terms of default point, there is no theory on how to choose an ideal default point. However, we can use all short-term debts plus the half of long-term debts as our default point. After we have the values of the MV of assets and its volatility, we can use the following equation to estimate the distance to default. The A and σ_A are from the output from equation 7. On the other hand, if the default point equals to E, we would have the following formula:

Equation 12

$$DD = -\frac{\ln\left(\frac{V_A}{D}\right)+\left(r-\frac{1}{2}\sigma_A^2\right)T}{\sigma_A\sqrt{T}}$$

According to the Black-Scholes model, the relationship between DD and DP (default probability) is given below.

Equation 13

$$DP\ (Default\ Probability) = N\ (-\ DD)$$

12.18. R Data Set Called credit.RData

We can load it by using the **load()** function.

```
load("c:/temp/credit.RData")
```

Currently **credit.RData** contains **equivalent3rating**, **moody5year_migration**, **one_year_migration**, and **yield_AAA**. Equivalent3rating is the same as table 12.2's. The data of **one_year_migration.RData** is the same as table 12.3's.

```
> one_year_migration
    AAA AA A BBB BB B CCC D
AAA 0.9081 0.0833 0.0068 0.0006 0.0008 0.0002 0.0001 0.0001
AA 0.0070 0.9065 0.0779 0.0064 0.0006 0.0013 0.0002 0.0001
A 0.0009 0.0227 0.9105 0.0552 0.0074 0.0026 0.0001 0.0006
BBB 0.0002 0.0033 0.0595 0.8593 0.0530 0.0117 0.0112 0.0018
BB 0.0003 0.0014 0.0067 0.0773 0.8053 0.0884 0.0100 0.0106
B 0.0001 0.0011 0.0024 0.0043 0.0648 0.8346 0.0407 0.0520
CCC 0.0021 0.0000 0.0022 0.0130 0.0238 0.1124 0.6486 0.1979
D 0.0000 0.0000 0.0000 0.0000 0.0000 0.0000 0.0000 1.0000
```

12.19. CreditMetrics in R

The R package called **CreditMetrics** is the package related to credit risk. First, let's look at a function called **cm.cs**, which offers credit spreads for a given one-year migration matrix and a given LGD (loss given default). If we use **CS** for credit spread, the present value of V_t will have the following form.

Equation 14

$$V_0 = PV(V_t) = V_t e^{-(r_f + CS)t}$$

where t is the time in year. In a risk-free world (under a riskless-probability measure), the value of a credit position at time t will be

Equation 15

$$V_0 = E[V_t]e^{-r_f t}$$

If we use $P_{default}$ for a default probability, we have

Equation 16

$$E[V_t] = (1 - P_{default}) * V_t + P_{default} * V_t [1 - LGD]$$

After combining the above equations and following transformation, we get the formula for a credit spread:

Equation 17

$$CS_t = -\ln(1 - LGD * P_{default})/t$$

For an AAA-rated bond with a default **probability=0.0001, LGD=0.45**, and **t=1**, we have

```
> -log(1-0.45*0.0001)
[1] 4.500101e-05
```

For a set of credit ratings, we have the following commands:

```
library(CreditMetrics)
load("c:/temp/credit.RData")
loss_given_default<- 0.45
> cm.cs(one_year_migration,loss_given_default)
   AAA     AA     A    BBB      BB       B       CCC
4.500e-05 4.50e-05 2.70e-04 8.103e-04 4.78e-03 2.368e-02 9.3236e-02
```

To make the result more readable, we convert it into basis point and keep only two decimal places. It means the spread for a BBB-rated bond is 8 basis-points.

```
> round(cm.cs(one_year_migration, loss_given_default)*10000,digit=2)
  AAA  AA   A  BBB   BB     B    CCC
 0.45 0.45 2.70 8.10 47.81 236.78 932.73
```

For a one-year migration, we have the following codes:

```
> t(one_year_migration[,8])
     AAA   AA   A   BBB    BB     B    CCC  D
[1,] 1e-04 1e-04 6e-04 0.0018 0.0106 0.052 0.1979 1
```

Thus, **credit spread = - log(1-0.45*0.0001)= 4.500101e-05=0.0045%**. For the CCC-rated bond, we have > -log(1-0.45*0.1979) # [1] 0.09327276.

Table 12.10. List of major functions included in CreditMetrics

Function	Description
cm.CVaR	Computation of the credit value at risk (CVaR)
cm.cs	Computation of credit spreads
cm.gain	Computation of simulated profits and losses
cm.hist	Profit/loss distribution histogram
cm.matrix	Testing for migration matrix
cm.portfolio	Computation of simulated portfolio values
cm.quantile	Computation of migration quantiles
cm.ref	Computation of reference value
cm.rnorm	Computation of standard normal distributed random numbers
cm.rnorm.cor	Computation of correlated standard normal distributed random numbers
cm.state	Computation of state space
cm.val	Valuation for the credit positions of each scenario

The function **cm.matrix()** is used to test whether the transition matrix has the property of the summation of probabilities being equal to one.

```
>library(CreditMetrics)
>load("c:/temp/credit.RData")
>cm.matrix(one_year_migration)
```

To double check, we can use **rowSums()** function.

```
> rowSums(one_year_migration)
AAA AA A BBB BB B CCC D
  1 1 1 1 1 1 1 1
```

The function called **cm.ref()** offers the present value of a credit value over one year for a given set of parameters such as credit rating, credit values, discount rate, and loss given default. Assume that we have a bond portfolio with just three bonds.

Bond	Values (million)	Rating
1	4	BBB
2	1	AA
3	10	BB

Assume further that the risk-free rate (T-yield) is 3% and the LGD is 0.45 with the previous oneyear migration matrix. To estimate three present values, we have the following codes.

```
>library(CreditMetrics)
>load("c:/temp/credit.RData")
>rf <- 0.03 # risk-free rate
>values <- c(4, 1, 10)*1e6 # credit values
>rating <- c("BBB","AA","B")
>loss_give_default<- 0.45
x<-cm.ref(one_year_migration,loss_given_default,values,rf,rating)
```

The output below shows that an initial value of $4 million, which has a credit risk with a BBB rating, one year later could be $3.88 million.

```
X
$constVal
  BBB AA B
3878637.9 970401.9 9477371.1
$constPV
[1] 14326411
```

The function **cm.CVaR()** offers the credit value at risk by simulated profits/losses. Assume the same bond portfolio as discussed above. The total value today is $15 million. The bond ratings for those three bonds are BBB, AA, and B. The LGD is 0.45. The correlation matrix for those three firms are given below:

```
> rho
       firm 1 firm 2 firm 3
firm 1 1.0 0.4 0.6
firm 2 0.4 1.0 0.5
firm 3 0.6 0.5 1.0
```

The credit VaR is estimated below:

```
>library(CreditMetrics)
>load("c:/temp/credit.RData")
>n <- 50000 # number of random numbers
>rf <- 0.03 # risk-free rate
>values <- c(4, 1, 10)*1e6 # credit values
>LGD<- 0.45 # LGD: loss given default
>rating <- c("BBB","AA","B") # rating of three firms
>alpha <- 0.99 # confidence level
>firmnames <- c("f1","f2","f3") # three names
>rho <-matrix(c( 1, 0.4, 0.6, # correlation matrix
  0.4, 1, 0.5,
  0.6, 0.5, 1),3,3,dimnames=list(firmnames,
  firmnames),byrow = TRUE)
>N<-length(values)
cm.CVaR(one_year_migration,LGD,values,N,n,rf,rho,alpha,rating)
  1%
4065061
```

The result indicates that our credit VaR for our three-bond portfolio is $4.1 million. Note that every time you run the above codes, a slightly different output results.

12.20. Credit Default Swap (CDS)

A lender can buy a so-called credit default swap (CDS) to protect him/her in an event of default. The buyer of the CDS makes a series of payments (the CDS "fee" or "spread") to the seller and, in exchange, receives a payoff if the loan defaults. It was reported that there was a contract worth $25.5 trillion in early 2012.

Here is a simple example. A pension fund just bought $100 million corporate bonds with a maturity of ten years. If the issuing firm does not default, the pension fund would enjoy interest payment every year plus $100 million at the end of the tenth year. However, the pension fund worries about possible default. To protect themselves, they entered a ten-year CDS contract with a financial institution. Based on the credit worthiness of the bond-issuing firm, the agreed spread is 80 basis points payable annually. This means that every year, the pension fund (CDS buyer) pays the financial institution (CDS seller) $80,000 over the next ten years.

If a credit event happens, the CDS seller would compensate the CDS buyer depending on their loss because of the credit event. If the contract specifies a physical settlement, the CDS buyer could sell their bonds at $100 million to the CDS seller. If the contract specifies a cash settlement, the CDS seller would pay Max($100m-X,0) to the CDS buyer, where X is the market value of the bonds. If the market value of the bonds is $70 million, then the CDS seller would pay the CDS buyer $30 million.

In the above case, the spreads or fees is strongly correlated with the default probability of the issuing firm. The higher the default probability, the higher the CDS spread. The following table presents such a relationship.

Table 12.11. Default probability and credit default swap—estimated five-year cumulative probability of default (P) and five-year credit default swaps (5Y CDS)

CDS	P	CDS	P	CDS	P	CDS	P	CDS	P	CDS	P	CDS	P
0	0.0%	100	7.8%	200	13.9%	300	19.6%	500	30.2%	500	30.2%	1000	54.1%
5	0.6%	105	8.1%	205	14.2%	310	20.2%	510	30.7%	525	31.4%	1025	55.2%
10	1.1%	110	8.4%	210	14.5%	320	20.7%	520	31.2%	550	32.7%	1050	56.4%
15	1.6%	115	8.7%	215	14.8%	330	21.2%	530	31.7%	575	33.9%	1075	57.5%
20	2.0%	120	9.1%	220	15.1%	340	21.8%	540	32.2%	600	35.2%	1100	58.6%
25	2.4%	125	9.4%	225	15.4%	350	22.3%	550	32.7%	625	36.4%	1125	59.7%
30	2.8%	130	9.7%	230	15.7%	360	22.9%	560	33.2%	650	37.6%	1150	60.9%
35	3.2%	135	10.0%	235	16.0%	370	23.4%	570	33.7%	675	38.8%	1175	62.0%
40	3.6%	140	10.3%	240	16.2%	380	23.9%	580	34.2%	700	40.0%	1200	63.1%
45	4.0%	145	10.6%	245	16.5%	390	24.5%	590	34.7%	725	41.2%	1225	64.2%
50	4.3%	150	10.9%	250	16.8%	400	25.0%	600	35.2%	750	42.4%	1250	65.3%
55	4.7%	155	11.2%	255	17.1%	410	25.5%	610	35.7%	775	43.6%	1275	66.4%
60	5.0%	160	11.5%	260	17.4%	420	26.0%	620	36.1%	800	44.8%	1300	67.5%
65	5.4%	165	11.8%	265	17.7%	430	26.6%	630	36.6%	825	46.0%	1325	68.6%
70	5.7%	170	12.1%	270	17.9%	440	27.1%	640	37.1%	850	47.2%	1350	69.7%
75	6.1%	175	12.4%	275	18.2%	450	27.6%	650	37.6%	875	48.3%	1375	70.7%
80	6.4%	180	12.7%	280	18.5%	460	28.1%	660	38.1%	900	49.5%	1400	71.8%
85	6.8%	185	13.0%	285	18.8%	470	28.6%	670	38.6%	925	50.6%	1425	72.9%
90	7.1%	190	13.3%	290	19.1%	480	29.1%	680	39.1%	950	51.8%	1450	74.0%
95	7.4%	195	13.6%	295	19.3%	490	29.6%	690	39.6%	975	52.9%	1475	75.1%
100	7.8%	200	13.9%	300	19.6%	500	30.2%	700	40.0%	1000	54.1%	1500	76.1%

Source: **http://workforall.net/CDS-Credit-default-Swaps.html**

12.21. R Package crp.CSFP (CreditRisk+Porfolio Model)

First, let us look at three data sets. The author thanks Kevin Jakob for supplying me those three data sets: rating.scale, sec.var, and portfolio. We can use the following codes to retrieve those three data sets.

```
> Path=system.file("data",package="crp.CSFP")
> portfolio=read.csv(paste(Path,"/portfolio.csv",sep=""))
> rating.scale=read.csv(paste(Path,"/rating_pd.csv",sep=""))
> sec.var=data.frame(Var=runif(3,0,2))
```

The first one is related to rating (see below). The first column is rating for seven different sections (industries). PD is default probability, and SD is standard deviation. The second input file gives ten section names and their corresponding VaR.

```
> head(rating.scale)        > head(sec.var)
  RATING  PD    SD               Var
1    1 0.015 0.0075        1 0.8028986
2    2 0.016 0.0080        2 0.4937825
3    3 0.030 0.0150        3 1.6125254
4    4 0.050 0.0250
5    5 0.075 0.0375
6    6 0.100 0.0500
```

The third input file is a portfolio's risk matrix (500 by 16). The 16 variables are **CPnumber, CPname, EXPOSURE, LGD, MATURITY, RATING, S1, S2**, to **S10**.

```
> head(portfolio)
  CPnumber CPname exposure      lgd maturity rating S1 S2 S3
1        1 NAME1   358475 0.9885447      365      8  1  0  0
2        2 NAME2  1089819 0.6076650      365      8  0  1  0
3        3 NAME3  1799710 0.5359004      365      6  0  1  0
4        4 NAME4  1933116 0.5905669      365      7  1  0  0
5        5 NAME5  2317327 0.4849782      365      7  0  0  1
6        6 NAME6  2410929 0.0263668      365      7  0  0  1
```

The unique maturity is 1. We indent to estimate various risk measure with those 500 bonds with a one-year maturity.

```
f_out<-"c:/temp"
port<-read.csv("c:/temp/portfolio.csv",header=T)
risk<-read.csv("c:/temp/rating_pd.csv")
sec.var<-read.csv("c:/test_R/pd_sector_var.csv",header=T)
y<-crp.init(PATH.OUT=f_out,portfolio=port,risk.
matrix=risk,sec.var=sec.var,LOSS.UNIT=1e6,CALC.RISK.CONT=T)
result<-crp.CSFP(y)
```

The part of the output is given below, including the graph.

```
Diversifible risk: 22459.73 Tril. Systematic risk: 8902.86 Tril.
Portfolio net exposure: 30.8 Bil.
Portfolio potential loss: 12.43 Bil.
Portfolio expected loss: 157.55 Mio.
Portfolio standad deviation: 177.09 Mio.
Max. exposure band per CP: 600
Calculate the loss distribution till 0.9999-confidence level is reached.
Loss unit: 1 Mio.
  it= 1000 CDF= 0.9973529 ;
Reached level of confidence: 0.9999004(iterations actually done: 1526 )
CR+ portfolio expected loss: 157.39 Mio.
Expected loss difference: -167.73 Thd.
CR+ Exceedance Probability of the expected loss: 0.3469207
CR+ portfolio standard deviation: 176.43 Mio.
CR+ portfolio Value-at-risk(0.999): 1.16 Bil.
CR+ portfolio economic capital(0.999): 1 Bil.
CR+ portfolio Expected Shortfall(0.999): 1.32 Bil.
CR+ portfolio mean expected loss exceedance: 353.4 Mio.
Calculating VaR and ES contributions….
CR+ Expected Shortfall TAU( 0.9973186 ): 1.16 Bil.
Scale Factor for TAU 1.000759
```

The corresponding graph is given below:

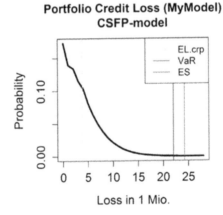

Exercises

12.1. What is the definition of credit risk?

12.2. What are the differences between credit risk and market risk?

12.3. What are the major credit-rating agencies in the United States?

12.4. Why do we care about treasury yields?

12.5. From where do we find the treasury yields?

12.6. What is the definition of credit spread?

12.7. How to find a credit spread?

12.8. What are the uses of zero curve?

12.9. Study the definitions of X_1, X_2, X_3, X_4, and X_5 for the z-score formula. Explain why the higher the z-score, the lower the probability of bankruptcy.

12.10. What is the one-year migration (transition) matrix?

12.11. What is the use of the one-year migration matrix?

12.12. What is the relationship between the credit rating and the default probability?

12.13. Use the concept of the present value of a bond being the discounted expected future cash flows to derive equation 1.

12.14. What are the values on the (main) diagonal line (from NW to SE) of a credit-transition matrix?

12.15. Generate an R data set with the following six data sets (CSV files).

File; Title; Units; Frequency; Seasonal Adjustment; Last Updated
DAAA.csv ;Moody's Seasoned Aaa Corporate Bond Yield; %; D; NA; 2011-04-29
AAA.csv ;Moody's Seasoned Aaa Corporate Bond Yield; %; M; NA; 2011-04-05
WAAA.csv ;Moody's Seasoned Aaa Corporate Bond Yield; %; W; NA; 2011-04-26
DBAA.csv ;Moody's Seasoned Baa Corporate Bond Yield; %; D; NA; 2011-04-29
WBAA.csv ;Moody's Seasoned Baa Corporate Bond Yield; %; W; NA; 2011-04-26
BAA.csv ;Moody's Seasoned Baa Corporate Bond Yield; %; M; NA; 2011-04-05

Note: To download the data, go to the following links:
- http://research.stlouisfed.org/fred2/categories/32348
  - Click IRCAB_csv_2.zip.
- http://research.stlouisfed.org/fred2/categories/119/downloaddata

12.16. Identify an issue with z_score and find a way to address the issue.

12.17. Download the corporate-bond spread data (CORPBONDSPREADS._csv_2.zip) at http://research.stlouisfed.org/fred2/categories/32297/downloaddata. Write an R program to generate a R data sets including all the following files:

File ;Title; Units; Frequency; Seasonal Adjustment; Last Updated
BAMLC7A0C1015Y.csv ;US Corporate 10-15 Year Option-Adjusted Spread; %; D; NA; 2011-05-02
BAMLC1A0C13Y.csv ;US Corporate 1-3 Year Option-Adjusted Spread; %; D; NA; 2011-05-02
BAMLC8A0C15PY.csv ;US Corporate 15+ Year Option-Adjusted Spread; %; D; NA; 2011-05-02
BAMLC2A0C35Y.csv;US Corporate 3-5 Year Option-Adjusted Spread; %; D; NA; 2011-05-02
BAMLC3A0C57Y.csv;US Corporate 5-7 Year Option-Adjusted Spread; %; D; NA; 2011-05-02
BAMLC4A0C710Y.csv ;US Corporate 7-10 Year Option-Adjusted Spread; %; D; NA; 2011-05-02
BAMLC0A1CAAA.csv;US Corporate AAA Option-Adjusted Spread; %; D; NA; 2011-05-02
BAMLC0A2CAA.csv ;US Corporate AA Option-Adjusted Spread; %; D; NA; 2011-05-02
BAMLC0A3CA.csv ;US Corporate A Option-Adjusted Spread; %; D; NA; 2011-05-02
BAMLC0A4CBBB.csv;US Corporate BBB Option-Adjusted Spread; %; D; NA; 2011-05-02
BAMLC0A0CM.csv ;US Corporate Master Option-Adjusted Spread; %; D; NA; 2011-05-02
BAMLH0A1HYBB.csv ;US High Yield BB Option-Adjusted Spread; %; D; NA; 2011-05-02
BAMLH0A2HYB.csv ;US High Yield B Option-Adjusted Spread; %; D; NA; 2011-05-02
BAMLH0A3HYC.csv ; US High Yield CCC or Below Option-Adjusted Spread; %; D; NA; 2011-05-02
BAMLH0A0HYM2.csv ;US High Yield Master II Option-Adjusted Spread; %; D; NA; 2011-05-02

12.18. Derive equation 17 from equations 14 to 16.

12.19. Walmart plans to issue $50-million (total face value) corporate bonds with a face value of $1000 for each bond. The bonds would mature in ten years. The coupon rate is 8% with an annual payment. How much could Walmart raise today? If Walmart manages to raise its credit rating by one notch, how much extracash could the firm raise?

CHAPTER 13

Bid-Ask Spread and Transaction Costs

An *ask price* is "the price at which an owner is willing to sell a security," while a *bid price* is "the price that a buyer (investor) is willing to pay." Their difference is called bid-ask spread or simply spread (S). To estimate bid-ask spread, we need high-frequency trading data (see chapter 15: "Using R to process TAQ (High-Frequency Data)").

Equation 1

$$S = Ask - Bid$$

Roll's (1984) spread is based on the serial covariance in price changes (i.e., using daily data instead of high-frequency data).

Equation 2

$$S = 2\sqrt{-cov(\Delta P_t, \Delta P_{t-1})}$$

where S is spread,

P_t is the closing price on day t,

and ΔP_t (= P_t - P_t-1) is the price change at t.

The following codes estimate IBM's spread by using its daily prices.

```
> ticker<-"IBM"
> t1<-'http://finance.google.com/financeihistorical?g=1
> t2<-paste(t1,ticker,'Sstartdate=Jun+02,+19701,sep=")
> x<-read.csv(paste(t2,1Senddate=Jul+10,+2012&output=csvi,sep="))
> x[1:2,]
      Date  Open   High   Low   Close   Volume
1 10-Jul-12 190.30 191.14 185.60 186.26 4690312
2 9-Jul-12 190.76 191.00 188.05 189.67 3988256
> p<-diff(x[1:500,5]) # using the latest 500 trading days
> n<-length(p)
> cov(p[1:(n-1)],p[2:n])
[1] -0.08933841
> 2*sqrt(-cov(p[1:(n-1)1,p[2:n]))
[1] 0.5977906
```

The above result shows that the covariance is -0.089 and the spread is 0.60. This suggests that a oneway transaction cost will be 30¢.

13.1. Introduction

Spread or bid-ask spread has many important practical and academic implications. For example, when rebalancing our portfolios, we should consider transaction costs. Usually spread (ask minus bid) is used to represent the cost of buying and selling (i.e., two transactions). Some finer and more accurate measures based on market microstructure data can be estimated, such as bid-ask spread, effective bid-ask spread, and price response to signed order flow. Thus, the bid-ask spread based on the high-frequency data is more accurate, and its various types of measure are used as benchmarks.

However, there are many disadvantages of using high-frequency data. First, the earliest year we can go is 1983 for American stocks while daily data goes as early as 1926. Because of this, researchers designed various liquidity measures based on daily data since they need a longer time series. Second, the size of high-frequency data is huge, about 1TB (1 terabyte = 1012 bytes) per month in 2010 for TAQ (New York Stock Exchange's trade and quote database). It requests huge amounts computing time. The size of daily data is much smaller. Third, it is extremely more expensive to purchase high-frequency data such as TAQ database.

13.2. Roll Spread (1984)

For the bid-ask spread, Roll (1984) shows that we could estimate it based on the serial covariance in price changes.

Equation 3

$$\begin{cases} S = 2\sqrt{-cov(\Delta P_t, \Delta P_{t-1})} \\ \% \ spread = \frac{S}{\bar{P}} \end{cases}$$

where P_t is the closing price of a stock on day t and $\bar{P}$ is the average share price in the estimation period. For example, we can use the following R codes to estimate the covariance between ΔP_t and ΔP_{t-1}.

The following R codes will estimate Roll's spread for a given ticker—DELL, in this case—by using last year's 252 trading days daily data from Yahoo Finance.

```
> ticker<-"DELL"
> n_days<-252
> t1c-Ihttp://finance.google.com/finance/historical?q=1
> t2<-paste(tlytickerf'Sstartdate=Jun+02,+1970',sep=")
> x<-read.csv(paste(t2,1Senddate=Sul+10,+2012&output=csv.,sep="))
> p<- -diff(x[f5])
> cov1<-cov(p[1:n_days],p[2:(n_days+1)])
> cov1 [1] -0.01107994
> 2*sqrt(-cov1)
[1] 0.2105226
```

Thus, the spread for DELL over the last year (252 trading days) based on the Roll model will be 0.21. The major assumption for the Roll's model is that the covariance between ΔP_t and ΔP_{t-1} is negative. When its value is positive, the Roll model would fail. In a real world, it is true for many cases. Usually there are two solutions. First, when the covariance is negative, we ignore those cases (stocks) or use other methods to estimate the spread. The second approach is to add a negative sign in front of a positive covariance. The result shown on the first page of this chapter indicates that the spread is 34¢, which is much higher than the result based on the TAQ database.

```
> ticker<-"IBM"
> t1<-'http://finance.google.com/finance/historical?g=.
> t2<-paste(t1,ticker,'Sstartdate=Jun+02,+19701,sep=")
>  x<-read.csv(paste(t2,1Senddate=Jun+10,+2017&output=csvi,sep="))
> p<- -diff(x[f5])
> n<-length(p)
> n1<-21
> cov1<-NA
> s<-NA
> for(i in 1:(n-n1)){
+     m1<-i
+     m2<-i+n1
+     cov0<-cov(p[m1:m2],p[(m1+1):(m2+1)])
+     covi[i]<-min(cov0,0)
+     s[i]<-2•sqrt(-covi[i])
+ }
> s2<-s[is.na(s)==F]
> mean(s2)
[1] 0.7096071
```

13.3. Corwin and Schultz's (2011) High-Low Spread

Corwin and Schultz (2011) designed a new method to estimate spread from the observed daily high (H) and low (L) (see below).

$$
\begin{cases}
S = \frac{2(e^\alpha - 1)}{1+e^\alpha} \\
\alpha = \frac{\sqrt{2\beta} - \sqrt{\beta}}{3 - 2\sqrt{2}} - \sqrt{\frac{\gamma}{3 - 2\sqrt{2}}} \\
\beta = \log(\frac{H}{L})^2_{daily} \\
\gamma = \log(\frac{H}{L})^2_{2\text{-}day\ period}
\end{cases}
$$

where S is the Corwin and Schultz–defined spread,
H is the daily high or high within a two-day window,
and L is the daily low or low within a two-day window.

Below are codes to estimate spread for IBM based on Corwin and Schultz (2011) methodology. Below we show how to get high-low ratio for a one-day and a two-day window manually.

```
> tl<-1http://finance.google.com/finance/historical?g=1
> t2<-paste(t1,1IBMSstartdate=Jun+02,+19701,sep=")
> x<-read.csv(paste(t2,1.Senddate=Dec+06,+2011&output=csv1,sep="))
> x[1:3,]
    Date    Open    High    Low   Close   Volume
1 6-Dec-11 190.65 193.53 190.32 192.94 4145053
2 5-Dec-11 191.18 193.61 190.38 190.84 5699392
3 2-Dec-11 189.92 191.33 189.45 189.66 4962414
```

On December 06, 2011 and for a one-day window, H will be 193.53, and L will be 190.84. For a twoday window, H will be 193.61—that is, **max(193.53, 193.61)**—and L will be 190.32—that is, **min(190.32 and 190.38)**.

```
x<-read.csv("http://canisius.edu/
~yany/data/ibmDaily.csv",header=T)
H<-x$High
L<-x$Low
n<-nrow(x)
s<-NA
for(i in 2:n){
    beta<-log(H[i]/L[i])^2
    H2<-max(H[i+1],H[i])
L2<-min(L[i+1],L[i])
    gamma<-log(H2/L2)^2
    t<-3-2*sqrt(2)
    alpha<-(sqrt(2*beta)-sqrt(beta))/t- sqrt(gamma/t)
    s[i-1]<-(2*exp(alpha)-1)/(1+exp(alpha))
}
s2<-s[is.na(s)==F]
mean(s2)
[1] 0.4825508
```

There are several issues with Corwin and Schultz's spread based on high and low stock prices. The assumption underlying Corwin and Schultz's methodology is continuous trading. When the trading is not continuous, we expect some discrepancy. The most important impact is the overnight return. The authors use the following formula to include the impact of overnight returns.

Equation 5

$$\begin{cases} if\ A_t < P_{t-1}\ then\ \Delta P = P_{t-1} - A_t \\ if\ B_t > P_{t-1}\ then\ \Delta P = B_t - P_{t-1} \\ \quad H_t = A_t + \Delta P \\ \quad L_t = B_t - \Delta P \end{cases}$$

We designed a question related to equation 5 (see the exercise at the end of this chapter).

13.4. Spread Estimated Based on High-Frequency Data

Spread is negatively correlated with the liquidity (i.e., the higher the spread, the lower the liquidity).

The bid-ask spread is the all-around transaction cost. In other words, when a trader buys one share then sells it, he/she would have to buy at high (ask) and sell at low (bid). Thus, we can treat the bid-ask spread as the transaction cost. On the other hand, the higher this spread, the lower the liquidity of the underlying stock.

Table 1 shows the first ten lines from TAQ.

Table 13.1. Ten lines from CT (consolidated trade, TAQ, January 2, 2004)

```
Obs SYMBOL DATE TIME PRICE SIZE G127 CORR COND EX TSEQ
1 A 20040102 9:30:16 29.25 31100 40 0 N 158291
2 A 20040102 9:30:17 29.25 300 0 0 M 0
3 A 20040102 9:30:18 29.25 300 0 0 M 0
4 A 20040102 9:30:18 29.25 1000 0 0 M 0
5 A 20040102 9:30:18 29.25 100 0 0 M 0
6 A 20040102 9:30:18 29.25 100 0 0 M 0
7 A 20040102 9:30:18 29.25 300 0 0 M 0
8 A 20040102 9:30:18 29.25 200 0 0 M 0
9 A 20040102 9:30:20 29.25 100 0 0 B 0
10 A 20040102 9:30:20 29.25 500 0 0 B 0
```

The first spread is the same as the bid and ask defined in equation 1. Usually researchers use a volumeweighted spread. The daily-trading volume-weighted spread is given below.

Equation 6

$$\begin{cases} S = \sum w_i * (A_i - B_i) \\ w_i = \dfrac{v_i}{\sum v_i} \end{cases}$$

where S is the spread,

w_i is the weight for the ith trade,

and v_i is its corresponding trading volume.

Instead of quote data, TAQ offers high-frequency trade data with the same time stamp of seconds. The following table shows the first ten lines from a TAQ data set.

Table 13.2. Ten lines from CQ (consolidated quote, TAQ, January 2, 2004)

```
Symbol Date    time     bid ofr bidSiz ofrSiz Mode EX MMID
1 A 20040102 8:00:01 0.00 0.00 0 0 12 P 0
2 A 20040102 8:00:06 0.00 0.00 0 0 12 P 0
3 A 20040102 8:08:15 0.01 0.00 1 0 12 P 0
4 A 20040102 8:19:05 0.01 58.48 1 1 12 P 0
5 A 20040102 8:26:11 28.30 58.48 2 1 12 P 0
6 A 20040102 8:30:01 0.00 0.00 0 0 12 T MADF 0
7 A 20040102 8:30:01 0.00 0.00 0 0 12 T TRIM 0
8 A 20040102 8:30:01 0.00 0.00 0 0 12 T SBSH 0
9 A 20040102 8:30:01 0.00 0.00 0 0 12 T SCHB 0
10 A 20040102 8:30:01 0.00 0.00 0 0 12 T STGI 0
```

From the TAQ data, we have both quote prices and transaction prices; thus, we can define various different spreads.

After matching trade and quote data for the same trading day, we can estimate an effective spread, which is defined below:

Equation 7

$$Effective\ spread = 2\ |\ log(P) - lag(log(MidQ))|$$

where P is the trading price,

lag is the lag operation,

and *MidQ* is the midpoint (average) of the bid and ask

On the other hand, a dollar-effective spread is defined below:

Equation 8

Dollar effective spread = *2*I*(P-midQ)*,

where I is a binary indicator: I = 1 (-1) for a buyer (seller)-initiated trade.

To determine the trade direction, we apply Lee and Ready's (1991) algorithm: a quote test first then a tick test. For a quote test, if the current trade price is higher than the midpoint of the latest quote, then it is a buyer-initiated trade. If it is lower than the midpoint, then it is a seller-initiated trade. If they are equal, we resort to the tick test: if the $P_t > P_{t-1}$ ($P_t < P_{t-1}$), then it is a buyer (seller)-initiated trade. The relative dollar spread is the dollar spread defined by the midquote.

Equation 9

Relative effective spread = dollar effective spread / MidQ

The following result show the daily mean spread, relative spread, and effective spread for IBM in January 2004.

```
      relative_  effective_
Obs symbol date spread n1 spread n2 spread n3
1  IBM 20040102 0.17047 40279 .001849 40279 .000610 5188
2  IBM 20040105 0.17497 47841 .001889 47841 .000705 5521
3  IBM 20040106 0.20079 51477 .002164 51477 .000842 5349
4  IBM 20040107 0.20798 48732 .002237 48732 .000685 4666
5  IBM 20040108 0.16538 37822 .001786 37822 .000681 5246
6  IBM 20040109 0.20104 52798 .002186 52798 .000858 6201
7  IBM 20040112 0.21274 78257 .002319 78257 .000902 5886
8  IBM 20040113 0.17791 57263 .001977 57263 .000782 6999
9  IBM 20040114 0.13584 26140 .001508 26140 .000655 4901
10 IBM 20040115 0.17635 44504 .001864 44504 .000706 8287
11 IBM 20040116 0.09802 34294 .001031 34294 .000355 6530
12 IBM 20040120 0.16956 27185 .001754 27185 .000696 6045
13 IBM 20040121 0.16418 35548 .001685 35548 .000712 5494
14 IBM 20040122 0.17113 33228 .001752 33228 .000823 4965
15 IBM 20040123 0.16479 37083 .001686 37083 .000759 5327
16 IBM 20040126 0.15984 32111 .001618 32111 .000896 5734
17 IBM 20040127 0.17076 36493 .001724 36493 .000758 5160
18 IBM 20040128 0.17923 42196 .001815 42196 .000723 5157
19 IBM 20040129 0.21802 65250 .002234 65250 .000702 6161
20 IBM 20040130 0.20131 38746 .002041 38746 .000925 5187
```

For IBM, the mean spread is 0.18 in January 2004.

```
symbol=IBM
The MEANS Procedure
  Analysis Variable : spread
  N Mean Std Dev Minimum Maximum

20 0.1760149 0.0276176 0.0980170 0.2180190
```

13.5. Chung and Zhang (2009)

To estimate spread, Chung and Zhang (2009) used two new variables added by CRSP (Center for Research in Security Prices) to the daily data. They then calculated the CRSP bid-ask spread of stock i on day using the following formula:

Equation 10

$$S = \frac{A_t - B_t}{\frac{A_t + B_t}{2}}$$

where A_t is the ask price of stock i on day t and B_t is the bid price of stock i on day t.

They find that the correlation of the CRSP spread and the TAQ spread is quite high.

Exercises

13.1. Why do we care about spread?

13.2. What is the formula to estimate a Roll's spread?

13.3. What is the main issue related to Roll's spread?

13.4 What are the advantages of using daily data measure spread?

13.5. What are the advantages and disadvantages of using high-frequency data to estimate spreads?

13.6. How do we measure spread by using daily data?

13.7. Write an R program for the Corwin and Schultz (2011) spread based on daily high and low considering the overnight return.

13.8. Is spread related to liquidity?

13.9. If you have an access of the TAQ database, what is the average bid-ask spread for the first fifty stocks in January 2004?

13.10. Repeat the above question to estimate relative spreads instead.

13.11. Use bid-ask spread as a benchmark, which measure of Amihud (2002) and Pastor and Stambaugh (2003) is a better measure?

CHAPTER 14

Liquidity Measures

Liquidity measures how quickly an investor could convert his/her investment into cash without losing much of its true value. According to Amihud (2002), liquidity reflects the impact of order flow on price. Since the illiquidity is the reciprocal of liquidity, the lower is an illiquidity value, and the higher is the liquidity of the underlying security. The daily illiquidity ratio is defined as below:

Equation 1

$$daily\ ratio = \frac{|R_t|}{P_t \cdot V_t},$$

where R_t is daily return at day t,
P_t is closing price at t,
and V_t is the daily trading volume at t.

Using following R codes, we can estimate IBM's one day illiquidity ratio.

```
> tl<-'http://finance.google.com/finance/historical?g='
> t2<-paste(t1,1IBMSstaxtdate=Jun+02,+19701,sep=")
> x<-read.csv(paste(t2,1Senddate=Dec+02,+2011&output=csv',sep="))
> x[1:2,]
    Date    Open    High    Low    Close    Volume
1 2-Dec-11 189.92 191.33 189.45 189.66 4962414
2 1-Dec-11 187.01 189.99 186.77 189.45 4862618
```

On December 02, 2011, we use two days' prices to estimate return then divide it by its corresponding dollar-trading volume (price times trading volume).

```
> abs((189.66-189.45))/189.45/(189.66*4962200)
[1] 1.177808e-12
```

Thus, IBM's one day illiquidity ratio is 1.177808e-12. We can interpret it as a trading of $100 million that day and would move the return by 0.012% (see codes below). For the same amount of dollar-trading volume, if its impact on return is smaller, the stock is more liquid.

```
> abs((189.66-189.45))/189.45/(189.66*4962200/1e8)*100
[1] 0.01177808
```

14.1. Introduction

Liquidity has many important practical and academic implications. Since liquidity is not observed directly but rather has a number of aspects that cannot be captured in a single measure, various proxies for liquidity have been used. Some easily obtained proxies are turnover, trading volume, or trading dollar value, firm size, etc. However, as pointed out by Lesmond (2002), these proxies may capture the effect of variables not related to liquidity. On the other hand, we can have finer and more accurate measures based on market microstructure data, such as bid-ask spread, amortized effective bid-ask spread, price response to signed order flow, and probability of information-based trading. Thus, the bid-ask spread based on the highfrequency data is more accurate.

Bid-ask spread and its variations are usually used as benchmarks. However, there are many disadvantages of using high-frequency data. First, the earliest year we can go is 1983 for American stocks while daily data can go as early as 1926. Because of this, many researchers design various liquidity measures based on daily data because they need a long history to time series. Second, the size of high-frequency data is huge, about 1T per month in 2010. It demands a huge amount of computing time if researchers plan to process all stocks' spread. The size of daily data is much smaller.

To measure liquidity of a stock (firm), researchers and practitioners use size of a firm, age of a firm, trading volume, dollar-trading volume, Amihud's illiquidity (2002), Pastor and Stambaugh's liquidity measure (2003), bid-ask spread, Liu (2006), number of financial analysts following a firm, and percentage of zero trading days, among others.

14.2. Size of a Firm

The bigger is a firm, the higher is the liquidity. The logic is that when a company has just started, its size will be relatively small. After it is listed on a stock exchange, its trading will be less frequent. In other words, its liquidity would be small. When a firm grows, its size will be growing as well. Its trading volumes will be become more active (i.e., more liquidity). Thus, the relative size will be good to measure liquidity. The *size* here is defined as "the price times the shares outstanding."

To find out the shares outstanding for IBM, we use the website of https://finance.yahoo.com/quote/IBM/key-statistics?ltr=1, see the following image.

Valuation Measures		Trading Information	
Market Cap (intraday) [5]	143.92B	**Stock Price History**	
Enterprise Value [3]	N/A	Beta	0.89
Trailing P/E	12.60	52-Week Change [3]	2.09%
Forward P/E [1]	11.01	S&P500 52-Week Change [3]	17.06%
PEG Ratio (5 yr expected) [1]	4.40	52 Week High [3]	182.790
Price/Sales (ttm)	1.81	52 Week Low [3]	142.500
Price/Book (mrq)	7.85	50-Day Moving Average [3]	153.684
Enterprise Value/Revenue [3]	N/A	200-Day Moving Average [3]	167.201
Enterprise Value/EBITDA [6]	N/A	**Share Statistics**	
		Avg Vol (3 month) [3]	4.55M
Financial Highlights		Avg Vol (10 day) [3]	4.3M
Fiscal Year		Shares Outstanding [5]	939.5M

14.3. Turnover

The *turnover* is defined as "the total trading volume divided by its corresponding market capitalization (price times the number of shares outstanding)." The higher is the turnover, the higher is the liquidity.

Assume two firms have the same market capitalization of $10 million. The first firm's annual turnover is 5 while the second firm's annual turnover is 1. Then we can claim that the first firm is more liquid than the second firm. To find out the current IBM stock price, we have a one-line code.

```
> t1<-'http://finance.google.com/finance/historical?g='
> t2<-paste(t1,1IBMSstaxtdate=Jun+02,+19701,sep=")
> x<-read.csv(paste(t2,'Senddate=Jun+16,+2017&output=csv',sep="))
> x[1:2,]
      Date    Open   High    Low   Close   Volume
1 15-Jun-17 153.29 154.69 153.29 154.22 4654297
2 14-Jun-17 153.97 154.94 152.94 153.81 3049726
>
> 939.5*154.22
[1] 144889.7
> 0.9395*154.22
[1] 144.8897
>
```

The size or market capitalization of IBM will be 145 billion on June 15, 2017.

14.4. Trading Volume

Here, the *trading volume* is defined as "the number of shares traded." Obviously the higher is the trading volume, the higher is the liquidity. The following codes will estimate the averages daily trading volumes for IBM and DELL. Since the trading volume for DELL is much higher than IBM, we can argue that DELL is more liquid.

```
> t1<-'http://finance.google.comifinance/historical?q=1
> t2<-paste(t1,1IBMSstartdate=Jun+02,+19701,sep=")
> x<-read.csv(paste(t2,1Senddate=Jun+16,+2017&output=csiP,sep="))
> mean(x[1:252,51)
[1] 162.5406
> t3<-paste(t1,'DELL&startdate=Jun+02,+19701,sep=")
> y<-read.csv(paste(t3,'&enddate=Jun+16,+2017&output=csiP,sep="))
> mean(y[1:252,51)
[1] 12.89635
```

To estimate the total trading volume in one year, such as in 2010, for DELL, we apply the following R codes:

```
> ticker<-"DELL"
> year<-2010
> tic-ihttp://finance.google.com/finance/historical?g='
> t2<-paste(tliticker,'&startdate=Jun+02,+1970',sep=")
> x<-read.csv(paste(t2,1&enddate=Dec+31,4-1,year,'&output=csvi,sep="))
> x[1,]
    Date Open High Low Close Volume
1 31-Dec-10 13.59 13.63 13.49 13.55 8352503
> x2<-data.frame(as.Date(x[,1],"%d-%b-%y"),x[,6])
> x2[,3]<-format(x2[,1],"%Y")
> colnames(x2)<-c("daten,"voln,myear")
> x2[1,]
date vol year
1 2010-12-31 8352503 2010
> x3<-subset(x2,x2$year==as.character(year))
> dim(x3)
[1] 4000 3
> sum(as.numeric(x36vol))/1e9
[1] 128.3438
```

14.5. Dollar-Trading Volume

Many argue that the number of shares traded is not a good measure of liquidity. For example, if we use dollar-trading volume, IBM is more liquid than DELL (see the results below).

```
> t1<-'http://finance.google.com/finance/historical?q=1
> t2<-paste(t1,1IBMSstartdaterun+02,+19701,sep=")
> x<-read.csv(paste(t2,1&enddate=Jun+16,-0,12017&output=csr,sep="))
> mean(x[1:252,6]*x[1:252,5])/10e6
[1] 61.51855
> t3<-paste(t1,1DELLSstartdate=grun+02,+1970',sep=")
> x2<-read.csv(paste(t3,1&enddate=ann+16,+',12017&output=csys,sep="))
> mean(x2[1:252,6]*x2[1:252,5])/10e6
[1] 416.4362
```

14.6. Impact of Trading on Price/Return

Assume that you are a mutual-fund manager. Because of some reasons, you want to buy $10 million of stock A. Since you cannot place an order of $10 million at once, you have to divide $10 million into several smaller trades. Now you worry about the impact of your first several trades on the price of the stock. If the first several trades push up the stock prices, your total trading cost will increase dramatically. The opposite is true when you intend to sell a large quantity of the same stock. The impact of one trade on the price will be a good measure of trading impact.

14.7. Amihud Illiquidity (2002)

Amihud's (2002) illiquidity (ILLIQ) is defined below:

Equation 4

$$ILLIQ = \frac{1}{N} \sum_{t-1}^{N} \frac{|R_t|}{DVOL_t}$$

where N is the number of trading day within one month,

R_t is the daily return,

and $DVOL$ is the dollar volume.

To estimate the illiquidity for IBM from March 21, 2011 to April 21, 2011, we have the following program:

```
> t1<-'http://financeogowle.com/finance/historical?q='
> t2<-paste(t1,1IBMstartdate=Mar+21,+20111,sep="")
> x<-read.csv(paste(t2,1Senddate=Apr+21,+','20116output=csvt,sep=""))
> n<-nrow(x)
> y<-data.frame(x[1:(n-1),5:6],(x[1:(n-1),5]-x[2:n,5])/x[2:n,5])
> colnames(y)<-c(npricenfmvoln,nret")
> illiq<-sum(abs(y$ret)/(y$price*y$vol))/nrow(y)
> illiq
[1] 6.566403e-12
```

ILLIQ is in monthly frequency based on daily data. The illiquidity measure designed by Amihud is quite simple since it does not need running regressions and there is no lag involved. Another advantage is that the measure can be used for a very short time, such as a couple of days. Of course, there are some disadvantages, such as the fact that stability of the measure is quite low. Amihud's illiquidity index is used by many researchers, such as Acharya and Pedersen (2004).

14.8. Pastor and Stambaugh's (2003) Measure

Based on the methodology and empirical evidence in Campbell, Grossman, and Wang (1993), Pastor and Stambaugh (2003) designed an excellent model to measure individual stock's liquidity and the market liquidity. Here is their model.

Equation 5

$$y_t = a + \beta_1 x_{1,t-1} + \beta_2 x_{2,t-1} + \varepsilon_t$$

where y_t is the excess daily stock return $(R_t - R_{m,t})$,

R_t is a stock's daily return,

$R_{m,t}$ is the return on the CRSP value-weighted market return;

$x_{1,t}$ is the stock's return,

$x_{2,t}$ is the signed dollar-trading volume, where the variable called sign is the sign of $(R_t - R_{m,t})$,

$prc_t * vol_t$ is the dollar-trading volume,

prc_t is the stock price,

and vol_t is the trading volume.

The regression is run based on daily data for each month. In other words, for each month, we get one β_2, which is defined as the liquidity measure for the underlying stock. The minimum number of observations for the regression should be larger than 15. Other constraints include using NYSE/AMEX stocks only. Stock prices should be between \$5 and \$1,000 at the end of the previous month, and only use common stocks with a share code of 10 or 11 from the CRSP database.

Although the paper does not specify, our empirical results suggest that a data filter is to delete observations with negative prices. An equivalent treatment is to delete the observations with zero volume. First, we download IBM and S&P 500 daily price data, estimate their daily returns, and merge them (see the R codes below).

```
> t1<-'http://finance.google.comifinancedthistorical?g=1
> t2<-paste(t1,1IBMSstartdate=Jun+02,+1970',sep=")
> d<-read.csv(paste(t2,1Senddate=Jun+16,+','2017&output=csvi,sep="))
> n<-nrow(d)  > ret<-d[1:(n-1),5]/d[2:n,5]-1
> x<-data.frame(as.Date(d[1:(n-1),1],"%d-M-%y"),d[1:(n-1),5:6],ret)
> colnames(x)<-c('DATE','PRICE','VOL','RET')
> x2<-subset(x,format(x$DATE,"%Th0)=="201601")
> loc<-url(ghttp://canisius.edu/-yany/RData/ffDaily.RDatan)
> load(loc)
> y<-data.frame(.ffDaily$DATE,.ffDaily$MKT_RF,.ffDaily$RF)
> y2<-subset(.ffDaily,format(.ffDaily$DATE,"%Y%mm)=="201601")
> z<-merge(x2,y2)
> head(z)
        DATE   PRICE    VOL             RET   METRE'    SMB     HML    RF
1 2016-01-04 135.95 5208900 -0.0121348641 -0.0159 -0.0086 0.0070 0
2 2016-01-05 135.85 3924793 -0.0007355645  0.0012  -0.002 0.0005 0
3 2016-01-06 135.17 4310939 -0.0050055208 -0.0135 -0.0015 0.0001 0
4 2016-01-07 132.86 7025760 -0.0170895909 -0.0244 -0.0031 0.0022 0
5 2016-01-08 131.63 4762706 -0.0092578654 -0.0111 -0.0048 0.0008 0
6 2016-01-11 133.23 4974436  0.0121552837 -0.0006 -0.0063 0.0040 0
```

After that, we run the Pastor and Stambaugh's regression by using one month data to find the coefficient of x2, which is our liquidity measure.

```
> y<-z$RET-(z$MET_RF+z$RF)
> xl<-z$RET-(z$MET_RF+z$RF)
> x2<-sign(x1)•z$PRICE*z$VOL
> x<-cbind(xl,x2)

> Im(y-x)
Call: lm(formula = y x)

Coefficients:
(Intercept)        xxl              xx2
0.000e+00  1.000e+00      2.827e-28
```

The liquidity measure in this case is 4.012e-11. We interpret that in the Pastor and Stambaugh's framework, a $100-million dollar-trading volume of IBM would move its excess return by 0.4%.

```
> 4.012e-11*1e8*100
[1] 0.4012
```

14.9. Liu (2006)

Liu (2006) designed a liquidity measure based on turnover and the number of zero daily trading days.

Equation 6

$$LMx = \left[days\ with\ zero\ tradign\ vlume + \frac{\frac{1}{x - month\ turnover}}{Deflator} \right] \cdot \frac{21x}{N}$$

where LMx is the liquidity measure, as the standardized turnover-adjusted number of zero daily trading volumes over the prior x months. The x-month turnover is turnover the prior x month, estimated as the sum of daily turnover over the prior x months. Daily turnover is the ration of the number of shares traded in a day to the number of shares outstanding at the end of the day. N is the total number of trading days in the market over the prior x months. The defector is chosen such that

Equation 7

$$0 < \frac{\frac{1}{x - month\ turnover}}{Deflator} < 1$$

14.10. Firm's Liquidity Divided by the Market Liquidity

There is no doubt that the liquidity of a firm might change over time. For example, using a certain measure, we find that a firm's liquidity has improved over the last year. Here, we can have two explanations: 1) the whole market is more liquid, or 2) the firm is more liquid while the whole market remains the same. Sometimes we have to distinguish between the two effects. For this very purpose, we can define a relative liquidity (or illiquidity) measure as the firm's liquidity divided by the market liquidity, which is a valueweighted individual liquidity. The weight will be the market capitalizations of individual firms.

14.11. Bid-Ask Spread from High-Frequency Data

High-frequency data means the transactions trade and quote data by seconds (or millisecond), such as TAQ (NYSE trade and quote) database. The market makers or dealers post their bid-and-ask price to increase the liquidity of the underlying stocks. The spread between bid-ask will be their profit. Spread represents the liquidity as well: the lower the spread, the higher the liquidity of the underlying security. For more details about TAQ, see chapter 15: "Using R to Process TAQ."

For many reasons, researchers and practitioners have developed many methods to estimate spread by using low-frequency data. One reason is the availability of high-frequency data. The second reason is that before 1983, there was no high-frequency data available for American stocks.

The most famous example is Roll (1984) using the daily serial autocovariance to estimate spread. The second example is Corwin and Schultz's (2010) high-low spread. They use two adjacent days' high and low prices to estimate the spread. For more details, see chapter 18: "Spread (Transaction Costs)."

Exercises

14.1. What is the common-sense definition of liquidity in terms of assets?

14.2. How do you measure the liquidity of assets?

14.3. Why do investors prefer more liquid assets?

14.4. What is the definition of turnover?

14.5. Using turnover, what do we try to measure?

14.6. Why does a typical investor care about liquidity?

14.7. How many ways can we measure a stock's liquidity?

14.8. What is the simplest way to estimate liquidity?

14.9. Which liquidity measure has the most power?

14.10. For a trading strategy, why do we care about impact of a trading?

14.11. How do you measure the impact of a trading?

14.12. For the following stocks, estimate their annual illiquidity (Amihud 2002) for 2010: IBM, DELL, MSFT, WMAT, and C.

14.13. For the above stocks, estimate their Pastor and Stambaugh (2003) measure.

14.14. Are Amihud (2002) and Pastor and Stambaugh (2003) negatively correlated?

14.15. Write an R program to estimate the sum of annual-trading volume for a set of input tickers such as fifty of them.

14.16. Write an R program to estimate an industry mean in terms of liquidity (or illiquidity).

14.17. Write an R program to estimate an equal-weighted monthly market liquidity from January 2010 to December 2010.

14.18. If you have an access of the TAQ database, what is the average bid-ask spread for the first fifty stocks in January 2004?

14.19. Repeat the above question to estimate relative spreads instead.

14.20. Using bid-ask spread as a benchmark, which measures of Amihud (2002) and Pastor and Stambaugh (2003) is a better measure? (Assume that you have access to the TAQ database.)

CHAPTER 15

Using R to Process TAQ (High-Frequency Data)

For a person who has never touched TAQ (NYSE trade and quote) binary data, he/she can print the first ticker within three minutes. Assume we have one binary index file called **T200411a.idx**, where T stands for trade and a represents the first trading day in a month. To retrieve the first ticker, we have three-line R codes.

```
> in.file<-file("c:/temp/T200411a.idx","rb")
> x<-readBin(in.file,character(),size=4,n=1,endian="little")
> substr(x,1,10)
[1] "A "
```

"**A**" is the ticker of the first stock from that index file. Below are a few records from the same index file. The first record indicates that line 1 to line 24686 from a corresponding data file (**T200411a. bin**) belong to **A** on November 1, 2004.

```
A 20041101 1 24686
AA 20041101 24687 57606
AAA 20041101 57607 59762
AABC 20041101 59763 60014
AAC 20041101 60015 60309
```

From the corresponding data file (**T200411a.bin**), the first three lines are given below.

```
time price size tseq g127 corr cond ex
9:30:18 24.95 19600 220946 40 0
9:30:19 24.95 400 0 0 0
9:30:19 24.95 100 0 0 0
```

15.1. Introduction to High-Frequency Data

Many hedge funds and Wall Street banks use certain high-frequency trading strategies by buying hundreds or thousands of stocks and selling them one or a few seconds later. With such a strategy, they can earn a tenth of a penny off each share. In 2009 and 2010, those financial institutions jointly earned $12.9 billion in profit. The data they used to test and implement their strategies is high-frequency transaction data, such as TAQ. Currently the demand of high-frequency trading specialists is quite high (see Web page at http://efinancialCareer.com by typing the keywords *high frequency*).

15.2. TAQ (NYSE Trade and Quote Data)

TAQ database contains high-frequency transaction data for stocks traded in the United States. The related research area is called market microstructure. Since TAQ became available in '90s, the related research has achieved many important discoveries. For example, Easley et al. (2002, 2010) show that private information, proxied by PIN (probability of informed trading), could be a priced risk factor in a multiple-factor model. Their PIN estimates are based on the output using TAQ. TAQ contains data from 1993 onward.

ISSM (the Institute for the Study of Security Markets) is another high-frequency database that has data from 1983 to 1992 for American equity. The size of TAQ data sets is huge. Over years, the volume of TAQ has grown exponentially. The joined size in January 1993 is about 350 megabytes while this value is 36 gigabytes in December 2005, a 10186% increase! The huge size definitely causes headaches to researchers and practitioners. Other ways to process TAQ is to use Fortran, C++ (C), or SAS. In this chapter, we will first demonstrate how to process one day's high-frequency data. Later we will show how to generate a loop to process multiple years' data.

15.3. One Day's Data (Four Data Sets)

For teaching, it is more than enough to have just one day's data showing how to retrieve data from an index file, from a binary data file, how to merge trade with quote, how to estimate spread, relative spread, realized spread, and trading direction (whether a trade is buyer- or seller-initiated). Most of the times, it is not adequate for most research topics by studying just one day's data. However, understanding how to process one day's high-frequency data is the key. After mastering it, processing multiple years' data would be a simple extension. I select November 1, 2004 as our day (see its four data sets below). Two index files have an extension of .idx, and two data files have an extension of .bin.

```
12/01/2004 04:03 PM 1,800,548,334 Q200411a.bin
12/01/2004 04:03 PM 182,424 Q200411a.idx
12/01/2004 04:08 PM 184,899,853 T200411a.bin
12/01/2004 04:08 PM 169,334 T200411a.idx
4 File(s) 1,985,799,945 bytes
```

T200411a.idx is an index file for consolidated trade (CT); T200411a.bin is its binary data file. Q200411a.idx is another index file for consolidated quote (CQ) while Q200411a.bin is its corresponding data file. The total size of those four files is close to 2 gigabytes. The letter a in the file names represents the first trading day in that month. Since there are twenty-one trading days in November 2004, the last letter will be a u, such as T200411u.idx.

```
> letters[21]
[1] "u "
> for(i in 1:26) if(letters[i]=='u')print(i)
[1] 21
```

15.4. Setup and Global Variables: idx.T, idx.Q, bin.T, and bin.Q

For each data set, we usually have two-line codes. The first line defines the location (path) and name of the data set while the next command defines a file handler.

```
> path_index_CT<-"c:/temp/T200411a.idx"
> index_CT<-file(path_index_CT, "rb")
```

For four data sets, we should have eight lines. It is quite often that we find ourselves confused since we are not sure of the difference between **path_index_CT** and **index_CT**. Why not write a function to define four global variables such as **idx.T**, **idx.Q**, **bin.T**, and **bin.Q** and use them in the rest of our program? Below is such a function.

```
setup<-function(path,day){
   idx.T<<-file(paste(path,'T',day,'.idx',sep=""),'rb')
   idx.Q<<-file(paste(path,'Q',day,'.idx',sep=""),'rb')
   bin.T<<-file(paste(path,'T',day,'.bin',sep=""),'rb')
   bin.Q<<-file(paste(path,'Q',day,'.bin',sep=""),'rb')
   return('Four global variables: idx.T, idx.Q, bin.T and bin.Q')
}
```

The double less-than signs, <<, define a global variable that can be accessed from anywhere within our program. For example, whenever we want to use a CT index, we use **idx.T**. The **file()** function defines a file handler, and **rb** means "read binary." We need to call this setup function after we launch our program.

```
>path<-"c:/temp/" # modify this part accordingly
>day<-"200411a " # modify this part accordingly
>setup(path,day) # run just once
```

15.5. Two Data Sets for CT

Each index data set contains four variables: ticker, date, beginning line (**BEGREC**), and ending line (**ENDREC**). Below, the first record from **T200411a.idx** indicates that the corresponding data file (**T200411a.bin**) has records from lines 1 to 3377 for stock A on November 1, 2004.

```
A 20041101 1 3377
```

Assuming the location of our four data sets is **c:\temp**, from R, we issue the following three lines to retrieve the first data item (first ticker):

```
# run setup program first
> x<-readBin(idx.T,character(),size=4,n=1,endian="little")
> substr(x,1,10)
[1] "A"
```

The **readBin()** function reads in data with a binary format. Since ticker is a string, we use **character()**. To get the next number, we the have following two-line codes.

```
> seek(idx.T,10)
> readBin(idx.T,integer(),size=4,n=1,endian='little')
[1] 20041101
```

The **seek(idx.T,10)** moves our pointer to the tenth byte from the beginning of the file defined by **idx.T**. For the next two integers (**BEGREC, ENDREC**), we call the **readBin()** function twice.

```
> readBin(idx.T,integer(),size=4,n=1,endian='little')
[1] 1
> readBin(idx.T,integer(),size=4,n=1,endian='little')
[1] 3377
```

15.6. Sequential and Random Access

The **seek()** function is critical for retrieving data efficiently. To print the one hundredth ticker on our screen, we can have two approaches: 1) Retrieve the first record then go to the next one until we reach the one hundredth ticker. Obviously this is not efficient since we don't need to reach the first ninetynine records. 2) Skip the first ninety-nine lines by using the **seek()** function. The first method is called sequential access while the second one is called random access. To show the one hundredth ticker, we have the following three lines:

```
> seek(idx.T,(100-1)*22)
> x<-readBin(idx.T,character(),size=4,n=1,endian='little')
> substr(x,1,10)
[1] "AD "
```

The first command line skips 2978 (99*22) bytes from the beginning of the data file. Obviously 22 is the length of one record (four variables). See table 1 for more details. To find its other three variables, we have fourline R codes.

```
> seek(ind.T,(100-1)*22+10)
[1] 2196
> readBin(ind.T,integer(),size=4,n=1,endian='little')
[1] 20041101
> readBin(ind.T,integer(),size=4,n=1,endian='little')
[1] 125645
> readBin(ind.T,integer(),size=4,n=1,endian='little')
[1] 126008
```

Those three outputs suggest that the one hundredth ticker is AD, and it has 364 lines of data from its data file (**T200411a.bin**). The starting line is **125645**, and the ending line is **126008**. Again, if we intend to read in those records from **T200411a.bin**, we simply skip the first (**125645-1**) lines by using the **seek()** function. Usually we don't search each ticker manually. However, typing those codes, we can familiarize ourselves with the structure of TAQ index files. To find out the last ticker, we have three-line codes.

```
> seek(idx.T,where=-22,origin='end')
> x<-readBin(idx.T,character(),size=4,n=1,endian='little')
> substr(x,1,10)
[1] "ZXZZT "
```

To find out how many tickers available from an index file, see codes below:

```
> seek(idx.T,where=0,origin='end')
[1] 169312
> p2<-seek(idx.T)
> p2/22
[1] 7697
```

Now we turn to the binary data file related to CT (see the following codes to get the first value, which is time). According to the TAQ manual, *time* is defined as "seconds from midnight."

```
# run the setup program
> readBin(bin.T, "integer",size=4,n=1,endian='little')
[1] 34218
```

Thus, **34218** stands for **9:30:18** (see codes below).

```
> h<-as.integer(34218/3600)
> h
[1] 9
> m<-as.integer((34218-h*3600)/60)
> m
[1] 30
> s<-34218-h*3600-m*60
> s
[1] 18
```

To show the time variable for the first ten observations, we have the following codes. Again, **29** is a critical value, which is the size of each record (see table 2 for more details).

```
for(i in 1:10){
  seek(in.file, (i-1)*29)
  print(readBin(in.file, "integer",size=4,n=1,endian='little'))
}
[1] 34218
[1] 34219
[1] 34219
[1] 34219
[1] 34222
[1] 34222
[1] 34222
[1] 34222
[1] 34223
[1] 34225
```

15.7. Time Format of H:M:S

We can write a function program to convert time in second into an H:M:S format.

```
hms<-function(x){
h<-as.integer(x/3600)
m<-as.integer(x/60)-h*60
s<-x-h*3600 - m*60
cat("h:m:s=",h,":",m,":",s,"\n")
}
> hms(34218)
h:m:s= 9 : 30 : 18
```

15.8. Several Small Programs

Most of times, we write and use small functions. A few examples are given below.

Example 1. The function **show_index_n1_n2()** takes just three inputs: **idx.T** (or **idx.Q**), beginning line, and ending line. Assume that we are interested in the first two lines from the CT index file.

```
# run setup program first
> show_index_n1_n2(idx.T,1,2)
A 20041101 1 3377
AA 20041101 3378 7413
```

Example 2. The show_last_ticker() function offers the last ticker and the number of stocks for a given index file.

```
# idx.T is defined
> show_last_ticker(idx.T)
last ticker n
=========== ====
ZXZZT 7696
```

Example 3. The function show_trade_n1_n2()

```
# run setup program first
> show_trade_n1_n2(bin.T,3378,3380)
time price size tseq g127 corr cond ex
==== ====== ===== ==== ==== ==== ==== ===
9 : 30 : 55 32.65 49500 216317 40 0
9 : 30 : 55 32.65 100 216320 40 0
9 : 30 : 56 32.65 100 0 0 0
```

From the index file, we know that stock AA has records from 3378 to 7413. Thus, the above observations belong to AA. Here is a general rule: for a given stock ticker, we search its index file to find the starting and ending lines. Then we go to the corresponding binary data file to retrieve the corresponding data.

Example 4. The get_trade_given_line_number() function

```
# run setup function first
> get_trade_given_line_number(12)
time price size tseq g127 corr cond ex
34230 24.89 100 220954 40 0 E
```

15.9. Two Data Sets Related to CQ

The structure of **Q200411a.idx** is exactly the same as that of **T200411a.idx**.

```
# run setup first
> show_index_n1_n2(idx.Q,1,5)
ticker date begrec endrec
==== ====== ===== ====
A 20041101 1 24686
AA 20041101 24687 57606
AAA 20041101 57607 59762
AABC 20041101 59763 60014
AAC 20041101 60015 60309
```

We have a function called **show_quote_n1_n2()** that can be used to retrieve CQ data.

```
# run setup()
> show_quote_n1_n2(2,20) # show lines 2 to 20
```

I wrote a function called **get_quote_given_line_number()**, which outputs corresponding record from a CQ binary file.

```
# run setup()
> get_quote_given_line_number(24686)
  time bid ofr qseq bidsiz ofrsiz mode ex MMID
1 72001 0 0 0 0 201326592 21504 T
```

From the index file, we know that line 24686 is the last record for A and that the next line of 24687 is the first line for AA. Thus, we should expect the time stamp of line 24686 to be bigger (since it is afternoon) than the time stamp of line 24687 (since it is in the morning). The following result confirms this (72001 > 28863).

```
> get_quote_given_line_number(24686)
time bid ofr qseq bidsiz ofrsiz mode ex MMID
1 72001 0.01 2000 0 1 1 12 T
> get_quote_given_line_number(24687)
time bid ofr qseq bidsiz ofrsiz mode ex MMID
1 28863 0.01 2000 0 1 1 12 T
```

Obviously those two quotes are not valid: the BID is 0.01 while the OFR is 2000! We can apply our hms() function to find out the time in the H:M:S format.

```
h:m:s= 20 : 0 : 1
> x<-72001
> hms(x)
h:m:s= 20 : 0 : 1
```

15.10. Adding Filters

It is important that we clean the TAQ data before we can possibly use it. For CT, usually we have thefollowing filters: 1) **price** >0, 2) **corr** = 0, and 3) **cond** not in ("O", "Z", "B", "T", "L", "G", "W", "J", "K").

CORR is defined as "correction indicator" (e.g., CORR=0: regular trade). COND is defined as "condition of sale" (e.g., **COND="O"**: an opening trade that occurs in sequence but is reported to the tape in a later time; **COND="B"**: bunched trade [aggregate of two or more regular trades executed within sixty seconds with same price]; **COND="G"**: a bunched trade not reported within ninety seconds).

For CQ, our filters will be: 1) **bid** >0, **ofr** >0, **ofr**>bid, 2) **size** : bidsiz>0 ofrsiz>0, and 3) **MODE** not in (4, 7, 9, 11, 13, 14, 15, 19, 20, 27, 28). MODE is defined as "quote condition" (e.g., **MODE=4**: regulatory halt [news dissemination]; **MODE=7**: nonregulatory halt [order imbalance]; and MODE=9: regulatory halt).

15.11. How to Merge Trade with Quote

It seems that we simply match trade and quote data sets for the same stock over the same day by time stamp (see codes below).

```
>x<-get_trade("ibm",500)
>y<-get_quote("ibm",500)
>z<-merge(x,y,all=T)
```

However, Lee and Ready (1991) argue that that the quote data is more active than trade data since investors look at quote data for the best choice while the record of a trade is just a routine bookkeeping.

15.12. Five-Second Rule, Two-Second Rule, and Zero-Second Rule

Based on their empirical results, Lee and Ready (1991) recommend a so-called five-second rule: move the time stamp of a trade by adding five seconds.

```
>x<-get_trade("ibm",500)
> x[1,]<-x[1,]+5
>y<-get_quote("ibm",500)
>z<-merge(x,y,all=T)
```

Madhavan et al. (2002) suggest a two-second rule after they tested different quote lags of zero, two, five, and ten seconds. Vergote (2005) suggests a two-second rule. Other researchers—such as Ellis, Michaely, and O'Hara (2000) and Peterson and Sirri (2002)—suggest no time lag (i.e., zero-second rule) in applying both the Lee and Ready algorithm based on the argument that the advance of technology would eliminate any lag during the reporting of trades.

15.13. Who Initiated a Trade?

The Lee and Ready methodology (1991) is widely used to identify who initiated a trade: a buyer or a seller. More specifically, we conduct a quote test first. If it is not satisfied, then we conduct a tick test. First, we merge trade data with quote data.

Quote test. If the price is bigger than the midpoint of bid and ask, the trade is buyer initiated. If the price is smaller than the midpoint, the trade is seller initiated. If the quote test fails, then go to tick test.

Tick test. If the price is greater than the previous price, it is buyer initiated. If the price is lesser than the previous price, it is seller initiated.

Ellis, Michaely, and O'Hara (2000) introduce another classification algorithm. They recommend that trades executed at the prevailing bid and ask quotes be classified as seller and buyer initiated. For all other trades (i.e., all trades inside or outside the prevailing bid-ask spread), a tick test is used. Therefore, the only difference between their algorithms and Lee and Ready's is the classification of trades executed at prices not equal to bid, ask, and midpoint prices.

15.14. Using a Quote Test in an R package of FinAsym

The description of the package says, "Classifies implicit trading activity from market quotes and computes the probability of informed trading." We will discuss the contents of probability of informed trading in the last subsection. According to the manual, we have the following example to classify the trading direction by using quotes only. The logic behind using the quote test only is that for the OTC (over-the-counter market), trade data is difficult and less reliable.

```
>library(FinAsym)
x<-matrix(c(4.56, 4.7, 4.57, 4.64, 4.53,
4.65, 4.59, 4.66, 4.55, 4.65, 4.59, 4.66, 4.59,
4.66, 4.55, 4.65, 4.55, 4.65, 4.55, 4.65, 4.59,
4.66, 4.55, 4.65, 4.59, 4.66, 4.59, 4.66),nrow=14, byrow=TRUE)
> classify_quotes(x,1,2, "2/2/2012")
[1] "Classification ok on trading day: 2/2/2012 "
$no_trades
[1] 4
$sell_trades
[1] 5
$buy_trades
[1] 4
```

When the midpoint at time t is lower than the previous one (at *t-1*), it is a buyer-initiated trade. If it is higher than the previous one, it is a seller-initiated trade. If they are equal, then we cannot decide who initiated the "trade."

```
>n_buy<-0
>n_sell<-0
>not_sure<-0
>n<-nrow(x)
for(i in 2:n){
  if(mean(x[i,])>mean(x[i-1,])){
  n_buy<-n_buy+1
  }else if (mean(x[i,])<mean(x[i-1,])){
  n_sell<-n_sell+1
  }else{
  not_sure<-not_sure+1
  }
}
> cat("not_sure",not_sure,"\n")
not_sure 4
> cat("n_sell",n_sell,"\n")
n_sell 5
> cat("n_buy",n_buy,  "\n")
n_buy 4
```

15.15. Mean Spread, Relative Spread, Realized Spread

To estimate a stock's spread based on quote, we deal with two data sets such as **Q200411a.idx** and **Q200411a.bin**. Actually there are three steps in this assignment. The first part is to print on screen five valid quotes for a random stock. Thus, we can check our average spread manually. This also gives students a taste of data. The next step is to get all stocks by using five (or another small number) valid quotes to estimate daily average spread for all stocks. The last step is to use all valid quotes for all stocks.

Effective spread. First, we have to match trade with quote first. Then we estimate the midpoint of bid and ask. Thus, at time *t*, we have P_t (trading price) and $midPoint_t$ ((bid+ask)/2). Using the Lee and Ready (1991) methodology, we identify the direction of a trade *D=1* for a buyer-initiated trade while *D=-1* for a seller-initiated trade. The effective spread is defined as

Equation 1

$$effective\ spread_t = 2 * D_t\ (P_t - midPoint_t)$$

The percentage-effective spread is defined below:

Equation 2

$$percentage\ effective\ spread_t = 2 * D_t\ \frac{(P_t - midPoint_t)}{midPoint_t}$$

15.16. PIN (Probability of Informed Trading)

Easley et al. (1996) assume that trading days are independent from one another. On any trading day, nature decides whether an information event occurs (with a probability of α) or not (with a probability of $1-\alpha$). Informed traders know the impact of the new information on the underlying securities. When an event occurs, it can be either bad (with a probability of δ) or good (with a probability of $1-\delta$). Trades arrive according to Poisson processes. Uninformed traders submit buy (sell) orders at the daily arrival rates of e_b (e_s). On an event day, informed traders buy at good news or sell at bad news with the same rate of m. The probability of observing B_i (buyer-initiated trades) and S_i (seller-initiated trades) on each trading day i is represented by the following equation:

Equation 3

$$L(\theta \mid B_i, S_i) = \alpha(1-\delta)e^{-(\mu+\varepsilon_b)}\frac{(\mu+\varepsilon_b)^{B_i}}{B_i!}e^{-\varepsilon_s}\frac{\varepsilon_s^{S_i}}{S_i!}$$

$$+\alpha\delta e^{-\varepsilon_b}\frac{\varepsilon_b^{B_i}}{B_i!}e^{-(\mu+\varepsilon_s)}\frac{(\mu+\varepsilon_s)^{S_i}}{S_i!}+(1-\alpha)e^{-\varepsilon_b}\frac{\varepsilon_b^{B_i}}{B_i!}e^{-\varepsilon_s}\frac{\varepsilon_s^{S_i}}{S_i!}$$

where $\theta = (\alpha, \delta, \mu, \varepsilon_b, \varepsilon_s)$, which is the parameter set researchers intend to estimate. PIN is defined as Equation 4

$$PIN = \frac{\alpha\mu}{\alpha\mu + \varepsilon_b + \varepsilon_s}.$$

Intuitively PIN measures the fraction of informed trades out of the total trades. First, let's look at a **B_S** data set here. B is the daily summation for all buyer-initiated trades while S is the daily (period) summation for all seller-initiated trade. Based on the output below, for the first day, we have N=9 (trades cannot be identified), B=6, and S=13.

```
x<-c(9,6,13)
B_S<- matrix(x,3,15)
> B_S[,1:5]
    [,1] [,2] [,3] [,4] [,5]
[1,] 9 9 9 9 9
[2,] 6 6 6 6 6
[3,] 13 13 13 13 13
```

The following example is adopted from the R package called **FinAsym**. Simplifying the program and the original PIN formula might be problematic.

```
>library(FinAsym)
>x<-c(9,6,13)
>B_S<- matrix(x,3,15) # structure of each column: N, B, S
>par0 <- c(0.4, 0.5, 0.5, 0.5)
>out <- optim(par0, pin_likelihood,gr=NULL,B_S)
>alpha <- out$par[3]
>mu <- out$par[2]
>delta <- out$par[4]
>epsi <- out$par[1]
>pin <- alpha*mu/(alpha*mu+ 2*epsi)
>print(pin)
 [1] 0.1414034
```

One issue is that the PIN will change when we choose different initial values. Try the following different initial values. For a more detailed discussion, see Yan and Zhang (2012).

```
> par0 <- c(0.4, 0.5, 0.5, 0.5)
> out <- optim(par0, pin_likelihood,gr=NULL,B_S)
> alpha <- out$par[3]
> mu <- out$par[2]
> delta <- out$par[4]
> epsi <- out$par[1]
> pin <- alpha*mu/(alpha*mu+ 2*epsi)
>
> pin
[1] 0.1779455
```

15.17. One Day vs. Multiple Years

For multiple years' data, we have a four-step approach.

Step 1. We generate a text file by using the following DOS command. Here we assume that we are saving all our binary data sets under the directory **e:\TAQ_binary_data**.

```
dir e:\TAQ_binary_data /b /s >t.txt
```

Step 2. Generate an index file with a date and its corresponding directory.

```
Date directory
20040102 2004/200401disk1_TAQ_JAN04_02_05/
20040103 2004/200401disk2_TAQ_JAN04_02_05/
20040104 2004/200401disk1_TAQ_JAN04_02_05/
20040105 2004/200401disk2_TAQ_JAN04_02_05/
20040106 2004/200401disk1_TAQ_JAN04_02_05/
20040109 2004/200401disk2_TAQ_JAN04_06_11/
20041101 2004/200411disk1_TAQ_NOV04_01_05/
20041102 2004/200411disk1_TAQ_NOV04_01_05/
20041103 2004/200411disk1_TAQ_NOV04_01_05/
```

Step 3. Write an R program to read this index file for a given date. For example, for **20040102**, our program outputs a path of **2004/200401disk1_TAQ_JAN04_02_05/** and a day of **200411a**.

Step 4. We call our **setup()** function to update our four global variables. In our main program, we generate a loop starting from our **date1** and conduct our tests. After that, we move to **date2**. We repeat this until we reach our last date.

15.18. How to Make Our Search More Efficient

When our data sets are relatively small, it is less critical in terms of the efficiency of our programs. However, since TAQ is huge, we should make our program as efficiently as possible. Here are several examples.

Example 1. Assume we have sixty days' data. We plan to retrieve five hundred stocks' data. If we call the **which_date()** function to convert **20041101** to **200411a**, we end up calling the function thirty thousand times (i.e., downloading a market index thirty thousand times). The efficient way is to just download the market index once.

Example 2. To search a binary index file, we have two ways: sequential and binary. If we use a sequential search, we read in about half of our observations for each search. Since **T200411a.idx** has 7,697 tickers, we read 3,848 lines to get our result. This is not efficient. The binary search is much more efficient (see related appendix).

Example 3. To find out who initiated a trade, the conventional thinking is that for a given stock and day, such as IBM on November 1, 2004, we retrieve CT and CQ first, clean them, merge them, and finally apply a function conducting Lee and Ready's (1991) test. However, such a procedure is extremely inefficient since for each trade (or quote), we have four passes. If we can read each trade and quote just once, our speed will increase by 400%! Another equally serious problem is that such an approach merges two big matrices. For example, for stock A on November 1, 2004, we match a trade matrix (3,377 by 8) with a quote matrix (24,686 by 9). For a more heavily traded stock, those two matrices will be even much bigger. For the solution, we have the next section.

15.19. A More Efficient Way to Find Trading Directions

We can have a more efficient way to do so in terms of speed and computer resource. We intend to apply Lee and Ready's (1991) method suing IBM data on November 1, 2004. Below is a general procedure:

Step 1. Find out **BEGREC** and **ENDRED** for both CT and CQ for IBM.

Step 2. A) Find the first valid trade and call it **previous trade**. B) Find the next valid trade and call it **current trade.**

Step 3. Find a valid quote from CQ; and if its time stamp is before our **current trade**, call it **previous quote**. Repeat this step many times until the following situation happens: the **previous** quote is before the **current trade** and the **current quote** is after the **current trade** (see below).

```
# previous trade ————————————
# ————————————————————— previous quote
# current trade ———————————
# ————————————————————— current quote
```

Step 4. Apply Lee and Ready's (1991) algorithm to assign a trading direction, such as **B=1** for a buyerinitiated trade, **B=-1** for a seller-initiated trade, and **B=NA** for a trade we cannot determine.

Step 5. Replace the **previous trade** with the **current trade** and go back to Step 2B until we reach the end of the record (**ENDREC**). The beauty of the above procedure is that we use each trade and each quote just once. Another critical feature is that at any time, we only have about six records in the memory. This method is way better than our conventional way.

Table 15.1. Structure of a binary index file (the size [bit] of an index file is 22 with 4 variables)

#	Name of the variable	Meaning	Size	Type
1	Ticker	Stock symbol	10	Character
2	Date	Trading date	4	Integer
3	Begrec	Beginning record	4	Integer
4	Endrec	Ending record	4	Integer

Table 15.2A. Structure of binary CT (consolidated trade) file before October 2008 (the size [bit] of a CT file is 29 with 8 variables)

#	Name of the variable	Meaning	Size	Type
1	Time	Trading time	4	Integer
2	Price	Trading price	8	Float
3	Tseq	Sequence number	4	Integer
4	Size	Trading size	4	Integer
5	G127	G127 rule	2	Integer
6	CORR	Correction	2	Integer
7	COND	Sale condition	4	Character
8	Ex	Exchange	1	Character

Table 15.2B. Structure of binary CT (consolidated trade) file after October 2008 (the size [bit] of a CT file is 19 with 7 variables)

#	Name of the variable	Meaning	Size	Type
1	Time	Trading time	4	Integer
2	Price	Trading price	4	Float
3	Tseq	Sequence number	4	Integer
4	Size	Trading size	4	Integer
5	G127	G127 rule	2	Integer
6	CORR	Correction	2	Integer
7	COND	Sale condition	4	Character

Table 15.3A. Structure of a binary CQ (consolidated quote) file before October 2008 (the size [bit] of a CQ file is 39 with 9 variables)

#	Name of the variable	Meaning	Size	Type
1	Time	Trading time	4	Integer
2	Price	Bid price	8	Float
3	Ofr	Ask price	8	Float
4	Qseq	Sequence number	4	Integer
5	Bidsiz	Bid size	4	Integer
6	Asksiz	Ask size	4	Integer
7	MODE	quote condition	2	Integer
8	EX	Exchange	1	Character
9	MMID	NASDAQ market maker	4	Character

Table 15.3B. Structure of a binary CQ (consolidated quote) file after October 2008 (the size [bit] of a CQ file is 27 with 8 variables)

#	Name of the variable	Meaning	Size	Type
1	Time	Trading time	4	Integer
2	Bid	Bid price	4	Float
3	Ofr	Ask price	4	Float
4	Bidsiz	Bid size	4	Integer
5	Asksiz	Ask size	4	Integer
6	MODE	Quote condition	2	Integer
7	EX	Exchange	1	Character
8	MMID	NASDAQ market maker	4	Character

Exercises

15.1. What is the use of TAQ (high-frequency data)?

15.2. Define a bid-ask spread.

15.3. Why do we care about a bid-ask spread?

15.4. What do CT and CQ stand for?

15.5. For each trading day, how many binary files should we access?

15.6. For the TAQ database, what is the relationship between an index file and a data file?

15.7. What is the difference between sequential access and random access?

15.8. What is the use of a binary search?

15.9. How do you write an R program to do a binary search?

15.10. How do you retrieve all quote data from 9:30 a.m. 10:50 a.m.?

15.11. How can I get the last trade for a given date from the TAQ?

15.12. How can I get both the trade data and the quote data for a list of firms for a given date?

15.13. I got a list of samples drawn from CRSP. How can I match them with the TAQ?

15.14. How do you get a list of all the firms (e.g., tickers or, better yet, CUSIP) in TAQ for any given month?

15.15. Which firm ID is the best choice to match CRSP with TAQ: CUSIP, TICKER, or others?

15.16. How do you retrieve S&P 500, S&P 100, DJIA, MSCI USA, and S&P futures, AMEX highfrequency (three-minute) data ?

15.17. How do you get data point every half an hour from TAQ?

15.18. What is the difference between accessing one-day TAQ data and accessing multiple-year TAQ data?

15.19. How can I identify preferred stocks?

15.20. Why is it that in the TAQ database for the stock with the ticker symbol PALM on March 2, 2000, the offer or ask price was actually smaller than bids and traded prices?

15.21. How do you retrieve all CUSIP from TAQ?

15.22. How can I randomly select 100 firms from TAQ?

15.23. Is it possible to retrieve the intraday data for a market index such as S&P 500?

15.24. After issuing the following codes, we have one record. Which stock does it belong to?

```
> in.file<-file("c:/temp/Q200411a.bin","rb")
> get_quote_given_line_number(in.file,5000)
time bid ofr qseq bidsiz ofrsiz mode ex MMID
1 38084 24.65 25.17 0 1 1 12 X
```

15.25. Assume that you have a one-day TAQ file (such as November 1, 2004). Print the first ten valid trades and the first twenty valid quotes for IBM on that day.

15.26. Assume that you have a one-day TAQ file (such as November 1, 2004). How many records both from CT and CQ were for DELL on that day? What are the percentages of valid records over the total records?

15.27. Write an R program called show_trade_index_n1_n2() to show n2-n1+1 lines, with the first record starting at n1.

CHAPTER 16

Two Dozen R Packages Related to Finance

Before reading this chapter, it is a good idea to read chapter 31: "Introduction to R Packages." To check the current stock information from Yahoo Finance, we have two-line R codes, where the first line loads an R package called **quantmod**. Assume that **quantmod** is preinstalled. If we get an error message saying **Error in library(quantmod)**, there is no package called **quantmod**. It means that the package is not preinstalled. Just click packages on the menu bar, choose a location, then install the package. Later in the chapter, we will discuss this R package in more detail.

```
> library(quantmod)
> getQuote("ibm",src='yahoo')
Trade Time Last Change % Change Open High Low Volume
ibm 2015-03-16 02:10:00 156.28 2 +1.30% 155.09 156.45 154.8 2034575
```

With the **getQuote()** function, we can use the output as an input for our further analysis. Assume that we are interested in the current stock price; then we can retrieve it easily.

```
> x<-getQuote("ibm",src='yahoo')
> length(x)
[1] 8
> x[2]
Last
ibm 161.996
```

On the other hand, to download the monthly prime rate, we have two lines as well. The function of **fredSeries()** downloads data from the Federal Research Bank of St. Louis.

```
2001-03-01 8.32
2001-04-01 7.80
> tail(x,2)
  MPRIME
2014-08-01 3.25
2014-09-01 3.25
```

16.1. Introduction

After understanding basic R concepts and syntaxes, we should utilize the packages developed by others since the uses of various packages would save us huge amount of time. Simply put, we should reinvent the wheel the second time.

To find out all R packages, we have the following steps:

1. Go to http://r-project.org/.
2. Click **CRAN** on the left under Download.
3. Choose a mirror Web site.
4. Click **Package** on the left-hand side.

To find out the many R packages related to finance, we go to the following Web page.

1. Go to http://cran.r-project.org/.
2. Click **Task Views**.
3. Choose **Finance, Economics**, and other related task views.

16.2. About Two-Dozen Packages for Finance

In this chapter, we will discuss briefly two dozen finance-related packages.

Table 16.1. A list of packages discussed briefly in this chapter

Package	Description	Section
CreditMetrics	Credit migration, credit VaR	16.16
fAsianOptions	Path dependent Asian options	16.10
fAssets	Related to assets selection and modeling	16.19
fBasics	Markets and basicsStatistics	16.12
fBonds	Two functions: Nelson-Siegel and Svensson (Nelson-Siegel-Svensson) term structure	16.13
fExoticOptions	Exotic options	16.11
fImport	Retrieve financial data	16.5
fOptions	Basic options, such as Black-Scholes-Merton model	16.9
MASS	Functions/data sets to support Modern Applied Statistics with S	16.27
metafolio	Portfolio construction	16.8
pdfetch	Retrieve public data	16.7
PerformanceAnalytics	Econometric tools for performance and risk analysis	16.25
quantmod	Quantitative finance modeling framework	16.6
RQuantLib	Quantitative finance, options, fixed income, and calendar functions	16.26
stockPorftolio	Portfolio	16.23
termstruc	Term structure of interest rate	16.14
timeDate	Calendar functions: timeDate(), dayOfWeek(), dayOfYear()	16.17
timeSeries	Time series	16.16
TTR	Technical trading rule	16.21
ttrTests	Back test for technical trading rules	16.22
tseries	Time series (for computational finance)	16.18
XML	Reading and analyses of various Web pages	16.24
YieldCurve	Yield curve construction	16.15
zoo	Regular and irregular time series	16.20

16.3. Download and Install all Packages Listed by Finance View

From the finance task views introduced in 16.1, we can find over two hundred packages related to finance. To install them all at once, we simply issue the following three-line codes.

```
> install.packages("ctv")
> library(ctv)
> install.views("Finance")
```

On August 12, 2015, it took the author less than ten minutes to install 277 packages. The related list can be found at http://canisius.edu/~yany/R/packagesInstalledBy3linesCodes.txt.

16.4. Package of fImport

The package is for economic and financial data import. The package has several functions that can be used to retrieve financial market data from the Federal Reserve Economic Data (FRED) at the Federal Reserve Bank of St. Louis (http://www.research.stlouisfed.org), exchange rate data from Oanda Corp (www.oanda.com), and historical trading data from Yahoo Finance (http://chart.yahoo.com).

To download the daily prime rate, we have just two lines.

```
> library(fImport)
> x<-fredSeries("DPRIME") # DPRIME for daily prime rate
```

For the monthly prim rate, we have similar commands.

```
> library(fImport)
> y<-fredSeries("MPRIME")
> head(y)
GMT
  MPRIME
2014-04-01 3.25
2014-05-01 3.25
2014-06-01 3.25
2014-07-01 3.25
2014-08-01 3.25
2014-09-01 3.25
```

Running the following codes would lead to an error message. Where is the problem?

```
>library(fImport)
>x<-yahooSeries('IBM',nDaysBack=500)
>n<-nrow(x)
>ret<-(x[1:(n-1),6]-x[2:n,6])/x[2:n,6]
Error in x[1:(n - 1), 6] - x[2:n, 6] : positions slot do not match
```

The following codes would correct such an error.

```
>library(fImport)
>x<-yahooSeries('IBM',nDaysBack=500)
>n<-nrow(x)
>p<-x[,6]
>rownames(p)<-1:n
>ret<-(p[1:(n-1)]-p[2:n])/p[2:n]
```

A few included data sets are quite useful since they list all stocks listed on various stock exchanges. Table 16.2. A set of listing data sets

Name	Description
amexListing	1,553 stocks listed on the AMEX
nyseListing	3,387 stocks listed on the NYSE
oandaListing	191 data items from OANDA
stoxxListing	2,328 stocks for European stocks
swxListing	2,085 stocks

Below is a simple example on how to use the **nyseListing** data set.

```
> library(fImport)
> head(nyseListing,2)
  Symbol Name MarketCap Exchange
1 A Agilent Technologies, Inc. $12,852.3 NYSE
2 AA Alcoa Inc. $28,234.5 NYSE
> dim(nyseListing)
[1] 3387 4
```

From the data set, we can easily collect all symbols traded on NYSE, their market capitalizations, which is defined as "the shares outstading times the stock price of the underlying stock."

16.5. Finding the Manual for the R Package fImport

We go to www.r-project.com then click CRAN. We then choose a mirror location then click Package on the left-hand side. After a list of all packages pops up, we find fImport by using Ctrl+F (see below).

Downloads:

Reference manual:	fImport.pdf
Package source:	fImport_3000.82.tar.gz

16.6. Package quantmod

The quantitative financial-modeling framework (quantmod) package includes a set of functions that facilitate statistics-based financial modeling.

It can be used to retrieve real-time financial data, construct concise numerical charts, and conduct technical analysis for trading purposes. To retrieve daily returns for individual stocks, we have the following codes:

```
> require(quantmod)
> getSymbols('ibm',src='yahoo')
[1] "IBM"
> x<-dailyReturn(IBM)
> head(x,2)
daily.returns
2007-01-03 0.0009261165
2007-01-04 0.0106918886
> tail(x,2)
  daily.returns
2015-03-12 0.00752551
2015-03-13 -0.02342069
```

The major functions include **GetFinanccials, GetOptionChain, GetQuote, GetDividends, addBbankds, AddMA, addRSI**, etc. Let's see how to estimate **Lag** and lead (**Next**).

```
> y<-cbind(x,Lag(x),Next(x))
> head(y,2)
daily.returns Lag.1 Next
[1,]  0.0009261165 NA 0.010691889
[2,]  0.0106918886 0.0009261165 -0.009052996
```

To get several income statements for the Apple company, see the following R codes. In the following codes, **IS** is for income statement while **A** is for annual.

Quarterly income statement for AAPL

```
> library(quantmod)
> getFinancials("AAPL")
 [1] "AAPL.f"
> x<-viewFin(AAPL.f,"IS","A")
Annual Income Statement for AAPL
> dim(x)
 [1] 49 5
```

To view the first couple of lines of x, we use the **head()** function.

```
> head(x)
2014-09-27 2013-09-28 2012-09-29 2011-09-24
Revenue 182795 170910 156508 108249
Other Revenue, Total NA NA NA NA
Total Revenue 182795 170910 156508 108249
Cost of Revenue, Total 112258 106606 87846 64431
Gross Profit 70537 64304 68662 43818
Selling/General/Admin.Expenses,Total 11993 10830 10040 7599
```

The **rownames()** function can be used to find out the names of those forty-nine data items. For more details on how to retrieve various data items and estimate various financial ratios, such as current ratio, please see chapter 4: "Financial-Statement Analysis."

```
> y<-rownames(x)
> head(y)
[1] "Revenue"
[2] "Other Revenue, Total"
[3] "Total Revenue"
[4] "Cost of Revenue, Total"
[5] "Gross Profit"
[6] "Selling/General/Admin. Expenses, Total"
> tail(y)
[1] "Effect of Special Items on Income Taxes"
[2] "Income Taxes Ex. Impact of Special Items"
[3] "Normalized Income After Taxes"
[4] "Normalized Income Avail to Common"
[5] "Basic Normalized EPS"
[6] "Diluted Normalized EPS"
```

16.7. Package pdfetch

The package is used to retrieve economic and financial data from pub resource http://cran.r-project.org/bin/windows/base/old/. Here is the example. We use the pdfetch_BLS() function to get inflation rates from the Bureau of Labor Statistics. EIUIR is the import/export price indexes for a one-month percent change (http://data.bls.gov/timeseries/EIUIR?output_view=pct_1mth).

```
> library(pdfetch)
> x<-pdfetch_BLS(c("EIUIR","EIUIR100"), 2005, 2014)
> head(x,2)
EIUIR EIUIR100
2005-01-31 104.6 141.2
2005-02-28 105.5 148.4
> tail(x,2)
EIUIR EIUIR100
2014-08-31 139.3 371.3
2014-09-30 138.6 363.7
```

The following table lists important functions included in this package that we can use to retrieve economic and financial data from various open sources.

Table 16.3. Various functions to retrieve data

Function	Description
pdfetch_BLS	Fetch data from US Bureau of Labor Statistics
pdfetch_BOE	Fetch data from the Bank of England Statistical Interactive Database
pdfetch_ECB	Fetch data from European Central Bank's Statistical Data Warehouse
pdfetch_EIA	Fetch data from the US Energy Information Administration
pdfetch_EUROSTAT	Fetch data from Eurostat
pdfetch_EUROSTAT_DSD	Fetch description for a Eurostat data set
pdfetch_FRED	Fetch data from St Louis Fed's FRED database
pdfetch_INSEE	Fetch data from the French National Institute of Statistics and Economic Studies (INSEE)
pdfetch_ONS	Fetch data from the UK Office for National Statistics
pdfetch_WB	Fetch data from the World Bank
pdfetch_YAHOO	Fetch data from Yahoo Finance

16.8. Package metafolio

This package deals with portfolio theory, such as constructing an optimal portfolio. The **plot_efficient_porfolio()** function creates mean-variance-efficient portfolios across possible asset weights, colors the efficient frontier, and shows the contribution of the different stocks/assets.

```
>library(metafolio)
>n<-3000 # number of simulation
>w<-create_asset_weights(n_pop=6,n_sims=n,weight_lower_limit=0.001)
>p<-monte_carlo_portfolios(weights_matrix=w,n_sims=n,mean_b=1000)
>col_pal<-rev(gg_color_hue(6))
>plot_efficient_portfolios(port_vals=p$port_vals,pal=col_pal,weights_matrix= w)
```

The related outputs are shown below.

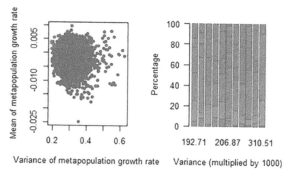

16.9. Package fOptions

The package called **fOptions** contains a set of R programs related to basic options, such as the Black-Scholes-Merton for European options, American options, the binomial tree model (CRR), and the Monte Carlo simulation. Several important functions are listed in the following table.

Table 16.4. Several functions in the **fOptions** package

Function	Description
GBSOption	Black-Scholes-Merton option model for European options
BSAmericanApproxOption	Bjerksund and Stensland approximation for an American option
CRRBinomialTreeOption	CRR Binomial Tree Option,
JRBinomialTreeOption	JR Binomial Tree Option
TIANBinomialTreeOption	TIAN Binomial Tree Option
BinomialTreeOption	Binomial Tree Option
BinomialTreePlot	Binomial Tree Plot
HNGOption	Heston-Nandi GARCH(1,1) option price
HNGGreeks	Heston-Nandi GARCH(1,1) option sensitivities
HNGCharacteristics	option prices and sensitivities
MonteCarloOption	Monte Carlo Simulator for options.
BlackScholesOption	a synonyme for the GBSOption
Black76Option	options on Futures
MiltersenSchwartzOption	options on commodity futures
NDF, CND, CBND	distribution functions,
unif.sobol	Sobol sequence
BAWAmericanApproxOption	Barone-Adesi and Whaley Approximation
BSAmericanApproxOption	Bjerksund and Stensland Approximation
RollGeskeWhaleyOption	Roll, Geske and Whaley Approximation
BAWAmericanApproxOption	Barone-Adesi and Whaley Approximation
BSAmericanApproxOption	Bjerksund and Stensland Approximation.

The option function for the Black-Scholes-Merton European options is **GBSOption()**. In the following codes, **c** is for a call option, **S** is the current stock price, **X** is the exercise price, **Time** is time to maturity, **r** is a risk-free interest rate, **b** is the annualized cost-of-carry rate (such as dividend yield), and **sigma** is the volatility of the underlying security.

```
>require(fOptions)
>GBSOption(TypeFlag="c",S=60,X=65,Time=1/4,r=0.08,b=0.08,sigma=0.30)
Option Price:
2.133372
```

For the Bjerksund and Stensland approximation for American options, we have the **BSAmericanApproxOption()** function.

```
> require(fOptions)
> BSAmericanApproxOption(TypeFlag ="c",S = 42, X = 40,
Time = 0.75, r = 0.04, b = 0.04-0.08, sigma = 0.35)
Option Price:
  5.270405
```

For the Roll-Geske-Whaley American calls on dividend-paying stock, we have the function RollGeskeWhaleyOption().

```
> library(fOptions)
> RollGeskeWhaleyOption(S = 80, X = 82, time1 = 1/4, Time2 = 1/3, r = 0.06, D = 4, sigma = 0.30)
Option Price:
   4.38603
```

16.10. Package fAsianOptions

Our European options, which exercise only on maturity dates, or American options, which are exercisable any time before or on maturity dates are path-independent options. It means that the final payoff has nothing to do with the path. On the other hand, Asian options are path dependent. For a call Asian option, we have the following odes. For the corresponding put option, we just change the **typeFlag**.

```
> library(fAsianOptions)
> MomentMatchedAsianOption(TypeFlag ="c",S = 100, X = 100,
Time = 1,r = 0.09, sigma = 0.30, table = NA, method = "LN")
 Option Price:
   8.885762
```

According Zhang's method, we have the following codes.

```
> ZhangAsianOption(TypeFlag = "c",S = 100, X = 100, Time = 1,r = 0.09, sigma =
0.30, table = NA, correction = TRUE, nint = 800,eps = 1.0e-8, dt = 1.0e-10)
[1] 8.814305
```

16.11. Package fExoticOptions

The package includes Asian options, barrier options, binary options, and currency-translated options. Below are several examples.

```
>library(fExoticOptions)
> GeometricAverageRateOption(TypeFlag="p",S = 80,X = 85,Time = 0.25,  r =
0.05, b = 0.08,sigma= 0.2)
Option Price:
   4.69222
```

The following function is for Levy's approximation for an Asian option.

```
> LevyAsianApproxOption(TypeFlag = "c",S = 100, SA = 100, X = 105,Time = 0.75,
time = 0.5, r = 0.1, b = 0.05, sigma = 0.15)
Option Price:
   0.3564905
```

For a barrier option, we have the following example:

```
> SoftBarrierOption(TypeFlag = "cdo",S = 100, X = 100, L = 70,
U = 95, Time = 0.5, r = 0.1, b = 0.05, sigma = 0.2)
Option Price:
  6.442895
```

16.12. Package fBasics

This package is a collection of functions to explore and investigate basic properties of financial returns and related quantities including explorative data analysis, distribution analysis, estimation, and hypothesis testing (see http://127.0.0.1:16484/library/fBasics/html/00fBasics-package.html).

```
> require(fBasics)
> set.seed(123)
> x<-timeSeries(matrix(rnorm(12)), timeCalendar())
```

We can use the function called **basicStats** to show the basic statistics of a time series (see the following simulated twelve monthly prices).

```
> basicStats(x)
   TS.1
nobs 12.000000
NAs 0.000000
Minimum -1.265061
Maximum 1.715065
1. Quartile -0.474365
3. Quartile 0.651708
Mean 0.194179
Median 0.099898
Sum 2.330152
SE Mean 0.267117
LCL Mean -0.393741
UCL Mean 0.782100
Variance 0.856218
Stdev 0.925321
Skewness 0.274851
Kurtosis -1.225650
```

To deal with missing data, one of the techniques is linear interpolation.

```
# Linear Interpolation:
if (require(akima)) {
  set.seed(1953)
  x = runif(999) - 0.5
  y = runif(999) - 0.5
  z = cos(2*pi*(x^2+y^2))
  ans = linearInterp(x, y, z, gridPoints = 41)
  persp(ans, theta = -40, phi = 30, col = ""steelblue",
  xlab = "x",ylab = "y",zlab = "z")
  contour(ans)
}
```

16.13. Package fBonds

The package includes two functions: **NelsonSiegel()** for the Nelson-Siegel term structure and **Svensson()** for the Nelson-Siegel-Svensson term structure. First, let's get the term structure of interest rate.

```
> library(XML)
> x<-readHTMLTable("http://finance.yahoo.com/bonds")[[2]][,1:2]
> x
  Maturity Yield
1  3 Month 0.00
2  6 Month 0.04
3   2 Year 0.38
4   3 Year 0.82
5   5 Year 1.49
6  10 Year 2.27
7  30 Year 3.05
```

Below, the example is related to the Nelson-Siegel term structure.

```
> require(fBonds)
> r<-as.numeric(as.matrix(x$Yield))/100
> r
[1] 0.0000 0.0004 0.0038 0.0082 0.0149 0.0227 0.0305
> mat<-c(3/12,6/12,2,3,4,10,30)
> NelsonSiegel(r, mat, doplot = TRUE)
$par
  beta0 beta1 beta2 tau1
   0.03258118 -0.03055480 -0.04893720 1.06024047
```

The corresponding graphs are given below:

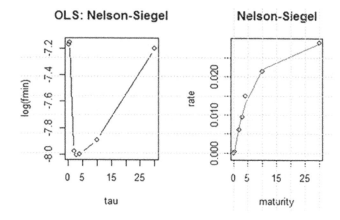

16.14. Package termstrc (Term Structure of Interest Rate)

Based on static and dynamic coupon bond and yield data, the package offers functions related to the term structure estimation: McCulloch (1971, 1975), Nelson and Siegel (1987), Svensson (1994), Diebold and Li (2006), and De Pooter (2007). It is very important to understand the structure of several data sets supplied by the package and used by various functions. In total, three data sets are included in the package. Their names and descriptions are given below.

Table 16.5 Three data sets in the package termstrc (all data sets have the structure of a list)

Name	Description	Length
govbonds	German, Austrian, and French government bonds	3
datadyncouponbonds	Dynamic German government coupon bonds	65
zyields	Zero-curve bond	17

Let's use the data set called **govbonds** as an example. The data set is a list with a length of 3 (see below).

```
> library(termstrc)
> data(govbonds)
> typeof(govbonds)
  [1] "list"
> length(govbonds)
  [1] 3
```

To generate a cash-flow matrix, we apply the **create_cashflows_matrix()** function if we use the included R data set called **govbonds**.

```
> data(govbonds)
> cf <- create_cashflows_matrix(govbonds[[1]])
> dim(cf)
[1] 32 52
> cf_p[1:5,1:5]
  DE0001141414 DE0001137131 DE0001141422 DE0001137149 DE0001135093
[1,] -104.089 -102.5757 -102.2312 -101.819 -102.4543
[2,] 104.250 103.0000 103.0000 103.250 104.1250
[3,] 0.000 0.0000 0.0000 0.000 0.0000
[4,] 0.000 0.0000 0.0000 0.000 0.0000
[5,] 0.000 0.0000 0.0000 0.000 0.0000
```

To estimate a bond price, we can apply the **bond_prices()** function (see below).

```
>data(govbonds)
>cf <- create_cashflows_matrix(govbonds[[1]])
>m <- create_maturities_matrix(govbonds[[1]])
>beta <- c(0.0511,-0.0124,-0.0303,2.5429)
>bond_prices(method="ns",beta,m,cf)$bond_prices
```

To estimate cash flows, we can use the following functions.

```
>data(govbonds)
>cf_p=create_cashflows_matrix(govbonds[[1]],include_price=TRUE)
>m_p=create_maturities_matrix(govbonds[[1]],include_price=TRUE)
>bond_yields(cf_p,m_p)
```

16.15. Package YieldCurve

The package models the yield curve with some parametric models, such as Nelson-Siegel, Diebold-Li, and Svensson. It also includes the data (term structure of interest rate) from the Federal Reserve Bank and the European Central Bank.

```
> library(YieldCurve)
> data(FedYieldCurve)
> head(FedYieldCurve,2)
  R_3M R_6M R_1Y R_2Y R_3Y R_5Y R_7Y R_10Y
1981-12-31 12.92 13.90 14.32 14.57 14.64 14.65 14.67 14.59
1982-01-31 14.28 14.81 14.73 14.82 14.73 14.54 14.46 14.43
> tail(FedYieldCurve,2)
  R_3M R_6M R_1Y R_2Y R_3Y R_5Y R_7Y R_10Y

2012-10-31 0.09 0.14 0.18 0.27 0.36 0.67 1.08 1.65
2012-11-30 0.07 0.12 0.16 0.26 0.35 0.70 1.13 1.72
```

To use the Federal Reserve Bank's data, the Nelson-Siegel would predict the following graph.

```
>data(FedYieldCurve)
>rate.Fed = first(FedYieldCurve, '5 month')
>maturity.Fed <- c(3/12, 0.5, 1,2,3,5,7,10)
>NSParameters <- Nelson.Siegel( rate= rate.Fed, maturity=maturity.Fed )
>y <- NSrates(NSParameters[5,], maturity.Fed)
>plot(maturity.Fed,rate.Fed[5,],main="Fitting Nelson-Siegel yield curve",
type="o")
>lines(maturity.Fed,y, col=2)
>legend("topleft",legend=c("observed yield curve","fitted yield curve"),
col=c(1,2),lty=1)
```

The output is shown below:

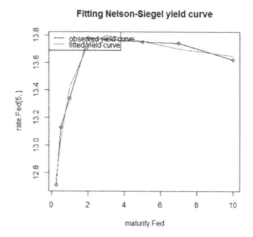

16.16. Package CreditMetrics

A one-year migration matrix can be entered manually.

```
# one year empirical migration matrix from standard&poors website
rc <- c("AAA","AA","A","BBB","BB","B","CCC","D")
M <- matrix(c(90.81,8.33,0.68, 0.06, 0.08, 0.02, 0.01, 0.01,
  0.70,90.65, 7.79, 0.64, 0.06, 0.13, 0.02, 0.01,
  0.09, 2.27, 91.05, 5.52, 0.74, 0.26, 0.01, 0.06,
  0.02, 0.33, 5.95, 85.93, 5.30, 1.17, 1.12, 0.18,
  0.03, 0.14, 0.67, 7.73, 80.53, 8.84, 1.00, 1.06,
  0.01, 0.11, 0.24, 0.43, 6.48, 83.46, 4.07, 5.20,
  0.21, 0, 0.22, 1.30, 2.38, 11.24, 64.86, 19.79,
  0, 0, 0, 0, 0, 0, 0, 100
)/100, 8, 8, dimnames = list(rc, rc), byrow = TRUE)
```

The one-year credit-migration matrix will be the following format. The probability of a AAA-rated bond has a 90.81% chance to remain AAA while its chance to downgrade to AA is 8.33%. The last column, under D, shows the default probability. For instance, for a BBB-rated bond, its default probability is 0.18% within one year.

```
> M
  AAA AA A BBB BB B CCC D
AAA 0.9081 0.0833 0.0068 0.0006 0.0008 0.0002 0.0001 0.0001
AA 0.0070 0.9065 0.0779 0.0064 0.0006 0.0013 0.0002 0.0001
A 0.0009 0.0227 0.9105 0.0552 0.0074 0.0026 0.0001 0.0006
BBB 0.0002 0.0033 0.0595 0.8593 0.0530 0.0117 0.0112 0.0018
BB 0.0003 0.0014 0.0067 0.0773 0.8053 0.0884 0.0100 0.0106
B 0.0001 0.0011 0.0024 0.0043 0.0648 0.8346 0.0407 0.0520
CCC 0.0021 0.0000 0.0022 0.0130 0.0238 0.1124 0.6486 0.1979
D 0.0000 0.0000 0.0000 0.0000 0.0000 0.0000 0.0000 1.0000
```

The function **cm.ref** computes the value of a credit in one year for each rating for a given exposure. Furthermore, the portfolio value in one year is the summation of individual value and is the last value called **constPV**.

```
>library(CreditMetrics)
> rf<-0.03 # M from previous operation
> exposure<-c(100,100)
> loss_given_default=0.5
> rating<-c("AAA","BBB")
> cm.ref(M, loss_given_default, exposure,rf,rating)
$constVal
  AAA BBB
97.03970 96.95721
$constPV
[1] 193.9969
```

To use the **cm.CVaR()** function (credit VaR), we have the following codes:

```
> library(CreditMetrics)
> n_firm <- 3
> ead <- c(4000000, 1000000, 10000000)
> rating <- c("BBB","AA","B")
> firmnames <- c("firm 1","firm 2","firm 3 ")
> rf <- 0.03
> rc <- c("AAA","AA","A","BBB","BB","B","CCC","D")
```

```
> loss_given_default <- 0.45
> alpha <- 0.99 # confidence level
> n <- 50000 # number of simulations
> rho<-matrix(c( 1, 0.4, 0.6,
  0.4, 1, 0.5,
  0.6,0.5,1),3,3,dimnames=list(firmnames, firmnames),
  byrow = TRUE)
> cm.CVaR(M,loss_given_default,ead,n_firm,n,rf,rho,alpha,rating)
  1%
3997328
```

16.17. Package timeDate

This package is related to various date formats that set a good environment for teaching financial engineering and computational finance.

```
> library(timeDate)
> Sys.timeDate()
 [1] [2011-12-29 01:29:31]
```

To convert a string into a date-and-time variable, we have the following codes:

```
> x<-"2011-12-28 20:20:10"
> timeDate(x)
GMT
[1] [2011-12-28 20:20:10]
> timeDate(x)+4
GMT
[1] [2011-12-28 20:20:14]
```

A function called **listFinCenter()** can be used to retrieve the name of a specific financial center. The use of the function is **listFinCenter("Keyword")**.

```
>library(timeDate)
> x<-listFinCenter("Asia")
> length(x)
[1] 75
> head(x,5)
[1] "Asia/Aden" "Asia/Almaty" "Asia/Amman" "Asia/Anadyr" "Asia/Aqtau"
> tail(x,3)
[1] "Asia/Yakutsk"    "Asia/Yekaterinburg" "Asia/Yerevan"
```

To find the holidays for NYSE, we have the following codes:

```
> holidayNYSE(2011)
NewYork
[1] [2011-01-17] [2011-02-21] [2011-04-22] [2011-05-30] [2011-07-04]
[6] [2011-09-05] [2011-11-24] [2011-12-26]
```

16.18. Package tseries

The package called tseries is for time-series analysis and computational finance. The first example is related to the augmented Dickey-Fuller test (ADF), which tests whether a unit root is present in an autoregressive model. The testing procedure for the ADF test is the same as for the Dickey-Fuller test but with the following model:

$$\Delta y_t = a + \beta t + Y y_{t-1} + \delta_1 \Delta y_{t-1} + \ldots + \Delta y_{p-1} \Delta y_{t-p+1}$$

where α is a constant,

β is the coefficient on a time trend,

and p is the lag order of the autoregressive process.

Imposing the constraints $\alpha = 0$ and $\beta = 0$ corresponds to modeling a random walk, and using the constraint $\beta = 0$ corresponds to modeling a random walk with a drift.

```
>require(tseries)
>require(quantmod)
>getSymbols('ibm',src='yahoo')
>x<-dailyReturn(IBM)
>adf.test(x)
```

The output is given below. The null hypothesis is that the underlying time series is not stationary. Since the p value is 0.01, we reject the null hypothesis. In other words, our results support the alternative hypothesis: the daily returns for IBM is stationary.

```
 Augmented Dickey-Fuller Test

data: x
Dickey-Fuller = -12.553, Lag order = 12, p-value = 0.01
alternative hypothesis: stationary

Warning message:
In adf.test(x) : p-value smaller than printed p-value
>
```

To test whether a stock return follows a normal distribution, we can use the Jarque-Bera normality test. If we use the returns for IBM as an example, we reject the null hypothesis (underlying stock follows a normal distribution). In other words, IBM daily returns do not follow a normal distribution.

```
> library(quantmod)
> getSymbols("IBM",src='yahoo')
> x<-dailyReturn(IBM)
> jarque.bera.test(x)
Jarque Bera Test
data: x
X-squared = 2767.52, df = 2, p-value < 2.2e-16
```

To remove NA, we can apply the **na.remove()** function.

```
> require(tseries)
> x<-c(100,20,NA)
> y<-na.remove(x)
```

To get the daily return for a given ticker, we have the following codes:

```
>require(tseries)
>require(quantmod)
>getSymbols('ibm',src='yahoo')
>x<-dailyReturn(IBM)
```

When the variance is not a constant, we can use the ARCH(q) model to describe where the series σ_t^2 are modeled by the following equation, where ε_t ε_t is the error term as time t.

Equation 2

$$\sigma_t^2 = \alpha_0 + \alpha_1 \epsilon_{t-1}^2 + \cdots + \alpha_q \varepsilon_{t-q}^2 = \alpha_0 + \sum_{i=1}^{q} \alpha_i \epsilon_{t-i}^2$$

Below, we use IBM's daily data to estimate its ARCH(1) process.

```
require(tseries)
require(quantmod)
getSymbols('ibm',src='yahoo')
x<-dailyReturn(IBM)
x2 <- ts(x[1:252])
out<-garch(x2,c(0,1))
```

Based on the following output, we know that **a0** is close to 0 and **a1** is 0.22.

```
> out
Call:
garch(x = x2, order = c(0, 1))
Coefficient(s):
  a0  a1
0.0001336 0.2213745
```

The GARCH(p, q) model has the following form:

Equation 3

$$\sigma_t^2 = \alpha_0 + \sum_{i=1}^{q} \alpha_i \epsilon_{t-i}^2 + \sum_{i=1}^{p} \beta_i \sigma_{t-i}^2$$

279

The next example shows how to estimate a GARCH(0,2) process; that is , ARCH(2).

```
>library(tseries)
>n <- 1100
>a <- c(0.1, 0.5, 0.2) # ARCH(2) coefficients
>set.seed(12345) # fix a seed
>e <- rnorm(n) # generate a set of random numbers
>x <- double(n) # make sure they are in a correct format
>x[1:2] <- rnorm(2, sd = sqrt(a[1]/(1.0-a[2]-a[3])))
>for(i in 3:n) { # generate ARCH(2) process
 x[i] <- e[i]*sqrt(a[1]+a[2]*x[i-1]^2+a[3]*x[i-2]^2)
}
>x <- ts(x[101:n]) # skip the first 100 numbers
>x.arch <- garch(x, order = c(0,2)) # Fit ARCH(2)
```

To show our final result, just type the name of the variable **x.arch**. By construction, we know that our final result should be close to 0.1, 0.5, and 0.13.

```
> x.arch
Call:
garch(x = x, order = c(0, 2))
Coefficient(s):
 a0 a1 a2
0.09906 0.53909 0.12911
```

Below, we use IBM's daily data to estimate its GARCH(1,1) process.

```
>require(tseries)
>require(quantmod)
>getSymbols('ibm',src='yahoo')
>x<-dailyReturn(IBM)
>x2 <- ts(x[1:252])
>garch(x2,c(1,1))
```

The output result is given below:

```
***** FALSE CONVERGENCE *****
 FUNCTION -9.715678e+02 RELDX 2.641e-15
 FUNC. EVALS 72 GRAD. EVALS 21
 PRELDF 6.254e-19 NPRELDF 2.932e-08
 I FINAL X(I) D(I) G(I)
 1 3.620630e-05 1.000e+00 7.085e-02
 2 1.377926e-01 1.000e+00 1.320e-01
 3 6.516555e-01 1.000e+00 2.801e-02
Call:
garch(x = x2, order = c(1, 1))
Coefficient(s):
 a0 a1 b1
3.621e-05 1.378e-01 6.517e-01
```

16.19. Package fAssets

The package is related to selecting assets and modeling. Let's look at an R data set called **LPP2005REC**.

```
>library(fAssets)
> dim(LPP2005REC)
 [1] 377 9
```

Let's look at the first two lines.

```
> head(LPP2005REC,2)
GMT
SBI SPI SII LMI MPI
2005-11-01 -0.000612745 0.008414595 -0.003190926 -0.001108882 0.001548062
2005-11-02 -0.002762009 0.002519342 -0.004117638 -0.001175939 0.000342876
   ALT LPP25 LPP40 LPP60
2005-11-01 -0.002572971 -0.000130008 0.000199980 0.000809672
2005-11-02 -0.001141604 -0.001561421 -0.001120404 -0.000469730
```

To find the outliers, we can use the following codes:

```
> x <-as.timeSeries(data(LPP2005REC))[, 1:2]
> head(x,2)
GMT
 SBI SPI
2005-11-01 -0.000612745 0.008414595
2005-11-02 -0.002762009 0.002519342
> assetsOutliers(x, colMeans(x), cov(x))
$center
 SBI SPI
-1.501522e-05 1.310444e-03
$cov
 SBI SPI
SBI 1.561119e-06 -8.879654e-07
SPI -8.879654e-07 4.218738e-05
$cor
 SBI SPI
SBI 1.0000000 -0.1094175
SPI -0.1094175 1.0000000

$quantile
[1] 10.8133
$outliers
2006-05-17 2006-05-22 2006-05-26 2006-06-06 2006-06-08 2006-06-13 2007-02-
27 2007-03-14
  142 145 149 156 158 161 346 357
```

To simulate several stock returns, we use the

```
> x<- 100/12 * assetsSim(n = 120, dim = 4)
> dim(x)
[1] 120 4
> head(x,2)
   V1       V2        V3        V4
1 -5.168976 -11.703047  6.210015 -0.6970412
2 -1.536524   7.743162 -9.979900 -2.0108360
```

The function **cumsum()** will calculate the accumulated sum (see the following example).

```
> x<-1:6
> x
[1] 1 2 3 4 5 6
> cumsum(x)
[1] 1 3 6 10 15 21
```

Combine those commands together, and we have the following codes:

```
>library(fAssets)
>price<- 100/12 * assetsSim(n = 120, dim = 4)
>cum_price<-apply(price,2,FUN = cumsum)
>ts.plot(prices,col = 1:4,ylim = c(-300, 300))
```

To control the scale, we have the following codes:

```
> library(fAssets)
> weight<-rep(1/4, 4)
> price<- 100/12 * assetsSim(n = 120, dim = 4)
> cum_price<-apply(price,2,FUN = cumsum)
> alpha = 0.10
> pfolioVaR(cum_price, weight, alpha)
  VaR
-29.112
```

To estimate the conditional VaR, we call the **pfolioCVaRplus()** function.

```
# Conditional Value at Risk Plus:
> pfolioCVaRplus(cum_price,weight, alpha)
  CVaRplus
-33.13043
```

16.20. Package zoo

The package is for infrastructure for regular and irregular time series. To remove the leading and trailing NA, we use the **na.trim()** function.

```
> x <- c(NA, 6,2, 4, 6,NA)
> na.trim(x)
[1] 6 2 4 6
```

The na.fill() function is very useful since it interpolates for NA between values and uses the leftist (rightest) values for end values.

```
> x<-c(NA,NA,1,NA,2,NA,4,NA,10,NA)
> x2<-na.fill(x,"extend")
> x2
 [1] 1.0 1.0 1.0 1.5 2.0 3.0 4.0 7.0 10.0 10.0
```

16.21. Package of TTR (Technical Trading Rule)

TTR stands for "technical trading rule," and the package includes functions and data to construct technical trading rules with R. To get the daily price data for IBM for a certain period, we use the getYahooData() function.

```
>library(TTR)
>x <- getYahooData("IBM",19990404, 20050607)
> head(x,3)
  Open High Low Close Volume Unadj.Close Div Split Adj.Div
1999-04-05 77.41187 79.54827 77.22159 79.54827 10681007 183.94 NA NA NA
1999-04-06 79.19797 80.76351 78.79145 79.14175 10108018 183.00 NA NA NA
1999-04-07 79.57422 81.14408 77.43782 80.65539 13483061 186.50 NA NA NA
```

We use the **momentum()** function to estimate the difference. The format of the function is given below:

```
# momentum(x, n=1, na.pad=TRUE)
# n is the number of periods
# na.pad asks whether to keep the first several observations
```

Here is an example in which we estimate two differences over one a one-day period and over a twoday period.

```
>library(TTR)
>x <- getYahooData("IBM")
> tail(x[,1:4],3)
Open High Low Close
2011-12-27 184.97 185.85 184.39 184.95
2011-12-28 185.19 185.40 183.34 183.99
2011-12-29 184.07 186.23 184.01 186.18
> diff<-momentum(x[,"Close"])
> head(diff,3)
Close
1962-01-02 NA
1962-01-03 0.02248993
1962-01-04 -0.02586342
```
```
> diff2<-momentum(x[,"Close"],2)
> head(y2,4)
[1] NA 0.005217675 -0.001081373 -0.014668471
```

The function of **ROC()**, rate of change, is used to estimate the percentage of change. The default type is "**continuous**".

To double check just one value, the first number, we have the following result. Remember that the default setting is "**continuous**".

```
> log(184.95/183.99)
[1] 0.00520411
```

If we use "**discrete**", our normal percentage change, we have the following example:

```
> y2 <- ROC(x[,"Close"],1,"discrete")
> head(y2,4)
[1] NA 0.005217675 -0.001081373 -0.014668471
```

The relative strength index (RSI) is used to measure the strength of a price movement. RSI=100 will be an upward movement, and RSI=0 will be a downward movement.

16.22. Package ttrTests (Standard Back Tests for Technical Trading Rules in Financial Data)

This package includes many useful functions for technical-trading-related tests. One quite useful function is called **deleteNA()**.

```
>library(ttrTests)
> x<-c(1,3,NA,3,5,NA)
> y<-deleteNA(x)
> y
[1] 1 3 3 5
```

For a given data set, we can resample it by using the **bootstrap()** function.

```
>require(ttrTests)
>x <- runif(100)
>mean(x)
>var(x)
>sample <- bootstrap(x)
>mean(sample)
>var(sample)
```

To make our job easier, we could a simple function called **bootstrap_f()**.

```
>set.seed(12345)
>x <- runif(100)
>n<-500
>d<-bootstrap_f(x,n)
```

To test data-snooping issue, we apply the **dataSnoop()** function (see an example below).

```
>library(ttrTests)
>data(spData)
>rc <- dataSnoop(spData,bSamples=3,test="RC")
>spa <- dataSnoop(spData,bSamples=3,test="SPA")
```

16.23. Package stockPortfolio

The package is used to construct various types of portfolios.

```
>require(stockPortfolio)
>data(stock94)
> data(stock99)
> data(stock94Info)
>sim1  <-  stockModel(stock94,  model='SIM',  industry=stock94Info$industry,
index=25)
```

16.24. Package XML

The package is related to reading and analyzing various HTML Web pages. To find the current term structure (zero curve), use the following two-line R codes.

```
> library(XML)
> readHTMLTable("http://finance.yahoo.com/bonds")[[2]][,1:2]
  Maturity Yield
1 3 Month 0.00
2 6 Month 0.02
3 2 Year 0.26
4 3 Year 0.40
5 5 Year 0.90
6 10 Year 1.91
7 30 Year 2.90
```

The function called **xmlParseDoc()** can be used to parse an HTML document (see an example below).

```
> f = system.file("exampleData","mtcars.xml",package="XML")
> f
[1] "C:/Users/PaulYan/Documents/R/win-library/2.14/XML/exampleData/mtcars.xml"
> x<-xmlParseDoc(f)
> typeof(x)
[1] "externalptr"
```

16.25. Package PerformanceAnalytics

The package contains econometric tools for performance and risk analysis. The package includes four R data sets. Their names and descriptions are given below.

Table 16.6. Data sets included in the package

Name	Description
managers	It is an xts object that contains columns of monthly returns for six hypothetical asset managers (HAM1 through HAM6), the EDHEC Long-Short Equity hedge fund index, the S&P 500 total returns, and total return series for the US Treasury 10-year bond and 3-month bill. Monthly returns for all series end in December 2006 and begin at different periods starting from January 1996.
edhec	> colnames(edhec) [1] "Convertible Arbitrage" "CTA Global" [3] "Distressed Securities" "Emerging Markets" [5] "Equity Market Neutral" "Event Driven" [7] "Fixed Income Arbitrage" "Global Macro" [9] "Long/Short Equity" "Merger Arbitrage" [11] "Relative Value" "Short Selling" [13] "Funds of Funds" > dim(edhec) [1] 152 13
weights	> colnames(weights) [1] "Convertible Arbitrage" "CTA Global" [3] "Distressed Securities" "Emerging Markets" [5] "Equity Market Neutral" "Event Driven" [7] "Fixed Income Arbitrage" "Global Macro" [9] "Long/Short Equity" "Merger Arbitrage" [11] "Relative Value" > dim(weights) [1] 8 11
prices	> dim(prices) [1] 120 4 > head(prices,1) V1 V2 V3 V4 [1,] -7.601416 -8.201054 3.205665 -15.22682

To estimate a CAPM beta, we can use the **CAPM.beta()** function.

```
>require(PerformanceAnalytics)
>stock<- managers[, "HAM2", drop=FALSE]
>mkt<- managers[, "SP500 TR",drop=FALSE]
>rf<- managers[, "US 3m TR",drop=FALSE]
>CAPM.beta(stock,mkt,rf)
> CAPM.beta(stock,mkt,rf)
[1] 0.3383942
```

To estimate bull and bear beta, we can use two functions. 1) The **CAPM.beta.bull()** function is a regression with only positive market returns while the 2) **CAPM.beta.bear()** function considers only negative market returns. The first function will show the potential behavior (beta) of the stock with a bull market while the second function shows the beta with a bear market.

```
> CAPM.beta.bull(stock,mkt,rf)
[1] 0.5226596
> CAPM.beta.bear(stock,mkt,rf)
[1] 0.0698255
```

To estimate a Sharpe ratio, we can apply the **SharpeRatio()** function.

```
>require(tseries)
>require(quantmod)
>require(PerformanceAnalytics)
>getSymbols('ibm',src='yahoo')
>x<-monthlyReturn(IBM)
> SharpeRatio(x, Rf=.035/12, FUN="StdDev")
 monthly.returns
StdDev Sharpe: (Rf=0.3%, p=95%) 0.1650061
```

The third variable **FUN=** can take several other values.

```
> SharpeRatio(x, Rf=.035/12, FUN="VaR")
 monthly.returns
VaR Sharpe: (Rf=0.3%, p=95%) 0.100431
```

The Treynor ratio is the excess return over beta.

```
> TreynorRatio(stock,mkt,rf)
[1] 0.3882701
```

To estimate VaR, we apply the VaR function.

```
>require(tseries)
>require(quantmod)
>require(PerformanceAnalytics)
>getSymbols('ibm',src='yahoo')
>x<-dailyReturn(IBM)
> VaR(x,p=0.95,method="gaussian")
 daily.returns
VaR -0.02605961
```

16.26. Package RQuantLib

The **RQuantLib** package includes option-pricing functions, fixed income, and general calendaring and holiday utilities.

```
>library(RQuantLib)
> x<-AmericanOptionImpliedVolatility(type="call",value=11.10, underlying=100,
strike=100, dividendYield=0.01, riskFreeRate=0.03, maturity=0.5, volatility=0.4)
> x[1]
$impliedVol
[1] 0.3805953
```

16.27. Package MASS

The package includes various functions and data sets to support the book titled *Modern Applied Statistics with S* by Venables and Ripley (2002, 4th ed.). In total, there are eighty-four data sets. We can **use library(help=MASS)** to view all those data sets.

```
> library(MASS)
> length(SP500)
[1] 2780
> head(SP500)
[1] -0.2588908 -0.8650307 -0.9804139 0.4504321 -1.1856666 -0.6629097
```

The function called **fitdistr()** can be used to find the parameters of a specific distribution. In the **fitdistr(vector, distribution)**, the variable *distribution* could take a value, case-insensitive, of "**beta**", "**cauchy**", "**chi-squared**", "**exponential**", "**f** ", "**gamma**", "**geometric**", "**log-normal**", "**lognormal**", "**logistic**", "**negative binomial**", "**normal**", "**Poisson**", "**t**", and "**weibull**".

```
> library(MASS)
> set.seed(123)
> x<-rnorm(10000)
> fitdistr(x,"normal")
 mean sd
 -0.002371702 0.998586702
 ( 0.009985867) ( 0.007061074)
```

To install views finance, we issue the following codes:

```
>install.packages("ctv")
>library("ctv")
>install.views("Finance")
```

16.28. No Updated Packages Available

Assume that our current version of R is 3.11. On October 27, 2014, we intend to install the R package called **ttrTests**. We will see the following error messages:

```
> library(ttrTests)
Error in library(ttrTests) : there is no package called 'ttrTests'

> install.packages('ttrTests')
Installing package into 'C:/Users/yany/Documents/R/win-library/3.1'
(as 'lib' is unspecified)
Warning message:
package 'ttrTests' is not available (for R version 3.1.1)
>
```

Usually we have three solutions: 1) wait for a few more months until the updated version of the R package is available, 2) use other similar R packages, and 3) uninstall R from our machine and install an old R version. For the third approach, check the following link to find all previous R versions: http://cran.rproject.org/bin/windows/base/old/.

Exercises

16.1. If we are dealing with valuing the price of a bond, what kind of R packages can we use and why?

16.2. Using holidayNYSE(2010), we can find out holidays in 2010 for the New York Stock Exchange. Download several stocks data from Yahoo Finance to confirm or reject those days.

16.3. From where can we find our information about the function of isBizday()?

16.4. How do we define an ARCH process and what kind of function(s) can we use?

16.5. What is the difference between an ARCH and a GARCH process?

16.6. How do we apply the GARCH $(1, 1)$ model to the daily returns for DELL in the past three years?

16.7. What kind of tests can we use to determine whether a time series is stationary or not?

16.8. What is the function name and package name to test how stationary a time series is?

16.9. Are IBM's monthly returns for the past ten years stationary?

16.10. From which package can we get the data set called govbonds? What are the contents of the data set?

16.11. Find out the time period of the following S&P 500 level.

```
>require(ttrTests)
> length(spData) # [1] 755
```

16.12. Regenerate stock94 and extend it to 2010.

```
> library(stockPortfolio)
>data(stock94)
```

16.13. How do we filter out observations with NA?

CHAPTER 17

R Basics

Starting from this chapter, the rest of the book will focus on R. To facilitate a quick learning, every chapter is kept very short, usually less than ten pages and covers a narrow topic. Even for those simple and narrow topics, we will discuss only essential features. The objective is to make learning R less time-consuming and more enjoyable. Since we have discussed the basic concepts related to R in chapters 1 and 2, there will be many overlapping topics between chapters 1 and 2 and chapters 17 and 18. Thus, if you have gone through the first two chapters, just skip chapters 17 and 18.

17.1. Installation of R

Based on the following steps, we can download and install R.

1. Go to http://www.r-project.org.
2. Click **Download** on the left-hand side.
3. Choose a mirror address.
4. Download the appropriate PC software (Windows, Mac).

17.2. Starting and Quitting R

To launch, we double-click the R icon on our desktops.

To quit R, type q() from the R prompt > (see below).

```
> q() # the first way to quit
```

Note that > is the R prompt. When quitting, you will be asked whether to save the work-space image. If you want to save your variables or programs for future use, then answer yes. At this stage, just choose no.

A leading # before a line or a phrase indicates that this is a comment.

```
> # this is a comment line
```

There are several other ways to quit R. The second way to quit is given below.

```
> quit() # the 2nd way to quit
```

Here is the third way to quit:

```
> # click "file" — >"exit" # the 3rd way to quit
```

```
> # click right-top "x" # the 4th way to quit
```

17.3. R Basics

The simplest way to assign a value to a variable is to use <-.

```
> x<-10
```

To show its value, simply type the variable name.

```
> x
[1] 10
```

You don't have to define a variable before assigning a value to it.

```
> # a variable is not formally defined before its assignment
> fv<-100 # you don't define the variable called fv
```

R is case sensitive. This means that X and x are two different variables.

```
> x<-1.234
> X
Error: object 'X' not found
```

A comma is not necessary after each command line when the command stands alone. However, if we put several commands in one line, we need to use a semicolon (;) to separate them.

```
> fv<-10; pv<-100; n<-10; rate<-0.05
```

We have the following easy way to assign a vector. In the following example, **c()** means column.

```
> x<-c(1,2.5,4,6) # assign a vector
> y<-1:50 # from small to big with increment of 1
> z<-10:0 # from big to small
```

It is always a good idea to list all variables (objects). For this purpose, we use **ls()**.

```
> ls()
```

When a variable is no longer useful, we can remove it from the memory.

```
> rm(x) # remove variable called x
> rm(x,y) # remove both x and y
> rm(list=ls()) # remove all objects (variables)
# the second way to remove all objects
# go to "Misc" on the menu bar -> "Remove all objects"
```

To make our typing easier, we use the up and down arrow keys to recall our previous commands.

```
# use upper (down) arrow keys to recall previous commands
```

To print one line on the screen, we can use **cat("our sentence here")**.

```
> cat("hello, world!\n") # \n is for new line
```

17.4. Finding Help

There are many ways to find information related to specific functions. Assume that we are interested in mean. We then issue **help(mean)**.

```
> help(mean) # find information related to mean
> ?mean # find information related to mean
> example(median) # show examples related to median
```

If you're not sure about the exact spelling of a function, we use the **apropos()** function instead.

```
> apropos("me") # find information related to "me"
# second way to use apropos
# click "Help" on the menu bar
# click "apropos ..."
# enter your phrase
> # file - -> about [see the version of the current R]
> help.start() # start help
> help.search("topic") # start help
```

An alternative way is to click **Help** on the menu bar (see the following graph).

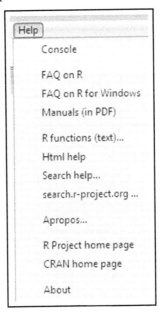

17.5. Using R as an Ordinary Calculator

We can use R to make calculations just like an ordinary calculator.

```
> x<-1:50
> mean(x)  # you can try max(), min(),median(),sd(),var(),range()
```

We can use the **ceiling()** and **floor()** functions to process our values.

```
> x<-9.5          > x<-9.5
> ceiling(x)      > floor(x)
[1] 10            [1] 9
```

We can use the as.integer() function to convert a real number into an integer.

```
> x<-9.5
> y<-as.integer(x)
> y
[1] 9
```

The following table summarizes a set of most widely used functions.

Table 17.1. A list of some basic functions

function	Meaning	Examples
mean(x)	Mean	x<-1:10 mean(x) # [1] 5.5
median(x)	Median	median(x) # [1] 5.5
min(x)	Minimum	min(x) # [1] 1
max(x)	Maximum	max(x) # [1] 10
var(x)	Variance	>var(x) # [1] 9.166667
sd(x)	Standard deviation	sd(x) # [1] 3.027650
exp(x)	Exponential function	exp(2.3) # [1] 9.974182
log(x)	Natural log function	log(4.5) # [1] 1.504077
log10(x)	Log function based on 10	log10(4.3) # [1] 0.6334685
sum(x)	Take the summation	sum(x) # [1] 55
sort(x)	Sort in ascending order	
range(x)	Range of a variable	x<-1.5:10 range(x) # [1] 1.5 9.5
diff(x)	Calculate the difference for a vector	x<-c(1,2.3,4.5) diff(x) # [1] 1.3 2.2
ceiling(x)	Get the smallest integer larger than x	x<-9.5 ceiling(x) # [1] 10
floor(x)	Get the largest integer smaller than x	x<-9.5 floor(x) # [1] 9
as.integer(x)	Take the integer value	x<-9.5 as.integer(x) # [1] 9
prod()	Get product of a vector >	x<-1:3 > prod(x) # [1] 6
quantile(x)	> quantile(x) 0% 25% 50% 75% 100% -2.3210170 -0.6862249 0.1460511 0.7151348 2.0682096	
	> quantile(x,probs=c(0.01,0.05,0.95,0.99)) 1% 5% 95% 99% -2.000058 -1.609246 1.256627 1.476727	

Sometimes we need to change the directory for convenience. The related procedure is given below.

```
# change the directory
# [click] File — > "Change dir…" [choose your working directory]
```

We can change our starting directory by modifying the properties of our R icon.

1. Right-click the R icon on your desktop.
2. Click **Properties**.
3. Choose your directory in **Start in** (e.g., **C:\test**).

Exercises

17.1. What are the advantages of using R?

17.2. What is the difference between functions **ls()** and **rm()**?

17.3. Generate a vector from 2 to 15 then from 20 to 40. Estimate its mean, standard deviation, and median.

17.4. What might be the disadvantages of using R?

17.5. How do we assign a value to a new variable?

17.6. Is R case sensitive?

17.7. Is R free?

17.8. How do we get help for R?

17.9. How do we add a comment?

17.10. Is it difficult to install R?

17.11. Will the R compiler compile a comment line?

17.12. Does a space play a role in R's commands?

17.13. How do we download manuals related to R?

CHAPTER 18

Simple Value Assignment

In this chapter, we will discuss different ways to assign a value or values to a variable. Again, if you read chapters 1 and 2, you can skip this chapter.

18.1. Several Ways to Assign a Value to a Variable

The simplest way to assign a value to a variable is to use <-.

```
> x<-10
```

To show the value of a variable, simply type its name.

```
> x
[1] 10
```

To assign a value to a variable, we can use = or -> as well.

```
> y=2
> 10->x
```

The -> assignment can make our debugging efforts easier. Assume that we want to test a program to estimate the present value of $100 received in two years with an 8% annual discount rate. We can have the following:

```
> 100/(1+0.08)^2
[1] 85.73388
```

After hitting the Enter key to get our result, we change our mind trying to sign the result to a variable, such as **pv**. To save time, we simply use the up arrow key to recall the previous command. Then we add **->pv** at the end of the above command.

```
> 100/(1+0.08)^2->pv
> pv
[1] 85.73388
```

To assign a set of values, we use **c(1,2.6,4.3,5.25)**, where c stands for "column."

```
# assign a vector (column values)
> X<-c(1,2,4,6)
```

To assign a set of consecutive integers, we can use n1:n2, such as 1:10.

```
> y<-1:50
> x<-c(1:5,8:12)
> x
[1]  1 2 3 4 5 8 9 10 11 12
```

We can input data from high to low (i.e., reverse the order).

```
> y<-5:1
```

The **rev()** function can be used to reverse an input data set.

```
> x<-5:1
> x<-rev(1:5)  # same as above
```

18.2. Viewing Objects Using the ls() Function

We can use the ls() function to list all objectives including variables.

```
> ls() # list all variables
```

18.3. The seq() Function

The **seq()** function is used to generate a set of values (see an example below).

```
> seq(1, 19, by = 2)
[1]  1 3 5 7 9 11 13 15 17 19
```

The following command uses pi as an incremental value.

```
> seq(1, 11, by = pi)
[1] 1.000000 4.141593 7.283185 10.424778
```

The complete command has the following format:

```
> seq(from=1,to=3, by =0.5)
```

18.4. Position and Keyword Approaches

There are two ways to input data: position and keyword. In the following one-line code, we use the position-variable approach. In other words, the meaning of the input variable depends on its position in the set of input variables.

```
> x<-seq(1,3,0.5) # position variable approach
```

For the keyword approach, we add a keyword in front of each input value, such as from=1. One advantage of the keyword approach is that the order of input variables does not play a role. The following three statements are equivalent.

```
> seq(from=1,to=3,by=0.5)  # they are equivalent
> seq(to=3,from=1,by=0.5)
> seq(by=0.5,to=3,from=1)
```

18.5. Inputting Data via scan()

Another easy way to input data from your keyboard is to use the **scan()** function.

```
> x<-scan()
1: 1
2: 3
3: 4
4: 2.5
5: 5
6:
Read 5 items
> x
[1] 1.0 3.0 4.0 2.5 5.0
```

If you plan to input multiple columns, you can input them as a vector first then use the **matrix()** function to convert it to what you need. The desired input format (two columns) is given in the right panel below.

```
> x<-scan()                          1 3
1: 1 3 3 6 5 6 7 8                   3 6
9:                                   5 6
Read 8 items                         7 8
> y<-matrix(x,4,2,byrow=T)
> y
     [,1] [,2]
[1,]  1    3
[2,]  3    6
[3,]  5    6
[4,]  7    8
```

In the above example, we input data according to row. On the other hand, if we input data according to column, we have to change our codes a little bit.

```
> x<-scan()
1: 1 3 5 7 3 6 6 8
9:
Read 8 items
> y<-matrix(x,4,2,byrow=F)  # or use default y<-matrix(x,4,2)
```

18.6. Getting Data from an Excel File

Assume that we have the following Excel spreadsheet (in the right panel below). To input the data into R, we can highlight and copy the data then issue **x<-read.table("clipboard")**.

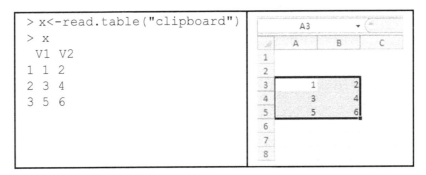

If the data set has headers (column names), just add **header=T**.

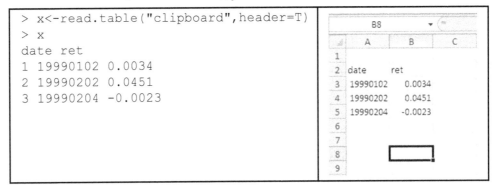

The above example is true when we open a Notepad or an MS Word file (see below).

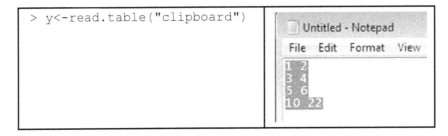

We should pay attention to the last row, which should be the entry only (see the comparison for the two formats below).

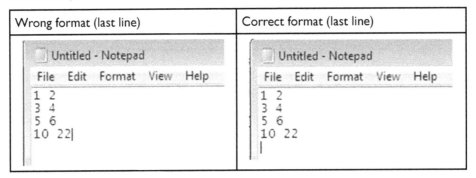

For the format shown in the above left panel, we will get the following warning message when issuing the command **x<-read.table("clipboard")**. Fortunately the variable will take values it is supposed to get.

```
> x<-read.table("clipboard")
Warning message:                   .
In read.table("clipboard"):
  incomplete final line found by readTableHeader on 'clipboard''
```

18.7. Precision of R

Most times, the precision of our R software is not an issue for most researchers for calculation. However, knowing how to find it would be helpful if you have such an issue in the future.

```
> .Machine$double.eps
[1] 2.220446e-16
```

Exercises

18.1. Use the **scan()** function to input twenty pairs of x and y.

18.2. Write an R program to input an Excel data set.

18.3. Input values for x ranging from 1 to 100 and 202 to 300.

18.4. Reverse the input values in 18.3.

CHAPTER 19

Inputting Data from External Sources

In this chapter, we introduce various ways to input data from external files or data sets. Reading data from external sources are common for researchers and practitioners since manually inputting data is not feasible for a reasonably sized data set, let alone for huge data sets that are the norm in financial analysis. For the counterpart of saving our data or results to an external file or data set, see chapter 32: "Reading and Writing Binary Data in R." A simple way to input data from a text file is to use the **read.table()** function (see below). The structure of an input file with a text format is in the right panel.

```
> x<-read.table("c:/test2.txt")    20110102 0.001
                                    20110104 0.002
```

The second example is related to the R data format, usually with an extension of **RData**. First, download and save a data set called **ibm.RData** to your PC then upload it by using the **load()** function.

```
# retrieve ibm.Rdata from CD
> load("c:/ibm.Rdata")
```

19.1. Reading Data from a Text File Using read.table()

Assume that we have a text file stored under the root directory of C drive (c:\). The file contains three observations with two variables (see the right panel below). The **header=T** will use the names of the first row of the input file as the column names.

```
> data<-read.table("c:/test.txt",header=T)    var1 var2
> data                                          29161 19761020
var1 var2                                       15763 19841229
1 29161 19761020                                10093 19830215
2 15763 19841229
3 10093 19830215
```

In the above codes, the single forward slash (/) can be replaced by a double backward slash (\\).

```
> data<- read.table("c:\\test.txt",header=T)
```

If there are some extralines at the top of an input file, such as a note, we have to skip those lines since they are not part of the data set we plan to input. Usually we call this type of note as a header. Since the **header=T** is referred to as the variable name, we don't use the word *header* to avoid potential confusion.

```
> # skip the first two lines          File name is test.txt
> x<- read.table("c:\\test2.txt",skip=2)  Generated 11/10/2010
                                       29161 19761020
                                       15763 19841229
                                       10093 19830215
```

19.2. Reading in the First Ten Rows to Explore

Sometimes we have no clue about the new data set. We like to explore the data set before processing it. We might like to input just ten observations. In those cases, we use **nrows=10**.

```
> d<- read.table("c:\\test.txt" ,skip=10,nrows=10)
```

19.3. Adding Column Names Using colnames() and col.names()

If an input data set has no names for any columns or we want to change the existing names, we use the **colnames()** function.

```
> x<-read.table("c:/test.txt ")
> colnames(x)<-c("ID","date")
```

To make our codes more condensed, we put the **col.names()** function in our **read.table()** function.

```
> x<-read.table("c:/test.txt",col.names=c("ID","date"))
```

Note that the **colnames()** and **col.names()** functions are used in different situations. We will explain their usages in other chapters.

19.4 Reading a CSV File

We use the **read.csv()** function to read an input file with a CSV format.

```
> x<-read.csv("c:/hsb.csv") # use default delimiter
```

For a comparison, if we use the **read.table()** function instead, we have to specify the delimiter (**sep=","**).

```
> x<-read.table("c:/hsb.csv",sep=',') # sep: separator
```

19.5. Reading from a Clipboard

First, we generate our simple input file. After launching Notepad, we type two lines of values then hit the **Enter** key (see below). In particular, the cursor is at the beginning of the third line, an empty line.

```
> x<-read.table('clipboard')
> x
V1 V2 V3
1  1  2  3
2  4  5  6
```

We highlight and copy the block (i.e., those two lines) then run the above R codes. If our cursor is at the end of the second line (i.e., after the value of 6—see the image below in the right panel), we would get a warning message after we issue the above R codes.

```
> read.table('clipboard')
V1 V2 V3
1  1  2  3
2  4  5  6
Warning message:
In read.table("clipboard"):
incomplete final line found by readTableHeader on 'clipboard'
```

Inputting from the clipboard this way is true for Excel. We can open an Excel file, generate a data set, then highlight and copy it. We can then issue the same R command **x<-read.table('clipboard')**.

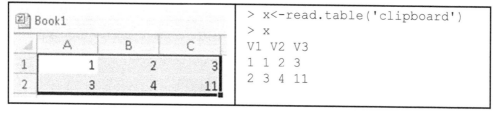

```
> x<-read.table('clipboard')
> x
V1 V2 V3
1  1  2  3
2  3  4  11
```

Copying files to Excel will be more complex. First, we generate a data set called y x, which is a matrix (see the codes below).

```
> x<-1:50
> y<-matrix(x,5,10)
> y
     [,1] [,2] [,3] [,4] [,5] [,6] [,7] [,8] [,9] [,10]
[1,]   1    6   11   16   21   26   31   36   41    46
[2,]   2    7   12   17   22   27   32   37   42    47
[3,]   3    8   13   18   23   28   33   38   43    48
[4,]   4    9   14   19   24   29   34   39   44    49
[5,]   5   10   15   20   25   30   35   40   45    50
> write.table(y,'clipboard')
```

Then we open an Excel file and right-click our mouse to paste it. We will end up with just one column of data (see below).

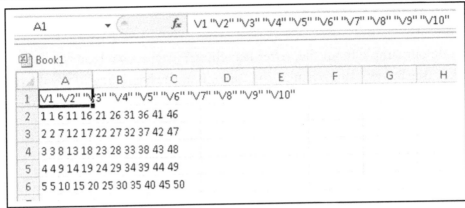

To separate the above one column into ten columns, we highlight the first column, click **Data** then **Text to columns**. Then we choose **delimited** and choose **space** as our delimiter (see below).

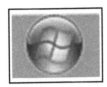

19.6. Input from a Delimited Input File

When retrieving files with a specific delimiter, we can use the **delim()** function.

```
> x<-read.delim("c:/temp/test2.txt",sep="*",header=T)
```

Alternatively we can use the **read.table()** function by specifying **sep='*'**.

```
> y<-read.table("c:/test2.txt",sep="*") # sep is separator
```

19.7. Input from a Fixed Width File read.fwf()

First, let's generate a text file called **test.txt**. The codes are in the left panel below while the final output is in the right panel.

```
>cat(file="c:/temp/test.txt","123456","987654",sep="\n")
```
```
123456
987654
```

The input format depends how we group those values. Assume that for each record, there are three different data items with lengths of 1, 2, and 3. Thus, for the first record, we have **data1=1**, **data2=23**, and **data3=456**. Then we can use **widths=c(1,2,3)**, as in the codes below:

```
> read.fwf(file="c:/temp/test.txt",widths=c(1,2,3))
  V1 V2 V3
1 1  23 456
2 9  87 654
```

To skip certain digits, a negative number is used. For the following codes, since the second one is negative, we end up with two data items only.

```
> read.fwf(file="c:/temp/test.txt",widths=c(1,-2,3))
  V1 V2
1 1 456
2 9 654
```

19.8. load() an R data set

First let's generate a binary R data set.

```
> x<-1:10
> save(x,file="c:/temp/test.Rdata")
```

To upload this data set, we use the **load()** function.

```
> rm(x)
> load("c:/test_R/test.Rdata") # x will be there
```

19.9. Extension .RData of an R Data Set Is Not Critical

In the following codes, we don't even give an extension to the R data set we generated.

```
> y<-1:100
> save(y,file="c:/test_R/abc")
> rm(y)
> load("c:/test_R/abc")
```

19.10. Reading from an Internet File

We can read a file from the Internet (see an example below).

```
> d<-read.csv("http://www.ats.ucla.edu/stat/R/notes/hsb2.csv",header=T)
> head(d)
   id female  race  ses schtyp   prog  read write math science socst
1  70   male white  low public general   57    52   41      47    57
2 121 female white middle public vocation 68   59   53      63    61
3  86   male white high public general   44    33   54      58    31
4 141   male white high public vocation  63    44   47      53    56
5 172   male white middle public academic 47   52   57      53    61
6 113   male white middle public academic 44   52   51      63    61
```

Next, let us try Yahoo Finance. First, go to the Yahoo Finance at http://finance.yahoo.com/. Then enter "IBM" in the Get Quote box. Click **Historical Prices** on the left-hand side. Go to the bottom of the Web page and click **Download to Spreadsheet**. Alternatively we can use a simple line of to get this file.

```
> x<-read.table('http://canisius.edu/~yany/data/ibm.csv',sep=',',header=T)
```

We can assign this data set to a new variable and show its first couple of lines.

```
> t1<-'http://finance.google.comifinance/historical?q='
> t2<-paste(t1,'IBM&startdateJun+02,+1970',sep='')
>x<-read.table(paste(t2,'&enddate=Jun+16,+','2017&output=csv',sep=''),sep=',')
> head(x)
     V1      V2     V3     V4     V5      V6
1    Date  Open  High  Low  Close  Volume
2 15-Jun-17 153.29 154.69 153.29 154.22 4654297
3 14-Jun-17 153.97 154.94 152.94 153.81 3049726
4 13-Jun-17 155.44 155.48 154.15 154.25 3523529
5 12-Jun-17 154.19 157.20 154.02 155.18 6471479
6 9-Jun-17 152.00 154.26 151.88 154.10 4361460
```

Of course we can use the **read.csv()** function to simplify our codes a little bit instead of using the **read.table()** function.

```
> t1<-'http://finance.google.com/finance/historical?q='
> t2<-paste(t1,'IBM&startdate=Jun+02,+1970',sep'')
> x<-read.csv(paste(t2,'&enddate=Jun+16,+','2017&output=csv',sep=''))
> head(x)
       Date     Open    High     Low   Close  Volume
1 15-Jun-17 153.29 154.69 153.29 154.22 4654297
2 14-Jun-17 153.97 154.94 152.94 153.81 3049726
3 13-Jun-17 155.44 155.48 154.15 154.25 3523529
4 12-Jun-17 154.19 157.20 154.02 155.18 6471479
5 9-Jun-17  152.00 154.26 151.88 154.10 4361460
6 8-Jun-17  151.00 152.82 150.92 152.10 3708962
```

19.11. Reading from canisius.edu/~yany

We keep many CSV files or R Data sets at the above Web site.

```
>x<-read.csv("http://canisius.edu/~yany/ibm.csv",head=T)
```

Again, to view the contents of the variable, we can use the **head()** function.

```
> head(x)
  Date Open High Low Close Volume Adj.Close
1 2010-12-03 144.25 145.68 144.25 145.38 3710600 145.38
2 2010-12-02 144.33 145.85 144.30 145.18 5374000 145.18
3 2010-12-01 143.61 145.13 143.51 144.41 6822800 144.41
4 2010-11-30 142.24 142.76 141.28 141.46 7674800 141.46
5 2010-11-29 143.53 143.67 141.50 142.89 5040300 142.89
6 2010-11-26 145.30 145.30 143.57 143.90 2081300 143.90
```

Here is another example:

```
>x<-read.table("http://canisius.edu/~yany/F-F_Research_Data_Factors2.
txt",skip=3,header=T)
> head(x)
 Mkt.RF SMB HML RF
192607 2.95 -2.46 -2.87 0.22
192608 2.63 -1.19 4.60 0.25
192609 0.38 -1.33 -0.23 0.23
192610 -3.24 -0.08 0.20 0.32
192611 2.54 -0.29 -0.24 0.31
192612 2.62 -0.20 -0.05 0.28
```

If we intend to retrieve several data sets from the same Web page, it is not convenient to specify the whole path every time. Thus, we are better off defining a variable that changes with different keywords. Below, a variable called **data_set** is such a variable.

```
> http<-"http://canisius.edu/-yany/data/"
> data_set<-"ffMonthly.txt" # change this one only
> location<-paste(http,data_set,sep="")
> x<-read.table(location, header=T)
```

19.12. Finding Help for Inputting Data from an External File

We can use the **help()** function to find the related information about those functions.

```
> help(read.table)
> help(read.csv)
> help(read.delim)
> help(read.fwf)
```

19.13. Some R Data Sets from the Internet

The data set called **ff.Rdata** has two data sets: Fama-French monthly factors and Fama-French daily factors (http://canisius.edu/~yany/RData/ff.RData). We can use the following codes to load the data set called **ff.RData**.

```
> con<-url('http://canisius.edu/~yany/RData/ff.RData')
> load(con)
> close(con)
> ls()
[1] "con " "ff_daily_factors " "ff_monthly_factors"
```

19.14. Inputting Files with Irregular Formats

Below, we try to write an R program to retrieve correct files by using the readLines() function. In the following input file, we need to input data lines that contain seven data items.

generated 12/12/2011

Date Open High Low Close Volume Adj.Close

2011-12-20 10.21 10.38 10.18 10.33 45218900 10.33

2011-12-19 10.25 10.39 9.99 10.02 45055000 10.02

2011-12-16 10.32 10.4 10.16 10.25 45882000 10.25

end of the file

After we use the **readLines()** function, we generate a variable with six data items, which represent the number of lines.

```
> x<-readLines("c:/temp/test.txt")
> x
[1] "generated 12/12/2011"
[2] "Date Open High Low Close Volume Adj.Close"
[3] "2011-12-20 10.21 10.38 10.18 10.33 45218900 10.33"
[4] "2011-12-19 10.25 10.39 9.99 10.02 45055000 10.02"
[5] "2011-12-16 10.32 10.4 10.16 10.25 45882000 10.25"
[6] "end of the file "
```

We know that the first line has two data items and is not a regular line, which have seven data items.

```
> k<-t(sapply(strsplit(x[1]," "),unlist))
> length(k)
[1] 2
> k<-t(sapply(strsplit(x[2]," "),unlist))
> length(k)
[1] 7
```

Now we have a way to get regular lines that contain only seven data items. Below is our complete program.

```
x<-readLines("c:/temp/test.txt ")
n<-length(x)
out<-NA
for(i in 1:n){
 k<-t(sapply(strsplit(x[i]," "),unlist))
 if(length(k)==7) out<-rbind(out,k)
 #print(length(k))
}
out2<-subset(out,!is.na(out[,1]))
> out2
 [,1] [,2] [,3] [,4] [,5] [,6] [,7]
 "Date " "Open" "High" "Low" "Close" "Volume" "Adj.Close"
 "2011-12-20" "10.21" "10.38" "10.18" "10.33" "45218900" "10.33"
 "2011-12-19" "10.25" "10.39" "9.99" "10.02" "45055000" "10.02"
 "2011-12-16" "10.32" "10.4" "10.16" "10.25" "45882000" "10.25"
```

There are many ways to generate a text file. For example, we can use Notepad. To launch Notepad, click. After that, we see the following setup:

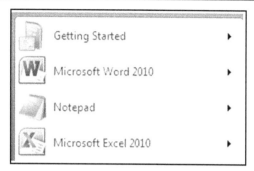

Click Notepad, type the following records, then save the output, such as **test.txt**.

29161 19761020
15763 19841229
10093 19830215

The second way to launch Notepad is to click **All Programs** then **Accessories** then **Notepad**. The third way to launch Notepad has two steps:

Type "notepad" in the following box (Search program and files).

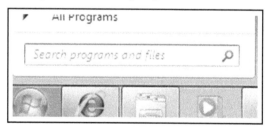

Exercises

19.1. Use Notepad to generate a text file and input it into R.
    -8.086741 10.011198 4.560525 -14.342503 -2.653048
    6.417692 -4.150210 -4.595757 -7.924940 -11.585391
19.2. Launch Excel to generate a file and save it with a CSV format. Input the file into R.
19.3. Go to Yahoo Finance and download DELL's historical price data and input it into R.
19.4. Based on the result from 19.3, estimate the returns for DELL.
19.5. We generated an R data set called **ff.Rdata**, which has two data sets (called **ff_monthly_factors** and **ff_daily_factors**). Please download it at http://canisius.edu/~yany/RData/ff.Rdata then upload and play with it.

19.6. Download the momentum factor from Professor French's data library. The name of the file is **F-F_momentum_Factor_CSV.zip**. Write an R program to retrieve the momentum factor and save it as an R data set.

CHAPTER 20

Simple Data Manipulation

In this chapter, we discuss ways to manipulate data, such as combining several columns to form a matrix, manipulating matrices, and choosing a subset from a big one.

20.1. The Functions head() and tail()

When a data set is big, it is a great idea to view the first and the last couple of lines. In this case, we use the **head()** and the **tail()** functions.

```
> x<-seq(1,500,1.5)
> head(x)
[1] 1.0 2.5 4.0 5.5 7.0 8.5
> tail(x)
[1] 491.5 493.0 494.5 496.0 497.5 499.0
```

We could specify number of lines we want to show, such as **head(x,20)** or **tail(x,20)**.

```
> tail(x,20)
[1] 470.5 472.0 473.5 475.0 476.5 478.0 479.5 481.0 482.5 484.0 485.5
[12] 487.0 488.5 490.0 491.5 493.0 494.5 496.0 497.5 499.0
>
```

20.2. The Function summary()

If **x** is a vector or matrix and we want to know more about the variable, we can use the **summary()** function.

```
> x<-1:500
> summary(x)
  Min. 1st Qu. Median Mean 3rd Qu. Max.
  1.0 125.8 250.5 250.5 375.2 500.0
```

20.3. Function ls() vs. ls(pattern='my_pattern')

While the **ls()** function is used to list all objectives, we use **ls(pattern="keyword")** to list objectives with a specified keyword or pattern.

```
> ls(pattern='my')
[1] "my_double" "my_pv"
```

20.4. Types of Variables

To know the types of variables, we can use **typeof(x)**.

```
> x<-1:5                > x<-'I love apples'> typeof(x)
> typeof(x)             [1] "character"
[1] "integer"
```

The following table lists different types of variables: definitions plus examples

Table 20.1. Types of variables

Name	Examples	Dimension
Scalar	>x<-10	> x<-10 > length(x) [1] 1
Vector	>y<-c(0.1,0.34,0.98) >x<-1:20 >t<-seq(1,10,by=0.5)	> x<-seq(1,50,2.34) > length(x) [1] 21
Matrix	> x<-1:100 > y<-matrix(x,2,50)	> x<-matrix(0,3,2) > dim(x) [1] 3 2
List	> x<-list(c(1,2,3),1:20,4)	> x<-list(c(1,2,3),1:20,4) > length(x) [1] 3
Factor	> x<-c(1,2,4,1,1,1,2) > y<-as.factor(x) > y [1] 1 2 4 1 1 1 2 Levels: 1 2 4	

20.5. The Function is.vector() and Similar Functions

We can use the **is.vector()** function and other similar functions to identify whether the variable is a vector, matrix, integer, or others.

```
> x<-1:10 # here are the answers
> is.vector(x)
[1] TRUE
> is.matrix(x)
[1] FALSE
> is.integer(x)
[1] TRUE
> is.list(x)
[1] FALSE
> is.real(x)
[1] FALSE
```

See a few similar examples below:

```
> is.character(2)
[1] FALSE
> is.numeric("Hi")
[1] FALSE
> x<-c(1,2,4,1,1,1,2)
> y<-as.factor(x)
> is.factor(y)
[1] TRUE
```

20.6. Functions length() vs. dim()

For a vector, we use the **length()** function to find out its number of values (length) while we use the **dim()** function to find out the dimensions of a matrix.

```
> x<-11:8
> length(x)
[1] 20 # there are 20 values
> y<-matrix(x,4,5)
> dim(y)
[1] 4 5 # dimensions of y is 4 by 5
```

20.7. The Function cbind()

We can use the **cbind()** function to combine two vectors (columns), as in the example below:

```
> x<-1:10
> y<-2:11
> cbind(x,y)
   x y
 [1,]  1  2
 [2,]  2  3
 [3,]  3  4
 [4,]  4  5
 [5,]  5  6
 [6,]  6  7
 [7,]  7  8
 [8,]  8  9
 [9,]  9 10
[10,] 10 11
```

When a vector is shorter than another, R recycles the values from the shorter vector.

```
> x<-1:5
> y<-c(0.2,0.3)
> cbind(x,y)
  x y
[1,] 1 0.2
[2,] 2 0.3
[3,] 3 0.2
[4,] 4 0.3
[5,] 5 0.2
Warning message:
In cbind(x, y) :
  number of rows of result is not a multiple of vector length (arg 2)
```

Sometimes we can use this property to add a constant (see below).

```
> x<-1:10
> cbind(20,x)
x
[1,] 20 1
[2,] 20 2
[3,] 20 3
[4,] 20 4
[5,] 20 5
[6,] 20 6
[7,] 20 7
[8,] 20 8
[9,] 20 9
[10,] 20 10
```

Since a matrix has the same data types for all its values, when a column is a character, , all columns become characters when using the **cbind()** function. This is true for the **rbind()** function.

```
> x<-1:5
> cbind("ibm",x)
x
                x
[1,] "ibm" "1"
[2,] "ibm" "2"
[3,] "ibm" "3"
[4,] "ibm" "4"
[5,] "ibm" "5"
```

20.8. Converting a Vector into a Matrix

Below, first we generate a vector then convert it into a matrix.

```
> x<-1:100
> y<-matrix(x,5,20) # nrow first and ncol second
```

We should pay attention when we convert a vector into a matrix: column first or row first. Since we know that **x** has values from 1, 2, 3, up to 100, we can see how the matrix is arranged by printing the first several lines (see the codes below).

```
> x<-1:100
> y<-matrix(x,50,5)
> dim(y)
[1] 20 5
> head(y)
     [,1] [,2] [,3] [,4] [,5]
[1,]  1   21   41   61   81
[2,]  2   22   42   62   82
[3,]  3   23   43   63   83
[4,]  4   24   44   64   84
[5,]  5   25   45   65   85
[6,]  6   26   46   66   86
```

Obviously the default setting is the column first. If we want to sort a vector into a matrix by row, we have to specify this condition by using **byrow=T**, where T stands for "true."

```
> y<-matrix(x,20,5,byrow=T)
> head(y)
     [,1] [,2] [,3] [,4] [,5]
[1,]  1    2    3    4    5
[2,]  6    7    8    9   10
[3,] 11   12   13   14   15
[4,] 16   17   18   19   20
[5,] 21   22   23   24   25
[6,] 26   27   28   29   30
```

To generate a matrix (n by m) with all zeros in it, we can use the following codes.

```
> x<-matrix(0,5,3)
> x
     [,1] [,2] [,3]
[1,]  0    0    0
[2,]  0    0    0
[3,]  0    0    0
[4,]  0    0    0
[5,]  0    0    0
```

20.9. Adding Column Names Using colnames()

It is a good programming practice to give columns meaningful names. It is quite convenient and sometimes critical especially when we have many columns.

```
> x<-1:5
> y<-rnorm(5) # assume those are returns
> z<-cbind(x,y)
> z
  x y
[1,] 1  0.7108900
[2,] 2  1.2676018
[3,] 3 -0.1431511
[4,] 4 -0.5150289
[5,] 5  1.4828912
> colnames(z)<-c("date","ret")
> z
  date ret
[1,] 1  0.7108900
[2,] 2  1.2676018
[3,] 3 -0.1431511
[4,] 4 -0.5150289
[5,] 5  1.4828912
```

After inputting a set of variables with their names (**header=T**), we can use the $ sign to refer to one specific column (see an example below). The input file is presented in the right panel.

```
> k<-read.table('clipboard', header=T)      date time
> k                                          1 2
date time                                    3 4
1 1 2
2 3 4
> k$date
[1] 1 3
```

20.10. Getting Specific Rows or Columns from a Matrix

Assume that x is a matrix. It is a good idea that we know the structure of the variable first by using **head()**, **tail()**, **summary()**, **length()**, or **dim()** to acquire basic knowledge related to this specific data set. For a specific column, we specify the second dimension.

```
> y<-x[,3:5] # get columns 3 to 5
```

Similarly we can choose specific rows.

```
> y<-x[1:100,3:5] # rows 1 to 100 for columns 3 to 5
```

20.11. Retrieving a Subset Based on Certain Conditions

Assume that we generate twenty random numbers and choose all positive ones.

```
> set.seed(12345)
> x<-rnorm(20)
> x
 [1]  0.5855288  0.7094660 -0.1093033 -0.4534972  0.6058875
 [6] -1.8179560  0.6300986 -0.2761841 -0.2841597 -0.9193220
[11] -0.1162478  1.8173120  0.3706279  0.5202165 -0.7505320
[16]  0.8168998 -0.8863575 -0.3315776  1.1207127  0.2987237
> y<-x[x>0]
> y
 [1]  0.5855288  0.7094660  0.6058875  0.6300986  1.8173120
 [6]  0.3706279  0.5202165  0.8168998  1.1207127  0.2987237
```

20.12. Row Names

Most of time, we care about the column names only. Occasionally we can use row names to save some space. In the following example, we use row names to separate data for different companies. Alternatively we can add an extracolumn called firm to accomplish the same task.

```
> x<-c(1,2,3,4)
> y<-c(0.23,0.14,-0.11,0.55)
> z<-cbind(x,y)
> z
     x y
[1,] 1  0.23
[2,] 2  0.14
[3,] 3 -0.11
[4,] 4  0.55
> rownames(z)<-c('firm1','firm2','firm3','firm4')
> z
      x y
firm1 1  0.23
firm2 2  0.14
firm3 3 -0.11
firm4 4  0.55
```

20.13. Converting a List into a Matrix

In the following example, we download the financial statement for IBM first then convert it into a matrix.

```
> library(XML)
x<-readHTMLTable("http://www.marketwatch.com/investing/stock/IBM/financials")
typeof(x)
> typeof(x)
[1] "list"
> length(x)
[1] 2
>x1<-as.matrix(x[[1]])
```

20.14. Combining Two Matrices By Row

The example below shows how to use the **rbind()** function to combine rows.

```
> library(XML)
x<-readHTMLTable("http://www.marketwatch.com/investing/stock/IBM/financials")
>x1<-as.matrix(x[[1]])
> dim(x1)
[1] 11 7
>x2<-as.matrix(x[[2]])
> dim(x2)
[1] 46 7
> y<-rbind(x1,x2)
> dim(y)
[1] 57 7
```

Exercises

20.1. When can we use the head() or tail() functions?

20.2. Assuming x is a matrix, how do we view its first twenty lines?

20.3. How can we be sure that x is a matrix?

20.4. Assuming y is a vector, how do we view the first sixteen data records?

20.5. How do we know the type of a variable?

20.6. Assuming there are three columns in x, could it be possible that those three columns have different types?

20.7. Generate random numbers of x and y drawn from a uniform distribution in order to form a twentyby-two matrix. The related random number function is **runif()**.

20.8. Generate 1,000 consecutive integers starting from -20. Convert them into a matrix with 500 by-2 dimensions. How many ways can we form such a matrix?

20.9. How do we add column names to a matrix?

20.10. What is the use of column names?

20.11. How do we add row names? What are their uses?

CHAPTER 21

R Loops

Loops are very important in R since we use various loops to manipulate data, get a subset, merge different data sets, or redirect the flows of our programs. The most used loops are the **for()** loop and the **while()** loop. Let's look at the simplest loop of printing three values on the screen.

```
> for(i in 1:3) print(i)
[1] 1
[1] 2
[1] 3
```

The **i in 1:3** means that the variable i will take one value at a time from 1 to 3. The above one-line codes are equivalent to the following two lines.

```
> x<-1:10
> for(i in x)print(i)
```

Below is a similar example but with a character vector instead. A vector is a column variable with n-by-1 dimensions.

```
> tickers<-c("DELL","IBM","C","MSFT")
> for(ticker in tickers) print(ticker)
[1] "DELL"
[1] "IBM"
[1] "C"
[1] "MSFT"
```

21.1. For Loop

In the following program, the variable of i (a scalar variable) will take one value at a time from 1 to n, where *n* is the number of the total observations of x, which itself is a vector variable.

```
> x<-5:15
> n<-length(x) # get the number of observations for x
> for(i in 1:n) print(x[i])# print each item from x
```

For a multiple-line program, we should use a pair of curly braces, { and }, to circle those command lines.

```
for(i in 1:10){
  #
  # add your codes here
  #
  print(i)
}
```

There are some predefined data sets in R. For example, a character data set called **LETTERS** contains twenty-six capital letters while the data set called **letters**, its counterpart, contains twenty-six lowercase letters.

```
> letters
 [1] "a" "b" "c" "d" "e" "f" "g" "h" "i" "j" "k" "l" "m" "n" "o" "p" "q" "r" "s"
[20] "t" "u" "v" "w" "x" "y" "z"
> typeof(letters)
               [1] "character"
> length(letters)
 [1] 26
```

The following codes show the variable called **letters**.

```
> for(letter in letters) print(letter)
```

Using the **cat()** function instead of the **print()** function. We will print all twenty-six letters one after another.

```
> for(letter in letters) cat(letter)
abcdefghijklmnopqrstuvwxyz>
```

If we intend to print one letter every line, we can add a new-line character ("\n").

```
> for(letter in letters) cat(letter, "\n")
```

The following program prints each ticker in a character vector called **tickers**.

```
> tickers<-c("IBM","DELL","MSFT")
> for(ticker in tickers)
> print(ticker)
```

21.2. Using Modulus Function to Shape the Output Format

Note that the function **%%** is the modulus function. It gives us the remainder **n %% m**. For instance, **11%% 10** will be 1, and **23 %% 10** will be 3. If we want to add a new line of "\n" every five letters, we can use the following codes.

| ```
n<-length(letters)
for(i in 1:n){
    cat(letters[i])
    if(i%%5==0) cat("\n")
}
# output shown on the right
``` | abcde<br>fghij<br>klmno<br>pqrst<br>uvwxy<br>z> |

21.3. Double Loops

For double loops, usually we use **[i,j]**, referring to those two loops. Again, properly indented codes are more readable.

```
n1<- 10
n2<- 50
for(i in 1:n1) {
    for(j in 1:n2){
        #
        # your codes here
        #
    }
}
```

For example, we intend to add 5 to the major diagonal variables **y[i, i]**, where **i=1, 2,..., 5** of a square matrix. The major diagonal line of a square matrix is from NW (northwest) to SE (southeast). First we generate a square matrix.

```
> x<-1:49 # x is a vector
> y<-matrix(x,7,7,byrow=T) # y is 7 by 7 matrix
> y
      [,1] [,2] [,3] [,4] [,5] [,6] [,7]
[1,]   1   2   3   4   5   6   7
[2,]   8   9  10  11  12  13  14
[3,]  15  16  17  18  19  20  21
[4,]  22  23  24  25  26  27  28
[5,]  29  30  31  32  33  34  35
[6,]  36  37  38  39  40  41  42
[7,]  43  44  45  46  47  48  49
```

Below are the codes to add a value of 5 to the data items on the major diagonal line.

```
n1<-nrow(y)
n2<-ncol(y)
for(i in 1:n1) {
   for(j in 1:n2){
   if(i==j) y[i,j]=y[i,j]+5
   }
}
```

To double check that we have indeed added 5 to those values, type **y**.

323
```

```
> y
     [,1] [,2] [,3] [,4] [,5] [,6] [,7]
[1,]  6   2    3    4    5    6    7
[2,]  8   14   10   11   12   13   14
[3,]  15  16   22   18   19   20   21
[4,]  22  23   24   30   26   27   28
[5,]  29  30   31   32   38   34   35
[6,]  36  37   38   39   40   46   42
[7,]  43  44   45   46   47   48   54
```

21.4. While Loop

Below is an example of a while loop:

```
i <- 0
while(i<15) {
        i<- i+2
        print(i)
}
```

Why are the following codes problematic?

```
i <- 0 # wrong codes
while(i<15) {
   print(i+2)
}
```

21.5. How to Stop (Cancel) an Execution

To stop a current computation, we can click **Misc** on the menu bar and choose **Stop current computation** (see below).

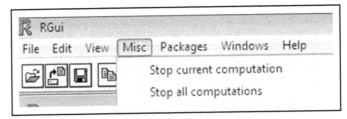

21.6. Stopping After Detecting an Error

Setting breaks would make our debugging efforts more efficient.

```
# add a break when an error happens
dd<-function(n){
     if (is.numeric(n)==FALSE) stop("Input should be numeric!")
     return(2*n)
}
```

After activating the function, we can test it by using the following two commands: one is for an integer input, and the other is for a character input.

```
> dd(2)
[1]  4
> dd("live")
Error in double("live")  :  Input should be numeric!
```

21.7. Length of a Vector vs. Dimension of a Matrix

A *vector* is defined as "a column variable," and we use the **length()** function to find out its number of observations.

```
> x<-c(1,2,4.5,7,9)
> x
[1]  1.0 2.0 4.5 7.0 9.0
> length(x)
[1]  5
```

A matrix is a two-dimensional data set (variable). We can use the **cbind()** function to join two vectors into a matrix such as **cbind(vectior1, vector2)**.

```
> x<-c(1,2,4.5,7,9)
> y<-c(0.3,0.2,0,4,5)
> z<-cbind(x,y)
> z
    x y
[1,] 1.0 0.3
[2,] 2.0 0.2
[3,] 4.5 0.0
[4,] 7.0 4.0
[5,] 9.0 5.0
```

In the above case, both x and y are vectors while z is a matrix. Sometimes we need to know how many data points (values) a vector contains (i.e., the length of a vector). In those cases, the **length()** function is used.

```
> x<-c(1:20,4:22,9)
> n<-length(x)
> n
[1]  40
```

For a matrix, we use the **nrow()** function for the number of rows and the **ncol()** function for the number of columns.

```
> x<-matrix(0,3,4)
> x
     [,1] [,2] [,3] [,4]
[1,]  0    0    0    0
[2,]  0    0    0    0
[3,]  0    0    0    0
> nrow(x)
[1] 3
> ncol(x)
[1] 4
```

Alternatively we can use the **dim()** function instead.

```
> dim(x)
 [1] 3 4
> n<-dim(x)
> n[1]
 [1] 3
> n[2]
 [1] 4
```

CHAPTER 22

If-Else, Logic OR, and Logic AND

Here is the simplest control using the **if()** function.

```
> x<-10
> if(x>0) print("x>0")
```

Assume that we have the following simple data set with just two columns.

```
> year<-c(1991,1992,1993,1994)    > data
> ret<-c(0.01,0.02,0.03,0.034)    year ret
> data<-cbind(year,ret)           [1,] 1991 0.010
                                  [2,] 1992 0.020
                                  [3,] 1993 0.030
                                  [4,] 1994 0.034
```

We want to get a subset of data, such as years after 1992.

```
> x<-subset(data,year>1992)
> x
 year ret
[1,] 1993 0.030
[2,] 1994 0.034
```

22.1. Introduction

Conditions—such as **if()** and **if()-else()** functions—are commonly used to manipulate data and/or redirect the flows of your programs. Assume that we have an R data set with daily return data for a thousand stocks over multiple years. We might be interested in just a few stocks for one year. To choose IBM for 2010, we can issue commands similar to the following codes: **if(ticker == "IBM" & year==2010)**, where & is logic AND.

22.2. The if() Function

In the following codes, we have a default value for the variable called **decision: reject**. When the NPV of our project is positive, we accept the project. From chapter 2, this is the NPV rule: if NPV>0, we accept the project; if NPV<0, we reject the project.

```
>decision<-"reject the project"
>if(npv>0) decision<-"accept the project"
>print(decision)
```

22.3. If-Else Function

If-else is another widely used structure (see the following example).

```
if(x>0){
  print("x>0")
  # your codes here
} else {
  print("x<=0")
  # your codes here
}
```

In the above codes, we classify **x** values into two groups.

22.4. If-Else–If-Else Function

For a multigroup classification, we can have multiple **if()** functions combined together. Below, we generate a function to convert a percentage grade into its corresponding letter grade.

```
letter_grade<-function(grade){
  if(grade>=90){
      final<-"A"
  } else if(grade>=80){
      final<-"B"
  } else if (grade>=70){
      final<-"C"
  } else if (grade>=60){
      final<-"D"
  } else{
      final<-"Fail"
  }
  return(final)
}
```

To call the function is easy.

```
> letter_grade(90)
[1] "A"
> letter_grade(89)
[1] "B"
> letter_grade(79)
[1] "C"
> letter_grade(50)
[1] "Fail"
```

22.5. The if() and stop() Pair

In our future-value function, an interest rate cannot be negative. In this case, we use the **if()** and **stop()** pair.

```
fv_f<-function(pv,r,n){
  if(r<0)stop("interest is negative")
  return(pv*(1+r)^n)
}
```

We can test this by entering a negative interest rate.

```
> fv_f(100,0.1,1)
[1] 110
> fv_f(100,-0.1,1)
Error in fv_f(100, -0.1, 1) : interest is negative
```

22.6. Logic OR

The logic OR means that if any of the given condition is met, we go to the next step (i.e., we do something).

```
> x=1
> y=-3
> if(x>0 | y>0) cat("x=",x,"y=",y,"\n")
x= 1 y= 3
```

Assume that we are trying to choose a sample data from a pool of all American stocks with publicly trading data. According to our research topic, we are interested in NYSE-listed or American-listed stocks. If we have a variable called **EXCHAGE** code—which takes the value of 1 for NYSE, 2 for AMEX, or 3 or NASDAQ—then we can have the following codes:

```
>x2<-subset(x,EXCHAGE==1 | EXCHAGE==2)
```

22.7. Logic AND

In R, we use an ampersand (**&**) to represent a logic AND.

```
> x<-1
> y <- -3
> if(x>0 & y>0) print("both positive")
```

22.8. Going to the Next Line After Every Ten Numbers

First, let's look at the modulus function **%%**. It gives us the remainder **n %% m** (e.g., **11 %% 10** will be 1, and **23 %% 10** will be 3). The following one-line codes would print 100 values on one line with a blank space between each adjacent numbers.

```
for(i in 1:100) cat(" ",i)
```

Now, we add a return after every ten numbers. The output looks much better now (see the right panel below).

```
for(i in 1:100){
  cat(" ",i)
  if(i%%10==0) cat("\n")
}
```

```
 1 2 3 4 5 6 7 8 9 10
 11 12 13 14 15 16 17 18 19 20
 21 22 23 24 25 26 27 28 29 30
 31 32 33 34 35 36 37 38 39 40
 41 42 43 44 45 46 47 48 49 50
 51 52 53 54 55 56 57 58 59 60
 61 62 63 64 65 66 67 68 69 70
 71 72 73 74 75 76 77 78 79 80
 81 82 83 84 85 86 87 88 89 90
 91 92 93 94 95 96 97 98 99 100
```

22.9. Combination of Various Conditions

When we have different types of combinations, we should test our codes. We have two variables (x, y). Our condition is that both should be positive and that x be an even number. If this is met, then we print pass.

```
> x<-7
> y<-9
> if((x>0 | y>0) & x%%2==1) print("pass")
```

How about the following codes?

```
> if(x>0 | y>0 & x%%2==1) print("pass")
```

Exercises

22.1. Assume that we have five hundred stocks in a data set. How do we randomly choose fifty stocks from it?

22.2. What is wrong with the following codes?

```
If(x=0) print("x is zero")
```

CHAPTER 23

Outputting to a File

To save data to a text file, use the following codes:

```
> x<-1:5
> write.table(x,file="c:/test.txt",quote=F,row.names=F)
```

The second example shows how to save an R data set, the best format of which is in R. The speed of retrieval is one of the major advantages of using the R-data format (RData). For more details, see chapter 43.

```
> x<-1:100
> y<-rnorm(200)
> save(x,y,file="c:/test.RData")
```

To upload an R data set, we use the **load()** function.

```
> load("c:/test.RData")
```

23.1. Writing to a Text File

There are several advantages of saving our results to a text file. First, it is easy to read since we can use Notepad or Microsoft Word to open such a file. Second, we can use other softwares to process the data further. Third, we can exchange data or results with other non-R users. To write a text file, we can use the **write.table(), write.csv(), write(), or cat()** functions which would be discussed later in the chapter.

23.2 The Function write.table()

This function is the most used R function to write a text file, including a CSV file. In the following example, pay attention to the double quotations and the first column in the right panel below, which are the row names.

```
> x<-100:1                              "x"
> write.table(x,'c:/temp/test.txt')    "1" 100
                                        "2" 99
                                        "3" 98
                                        "4" 97
```

However usually we don't need double quotation marks and row names. In this case, we add **quote=F**, **row.names=F**, where F stands "false."

	x
```> x<-1:100``` ```> write.table(x,'c:/temp/test.txt',quote=F,row.names=F)```	1 2 3 4

23.3. Writing a CSV (Comma Separate Value) File

A CSV file is a special format among text files. The advantage of a CSV file is that it saves space since we don't need blanks to make our output files more readable. Second, reading or writing a CSV file is quite common for almost all softwares. Third, it is quite easy to use Excel to input a CSV file.

23.4. The write.csv() Function

Below, we generate a vector from 1 to 100 then save it to a file called **test.dat.**

```> x<-1:100```
```> write.csv(x,'c:/test.dat')```
	```"","x"```
	```"1",1```
	```"2",2```
	```"99",99```
	```"100",100```

Again, double quotations and row names are usually not necessary.

```x<-1:10```
```> y<-rev(x)```
```> z<-cbind(x,y)```
```> write.csv(z,"c:/t.csv",quote=F,row.names=F)```
	```x,y```
	```1,10```
	```2,9```
	```3,8```
	```4,7```

	```5,6```
	```6,5```
	```7,4```
	```8,3```
	```9,2```
	```10,1```

There are two ways to retrieve such data from Excel. The first is to start Excel then open the above output file called **t.csv.** For the second method, we save our data to a clipboard first.

```
x<-1:10                                                      x,y
> y<-rev(x)                                                  1,10
> z<-cbind(x,y)                                              2,9
> write.csv(z, "clipboard",quote=F,row.names=F)             3,8
                                                             4,7
                                                             5,6
                                                             6,5
                                                             7,4
                                                             8,3
                                                             9,2
                                                             10,1
```

Go to Excel and paste it. Highlight the output then click **Data** then **Text to Column**. Choose **Delimiter** then **comma**.

	A
1	x,y
2	1,10
3	2,9
4	3,8
5	4,7
6	5,6
7	6,5
8	7,4
9	8,3
10	9,2
11	10,1

It is better to show the result if we have a matrix (multiple columns). The output is shown in the right panel.

```
> x<-1:10                                      "","x","y"
> y<-11:2                                      "1",1,11
> z<-cbind(x,y)                                "2",2,10
> write.csv(z,'c:/temp/test.txt')             "3",3,9
                                               "4",4,8
                                               "5",5,7
                                               "6",6,6
                                               "7",7,5
                                               "8",8,4
                                               "9",9,3
                                               "10",10,2
```

23.5. The write() Function

Below, we generate two vectors, combine them, and save the final results by using the **write()** function.

```
> x<-1:5                                          1 2
> y<-11:7                                          3 4
> z<-cbind(x,y)                                    5 6
> z                                                7 8
x y                                               9 10
```
```
[1,] 1 11                                         11 10
[2,] 2 10
[3,] 3 9
[4,] 4 8
[5,] 5 7
> write(z,'c:/temp/test.txt',ncolumns=2)
```
```
> write(x, "c:/test.txt") # double quotations
```
```
> write(x, "c:\\test.txt") # use \\ instead of /
```

If we use the **write()** function instead of the **write.table()** function, we will get a different output (see the right panel below).

```
> x<-1:100                          1 2 3 4 5
> write(x,'c:/test.dat')            6 7 8 9 10
                                    91 92 93 94 95
                                    96 97 98 99 100
```

We can save the column names as well.

```
> x<-c(19900102, 0.023, 19900102, 0.001)
> x2<-t(matrix(x,2,2))
> x2
   [,1] [,2]
[1,] 19900102 0.023
[2,] 19900102 0.001
> colnames(x2)<-c("date","ret")
> write.table(x2,file="c:/test.dat",col.names=TRUE)
```

We can use the **read.table()** function to read the output saved by the above program.

```
> read.table("c:/test.dat")
  date ret
1 19900102 0.023
2 19900102 0.001
```

We can define a variable representing the name of the output file.

```
> outfile<-"c:/test.txt"
> write.table(x,outfile)
```

23.6. Writing and Loading an R Data Set

To save an RData set, we use the **save()** function.

```
> x<-1:1000
> save(x,file="c:/temp/test.RData")
```

334

To retrieve the data set, we use the **load()** function.

```
> load("c:/temp/test.RData")
```

The extension of an R data set is not critical. You can try the following codes.

```
> x<-1:1000
> save(x,file="c:/temp/test")
> rm(x)
> load("c:/temp/test")
> x
> help(write.table) #get complete information about write.table()
write.table(x, file = "", append = FALSE, quote = TRUE, sep =
" ",eol = "\n", na = "NA", dec = ".", row.names = TRUE,col.
names = TRUE, qmethod = c("escape", "double"))
```

One of the advantages of using the **save()** function is that we can save multiple data sets simultaneously.

```
> x<-1:10
> y<-rnorm(100)
> save(x,y,file="c:/temp/test.RData")
```

23.7. Appending Data to an Existing Text File

It is quite often that we need to append data to an existing file.

```
> write.table(x,"c:/temp/test.txt")
> write.table(y,"c:/temp/test.txt",append=TRUE)
# For some reason "append=T" is not working for write.csv()
```

23.8. The dot-Rdata File (.Rdata)

The R data set called .RData under your working directory would save the data after you answer yes when quitting.

```
> # when quit answer yes to save the current settings (variables)
```

23.9. Using cat()

Here is another way to save data to a text file.

```
> cat("1 3 4 5","7 17 6 1",file="c:/test.txt",seq="\n")
>cat(file="c:/temp/test.txt","123456","987654",sep="\n")    123456
                                                             987654
```

23.10. Writing a Binary File

There are many ways to write a binary file. Using the **save()** function is one of them. The advantage of writing a binary file is the speed. It is extremely efficient to retrieve a binary data set compared to retrieving data from a text file. For more details, see chapter 32.

23.11. Saving a PDF File

In the following program, we generate a PDF file.

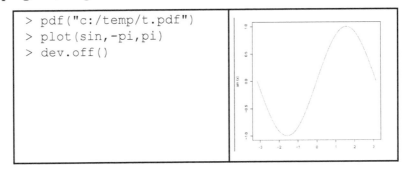

```
> pdf("c:/temp/t.pdf")
> plot(sin,-pi,pi)
> dev.off()
```

23.12. Writing Data to a Clipboard

We all know that we can high copy when we use Excel, MS Word, or Notepad. When we are doing so, we copy the highlighted contents to a clipboard. We can do so in R.

```
> x<-1:10                                    "","x","y"
> y<-rev(x)                                  "1",1,10
> z<-cbind(x,y)                              "2",2,9
> write.csv(z,"clipboard")                   "3",3,8
# you can paste it to MS Word or Excel       "4",4,7
                                             "5",5,6
                                             "6",6,5
                                             "7",7,4
                                             "8",8,3
                                             "9",9,2
                                             "10",10,1
```

Again, if we don't like quotation marks and row numbers, we can remove them by specifying those conditions. The corresponding output is given in the right panel.

```
> write.csv(z,"clipboard",quote=F,row.names=F)      x,y
                                                    1,10
                                                    2,9
                                                    3,8
                                                    4,7
```

23.13. Row Names and Column Names

Assume that we have the following input saved as a text file **c:/temp/test.txt**.

    IBM 19900101 0.1
    IBM 19990102 0.2

The following program retrieves and saves the data. The saved data is shown in the right panel.

```
x<-read.table("c:/temp/test.txt")          "ticker" "date" "ret"
> x                                         "1" "IBM" 19900101 0.1
V1 V2 V3                                     "2" "IBM" 19990102 0.2
1 IBM 19900101 0.1
2 IBM 19990102 0.2
> colnames(x)<-c("ticker","date","ret")
> write.table("c:/temp/test1.txt")
```

If we don't want the double quotation marks, we can specify **quote=F**. On the other hand, the row numbers seem redundant. To do without printing them, we specify **row.names=F**. The new output is shown in the right panel.

```
> write.table(x, "c:/temp/test1.txt",quote=F,row.names=F)   ticker date ret
                                                            IBM 19900101 0.1
                                                            IBM 19990102 0.2
```

23.14. The sink() Function

First, we should use the **sink()** function in pair, **sink("output_file_name")**, to initiate the operation and **sink()** to end the operation. After we issue **sink("output_file_name")**, all output will be saved to the output file the function has specified. The last **sink()** will finish this operation.

```
> x<-1:100
> sink("test.txt") # save subsequent print to this file
> x # nothing shown on the screen
> print(x) # again nothing shown
> sink() # end of the sink operation
> unsink("test.txt") # close the file
```

23.15. Temporary File tempfile()

The good thing about a temporary file is that after you quit R, the temporary file will vanish as well.

```
> help(tempfile)
> ff<-tempfile()
> ff
[1] "C:\\Users\\yyan\\AppData\\Local\\Temp\\RtmpYwK05b\\file46f33db4"> x<-10
> write.table(x,ff)
```

Exercises

23.1. Generate 100 random numbers from a standard normal distribution and save them to a text file by using **write.table()**.

```
> x<-rnom(100)
```

23.2. Generate a matrix with 10*4 and save them to an Rdata file.

23.3. Go to finance.yahoo.com to download IBM's monthly price data and save them to a text file.

C H A P T E R 2 4

Data Frame and List

Below, we download IBM daily data and assign it to **x**. We use the **class()** function and the **typeof()** function to view x's properties.

```
>   x<-read.csv("http://canisius.edu/~yany/data/ibm.csv",header=T)
>   class(x)
[1] "data.frame"
>   typeof(x)
[1] "list"
```

24.1. Introduction

Data frame is one of the most used data types in R, and it is part of a more general type called list. Assume that we have the following input:

ticker year return
ibm 1990 0.01
ibm 1991 0.04

Since the three columns have different types (character, integer, and real), we cannot combine those three columns into a matrix since it will *force* all columns to possess the same format (i.e., character). In this case, data frame is a better choice.

```
> x<-c(1990,0.01,1991,0.04)
> y<-matrix(x,2,2,byrow=T)
> z<-data.frame("ibm",y)
> colnames(z)<-c("ticker","year","ret")
> z
  ticker year ret
1 ibm 1990 0.01
2 ibm 1991 0.04
```

A list can consist of a numerical vector, a logic vector, a matrix, a complex vector, a character array, or a function. There is no particular need for the components to be of the same mode or type. The lengths of different components could differ.

24.2. The data.frame() Function

The data frame shares the properties of matrices and lists and is used as the fundamental data structure by most of R's packages.

```
> x<-matrix(1:10,5,2) # generate a 5 X 2 matrix
> x # default setting is by column
  [,1] [,2] # i.e., byrow=F
[1,] 1 6
[2,] 2 7
[3,] 3 8
[4,] 4 9
[5,] 5 10
```

The following two lines are equivalent.

```
> x<-matrix(1:10,5,2) # default is by column
> x<-matrix(1:10,5,2,byrow=F)
```

To convert the above matrix into a data frame with an extra column of ticker, we have the following R codes:

```
> data.frame('ibm',x) # convert it into a data frame
  X.ibm. X1 X2
1 ibm 1 6
2 ibm 2 7
3 ibm 3 8
4 ibm 4 9
5 ibm 5 10
```

24.3. Recycling Rule Apply

When the long vector is n times the short vector, the recycling rule applies.

```
> y<-1:6
> x<-2:3
> data.frame(x,y)
  x y
1 2 1
2 3 2
3 2 3
4 3 4
5 2 5
6 3 6
```

However, when the long vector is not a multiple of the short vector, an error message appears.

```
> x<-2:5
> y<-1:6
> data.frame(x,y)
Error in data.frame(x, y) :
  arguments imply differing number of rows: 4, 6
```

24.4. Adding Column Names

We can use the **colnames()** function to add names to each column and use **var$colname** to refer to an individual column.

```
> y<-data.frame('ibm',matrix(0:9,5,2))
> colnames(y)<-c("ticker","year","ret")
> y$ticker
[1] ibm ibm ibm ibm ibm
Levels: ibm
```

24.5. Using attach() to Make Columns Accessible Directly

The function called **attach()** would make columns available from a data set.

```
> y<-data.frame('ibm',matrix(0:9,5,2))
> colnames(y)<-c("ticker","year","ret")
> ticker # not available
Error: object 'ticker' not found
> attach(y)
> ticker
[1] ibm ibm ibm ibm ibm
Levels: ibm
```

To make columns within a variable unavailable, we use the detach() function.

```
> detach(y)
> ticker
Error: object 'ticker' not found
> a<- c(2.0, 0.3, 2.5)
> b<- c("ticker","date","ret")
> c<- c(T, T,FALSE)
> x<-data.frame(a, b,c)

> x
  a b c
1 2.0 ticker TRUE
2 0.3 date TRUE
2.5 ret FALSE
```

To merge two data sets together, we use the **merger()** function.

```
>z<-merge(stock,index,by="date")
```

24.6. The Data Type of the Data Frame is List

Again, the data type of the data frame is list.

```
> x<-matrix(1:10,5,2)
> typeof(data.frame('ibm',x)) #convert a matrix into a data frame
[1] "list"
```

24.7. Reading Data from an Input File

We can use the following program to download the historical price data from Yahoo Finance for IBM. Let's call the output as ibm.csv (http://canisius.edu/~yany/ibm.csv). The first couple of lines are shown below:

Date,Open,High,Low,Close,Adj Close,Volume
1962-01-01,7.713330,7.713330,7.003330,7.226670,2.077532,8760000
1962-02-01,7.300000,7.480000,7.093330,7.160000,2.058365,5737600
1962-03-01,7.186670,7.413330,7.070000,7.103330,2.042351,5344000
1962-04-01,7.100000,7.100000,6.000000,6.053330,1.740457,12851200
1962-05-01,6.053330,6.530000,4.733330,5.233330,1.504688,49307200
1962-06-01,5.213330,5.213330,4.000000,4.523330,1.300755,68451200
1962-07-01,4.523330,5.246670,4.513330,5.160000,1.483839,41052800

After we download it, we can use the **read.csv()** function to retrieve it.

```
> x<-read.csv("ibm.csv",header=T)
> typeof(x)
[1] "list"
> typeof(x)
[1] "list"
> head(x)

    Date  Open  High  Low  Close  Volume  Adj.Close
1 2010-12-06 144.54 145.87 144.52 144.99 3321800 144.99
2 2010-12-03 144.25 145.68 144.25 145.38 3710600 145.38
3 2010-12-02 144.33 145.85 144.30 145.18 5374000 145.18
4 2010-12-01 143.61 145.13 143.51 144.41 6822800 144.41
5 2010-11-30 142.24 142.76 141.28 141.46 7674800 141.46
6 2010-11-29 143.53 143.67 141.50 142.89 5040300 142.89
```

We can add the ticker symbol as "IBM" to the above data set (see the codes below).

```
> x<-read.csv("ibm.csv",header=T)
> y<-data.frame("ibm",x)
> y[1:2,]
  X.ibm. Date Open High Low Close Volume Adj.Close
1 ibm 2010-12-06 144.54 145.87 144.52 144.99 3321800 144.99
2 ibm 2010-12-03 144.25 145.68 144.25 145.38 3710600 145.38
```

Actually we can combine several command lines into just one line.

```
> x<-data.frame("ibm",read.csv("http://canisius.edu/~yany/data/ibm.csv",header=T))
> x[1:2,]
  X.ibm.       Date    Open    High     Low   Close Adj.Close  Volume
1    ibm 1962-01-01 7.71333 7.71333 7.00333 7.22667  2.077532 8760000
2    ibm 1962-02-01 7.30000 7.48000 7.09333 7.16000  2.058365 5737600
```

Here is an example related to the **data.frame()** function.

```
x <- data.frame(cbind(x=1, y=1:10))      data.frame(…, row.names = NULL, check.
> x                                      rows = FALSE,
  x y                                      check.names = TRUE,
1 1 1                                      stringsAsFactors =
2 1 2                                      default.stringsAsFactors())
3 1 3
4 1 4
5 1 5
6 1 6
7 1 7
8 1 8
9 1 9
10 1 10
```

24.8. Converting a Data Frame into a Data Matrix

Below, we generate a data frame first then convert it into a data matrix.

```
> x <- data.frame(a=1:3, b=letters[10:12],
+ c=seq(as.Date("2004-01-01"), by = "week",len = 3),
+ stringsAsFactors = TRUE)
> x
  a b c
1 1 j 2004-01-01
2 2 k 2004-01-08
3 3 l 2004-01-15
```

We can use the **data.matrix()** function to convert a data frame.

```
> data.matrix(x)
     a b c
[1,] 1 1 12418
[2,] 2 2 12425
[3,] 3 3 12432
```

The package **xts** stands for "extensible time series." This package provides for uniform handling of R's different time-based data classes by extending zoo, maximizing native-format information preservation, and allowing for user-level customization and extension while simplifying cross-class interoperability. The package includes several data sets. One of them is **sample_matrix**.

```
> library(xts) # load the package
> data(sample_matrix) # load the data set
> typeof(sample_matrix)
[1] "double"
> x<- data.frame(sample_matrix)
> typeof(x)
[1] "list"
```

In the following program, we estimate monthly mean return for each stock year. The program has two loops. The first loop is for different tickers while the second loop is for the different years for each ticker. For example, if there are two unique tickers, the first loop will run twice. If for the first ticker there are twenty years' data, then there will be twenty runs for it.

```
x2<-subset(x,is.na(ret)==F)              A 1926 0.003002917 12
tickers<-unique(x$ticker)                A 1927 0.0238755 12
for(tt in tickers){                      A 1928 0.06985583 12
  x3<-subset(x2,ticker==tt)              A 1929 -0.008491583 12
  years<-unique(as.integer(x3$date/10000)) A 1930 -0.0613575 12
  for(i in years){                       A 1931 -0.06221842 12
  x4<-subset(x3,i==as.integer(x3$date/10000)) A 1932 0.05964108 12
  cat(tt,i,mean(x4$ret),length(x4$ret), "\n") A 1933 0.09254633 12
  }
}
```

24.9. Generating a List

Here is an example of generating a variable in a list type.

```
>x<-list(name="John",spouse="Mary",no.children=2,child.ages=c(14,9))
> class(x)
[1] "list"
```

To show the contents, just type its name.

```
> x
$name
[1] "John"
$spouse
[1] "Mary"
$no.children
[1] 2
$child.ages
[1] 14 9
```

24.10. Length and Size of a List

The length of a list gives the number of items at the highest level. In the above case, the length will be 4 (i.e., name, wife, number of children, and ages).

```
> length(x)
[1]  4
```

To get the balance sheet for IBM from marketwatch.com, we have the following codes:

```
> library(XML)
>        x<-readHTMLTable("http://www.marketwatch.com/investing/stock/IBM/financials/
balance-sheet")
> typeof(x)
[1] "list"
> length(x)
[1] 3
> head(x[[11]])
Error in x[[11]] : subscript out of bounds
> head(x[[1]])
Fiscal year is January-December. All values USD millions.
  2007 2008 2009 2010 2011 5-yeartrend
1 Cash & Short Term Investments 16.15B 12.91B 13.97B 11.65B 11.92B
2 Cash Only 14.99B 2.73B 2.91B 2.86B -
3 Short-Term Investments 1.16B 10.18B 11.07B 8.79B -
4 Cash & Short Term Investments Growth -20.06% 8.27% -16.62% 2.33%
5 Cash & ST Investments / Total Assets 13.41% 11.78% 12.82% 10.27% 10.24%
6 Total Accounts Receivable 28.79B 27.56B 26.79B 28.23B 29.56B
```

24.11. Calling Elements of a List

To refer to each item in a list, we use [[ ]], such as x[[1]] for the first item.

```
> x[[1]]         > x[[4]]
[1] "John"       [1] 14 9
```

The second way to call the elements of a list is to use x$name or x[[name]].

```
> x$name         > x[["name"]]
[1] "John"       [1] "John"
```

24.12. Difference Between x[1] and x[[1]] When x Is a List

It is vital to separate x[[1]] from x[1]. The [[...]] is used to select a single element whereas [...] is a general subscription operator. Thus, the former is the *first* object in the list x; and if it is a named list, the name is *not* included. The latter is a *sublist* of the list x consisting of the first entry only. If it is a named list, the names will be transferred to the sublist.

```
> x[[1]]              > typeof(x[[1]])
[1] "John"            [1] "character"
> x[1]                > typeof(x[1])
$name                 [1] "list"
[1] "John"
```

We know that the fourth data item has two data points: 14 and 7.

```
> x[[4]]
[1] 14 9
```

To go to the next level, we use the **[[]][]** structure. To get the first item (i.e., 14), we use **x[[4]][1]**.

```
> x[[4]][1]
[1] 14
```

24.13. Adding More Data to an Existing List

It is easy to add more data to a variable that contains data.

```
> x[[1]][2]<-"Paul"
```

24.14. Long Names and Their Minimum Numbers of Distinguishable Letters

For a long name, we only need enough letters to identity it. We use the same example to illustrate. We have four variable names: **name**, **spouse**, **no.chldren**, and **child.ages**.

```
>x<-list(name="John",spouse="Mary",no.children=2,child.ages=c(14,9))
```

We can use **$name** to specify the first item.

```
> x$name
[1] "John"
```

Since there are two names starting with a letter n, we need more letters to distinguish them. In this case, two letters is enough.

```
> x$na
[1] "John"
```

Since there is only one name starting with the letter *s* (**spouse**), we need only one letter.

```
> x$s              > typeof(x[[1]])
[1] "Mary"         [1] "character"
```

24.15. Adding More to the Top Level

For example, in the above case, x has a length of 4. If we want to add home address, we simply use x[[5]].

```
> x[[5]]<-list(home.address="123, Board St, Philadelphia, PA 12245")
```

24.16. The class() Function

The possible outcomes for the **class()** function are numeric, logical, character, list, matrix array, factor, and data frame.

```
>   y<-read.csv("http://canisius.edu/~yany/data/ibm.csv",header=T)
>   class(y)
[1]  "data.frame"
```

24.17. Concatenating Lists

We can add one list to another one.

```
> list.x<-list(name="John",spouse="Mary",no.children=2,child.ages=c(14,9))
> list.y<-list(name="Peter")
> list.z<-list(name="Paul",spouse="Jen")
> k<-c(list.x,list.y,list.z)
> length(k)
[1] 7
```

Exercise

24.1. Both a matrix and a data frame can have different types of data.
   a) True
   b) False
24.2. Download monthly historical price data for DELL, IBM, and Microsoft and combine them into a single data set.
24.3. How do you convert a matrix into a data frame?
24.4. What are the advantages of using a data frame instead of a matrix?

CHAPTER 25

Subsetting

It is quite often that we input a big data set first. Then we slice it according to our need. In this chapter, we discuss various ways to do so. Assume that we have the following vector of **x**.

```
> x<-seq(1,5,by=0.123)
> x
 [1] 1.000 1.123 1.246 1.369 1.492 1.615 1.738 1.861 1.984 2.107
[11] 2.230 2.353 2.476 2.599 2.722 2.845 2.968 3.091 3.214 3.337
[21] 3.460 3.583 3.706 3.829 3.952 4.075 4.198 4.321 4.444 4.567
[31] 4.690 4.813 4.936
```

For a subset of **x**, we use the following codes:

```
> y<-x[1:10]
> y
 [1] 1.000 1.123 1.246 1.369 1.492 1.615 1.738 1.861 1.984 2.107
```

For a matrix, we can choose certain columns and/or rows. Assume x is an n-by-m matrix.

```
> a<-x[,1] # choose the first column
> b<-x[1:100,1:2] # choose the first 100 rows & columns 1 and 2
```

25.1. Introduction

In this chapter, we discuss how to retrieve part of a data set for further analysis. For example, we have an R data set called **retD50.RData** with only three columns (ticker, date, and return). The data set can be downloaded by using the link at http://canisius.edu/~yany/RData/retD50.RData. We can save it to a specific subdirectory. Then we change our working directory by clicking **File** then **Change dir…** and choose your correct directory. Below, we load the R data set from our working directory.

```
> web<-url("http://canisius.edu/~yany/RData/retD50.RData")
> load(web)
> close(web)
> head(retD50)
   ticker date ret
1883624 IBM 1962-01-02 -99.000000
1883625 IBM 1962-01-03 0.007663
1883626 IBM 1962-01-04 -0.011407
1883627 IBM 1962-01-05 -0.019231
1883628 IBM 1962-01-08 -0.019608
1883629 IBM 1962-01-09 0.012000
```

To choose a specific stock, we apply an equal condition (==) to column 1.

```
> load(retD50.RData)
> ibm<-subset(retD50,retD50[,1]== "IBM")
```

The **unique()** function can be used to show all unique value such as number of stocks available in the data set.

```
> y<-unique(retD50[,1])
> length(y)
[1] 50
```

25.2. Scalar, Vector, and Matrix

The scalar is a variable that takes many different values at different times. However, at one specific time, it takes one value only.

```
> x<-10
```

A vector is a column of data n by 1 (i.e., it has n data items).

```
> x<-1:10
```

A matrix has n rows and m columns (n by m). Thus, a matrix has n*m data items.

```
>x<-1:12
> y<-matrix(x,3,4,byrow=T)
> y
   [,1] [,2] [,3] [,4]
[1,] 1 2 3 4
[2,] 5 6 7 8
[3,] 9 10 11 12
```

There is only one data type for a matrix. Obviously the y variable from the above codes is an integer type.

```
> typeof(y)
[1] "integer"
```

However, if we assign a string to just one data item, the whole matrix becomes string instead of numeric.

```
> y[1,1]<-"good"
> y
     [,1]   [,2] [,3] [,4]
[1,] "good" "2"  "3"  "4"
[2,] "5"    "6"  "7"  "8"
[3,] "9"    "10" "11" "12"
> typeof(y)
[1] "character"
```

25.3. Getting a Subset from a Vector

The easiest way to get a subset is to specify the beginning and ending positions.

```
> x<-rnorm(50)
> y<-x[1:10] # retain the first 10 values
```

A negative-vector index indicates exclusion. Assume that a vector of x has fifty values; x[10] indicates the tenth value while x[-10] has forty-nine values except the tenth value.

```
> x<-rnorm(50)
> y<-x[-10]
> length(y)
[1] 49
```

25.4. Getting a Subset from a Matrix

Below, we show three ways to retrieve a subset from a matrix.

```
X[1:2,] # the first two rows
X[1,] # the first row
X[1: (n-1),5] # rows from 1 to n-1 and 5th column
```

The subset() function allows us to choose a subset from a given data set based on certain conditions.

```
> ibm<-subset(x,x[,1]=='IBM')
```

25.5. Getting a Specific Year's Data

If a variable related to the date is defined by the **as.Date()** function, then the codes will be simple. First, we download and save an R data set called **retDIMB.RData** from the Web page http://canisius.edu/~yany/RData/retDIBM.RData. For a specific subtime period, we can use the following program:

```
> load("retDIBM.RData")
> date1<- as.Date("2011-02-02")
> date2<-as.Date("2011-02-11")
> x<-subset(ibm,ibm[,1]>=date1 & ibm[,1]<=date2)
```

After we change our working directory that contains the above data set, we issue the following codes. The **load()** function is used to upload an R data set.

```
> load("retDIBM.RData")
> ls()
[1] "EDM1" "ibm" "sp500" "x" "y"
> head(ibm)
  date ret
1 1962-01-02 -99.000000
2 1962-01-03 0.007663
3 1962-01-04 -0.011407
4 1962-01-05 -0.019231
5 1962-01-08 -0.019608
6 1962-01-09 0.012000
> x<-subset(ibm,format(ibm[,1], "%Y ")==2000)
> dim(x)
[1] 252 2
```

With two conditions (conditions A and B) to filter out our data, we use & for an *and* condition (i.e., both A and B conditions must be true) and | for an *or* condition (i.e., at least one condition is true). For example, if we want to retrieve IBM's return for the period from **date1** to **date2**, we use the following codes:

```
> load("retDIBM.RData ")
> date1<-as.Date("2000-02-02")
> date2<-as.Date("2000-02-10")
> x<-subset(retD50,retD50[,1]== "IBM " & retD50[,2]>date1 & retD50[,2]<date2)
> x
  ticker date ret
1893215 IBM 2000-02-03 0.031870
1893216 IBM 2000-02-04 -0.012821
1893217 IBM 2000-02-07 -0.012987
1893218 IBM 2000-02-08 0.042265
1893219 IBM 2000-02-09 -0.012146
```

If the date-related variable is defined as an integer, we can use the following codes. For example, **19260113/10000= 1926.0113**. Its integer will be 1926.

```
> y<-subset(x,ticker=='A' & as.integer(date/10000)==1926)
```

Exercises

25.1. How do you get the dimensions of a matrix?

25.2. How do you get rows 25 to 50 and columns 1 to 20 from a matrix of x?

25.3. You are given a matrix of x. How do you print the first and last several lines of x?

25.4. What are the advantages and disadvantages of a data frame versus a matrix?

25.5. Can a matrix hold different types of data?

25.6. Download the **retD50.Rdata** and retrieve two stocks' data, such as IBM's and DELL's, from http://canisius.edu/~yany/RData/retD50.RData.

CHAPTER 26

Combine and Merge Data Sets

The opposite of choosing a subset from a big set is to combine different data sets according to our need. The simplest way to combine two columns into a matrix is to use the **cbind()** function. In the following case, z becomes a three-by-two matrix.

```
> x<-c(1,2,4.5)            > z
> y<-c(0.3,0.2,0)            x y
> z<-cbind(x,y)           [1,] 1.0 0.3
                          [2,] 2.0 0.2
                          [3,] 4.5 0.0
```

26.1. Introduction

Data manipulation is quite important. In this book, we devote four chapters on this topic: chapter 29 on simple data manipulation; chapter 34 on subsetting, which can be viewed as the opposite of this chapter; chapter 39 on string manipulation, in addition to the current chapter.

26.2. Combining Columns Using cbind()

It is quite common that researchers want to add an extra column to their data set. The following codes are used to download IBM's daily price from Yahoo Finance.

```
>x<-read.csv("http://canisius.edu/~yany/data/ibmDaily.csv",header=T)
```

The **head()** function is used to view the first couple of observations. Most of the time, we need returns. To estimate returns, we should use the adjusted closing price instead of the closing price. After that, we combine it with our x variable.

```
> head(x)
   Date Open High Low Close Volume Adj.Close
1 2011-09-28 177.97 180.75 177.08 177.55 7732200 177.55
2 2011-09-27 176.82 179.62 176.43 177.71 7638800 177.71
3 2011-09-26 170.96 174.70 169.86 174.51 6745700 174.51
4 2011-09-23 166.99 169.54 165.76 169.34 5586600 169.34
5 2011-09-22 168.33 169.97 166.50 168.62 8195600 168.62
6 2011-09-21 175.00 177.67 172.62 173.02 7043100 173.02
```

26.3. Recycling Rule When Using cbind()

We should be careful when applying the cbind() function, or one or more column might not have full range.

```
> x<-1:5
> y<-10:12
> z<-cbind(x,y)
Warning message:
In cbind(x, y):
  number of rows of result is not a multiple of vector length (arg 2)
> z
  x y
[1,] 1 10
[2,] 2 11
[3,] 3 12
[4,] 4 10
[5,] 5 11
```

In the above result, we are given a warning message. When the length of the long vector is a multiple of a shorter vector, we would not receive any warning message. Unfortunately it can be a potential disaster for a researcher who is not aware of this *terrible* property.

```
> x<-1:6
> y<-2:0
> cbind(x,y)
  x y
[1,] 1 -2
[2,] 2 -1
[3,] 3 0
[4,] 4 -2
[5,] 5 -1
[6,] 6 0
```

26.4. Removing the Recycling Rule

For researchers, the recycling rule is "dangerous" when applying the **cbind()** function to combine two or more vectors together. Usually we prefer to fill some kind of missing codes for the short vector. In the following program, we extend the length of a shorter vector to make it equal to the length of the longer one before we apply the **cbind()** function.

```
cbind2<-function(x,y,missing_code=NA){
    n_x<-length(x)
    n_y<-length(y)
    n <-max(n_x,n_y)
    if(n_x<n) x[(n_x+1):n]<-missing_code
    if(n_y<n) y[(n_y+1):n]<-missing_code
    return(cbind(x,y))
}
```

Below are two results by calling the above function:

```
> x<-1:3                    > cbind2(x,y,missing_code=-99)
> y<-1:2                    x y
> cbind2(x,y)              [1,] 1 1
 x y                       [2,] 2 2
[1,] 1 1                   [3,] 3 -99
[2,] 2 2
[3,] 3 NA
```

26.5. Adding Rows

Similarly we can combine rows by applying the **rbind()** function.

```
> x<-c(1990,0.01,1991,0.04)
> y<-matrix(x,2,2,byrow=T)
> z<-data.frame("ibm",y)
> x2<-c(2000,0.03,2001,0.05)
> y2<-matrix(x2,2,2,byrow=T)
> z2<-data.frame("ibm",y2)
> rbind(z,z2)
  X.ibm. X1 X2
1 ibm 1990 0.01
  ibm 1991 0.04
  ibm 2000 0.03
4 ibm 2001 0.05
```

We can use the **colnames()** function to add the names to all the columns.

```
> final<-rbind(z,z2)
> colnames(final)<-c("ticker","year","ret")
> final
  ticker year ret
ibm 1990 0.01
ibm 1991 0.04
ibm 2000 0.03
4 ibm 2001 0.05
```

If two data sets have different variables, then either delete the extravariables in data frame A or create the additional variables in data frame B and set them to NA (missing) before joining them with the **rbind()** function.

26.6. Merging Two Data Sets with One Common Variable

The **merge()** function combines two data sets by a common variable.

```
> d1<- data.frame(id=1:3, ret=0.1:3)          id      ret
                                              1       0.1
                                              2       1.1
                                              3       2.1

> d2<-data.frame(id=2:3,value=c(0.4,0.3))     id      value
                                              2       0.4
                                              3       0.3

> d3<-merge(d1,d2,by="id")                    id ret value
                                              2 1.1 0.4
                                              3 2.1 0.3
```

Since there is only one common variable, we can simplify our codes by omitting **by="ID"**.

```
> d3<-merge(d1,d2)
```

Assume that we have two data sets. The first one is related to a stock while the second one is for an index.

```
> x<-data.frame(c(1990,1991),c(0.02,0.03))
> stock<-data.frame("ibm",x)
> stock >
colnames(stock)<-c("ticker","year","ret")
    ticker year ret
       32 Ibm 1990 0.02
2 ibm 1991 0.03
```

Again, the second data set is related to an index.

```
> index<-data.frame(1990,0.03)
> colnames(index)<-c("year","mkt_ret")
> index
year mkt_ret
1 1990 0.03
```

Next, we merge them by year using **by="year"**.

```
> merge(stock,index,by="year")
year ticker ret mkt_ret
1 1990 ibm 0.02 0.03
```

Since there is only one common variable, we can ignore **by="year"**.

```
> merge(stock,index)
  year ticker ret mkt_ret
1 1990 ibm 0.02 0.03
```

We can generate an R function to achieve this.

```
# merge two dataframes by date
merge_two<- function(d1,d2,by="date"){
  return(merge(d1,d2,by=by))
}
> merge_two(stock,index,by="year")
```

When we want to merge two data sets by two commonly shared variables, we can use by=c("item_1", "item_2").

```
# merge two dataframes by ID and Country
> total <- merge( dataA,dataB,by=c("ticker","date"))
> final
 ticker year ret
32    ibm 1990 0.01
32    ibm 1991 0.04
32    ibm 2000 0.03
4 ibm 2001 0.05
> index
year vwretd
1 1990 0.01
> merge(final,index,by="year")
year ticker ret vwretd
1 1990 ibm 0.01 0.01
```

26.7. Keeping All Cases for merge()

In the above example, the final merged data set includes only merged cases (overlapping cases)—that is, it exists in both data sets. If we want to keep all cases, we should use **all=T**.

```
> first <- data.frame(a=1:3, id=4:6)
> second <- data.frame(id=6:9, c=9:12)
>x<-merge(first,second,by="id",all=T)
> x
id a c
1 4 1 NA
2 5 2 NA
3 6 3 9
4 7 NA 10
5 8 NA 11
6 9 NA 12
```

Assume that we want to merge two data frames **data1** and **data2** by **id**, which is common to both data frames. Another condition is that we keep all observations in **data1**.

```
> set.seed(100)
> data1 <-data.frame(id=c(1,3,5),x=rnorm(3)) # 3 x 2
> data2 <-data.frame(id=1:10, y=runif(10)) # 10 x 2
> merge(data1, data2, by="id", all.x=TRUE, all.y=FALSE)
 id        x         y
1 1 -0.50219235 0.8124026
2 3  0.13153117 0.5465586
3 5 -0.07891709 0.6249965
```

26.8. Merging Three Data Sets

One major issue is that in R, we cannot merge three data sets at the same time. Thus, we have a two-step approach: merge only two data sets at a time.

```
> first <- data.frame(a=1:3, b=4:6)
> second <- data.frame(b=7:9, c=10:12)
> third<-merge(first,second,by="b",all=TRUE)
> third
  b a c
1 4 1 NA
2 5 2 NA
3 6 3 NA
4 7 NA 10
5 8 NA 11
6 9 NA 12
```

The data sets are given below:

Data set 1	Data set 2	Data set 3
id age gender	id time x1	id time x2
01 12 M	01 1 0.25	01 1 0.34
03 15 F	01 2 0.27	01 2 0.55
04 19 M	01 3 0.29	01 3 0.79
	03 1 0.15	03 1 0.12
	03 2 0.18	03 2 0.23
	04 2 0.22	04 2 0.45
	04 3 0.54	04 3 0.56

After we generate those three data sets according to the above inputs, we can use the following codes to merge them:

```
> d1<-data.frame(read.table("clipboard",header=T))
> d2<-data.frame(read.table("clipboard",header=T))
> d3<-data.frame(read.table("clipboard",header=T))
```

In the codes below, we ignore the **by=id** since three data sets have only one common variable.

```
> merge(merge(d1,d2),d3)
  id age gender x y time x2
1 1 12 M 0.2478879 0.5236215 1 0.34
2 1 12 M 0.2478879 0.5236215 2 0.55
3 1 12 M 0.2478879 0.5236215 3 0.79
4 3 15 F 0.4164897 0.2122381 1 0.12
5 3 15 F 0.4164897 0.2122381 2 0.23
```

Please pay attention to the following program:

```
> merge(merge(d1,d2,all=T),d3)
  id age gender x y time x2
1 1 12 M 0.2478879 0.5236215 1 0.34
2 1 12 M 0.2478879 0.5236215 2 0.55
3 1 12 M 0.2478879 0.5236215 3 0.79
4 3 15 F 0.4164897 0.2122381 1 0.12
5 3 15 F 0.4164897 0.2122381 2 0.23
6 4 19 M NA NA 2 0.45
7 4 19 M NA NA 3 0.56
```

There is a minor difference between the following program and the one above.

```
> merge(merge(d1,d2,all=T),d3,all=T)
  id age gender x y time x2
1 1 12 M 0.2478879 0.5236215 1 0.34
2 1 12 M 0.2478879 0.5236215 2 0.55
3 1 12 M 0.2478879 0.5236215 3 0.79
4 3 15 F 0.4164897 0.2122381 1 0.12
5 3 15 F 0.4164897 0.2122381 2 0.23
6 4 19 M NA NA 2 0.45
7 4 19 M NA NA 3 0.56
8 5 NA <NA> 0.1007910 0.6727800 NA NA
```

26.9. Merging Two Data Sets with One Common Variable with Different names in Two Data Sets

Assume we merge two data sets by using id. The problem is that the id in those data sets have different names.

```
> d1<-data.frame(id=c(1,2,3),gender=c("m","f","f"))
> d2<-data.frame(p.id=c(1, 2), income=c(4551, 3000))
> merge(d1,d2,by.x="id", by.y="p.id")
  id gender income
1 1 m 4551
2 2 f 3000
```

26.10. Merging with Two Common Variables

Sometimes we need to merge two data sets with two criteria, such as ticker and date.

```
> >merge(x,y,by=c("ID1","ID2"))
```

Exercises

26.1. From Yahoo Finance, download IBM's and S&P 500's monthly price data then merge them. The related Web page is http://finance.yahoo.com/.

26.2. Download the daily price data from IBM, DELL, and MSFT and merge them.

26.3. We have two data sets: **x1** and **x2** (see codes below).

```
time1<-c(1,7,5,12,14,19,10,211)
data1<-c(17,16,15,14,10,7,47,1)
x1<-cbind(time1,data1)
time2<-c(1,7,5, 13)
data2<-c(5,5,14,25)
x2<-cbind(time2,data2)
```

Compare the following different ways to merge the two data sets.

```
> merge(x1,x2)
>merge(x1,x2,by.x="time1",by.y="time2")
> merge(x1,x2,by.y="time1",by.x="time2")
> merge(x1,x2,by.x="time1",by.y="time2",all=T)
```

26.4. Explain the following codes:

```
> library(zoo)
> time1<-c(1,7,5,12,14,19,10,211 )
> data1<-c(17,16,15,14,10,7,47,1)
> z1<-zoo(time1,data1)
> time2<-c(1,7,5, 13)
> data2<-c(5,2,14,25)
> z2<-zoo(time2,data2)
> merge(z1, z2, fill = 0)
```

CHAPTER 27

Date Variable

One of the most important elements in handling time series is called date variable. In this chapter, we show why it is important, how to define it correctly, and how it is used. For various financial databases and data manipulation, the date variable (or other names) plays a unique role since we need such a variable for many purposes such as choosing a specific weekday or final day at the end of each month and merging individual stock returns with a market index. There exist many ways to generate such a date variable. Among them, the best is to use the **as.Date()** function

If x is defined as the last day of January, then **x+1** should be the first day of February. In the first line below, **"%Y-%m-%d"** is the format that depends on the structure of the input value.

```
> x<-as.Date("2011-01-31","%Y-%m-%d")
> x+1
[1] "2011-02-01"
```

To retrieve a year variable from the formatted **x**, use the **format(x,"%Y")** function.

```
> y<-as.integer(format(x, "%Y"))
> y+1 # format(x, "%Y") is a character
[1] 2012
```

27.1. Converting a String into a Date Variable Using as.Date()

Here are several reasons for the use of the **as.Date()** function. First, if **x** is defined as the last of day of March, then **x+1** should be the first day of April.

```
> x<-"2011-03-31"
> date<-as.Date(x, "%Y-%m-%d")
> date+1
[1] "2011-04-01"
```

Second, if a date is not valid, the **as.Date()** function would say so. For example, **"2012-02-30"** is invalid when we apply the **as.Date()** function.

```
> x<-"2012-2-30"
> as.Date(x)
Error in charToDate(x):
  character string is not in a standard unambiguous format
> x<-"2012-2-28"
> as.Date(x)
[1] "2012-02-28"
> as.Date("2011-02-30")
Error in charToDate(x):
  character string is not in a standard unambiguous format
```

Third, it is easy to retrieve year, month, day, and weekday from such a variable defined via **as.Date()**. Fourth, it makes defining vector with many dates, such as a whole year, quite simple. Below are some examples. Please pay attention to various input formats.

```
> date<-as.Date("2011-01-31","%Y-%m-%d")
> date<-as.Date("2011/01/31","%Y/%m/%d")
> date<-as.Date("31/01/2011","%d/%m/%Y")
> date<-as.Date("01/31/2011","%m/%d/%Y")
> date<-as.Date("01/31/98","%m/%d/%y") # lower case y!!!!
> date<-as.Date("20110131","%Y%m%d")
```

There are some default settings as well (i.e., we can ignore the format).

```
> date<-as.Date("2011-01-31")
> date+1
[1] "2011-02-01"
> date<-as.Date("2011/01/31")
> date+1
[1] "2011-02-01"
```

For the special format of "**01Jan2000**", see the codes below:

```
> x <- c("1jan1970","2jan1982","31mar1992","30jul2010")
> y <- as.Date(x, "%d%b%Y")
> y
[1] "1970-01-01" "1982-01-02" "1992-03-31" "2010-07-30"
```

27.2. Converting an Integer into a Date

The **as.Date()** might be one of the most used functions in R.

```
> x<-as.Date(as.character(20110131), "%Y%m%d")
> x
[1] "2011-01-31"
```

27.3. Defining a Date Variable as an Integer

As we have discussed before, this is not a good way to use the function.

```> date<-19900101``` ```> year<-as.integer(date/10000)```	```> year``` ```[1] 1990```

27.4. Defining a Date Variable as an Ordinary String

Sometimes the input variable related to date is a character variable. Thus, we need other ways to convert those characters into a useful date variable.

```
> x<-"1990-01-02"
> year<-substr(x,1,4) # from 1 to 4
> month<-substr(x,6,7) # from 6 to 7
> day<-substr(x,9,10)
> date<-paste(year,month,day,sep="") # paste() combine strings
> date # sep is for separator
[1] "19900102"
```

We can process the data further (e.g., "get" date and calculate returns).

```
x<-read.csv('ibm.csv',header=T)
y<-substr(x[,1],1,4) # year
m<-substr(x[,1],6,7) # month
d<-substr(x[,1],9,10) # day
date<-as.integer(as.character(paste(y,m,d,sep="")))
data<-cbind(date,x[,7]) # combine date and price
```

The function **gsub()** is used for the global substitution (i.e., replace all characters with a new one).

```
> x<-"1990-01-02"
>date<-gsub("-","",x) # replace all - with nothing
> date # i.e., remove all -
[1] "19900102"
> as.integer(date)
[1] 19900102
```

27.5. Retrieving Year, Month, and Day from an as.Date()-Defined Variable

In the following example, we want to retrieve the year variable. We should be aware that such a variable is a string rather than an integer.

```
> x<-as.Date("2011-01-31","%Y-%m-%d")
> format(x, "%Y") # here the output is a string
[1] "2011"
```

27.6. Converting a Character Variable into an Integer or a Real Number

To convert a character such as **2010**, we use the **as.integer() function.**

```
> x<-"2010"
> as.integer(x)+1
[1] 2011
> x<-"201.1"
> as.numeric(x)
[1] 201.1
```

If we want to convert a string date variable into an integer, we use the **as.integer()** function.

```
> x<-as.Date("2011-01-31","%Y-%m-%d")
> as.integer(format(x,"%Y")) # convert string to integer
[1] 2011
> as.integer(format(x,"%m"))
[1] 1
> as.integer(format(x,"%d"))
[1] 31
```

27.7. Combining Two or More Character Variables

For string manipulation, the **paste()** function is vitally important.

```
> x<-"hello"
> y<-"world!"
> paste(x,y,sep=" ") # sep is separator
[1] "hello world!"
```

If we don't want any space between we use **sep=**

```
> x<-"hello"
> y<-"world!"
> paste(x,y,sep="") # sep is separator
[1] "helloworld!"
```

27.8 Converting a String into an Integer Date

In the following codes, the last one combined two separate operations.

```
> x<-"2011-01-31"              > date
> y<-substr(x,1,4)            [1] 20110131
> m<-substr(x,6,7)
> d<-substr(x,9,10)
> date<-as.integer(paste(y,m,d,sep=""))
```

27.9. Converting a String into a Date as an Integer

To compare the **sub()** function (single substitution) and the **gsub()** function (global substation), see below:

```
> x<-"2011-02-25"
> sub("-","",x) # replace "-" with nothing
[1] "201102-25"
> x<-"2011-02-25"
> gsub("-","",x) # replace all "-" with nothing
[1] "20110225"
```

Since we usually need an integer output, we use the **as.integer()** function.

```
> x<-"2011-01-31"
> as.integer(gsub("-","",x))
```

27.10. Choosing Many Dates Before date1 and date2

We can specify a range and choose certain days between.

```
> d1<-as.Date("19900101",format="%Y%m%d")
> d2<-as.Date("19901231",format="%Y%m%d")
> days<-seq(d1,d2,by=1)
> length(days)
[1] 365
> days <- seq(as.Date("2005/1/1"),as.
Date("2005/10/30"), "days")
```

27.11. Choosing the Last Day of Each Month

When converting daily prices to estimate monthly returns, we might need the end of monthly stock price.

```
x<-seq(as.Date("2005/1/1"),as.Date("2005/10/30"), "days")
> n<-length(x) # note: days is the keyword
> m<-format(x,"%m") # generate a month variable
> y<-data.frame(x,m)
> y2<-subset(y,y[1:(n-1),2]!=y[2:n,2])
> y2[1:5,]
x m
31 2005-01-31 01
59 2005-02-28 02
90 2005-03-31 03
120 2005-04-30 04
151 2005-05-31 05
```

27.12. Choosing Specific Weekdays

When testing the so-called weekday effect, we need to group daily stock returns into different weekdays.

```
> x<-"2011-2-13"
> weekdays(as.Date(x))
[1] "Sunday"
```

The following codes show how to get Monday-only observations.

```
> x<-read.csv("http://canisius.edu/~yany/data/ibmDaily.csv",header=T)
>  n<-nrow(x)
>  d<-data.frame(as.Date(x[2:n,1]),x[2:n,6]/x[1:n-1,6]-1)
>  colnames(d)<-c("date","ret")
>  y<-subset(d,weekdays(d[,1])=="Monday")
> head(y)
          date          ret
4  1962-01-08 -0.0187494740
9  1962-01-15  0.0044319756
14 1962-01-22 -0.0018067003
19 1962-01-29 -0.0170903326
24 1962-02-05 -0.0125449129
29 1962-02-12  0.0008981263
```

27.13. The Function cbind() vs. data.frame()

When using the **cbind()** function to join columns with different types, we might have an unexpected result.

```
> x<-as.Date("1990-01-02",format="%Y-%m-%d")
> y<-as.integer(format(x, "%Y"))
> data<-cbind(x,y)
> data
  x y
[1,] 7306 1990

> x<-as.Date("1990-01-02",format="%Y-%m-%d")
> y<-as.integer(format(x,"%Y"))
> data<-data.frame(x,y)
> data
  x y
1 1990-01-02 1990
```

The major reason that the **cbind()** function generates unexpected results is that it produces a matrix that requires all columns to have the same type (i.e., all numeric or all characters).

```
> x<-2001              > x<-"2001"
> y<-2009              > y<-2009
> cbind(x,y)           > cbind(x,y)
x  y                   x  y
[1,] 2001 2009         [1,] "2001" "2009"
```

Thus, it is a good idea to use **data.frame()** to combine columns with different data types.

27.14. The Function seq(as.Date())

To generate days between **date1** and **date2**, see the codes below:

```
> seq(as.Date("2010/1/1"), as.Date("2010/12/31"), "days")
```

To generate the first day for each month or each year, use the following program:

```
>seq(as.Date("2010/1/1"), as.Date("2010/12/31"), "months")
>seq(as.Date("1910/1/1"), as.Date("1999/1/1"), "years")
```

27.15. R Package timeDate

This package is for more advanced data manipulation. If we want to know today's date and time, we can use the following command.

```
> library(timeDate)
> Sys.timeDate()
GMT
[1] [2011-07-04 22:41:00]
```

Exercises

27.1. For a="1990/02/03", generate its corresponding date variable as an integer.

27.2. For the same date in 27.1, define it as a date variable by using the as.Date() function.

27.3. Generate all days between January 1, 2000 to December 31, 2007 by using the as.Date() function.

27.4. Generate the corresponding year, month, and day for the time series in 27.3.

27.5. How many days are there between July 1, 1975 and December 31, 2010?

27.6. Is 2000 a leap year? A leap year is defined as having 366 days instead of 365.

27.7. Download the daily price of IBM from Yahoo Finance then generate a date variable by using the as.Date() and data.frame() functions.

27.8. Retrieve all end-of-the-month records from 27.7 then estimate the monthly returns.

27.9. Try the following codes first then explain the function.

```
>X <- as.Date(paste(1999:2009, "-12-31",sep=""))
```

27.10. Retrieve the daily price data for DELL from Yahoo Finance then estimate the annual returns.

27.11. What is wrong with the following command?

```
> date<-as.Date("01/31/2011","%m-%d-%Y")
```

```
> z<-as.Date("01/31/2011","%d/%m/%Y")
> z
[1] NA
```

27.12. Explain the following codes and results:

```
> days<- seq(as.Date("2005/1/1"),as.Date("2005/1/10"), "days")
> days
 [1] "2005-01-01" "2005-01-02" "2005-01-03" "2005-01-04" "2005-01-05"
 [6] "2005-01-06" "2005-01-07" "2005-01-08" "2005-01-09" "2005-01-10"
>w<-format(days, "%W")
> w
 [1] "00" "00" "01" "01" "01" "01" "01" "01" "01" "02"
```

27.13. Download DELL's daily price data from Yahoo Finance and compare the mean returns on Mondays and Tuesdays. Are they statistically different?

CHAPTER 28

Matrix and Its Manipulation

A matrix is a collection of data items in a two-dimensional format. Matrices are one of the most used data formats in R and in any other language.

$$a = \begin{bmatrix} 1 & 2 & 3 \\ 3 & 6 & 7 \end{bmatrix}$$

The following one-line codes are used to generate the above matrix.

```
> x<-matrix(c(1, 2, 3, 3, 6, 7),2,3,byrow=T)
> x
  [,1] [,2] [,3]
[1,] 1 2 3
[2,] 3 6 7
```

Below is an example of generating a 3-by-2 matrix with all zeros in it.

```
> x<-matrix(0,3,2) # 3 by 2 with all zeros
> x
  [,1] [,2]
[1,] 0 0
[2,] 0 0
[3,] 0 0
```

28.1. Combining Vectors into a Matrix Using cbind()

We could use the **cbind()** function to combine two or multiple vectors into a matrix.

```
> x<-c(1,2,3)
> y<-c(100,123,717)
> z<-cbind(x,y)
> z
x y
[1,] 1 100
[2,] 2 123
[3,] 3 717
```

28.2. Recycling Rule

When two or more vectors with different lengths are combined into a matrix, the recycle rule applies: the data items in the short vector will be recycled.

```
> a<-1:10 # length is 10
> b<-100:105 # length is 6
> z<-cbind(a,b)
```

The following output shows that the items in the shorter vector are recycled.

```
> z
      a  b
 [1,]  1 100
 [2,]  2 101
 [3,]  3 102
 [4,]  4 103
 [5,]  5 104
 [6,]  6 105
 [7,]  7 100
 [8,]  8 101
 [9,]  9 102
[10,] 10 103
```

Another example is given below. The values of 1 to 5 are recycled.

```
> x<-1:10
> matrix(x,3,5)
     [,1] [,2] [,3] [,4] [,5]
[1,]  1   4   7  10   3
[2,]  2   5   8   1   4
[3,]  3   6   9   2   5
Warning message:
In matrix(x, 3, 5) :
  data length [10] is not a sub-multiple or multiple of the number of rows [3]
```

28.3. Same Type in a Matrix

When one vector is a character, then the final matrix will be a character matrix (i.e., all noncharacter vectors will be converted into character vectors).

```
> a<-c("a","b","c")
> b<-c(1,2,5)
> c<-cbind(a,b)
> c
     a   b
[1,] "a" "1"
[2,] "b" "2"
[3,] "c" "5"
```

28.4. Converting a Vector into a Matrix

Another easy way to generate a matrix is to convert a vector into a matrix. Below, we generate a vector that takes values from 1 to 10. Obviously it has a length of 10. We convert it into a matrix with a dimension of 5 by 2.

```
> x<-1:10
> y<-matrix(x,5,2)
```

There are two ways to arrange those 10 values in a matrix: by row or by column. The default is by column (i.e., fill in the first column first then the second column and so on).

```
> x<-1:10
> y<-matrix(x,5,2)
> y
     [,1] [,2]
[1,]  1    6
[2,]  2    7
[3,]  3    8
[4,]  4    9
[5,]  5   10
```

To arrange those value in a matrix by row, we specify **byrow=TRUE** or **byroww=T**.

```
> y<-matrix(x,5,2,byrow=T)
> y
     [,1] [,2]
[1,]  1    2
[2,]  3    4
[3,]  5    6
[4,]  7    8
[5,]  9   10
```

To show the dimension of a matrix, we use the **dim()** function.

```
> dim(y) # to show the dimension of a matrix
[1] 5 2
```

Alternatively use the **nrow()** and the **ncol()** functions to get the dimension of a matrix.

```
> nrow(y)
[1] 5
> ncol(y)
[1] 2
```

28.5. Double Loop for a Matrix

One use of the dimension of a matrix is to write double loops to get each data item in the matrix. (See chapter 30: "R Loops" for more information related to loops.)

```
n_row<-nrow(y)
n_col<-ncol(y)
for(i in 1:n_row){
    for(j in 1:n_col){
            # your codes here
    }
}
```

Of course you can simplify the above codes.

```
for(i in 1:nrow(y)){
    for(j in 1:ncol(y)){
            # your codes   here
    }
}
```

In the following codes, we plan to generate a two-by-three matrix (i.e., two rows and three columns). Please pay attention to **byrow=TRUE**.

```
> x <- matrix(c(1,2,3,9,2,3), nrow = 2, ncol=3, byrow=TRUE)
> x

[,1] [,2] [,3]
[1,] 1 2 3
[2,] 9 2 3
```

Please try the following codes (**byrow=FALSE**):

```
> x <- matrix(c(1,2,3,9,2,3), nrow = 2, ncol=3, byrow=FALSE)
```

The default value for the **byrow** variable is **FALSE**.

```
> x<-matrix(c(1,2,3,9,2,3), nrow = 2, ncol=3)# default is byrow=F
```

28.6. Converting a List (Data Frame) into a Matrix Using as.matrix() and is.matrix()

The **as.matrix()** function can be used to convert a data set in the format of a list.

```
> x<-read.table("clipboard") # input in right panel      1 2
> typeof(x)                                               3 4
[1] "list"
> y<-as.matrix(x)
> is.matrix(y)
[1] TRUE
```

28.7. Subset of a Matrix

Assume that x is a matrix. To get the first column, we use the following codes:

```
> x[1,]
```

Similarly, for the rows 1:10 and columns 2:4, we have

```
> x[1:10,2:4] # rows 1:10 and columns 2:4
```

Based on the following codes, we can view the matrix by printing its values.

```
x<-matrix(rnorm(20),4,5)
for(i in 1:nrow(x))
for(j in 1:ncol(x))
print(x[i,j])
```

A negative number indicates exclusion. For example, we exclude the second column in the following codes:

```
> x<-matrix(1:12,3,4)
> x
     [,1] [,2] [,3] [,4]
[1,]  1   4   7  10
[2,]  2   5   8  11
[3,]  3   6   9  12
> x[,-2]
     [,1] [,2] [,3]
[1,]  1   7  10
[2,]  2   8  11
[3,]  3   9  12
```

28.8. Adding Column Names to a Matrix

The **colnames()** function is used in this case.

```
> colnames(A)<-c("ticker","date","return")
```

28.9. Using the Name of the Columns

We can call a specific column by using the dollar-sign ($) variable and the name of the column.

```
> x<-matrix(1:12,3,4)
> colnames(x)<-c("a","b","c","d")
> y<-data.frame(x)
> y$a
[1] 1 2 3
```

To make a, b, c columns available, we can use the **attach()** function.

```
> x<-matrix(1:12,3,4)
> colnames(x)<-c("a","b","c","d")
> y<-data.frame(x)
> a
Error: object 'a' not found
> attach(y)
> a
[1] 1 2 3
```

The opposite of the **attach()** function is the **detach()** function.

```
> detach(y)
> a
Error: object 'a' not found
```

28.10. Solving a Linear Equation[2]

Assume that we have the following equations:

$$3x_1 + 2x_2 - x_3 = 0$$
$$3x_1 - x_2 + x_3 = 1$$
$$-x_1 + 4x_2 + 0.5x_3 = -1$$

We can define **A** and **b** as shown below:

$$A = \begin{bmatrix} 3 & 2 & -1 \\ 3 & -1 & 1 \\ -1 & 4 & 0.5 \end{bmatrix}$$

$$x = \begin{bmatrix} x_1 \\ x_2 \\ x_3 \end{bmatrix}$$

$$b = \begin{bmatrix} 0 \\ 1 \\ -1 \end{bmatrix}$$

$$A * x = b$$

Assign **A** and **b** and double check their values.

```
> a<-c(3,2,-1,3,-1,1,-1,4,0.5)
> A<-matrix(a,3,3)
> A
     [,1] [,2] [,3]
[1,]  3    3   -1.0
[2,]  2   -1    4.0
[3,] -1    1    0.5
> b<-c(0,1,-1)
> b
[1] 0 1 -1
```

To solve the above linear equation, we use the **solve(A,b)** function.

```
> x<-solve(A,b)
> x
[1]  0.4576271 -0.4915254 -0.1016949
```

---

2 To solve linear inverse models in R, we can use a package called **limSolve**.

To double check the result, we use **A%*%x**, where **%*%** is matrix multiplication.

```
> A%*%x
  [,1]
[1,] 6.938894e-17 # very close to zero
[2,] 1.000000e+00
[3,] -1.000000e+00
```

28.11. Inverse of a Matrix

If x is a nonzero scalar, the inverse of **x** will be **y=1/x**. In other words, **x*y=x*1/x=1**. For the inverse of a matrix, we define an *identity matrix* first. An identity matrix is a square matrix with 1 on its major diagonal line (from northwest to south east) and zeros for other data items. Below is a three-by-three identity matrix.

$$\begin{bmatrix} 1 & 0 & 0 \\ 0 & 1 & 0 \\ 0 & 0 & 1 \end{bmatrix}$$

Assume that **A** is a square matrix. We use the **solve(A)** function to get its inverse.

```
> solve(A) # get the inverse of A
```

With **inverse(A)*A**, we will get an identity matrix (i.e., there are 1s on the major diagonal line **x(i,i)** and zeros otherwise).

```
> A<-matrix(c(3,2,-1,3,-1,1,-1,4,0.5),3,3)
> inv_A<-solve(A)
> inv_A%*%A
  [,1] [,2] [,3]
[1,] 1.000000e+00 -5.551115e-17 -5.551115e-17
[2,] -1.110223e-16 1.000000e+00 2.775558e-17
[3,] -5.551115e-17 5.551115e-17 1.000000e+00
```

28.12. Testing Different Types of Data Format

We have a set of functions starting with **is.** (there is a dot after **is**).

```
> is.numeric(x)
> is.character(x)
> is.vector(x)
> is.matrix(x)
> is.data.frame(x)
> as.numeric(x)
> as.character(x)
> as.vector(x)
> as.matrix(x)
> as.data.frame(x)
```

Exercises

28.1. List a few ways we can generate a matrix.

28.2. Can a matrix have different types of data?

28.3. If we combine two vectors with a length of 10 and 6, what dimensions of the final matrix should we expect? How about the data arrangement?

28.4. If we combine three vectors with lengths of 10, 5, and 6, what will be our final matrix?

28.5. If the length of a vector is 20 and the dimension of our final matrix is 6 by 4, what will our final matrix look like?

28.6. How do we tell the dimensions of a matrix?

28.7. How do we run a loop to go through each data item as a matrix?

28.8. Explain the following codes:

```
ma <- matrix(1:12, 3, 4)
nrow(ma)
ncol(ma)
```

28.9. Explain how to convert a vector into a matrix and give an example.

28.10. Explain how to join two vectors into a matrix and give an example.

28.11. What is the difference between a vector and a matrix?

28.12. How do we determine that a variable is a matrix?

28.13. Solve the following linear equations:

$$x_1 + x_2 - 2x_3 = 0.5$$
$$1.5x_1 + 2x_2 - x_3 = 1.2$$
$$-2x_1 - 3x_2 + 0.5x_3 = 2$$

28.14. Continuing from 28.13, what is the difference between A*solve(A,b) and A%*%solve(A,b)?

CHAPTER 29

Simple Plot and Graph

A simple picture is worth a million words. In this chapter, we discuss simple plots. The first one has just one line.

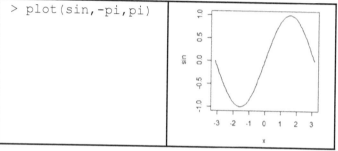

```
> plot(sin,-pi,pi)
```

In the above example, we have a function with a range. The most used plots are to variables of x and y (see below).

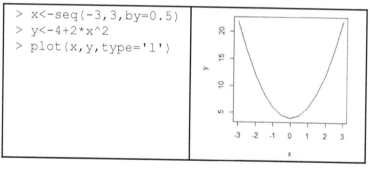

```
> x<-seq(-3,3,by=0.5)
> y<-4+2*x^2
> plot(x,y,type='l')
```

29.1. Plot for a Single Graph

To have a single graph is quite easy (see the codes below).

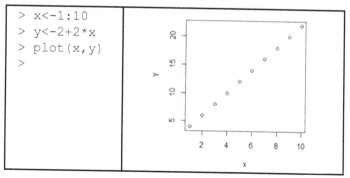

```
> x<-1:10
> y<-2+2*x
> plot(x,y)
>
```

29.2. Adding Labels on Horizontal and Vertical Axes

To add various labels on both axes, we use **xlab="This is x axis"** and **ylab="This is y axis"**.

```
> plot(x,y,xlab="time",ylab="Income")
```

29.3. Shading Certain Areas

In the following example, we shade the area when z is less than -2.33 for a standard normal distribution. The following codes can be used to show the 1% left tail of a standard normal distribution.

```
>x<-seq(-4,4,length=200)
>y<-dnorm(x,mean=0,sd=1)
> plot(x,y,type="l",lwd=2,col="red")
>x<-seq(-4,-2.33,length=200)
>y<-dnorm(x,mean=0,sd=1)
> polygon(c(-4,x,-
2.33),c(0,y,0),col="gray")
```

29.4. Putting Several Graphs Together

We can put several graphs together to make our output more efficient or clearer.

```
>attach(mtcars)
>x<- matrix(c(1,1,2,3),
2, 2, byrow = TRUE)
> layout(x,widths=c(3,1),heights=c(1,2))
> hist(wt)
> hist(mpg)
> hist(disp)
```

29.5. Greek Letters

Occasionally we need to add Greek letters to our output.

```
> plot(1,1,xlab=expression(alpha[i])
,ylab=expression(delta[j]));
```

The output is shown below.

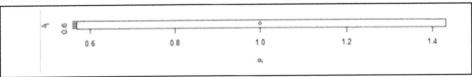

29.6. Saving a PDF File

In the following program, we generate a graph and save it to a PDF file.

```
> pdf("c:/temp/t.pdf")# specify an output file
> plot(sin,-pi,pi)
> dev.off() # disconnect the output file
```

29.7 Outputting High-Resolution Images

Nowadays, we like to include more and more images into our academic papers or articles since a good picture worth a million words. However, most publishers require the quality of an image has at least 300 DPI. If we use the following codes, we would find that the DPI is 92.

jpeg('test.jpg') plot(sin,-pi,pi) dev.off()	Dimensions	480X480
	Width	480 picels
	Height	480 pixels
	Horizon resolution	96 dpi
	Vertical resulation	96 dpi

Find the output and right click it. Then choose "Detail." You will find that the resolution is only 96 DPI.

```
jpeg('test.jpg', width = 4, height =
4, units = 'in', res = 600)
plot(sin,-pi,pi)
dev.off()
```

See below.

Dimensions	2400X2400
Width	2400 picels
Height	2400 pixels
Horizon resolution	600 dpi
Vertical resulation	600 dpi

29.8 Overlapping Graphs

Let's look at the following simplest one.

```
x <- c(7,9,10,10,12,11,11,13,13,12)
y <- c(9,12,12,11,13,14,15,10,15,1)
plot(density(x))
lines(density(y))
```

29.9 Putting an Efficient Frontier and CAPM Together

Sometimes, we need to put two graphs together, see the codes below.

```
rf<-0.16
x<-seq(0,0.7,0.05)
y<-rf+1.7*x
y2<-0.01 +x^0.5+0.2*(x-0.1)
plot(x,y2,type='l',main="Efficient Frontier and
CAPM",xlab=expression
(paste(sigma," (risk)")),ylab="Rp (Portfolio Return)",lwd=4)
lines(x,y,lwd=3)
text(0.09, 0.45, labels=expression("Rm") ,cex = 1)
```

To generate a high-resolution image, we have the following codes.

```
jpeg('test.jpg', width = 4, height = 4, units = 'in', res = 600)
rf<-0.175
x<-seq(0,0.7,0.05)
y<-rf+1.7*x
y2<-0.01 +x^0.5+0.2*(x-0.1)
plot(x,y2,type='l',main="Efficient Frontier and
CAPM",xlab=expression
(paste(sigma," (risk)")),ylab="Rp (Portfolio Return)",lwd=4)
lines(x,y,lwd=3)
text(0.09, 0.45, labels=expression("Rm") ,cex = 1)
dev.off()
```

29.10 Exporting High-Resolution Image with Sentences

We have the following steps.

Step 1: Run the following codes.

```
par(bg = "white")
x<-c(0.1,0.3,0.5,0.5,0.7,1)
y<-c(0.1,0.5,0.3,0.7,0.5,1)
plot(x, y,type='n',lwd=0.1,ann=FALSE,axes=FALSE, frame.plot=FALSE)
rect(par("usr")[1], par("usr")[3], par("usr")
[2], par("usr")[4],col= "grey")
text(0.3, 0.7, labels="FINANCIALS") , adj = c(0.2,0),cex = 4)
text(0.3, 0.6, labels="Income Statement", adj = c(0.1,0),cex = 3 )
text(0.3, 0.5, labels="Balance Sheet", adj = c(0.1,0),cex = 3 )
text(0.3, 0.4, labels="Income Cash Flow", adj = c(0.1,0),cex = 3 )
```

Step 2: Right click the image "Print," choose a PDF printer. For example, saved as test.pdf

Step 3: Launch GIMP to open test.pdf and export it as test.jpg, with a resolution of 600

Step 4: Export it as test.jpg

 i) Choose jpg and type the extension.

 ii) Set quality 100.

29.11 Adding a Shaded Area

The following codes adds a shaded area.

```
n <- 100
x <- c(0:n, n:0)
y <- c(c(0,cumsum(stats::rnorm(n))), rev(c(0,
cumsum(stats::rnorm(n)))))
plot    (x, y, type = "n", xlab = "Time", ylab = "Distance")
polygon(x, y, col = "gray", border = "blue")
title("Distance Between Brownian Motions")
```

CHAPTER 30

String Manipulation

To combine two strings, we use the **paste()** function with **sep='pattern'**, where **sep** stands for "separator."

```
> paste("I love"," dogs", sep=",") # separated by a comma
[1] "I love, dogs"
```

If we want to replace a character (value) with another one just once, we use the **sub()** function.

```
> sub("a","9","aacd") # replace 'a' with '9' just once
[1] "9acd"
```

To replace a pattern multiple times, use the **gsub()** function (global substitution).

```
> gsub("a","9","aacd") # replace all 'a' with '9'
[1] "99cd"
```

To remove all nonnumeric values, we use the following R codes. The command **[12]** means 1 or 2 and **[0-9]** means 0 or 1 or 2 up to 9. The symbol of ^ is a logic NO.

```
> gsub("[^0-9]", "","abcd2349")
[1] "2349"
```

In this chapter, we discuss how to manipulate a string/character variable. Here *string* and *character* are interchangeable.

30.1. Assigning a String Variable

We can use double quotation marks or single quotation marks to assign a character variable.

```
> x<-"this is"
> x
[1] "this is"
```

30.2. Checking Whether a Variable is a Character

The following example shows how to use the **is.chatacter()** function.

```
> is.character(1)
[1] FALSE
> is.character("Hello ")
[1] TRUE
```

30.3. Capital vs. Lowercase Letters toupper() and tolower()

Remember that R is case sensitive.

```
> tolower("Very good ")        > toupper("International Business ")
[1] "very good "              [1] "INTERNATIONAL BUSINESS "
```

30.4. The Length of a String nchar()

The **length()** function is used to check how many data items are there within a variable while the **nchar()** is used to check how many letters (number of characters) are within each data item.

```
> nchar("International Business ")
[1] 22
```

30.5. Choosing Part of a String Using substr() and substring()

Assume that we have a string. We plan to retrieve a substring of it.

```
> x<- "I love apples "
> substring(x,1,5) # start from 1, ends with 5
[1] "I lov"
> substr(x,5,5)
[1] "v"
```

From a specific position to the end of the string, we can ignore the third parameter.

```
> x<- "I love apples "
> substring(x,3,)

[1] "love apples "
```

30.6. Combining Two Strings Together Using paste()

We can use the paste() function to put two strings together (see below).

```
> x<- "2000"
> paste("year",x,sep="")
[1] "year2000"
```

When a variable is a vector, we combine each data item from this vector with the second string.

```
> x<-2000:2003
> y<-paste("year",x,sep="")
> y
[1] "year2000" "year2001" "year2002" "year2003"
```

The above codes are the same as the following codes:

```
> x<-as.character(2000:2003)
> x
[1] "2000" "2001" "2002" "2003"
> paste("year",x,sep="")
[1] "year2000" "year2001" "year2002" "year2003"
```

When **sep** is omitted, the default separator is a blank

```
> x<-2000:2003
> paste("year",x)
[1] "year 2000" "year 2001" "year 2002" "year 2003"
```

30.7. Removing Leading or Trailing Blanks from a String

Assume that we have the following string. We intend to remove the leading blanks, training blanks, or all blanks.

```
> x<-' this is a try '
> x
[1] " this is a try "
```

To remove one leading blank, we use ^ , where ^ indicates the beginning of a string.

```
> nchar(x)
[1] 19
y<-gsub("^ ","",x)
> y
[1] "this is a try "
> nchar(y)
[1] 18
```

To remove all leading blanks, we use ^ *, where * means one or more.

```
> gsub("^ *","",x)
[1] "this is a try "
```

To remove all trailing blanks, use the following codes, where $ indicates the end of the string.

```
> gsub(" * $","",x)
[1] " this is a try"
```

To remove all the blanks, use the following codes. By the way, we might not like this result.

```
> gsub(" ","",x)
[1] "thisisatry"
```

30.8. Repeating Indicator *, +, ?, and.

The following table shows the meanings of those so-called repeat indicators.

Table 30.1. Table definitions of repeat indicators

Symbol	Description
*	Repeat 0, 1, 2,..., n times
+	Repeat 1, 2,..., n times
?	Repeat 0 or 1 once
.	Any character repeat once

We can try different ways by specifying one of the above indicators. If we want to remove everything from a fixed phrase, we use "(phrase).*", which means any symbol after our fixed phrase and repeat any times (including zero time).

```
> x<-"You have successfully logged off from Inside Loyola."
> gsub("(logged off).*" ,"",x)
[1] "You have successfully
```

30.9. Convert a Number into a Character Variable Using as.character()

We can use the **as.character()** function to convert a number into a string.

```
> x<-1:10
> as.character(x)
[1] "1" "2" "3" "4" "5"
"6" "7" "8" "9" "10"
```

Alternatively we can use the **paste()** function to change the type.

```
> x<-2000:2003
> paste(x)
[1] "2000" "2001" "2002" "2003"
```

The third way is to use the **toString()** function.

```
> toString(1)
[1] "1"
```

30.10. Converting a String Variable into a Numerical One Using as.numeric()

```
> x<-"1990" # x is defined as a character variable
> as.numeric(x)+1
[1] 1991
```

The R function called **date()** will give us today's date and time. It is a string variable, and we can use the **typeof()** function to double check.

```
> typeof(date())
[1] "character"
```

We can use the **paste()** function to add a few words in front of it.

```
> paste("Today is", date())
[1] "Today is Thu May 28 10:16:45 2015"
```

30.11. String Matching

First, from http://canisius.edu/~yany/RData/retD50.RData, we download an R data set called **retD50.Rdata**. In the following codes, we choose stocks that has names equal to IBM's. We use double equal signs (==) for an equality

```
> load("retD50.Rdata")
> head(retD50)
  ticker date ret
1883624 IBM 1962-01-02 -99.000000
1883625 IBM 1962-01-03 0.007663
1883626 IBM 1962-01-04 -0.011407
1883627 IBM 1962-01-05 -0.019231
1883628 IBM 1962-01-08 -0.019608
1883629 IBM 1962-01-09 0.012000
> x<-subset(retD50,retD50[,1]=="IBM")
> dim(retD50)
  [1] 293373 3 # a big number
since multiple stocks
> dim(ibm)
  [1] 12386 3 # a small number
since just one stock
```

30.12. Logic OR []

If we want to replace **a** or **d** with **"9"**, we can use [] to include a and d.

```
> gsub("[ad]","9","abcd")
[1] "9bc9"
```

From **a, b, c** to **d**, we use [a-d]; and from **a, b,…,** up to **z**, we use [a-z]. In the following codes, we replace any letter from **a** to **z** with nothing. In other words, we remove any letter from **a** to **z**.

```
> gsub("[a-z]", "","abcd9")
[1] "9"
```

30.13. Logic NOT (^)

Keeping all alphabetic letters is equivalent to removing all nonalphabetic letters (i.e., replacing them with nothing).

```
> gsub("[^a-z]","","abcd9")
[1] "abcd"
```

30.14. Existence of a Pattern

The format will be **grep("pattern",your string")**. If the pattern exists, the function returns a value of 1; otherwise, it returns a zero.

```
> grep("Inter","Machine")
integer(0)
> grep("Inter","International Business")
[1] 1
```

30.15. Converting a String into an Integer Using strtoi()

The **strtoi()** function is used to convert a string into an integer.

```
> x<-"9"
> x+1
Error in x + 1 : non-numeric
argument to binary operator
> strtoi(x)+1
[1] 10
```

When x is a string variable that contains a noninteger, the **strtoi()** function will not work.

```
> x<-"9.9"
> strtoi(x)
[1] NA
> strtoi("year2001")
[1] NA
> strtoi("2001.")
[1] NA
```

30.16. The Names of Vectors (Matrix) are Strings

The column names and row names are string.

```
> load("retD50.Rdata")
> x<-subset(retD50,retD50[,1]=="IBM")
> colnames(x)
[1] "ticker" "date" "ret"
```

30.17. Two Predetermined Data Sets of letters and LETTERS

There are two default, predetermined variables called **letter** and **LETTERS**.

```
> LETTERS
[1]  "A" "B" "C" "D" "E" "F" "G" "H" "I" "J"
"K" "L" "M" "N" "O" "P" "Q" "R" "S"
[20] "T" "U" "V" "W" "X" "Y" "Z"
> letters
[1]  "a" "b" "c" "d" "e" "f" "g" "h" "i" "j"
"k" "l" "m" "n" "o" "p" "q" "r" "s"
[20] "t" "u" "v" "w" "x" "y" "z"
```

To print all twenty-six letters, we can issue the following command:

```
> for(letter in letters)
print(letter)
[1] "a"
[1] "b"

[1] "z"
```

Alternatively we can use the **cat()** function instead of the **print()** function.

```
> for(letter in letters)
cat(letter)
> for(letter in letters) {
+ if(letter=="z")
+ print(letter)
+ }
[1] "z"
```

(Note: the data set (variable) called **state.name** is a predetermined string vector.)

```
> typeof(state.name)
[1] "character"
> length(state.name)
[1] 50
```

30.18. Using Short Names with abbreciate()

Sometimes we want to use a short name in place of a long name. In those cases, we can use the function called **abbreciate()**.

```
> state.name
 [1] "Alabama"    "Alaska"   "Arizona"    "Arkansas"
 [5] "California" "Colorado"  "Connecticut" "Delaware"
 [9] "Florida"   "Georgia"  "Hawaii" " Idaho"
[13] "Illinois"  "Indiana"  "Iowa"  "Kansas"
[17] "Kentucky"  "Louisiana" "Maine"  "Maryland"
[21] "Massachusetts" "Michigan"  "Minnesota" "Mississippi"
[25] "Missouri"  "Montana"  "Nebraska"   "Nevada"
[29] "New Hampshire"  "New Jersey"  "New Mexico"  "New York"
[33] "North Carolina"  "North Dakota"  "Ohio"  "Oklahoma"
[37] "Oregon"  "Pennsylvania" "Rhode
Island" "South Carolina"
[41] "South Dakota" "Tennessee"  "Texas"   "Utah"
[45] "Vermont"   "Virginia"  "Washington"  "West Virginia"
[49] "Wisconsin"  "Wyoming"
```

If we look at the three-letter abbreviation, we have the following codes:

```
> abbreviate(state.name,3)
Alabama     Alaska  Arizona   Arkansas   California
"Alb"       "Als"   "Arz"     "Ark"      "Clf"
Colorado    Connecticut  Delaware  Florida   Georgia
"Clr"       "Cnn"        "Dlw"     "Flr"     "Grg"
Hawaii      Idaho   Illinois Indiana   Iowa
"Haw"       "Idh"   "Ill"    "Ind"     "Iow"
Kansas      Kentucky Louisiana Maine   Maryland
"Kns"       "Knt"    "Lsn"     "Man"   "Mry"
Massachusetts  Michigan  Minnesota
Mississippi  Missouri
"Mssc"       "Mch"     "Mnn"     "Msss"     "Mssr"
Montana     Nebraska Nevada  New Hampshire New Jersey
"Mnt"       "Nbr"   "Nvd"     "NwH"        "NwJ"
New Mexico  New York   North
Carolina    North Dakota   Ohio
"NwM"       "NwY"    "NrC"     "NrD"      "Ohi"
Oklahoma    Oregon  Pennsylvania
Rhode Island                        South Carolina
"Okl"       "Org"   "Pnn"     "RhI"      "StC"
South  Dakota Tennessee Texas Utah      Vermont
"StD"       "Tnn"    "Txs" "Uth"        "Vrm"
Virginia    Washington West Virginia Wisconsin Wyoming
"Vrg"       "Wsh"        "WsV"       "Wsc"    "Wym"
```

Exercises

30.1. Why does the following result give us a wrong answer?

```
> is.character("1")
[1] TRUE
```

30.2. Explain the following result:

```
> sub("g?","%","abcdefggggg")
[1] "%abcdefggggg"
```

30.3. What is the difference between the **nchar()** and **length()** functions?

```
> x<-"this is a try"
```

30.4. When we download a financial statement from marketwatch.com, we observe the values 32B and 19.3M. How do we convert them into numeric values such as **32*10^9** and **19.3*10^6**?

30.5. With the following three-line codes, we download IBM's income statement for several years from marketwatch.com.

```
> library(XML)
> t<-"http://www.marketwatch.com/
investing/stock/IBM/financials"
> x<-readHTMLTable(t)
```

To view a few lines of the first table, we use the **head()** function.

```
> head(x[[1]])
Fiscal year is January-December. 2007 2008
2009 2010 2011 5-year trend
1 Sales/Revenue 98.79B 103.63B 95.76B 99.87B 108.02B
2 Sales Growth-4.90% -7.60% 4.29% 8.16%
3 Cost of Goods Sold (COGS) incl. D&A
57.69B 58.6B 52.56B 54.42B 56.78B
4 COGS excluding D&A 52.49B 53.15B 47.56B 49.59B 56.78B
5 Depreciation & Amortization Expense 5.2B 5.45B 4.99B 4.83B -
6 Depreciation 4.04B 4.14B 3.77B 3.66B-
```

Write an R function to convert all values into numeric values.

CHAPTER 31

Introduction to R Package

Assume that we want to download the last seven days' daily data for IBM from Yahoo Finance. We have the following two-line R codes.

```
> library(fImport) # load fImport
>x<-yahooSeries("IBM",nDaysBack=7)#
use yahooSeries function
```

However, it is quite common that after issuing the first command to upload fImport, we receive the following error message:

```
> library(fImport)
Error in library(fImport) : there is
no package called 'fImport'
```

The error message tells us that the package called fImport is not preinstalled. The first way to install an R package is accomplished with the following one-line codes:

```
> install.packages("fImport")
```

After successfully installing the package, try the above two lines, which would lead to the following output:

```
> library(fImport)
> yahooSeries("IBM", nDaysBack=7)
GMT
  IBM.Open IBM.High IBM.Low IBM.
Close IBM.Volume IBM.Adj.Close
2014-10-24 162.08 162.44 161.45 162.08 6652100 162.08
2014-10-23 162.12 162.83 161.54 162.18 7599400 162.18
2014-10-22 162.41 165.41 161.10 161.79 11084800 161.79
2014-10-21 166.40 166.68 161.68 163.23 20949800 163.23
```

31.1 Introduction

An R package is a set of R programs (functions) serving a specific objective written by one or several experts or some users. For example, a package called **fOptions** has more than a dozen R functions that can be used to price various types of options. Currently, there are 5,983 packages available as of October 23, 2014. On average, two new packages are generated every day.

31.2. Loaded vs. Preinstalled Packages

To find out all loaded packages, use the **search()** function.

```
> search()
[1] ".GlobalEnv"  "package:stats"  "package:graphics"
[4] "package:grDevices" "package:datasets"
"package:utils"
[7] "package:methods"  "Autoloads"   "package:base"
```

Those seven packages are automatically uploaded when we launch R. To find out all preinstalled packages, we use the **library()** function.

```
> library() # show all installed packages
```

The difference between a loaded package and a preinstalled package is that if a package is loaded, you can use its related functions. If a package is not loaded but preinstalled, we can use the **library()** function to load it. If a package is not preinstalled, we have to install it before we can load it. Using appropriate packages makes programming much easier. For example, to download various foreign exchange rates, we can use the **readHTMLTable()** function from the XML package. The last command of **Sys.Date()** shows the date of *today* (i.e., those exchange rates are quoted on March 27, 2015).

```
> library(XML) # upload the package
> t<-"http://www.marketwatch.com/
investing/stock/IBM/financials"
> x<-readHTMLTable(t)
> typeof(x) # find the type of data
[1] "list"
> length(x) # find the length of a data set
[1] 2
> y<-as.matrix(x[[1]])
> dim(y)
[1] 10 3
> head(y)

US Dollar 1.00 USD inv. 1.00 USD
[1,] "Euro" "0.920632" "1.086210"
[2,] "British Pound" "0.672163" "1.487734"
[3,] "Indian Rupee" "62.522325" "0.015994"
[4,] "Australian Dollar" "1.283933" "0.778857"
[5,] "Canadian Dollar" "1.250604" "0.799614"
[6,] "Singapore Dollar" "1.369120" "0.730396"
> Sys.Date()
[1] "2015-03-27"
```

31.3. The Second Way to Install a Package

The second way involves using the menu bar.

1. Click **Packages** on the menu bar.
2. Choose a mirror location.
3. Click a desired package to install it.

31.4. The Third Way to Install a Package

The third way is to install a package based on a locally saved zip file. Obviously we need to save the zip file on our computers. Below, several steps are given if we plan to install the **quantmod** package from a locally saved zip file.

1. Go to http://www.r-project.org/.
2. Choose a mirror server.
3. Click **Packages** on the left-hand side.
4. Use **Ctrl+F** to search **quantmod**.
5. Download it to your PC.
6. Click **Packages** on the menu bar.
7. Install the package from our local files (just downloaded).

31.5. Can't Install an R Package

If we observe the following error message, it means the person trying to install certain R packages does not have a right to write to the library.

```
> utils:::menuInstallPkgs()
Warning in install.packages(NULL, .libPaths()
[1L], dependencies = NA, type = type) :
  'lib = "C:/Program Files/R/R-2.15.2/library"' is not writable
Error in install.packages(NULL, .libPaths()
[1L], dependencies = NA, type = type) :
  unable to install packages
```

To correct this problem, we change the permission.

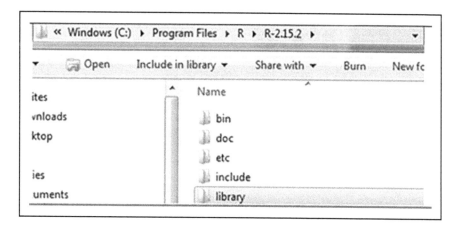

Choose **Library** and right-click the mouse and choose **Properties**. Then we change the permission (see below).

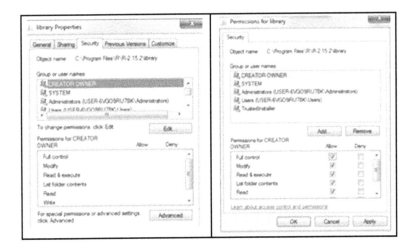

31.6. Using the .libPaths() Function

One way to avoid the above issue of administration privilege is to use the **.libPaths()** function. Be careful since there is a dot in front of **libPath()**. When I was teaching financial analysis with R at a school, I could not install any R package. The drive of my memory stick was e:\. Then after issuing the following R commands, I could install any R package I chose.

```
>.libPaths("e: / ")
>install.packages("XML ")
```

31.7. Three Ways to Load a Package

There are three ways to load a specific package.

```
> library(fImport) # Method I
> require(fImport) # Method II
# Click "Packages"[menu bar], "Load
packages" # Method III
```

31.8. Finding the Manual for a Specific Package

To find and download the manual for **fImport**, we can do the following steps:

Go to http://www.r-project.org/. Click CRAN. Choose a mirror. Click Packages on the left-hand side (under Software). Find a specific package. Use Ctrl+F to search. Download the manual in a PDF format to your PC.	**Reference manual:** flmport.pdf **Package source:** flmport_3000.82.tar.gz **Windows binaries:** r-devel: flmport_3000.82.zip, **OS X Snow Leopard binaries:** r-release: flmport_3000.82.tgz **OS X Mavericks binaries:** r-release: flmport_3000.82.tgz **Old sources:** flmport archive

31.9. Most Used Commands Related to Packages

R packages are the most important tools for using R. Usually we list all available packages then pick up the packages related to finance or the packages we need. However, for a new user, the following approach might be more appropriate: First, find out all loaded packages. Second, find out the contents of a loaded package. Third, search for more information related to its specific function in terms of use and examples. The following table presents the most used commands related to packages.

Table 31.1. Getting information about preinstalled, loaded packages

Description	R command
Find out all loaded packages	>search()
Find out whether a specific package is loaded or not	> library(XML) > "package:XML" %in% search() [I] TRUE
Find out all preinstalled packages	>library()
	>.packages(all.available=T)
Find out whether a specific package is preinstalled	> library(XML) > "XML" %in% .packages(all.available=T) [I] TRUE
Load a preinstalled package	> library(flmport)
	> require(financial)
Unload a package	> detach(package:flmport) detach("package:flmport",unload=TRUE)
Get information about a package	> help(package="timeDate") > library(help="timeDate")
Check all available packages	Go to http://www.r-project.org/. Click CRAN. Choose a location. Click Packages.

Exercises

31.1. What is the difference between a loaded package and a preinstalled one?

31.2. How do you load an R package?

31.3. How do you find all loaded R packages?

31.4. How do you find all preinstalled R packages?

31.5. How do you install an R package?

31.6. How do you find the manual for a specific R package?

31.7. How many R packages are available today?

31.8. How many ways can you install an R package?

31.9. How many functions are available for quantmod?

31.10. Download analyst recommendations for IBM, DELL, and MSFT.

31.11. Analyze the results from the above question.

31.12. What is the exchange rate between the US dollar and the Russian ruble on November 1, 2011?

31.13. Write an R program to put four exchanges rate side by side (e.g., you can use USD/GBP, USD/DEM, USD/FRF, and SD/CNY). Estimate how strongly they are correlated.

31.14. Download the prime rate and USD/GBP. What is the correlation between them?

31.15. What is the correlation coefficient between the prime rate and S&P 500 (use ^GSPC to retrieve daily data from Yahoo Finance for S&P 500)?

31.16. Write an R program to retrieve n trading days from today.

```
> library(fImport) # load the package called fImport
> x<-yahooSeries("IBM", nDaysBack=365)
# y<-yahooSeries2("IBM", nTradingDaysBack=252)
```

31.17. In the following codes, test whether 252 is a calendar day or a trading day. If it is a calendar day, how do you retrieve 252 calendar days' data? If it is a trading day, how do you retrieve 365 calendar days' data?

```
> library(fImport)
> d<-yahooSeries("IBM", nDaysBack=252)
```

CHAPTER 32

Reading and Writing Binary Data in R

Why should we care about reading from or writing to a binary file? The major reason is speed. By writing or reading from a binary file instead of a text (ASCII) file, we can increase our speed by ten folds or more. For example, based on the data below, you will realize that reading from a binary file is twenty-three times faster than reading from a text file. Later in the chapter, we will show you how to get those numbers.

	User time	System time	Total time
Read a csv file	6.80	0.05	6.85
Read a binary file	0.28	0.00	0.28

32.1. Writing and Reading a Binary File

To save an R binary data set, we can use the **save()** function. For example, we have a vector of x from 2 to 100. We can save it to a binary data set called **test.Rdata**.

```
>x<-2:100
> save(x,file="c:/temp/test.Rdata")
```

The extension is not critical, and we don't even need an extension in the first place. We can also save multiple variables at the same time.

```
>x<-2:100
> y<-c("this", "is"," a test")
> save(x,y,file="c:/temp/test2")
```

To retrieve a R binary data set, we use the **load()** function (see an example below).

```
>load("c:/temp/test2")
```

To remove a saved data set, we use the **unlink()** function.

```
> unlink("c:/temp/test2")
```

32.2. Comparison of Speed

Below, we test the speeds of writing to/reading from a CSV file and a binary file. First, we simply test those codes to see if they are bug free. The function of **rnorm(n)** delivers n random numbers from a standard normal distribution while **pnorm()** is for the cumulative standard normal distribution.

```
>n<-500000
>x<-data.frame(x1=rnorm(n),x2=rnorm(n),x3=pnorm(n))
>write.table(x,file="c:/temp/temp.csv",sep=",",col.names=NA)
> cat("first summary of x\n")
>summary(x)
> y<-read.table("c:/temp/temp.csv",header=TRUE,sep=",",row.names=1)
> save(x,file="c:/temp/temp.binary")# write binary
>rm(x)
> load("c:/temp/temp.binary")
> cat("2nd summary of x\n")
summary(x)
```

After we find no errors, we can use the function **system.time** (command lines) to give the three values: user time, system time, and total time.

```
>n<-500000
>x<-data.frame(x1=rnorm(n),x2=rnorm(n),x3=pnorm(n))
>cat("Time: write a text file\n")
>system.time(write.csv(x,file="c:/temp/t.csv",col.names=NA))
>cat("Time: read a text file\n")
>system.time(x<-read.csv("c:/temp/t.csv",header=TRUE,row.names=1))
>cat("Time: write a binary file\n")
>system.time(save(x,file="c:/temp/t.bin"))
>cat("Time: read a binary file\n")
>system.time(load("c:/temp/t.bin"))
```

The above results are summarized in the following table.

Table 32.1. System times for reading/writing a text and binary file

	User time	System time	Total time
Writing the CSV file	5.82	0.11	5.93
Read the CSV file	6.80	0.05	6.85
Writing the binary file	0.68	0.01	0.70
Reading (loading) the binary file	0.28	0.00	0.28

32.3. Writing a Binary File Using writeBin()

Here is a simple example to write a binary file called **test.bin**. Taing, the exact extension is not critical. There is only one variable (**x**), and it has values from 1 to 10. In the first line below, **wb** indicates "write" and "binary."

The **writeBin()** function is used to write a binary data set while the **close()** line disconnects our connection with our output file.

```
>out_f<- file("test.bin","wb")
>writeBin(1:10, out_f)
>writeBin(pi,out_f, endian="swap")
>writeBin(pi, out_f, size=4)
>close(out_f)
```

Endianness is how a machine stores its data. To check the endianness, we can issue **.Platform$endian**.

```
.Platform$endian
[1] "little"
```

32.4. Reading a Binary File Using readBin()

In the following example, we assume that **testbin** is available under the current working directory (see the previous section to see how to generate it). The function we use to retrieve data from a binary file is the **readBin()**. *Bin* stands for "binary."

```
> in_f <- file("test.bin","rb")
> readBin(in_f, integer(), 4)
[1] 1 2 3 4
```

The following codes read the first two data records; **readBin()** is the function we use to read a binary data set. Since our PC environment is "little endian," we have to use **endian=little**.

```
> in.file<-file("c:/temp/test.bin","rb") # open a file
>readBin(in.file,integer(),size=4,endian='little')
  [1] 1
>readBin(in.file,integer(),size=4,endian='little')
  [2] 2
>close(in.file)
```

Using a wrong format will lead to a wrong input. Since our PC is a little endian, the data saved should have the same format. If we use an **endian='big'** to read the first value (which we know is 1), we would get a value of 16777216 (see codes below).

```
> in.file<-file("c:/temp/test.bin","rb") # open a file
> readBin(in.file,integer(),size=4,endian='big')
  [1] 16777216
close(in.file)
```

32.5. Writing a Binary Data File

To download daily data for IBM, we go to finance.yahoo.com. Input "IBM" in the Get Quote box, click **Historical Data** then **Save to Spreadsheet** at the bottom of the screen. Thus, we have an input file called IBM.csv, which has seven columns: date, open price, high price of the day, low price of the day, closing price of the day, trading volume, and adjusted closing price. Each variable is separated by commas (see a few lines below).

Date,Open,High,Low,Close,Volume,Adj Close

2010-12-06,144.54,145.87,144.52,144.99,3321800,144.99
2010-12-03,144.25,145.68,144.25,145.38,3710600,145.38
2010-12-02,144.33,145.85,144.30,145.18,5374000,145.18
2010-12-01,143.61,145.13,143.51,144.41,6822800,144.41
2010-11-30,142.24,142.76,141.28,141.46,7674800,141.46
2010-11-29,143.53,143.67,141.50,142.89,5040300,142.89
2010-11-26,145.30,145.30,143.57,143.90,2081300,143.90
2010-11-24,143.95,146.44,143.82,145.81,4874100,145.81

Assume that the location of the file is c:/temp/. Then we can use the following codes to retrieve the data set.

```
> x<-read.csv("c:/temp/ibm.csv",header=T)
```

Again, we can use the **head()** function to view the first several lines of the data set (see below).

```
> head(x)
  Date Open High Low Close Volume Adj.Close
1 2010-12-06 144.54 145.87 144.52 144.99 3321800 144.99
2 2010-12-03 144.25 145.68 144.25 145.38 3710600 145.38
3 2010-12-02 144.33 145.85 144.30 145.18 5374000 145.18
4 2010-12-01 143.61 145.13 143.51 144.41 6822800 144.41
5 2010-11-30 142.24 142.76 141.28 141.46 7674800 141.46
6 2010-11-29 143.53 143.67 141.50 142.89 5040300 142.89
```

Similarly, we use the **tail()** function to view the last several lines. The last number *12318* is the number of observations.

```
> tail(x)
  Date Open High Low Close Volume Adj.Close
12313 1962-01-09 552.0 563.0 552 556.00 491200 2.54
12314 1962-01-08 559.5 559.5 545 549.50 544000 2.51
12315 1962-01-05 570.5 570.5 559 560.00 363200 2.56
12316 1962-01-04 577.0 577.0 571 571.25 256000 2.61
12317 1962-01-03 572.0 577.0 572 577.00 288000 2.64
12318 1962-01-02 578.5 578.5 572 572.00 387200 2.62
```

Actually we can use the **dim()** function to determine the number of observations and the number of variables (columns). The output from **dim(x)** shows that we have 12,318 observations and 7 variables.

```
> dim(x)
[1] 12318 7
```

A more complex program is given below:

```
> x<-read.csv("c:/temp/ibm.csv",header=T)
>y<-dim(x)
> out.file<-file("c:/temp/ibm.bin","wb")
>writeBin(y[2],out.file) # number of columns
>writeBin(y[1],out.file) # number of obs
>y<-as.integer(as.Date(x$Date))

>writeBin(y,out.file)
>writeBin(x$Open,out.file)
>writeBin(x$High,out.file)
>writeBin(x$Low,out.file)
>writeBin(x$Close,out.file)
>writeBin(x$Volume,out.file)
>writeBin(x$Adj.Close,out.file)
>close(out.file)
```

The size of the binary file in this case is slightly smaller.

12/07/2010 10:54 PM 591,272 ibm.bin
12/07/2010 04:44 PM 631,999 ibm.csv

To write a character to an output binary file, use the **writeBin** function (see a few lines below).

```
>out.file<-file("c:/temp/ibm3.bin","wb")
>writeBin("IBM",out.file)
>close(out.file)
```

To check the output from the above program, we can use the following program to print the only character saved in the output file, which is now the input file instead.

```
> in.file<-file("c:/temp/ibm3.bin","rb")
> readBin(in.file,character(),size=4,endian='little')
[1] "IBM"
> close(in.file)
```

Alternatively we can use the following method:

```
>out.file<-file("c:/temp/ibm2.bin","wb")
>writeChar("IBM",out.file,nchar=4)
>close(out.file)
>in.file<-file("c:/temp/ibm2.bin","rb")
>readChar(in.file,n=1)
>readChar(in.file,nchar=4)
>close(in.file)
```

We can also write the names of each variable (see the codes below).

```
>x<-read.csv("c:/temp/ibm.csv",header=T)
>y<-dim(x)
>out.file<-file("c:/temp/ibm.bin","wb")
>writeBin(y[2],out.file) # write the number of columns
>writeBin(y[1],out.file) # write the number of observations
>writeBin(colnames(x),out.file)# write the names of all columns
>close(out.file)
```

(Note: if we export the seven names to our output file, we have to retrieve those seven characters when we read the data from the same binary file.)

32.6. Reading a Binary Data File

Assume that we know the format of an input binary data set. The first line has two numbers: the number of variables and the number of observations. In addition, the binary data set is arranged by the data items. Assume that we have m variables and n observations. Thus, the first n inputs will be the first variable.

```
>in.file<-file("c:/temp/ibm.bin","rb")
>n_vars<-readBin(in.file,integer(),n=1,endian='little')
>n_obs<-readBin(in.file,integer(),n=1,endian='little')
>date<-readBin(in.file,integer(),n=n_obs,endian='little')
>open<-readBin(in.file,double(),n=n_obs,endian='little')
>high<-readBin(in.file,double(),n=n_obs,endian='little')
>low<-readBin(in.file,double(),n=n_obs,endian='little')
>close<-readBin(in.file,double(),n=n_obs,endian='little')
>vol<-readBin(in.file,integer(),n=n_obs,endian='little')
>adj.close<-readBin(in.file,double(),n=n_obs,endian='little')
>data<-cbind(as.Date(date,origin='1970-01-01'),open,high,low,close,vol,
adj.close)
>close(in.file)
```

Exercises

32.1. When do we need to input a binary data set?

32.2. How do we write our data to a binary output file?

32.3. What is the function we use to input a binary data?

32.4. From where can we get a binary data set?

32.5. Compared with a text file, what are the advantages and disadvantages of using binary data?

CHAPTER 33

Excel and R

Up to today, Excel has been quite popular in most financial-modeling courses since it is used almost exclusively as the computational tool (see *Financial Modeling* by Benninga [2009], *Financial Modeling with Crystal Ball and Excel* by Charnes [2009], *Professional Financial Computing Using Excel and VBA* by Lai et al. [2008], *Financial Analysis and Modeling Using Excel and VBA* by Senqupta [2009]), among others). Since R can be the main computational tool for the next-generation financial-modeling courses, we need a bridge between them. This chapter serves that purpose. In this chapter, we discuss several ways to transfer data between Excel and R.

33.1. Installation of Several Excel-Related R Packages

In this chapter, we will use various functions included in four R packages that are associated with Excel: **WriteXLS, XLConnect, xlsx**, and **excel.link**. To install these packages, we have the following codes. Note that when we install each package, we need to use double (or single) quotation marks. However, when uploading those packages, both ways would work—with or without quotation marks.

```
> install.packages("WriteXLS")
> install.packages("xlsx")
> install.packages("excel.link")
> install.packages("XLConnect")
```

Alternatively we can click **Packages** on the menu bar then **Install Package(s)...** When we load the **excel.link**, we would receive the following message. Because of it, we should install another R package called **RDCOMClient**.

```
> library(excel.link)
Loading required package: RDCOMClient
> install.packages("RDCOMClient") # for excel.link
```

This is true when uploading the **XLConnect** package.

```
> library(XLConnect)
Loading required package: XLConnectJars
```

33.2. Manuals for Excel-Related Packages

The best way to find the manuals for these packages is to go to http://r-project.org. Choose **CRAN** on the left-hand side. After selecting a mirror address, click **Packages** on the left. From the list of the all R packages, find your specific package. Click it then choose **Manual with a PDF Extension** (reference manual).

The second way is to find the location first. After you install one package, you already would have saved the document on your local computer. Here is an example of finding the manual related to fImport. First, we try to find the location of the package.

```
> path.package('fImport', quiet = FALSE)
[1] "C:/Users/yany/Documents/R/win-library/3.1/fImport"
```

After locating the specific subdirectory, we would see the following directories on the left side. The right panel shows the files under /**doc**.

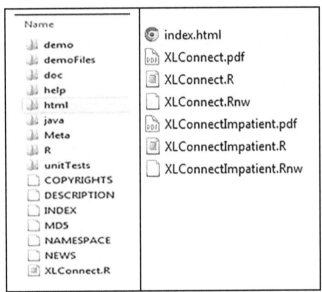

For the **XLConnect**, we can use the **vignette()** function.

```
> library(XLConnect)
> vignette("XLConnect")
```

33.3. Retrieving Data from Excel

In this section, we focus on various ways to retrieve data from Excel, such as the **read.table("clipboard")** discussed in chapter 5: "Open Data." We start from simple methods, especially the ones we know already.

33.3.1. Using read.table("clipboard")

Assume that we have the following Excel spreadsheet (in the right panel below). To input the data into R, we highlight and copy the Excel data first then issue x<-read.table("clipboard").

```
>read.table("clipboard")
> x
V1 V2
1 1 2
2 3 1
3 -1 5
```

	A	B
1	1	2
2	3	1
3	-1	5

If the Excel data set has a header (column names), we add **header=T**. Before we copy, remember that we have to highlight both header and data if we have **header=T** in our command.

```
> x<-read.table("clipboard",header=T)
> x
date ret
1 20010203 0.01
2 20010204 -0.02
3 20010205 0.05
```

	A	B
1	1	2
2	3	1
3	-1	5

This method works perfectly for a small data set. A user can just type a few observations to test it. However, for a big data set, we have to export the data set from Excel first; save the data set as, for example, a CSV (comma-separated values) file; then, from R, use the **read.table()** or **read.csv()** function to retrieve it.

33.3.2. Using the read.table() and read.csv() Functions

Assume that we have saved the above data with the variable names to a file called test.csv, which is under **c:/temp/**. The following codes can be used to retrieve the data.

```
> x<-read.csv("c:/temp/test.csv",header=T)  # Method 1
> x<-read.table("c:/temp/test.csv",header=T, sep=',')  # Method 2
```

33.3.3. Using the readWorksheetFromFile() Function

The related package is called **XLConnect**. If we have a very simple data set in Excel called test.xlsx (see the following right panel), we can issue two-line R codes to read it. Note that the value of the last input variable is 1—meaning, the first spreadsheet.

```
> library(XLConnect)
>    x<-readWorksheetFromFile("c:/test/
test.xlsx",sheet=1)
> x
date ret
1 20010203 0.01
2 20010204 -0.02
3 20010205 0.05
```

	A	B
1	date	ret
2	20010203	0.01
3	20010204	-0.02
4	20010205	0.05

If we know the name of the spreadsheet, such as **Sheet1,** it would be a good idea to specify its name in full in the codes.

```
> library(XLConnect)
> x<-readWorksheetFromFile("c:/test/test.xlsx",sheet='Sheet1')
```

We can use the following sets of commands to retrieve the included data in the **XLConnect** package.

```
>library(XLConnect)
> f<- system.file("demoFiles/mtcars.xlsx",package ="XLConnect")
>f2<-loadWorkbook(f)
> name<- getTables(f2, sheet = "mtcars_table")
> x<-readTable(f2,sheet="mtcars_table",table=name)
> head(x)
mpg cyl disp hp drat wt qsec vs am gear carb
1 21.0 6 160 110 3.90 2.620 16.46 0 1 4 4
2 21.0 6 160 110 3.90 2.875 17.02 0 1 4 4
3 22.8 4 108 93 3.85 2.320 18.61 1 1 4 1
4 21.4 6 258 110 3.08 3.215 19.44 1 0 3 1
5 18.7 8 360 175 3.15 3.440 17.02 0 0 3 2
```

It is very convenient that we can use the data sets included in the **XLConnect** package. In total, there are seven demo data sets (see a list below).

Table 33.1. List of data sets included in the **XLConnect** package

Data	Meaning
errorCell.xlsx	Contain some error message, C11=C7+C8, but C7 and C8 are strings Name of sheet: MySheet One named data set: Mydata
mtcars.xlsx	Three spreadsheets: mtcars, mtcars2, and mtcars3 One named data set: mtcars
multiregion.xls (old Excel format)	Two spreadsheets: FirstSheet and Secondsheet Three named data sets: Calendar, IQ, and Iris
multiregion.xlsx	Two spreadsheets: FirstSheet and Secondsheet Three named data sets: Calendar, IQ, and Iris
mydata.xlsx	One spreadsheet: mydata One named data set: mydata
template.xlsx	One spreadsheet: mtcars One named data set: mtcars
template2.xlsx	One spread sheet: mtcars One named data set: mtcars Several graphs

Again, to find the location of the demo files, we use the **path.package()** function.

```
> path.package('XLConnect', quiet = FALSE)
[1] "C:/Users/yany/Documents/R/win-library/3.1/XLConnect"
```

Based on the path, we can find the names of all related demo data sets under **demoFiles** (see below).

Here is a better way to find all sample Excel files under the **XLConnect** subdirectory. Note that if we use **pattern='.xlsx'** in the command, we would miss files with an extension of **.xls**.

```
> library(XLConnect)
> x<-path.package('XLConnect', quiet = FALSE)
> y<-list.files(x, recursive = T,pattern='.xls')
> length(y)
[1] 53
```

In total, we have fifty-three sample Excel programs.

```
> head(y)
[1] "demoFiles/conversion.xlsx" "demoFiles/errorCell.xlsx"
[3] "demoFiles/mtcars.xlsx"     "demoFiles/multiregion.xls"
[5] "demoFiles/multiregion.xlsx" "demoFiles/mydata.xlsx"
> tail(y)
     [1] "unitTests/resources/testWorkbookRemoveSheet.xls"
[2] "unitTests/resources/testWorkbookRemoveSheet.xlsx"
[3] "unitTests/resources/testWorkbookSetActiveSheet.xls"
[4] "unitTests/resources/testWorkbookSetActiveSheet.xlsx"
[5] "unitTests/resources/testWorkbookSheets.xls"
[6] "unitTests/resources/testWorkbookSheets.xlsx"
```

33.3.4. Using a Region Instead of the Whole Spreadsheet

Below is the general format for the **readWorksheetFromFile()** function.

```
>library(XLConnect)
> x<- readWorksheetFromFile(demoExcelFile,sheet=1,header=FALSE,
startCol=2, startRow=2,endCol=3,endRow=3)
```

33.4. Writing Data to Excel

This is opposite of retrieving data from an Excel file. The simplest way is to use **write.table('clipboard')** discussed in before. Another way is to generate a text file, such as a CSV file, which can be used by Excel for further analysis.

33.4.1. Using write.table('clipboard')

The simplest way to copy a small data set to Excel is to use the **write.table("clipboard")**. First, we generate a five-by-ten matrix (see the codes below).

```
> x<-1 :50
> y<-matrix(x,5,10)
> write.table(y,'clipboard')
```

Then we open an Excel file and right-click our mouse to paste it, as seen below (hint: just one column.)

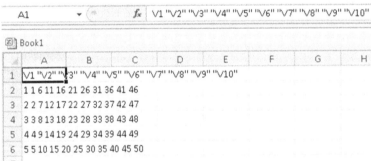

To cut one column of text into ten columns, we highlight the first column, click **Data** then **Text to Columns.** Choose **delimited** and choose **space** as our delimiter (see below).

A	B	C	D	E
1	12/31/2014	12/31/2013	12/31/2012	12/31/2011
2 Revenue	92793	98367	104507	106916
3 Other Revenue; Total	NA	NA	NA	NA
4 Total Revenue	92793	98367	104507	106916
5 Cost of Revenue; Total	46386	49683	54209	56778
6 Gross Profit	46407	48684	50298	50138
7 Selling/General/Admin. Expenses; Total	23180	23451	22934	22865

In the rest of the chapter, we discuss four R packages associated with Excel: **XLConnect**, **WriteXLS**, **xlsx**, and **excel.link**.

33.4.2. Writing a CSV File First

There are several advantages of generating a CSV file, which can be retrieved from Excel. First, it is straightforward. Second, we learn how to write a CSV file. Third, we can use any word editors such as Notepad or MS Word to open it. In the following example, we show how to retrieve the last several years' income statement for IBM and save the data as a CSV file.
The key function used is **write.csv()**.

```
> library(quantmod)
>y<-viewFin(getFin("IBM",auto.assign=FALSE),"IS","A")
>rownames(y)<-gsub(",",";",rownames(y))
>write.csv(y,file='ibm_is.csv',quote=F)
```

The package used is called **quantmod**, which stands for "quantitative financial method." **IS** is for "income statement," and **A** is for "annual." If we use Excel to open the output file, we will see something like the following image:

	A	B	C
1	ticker	year	beta
2	ibm	2010	
3	ibm	2009	
4	dell	2010	
5	dell	2009	
6	c	2008	
7	c	2007	

Here is another program.

```
>library(XML)
> x<-readHTMLTable("http://www.marketwatch.com/investing/stock/IBM/financials")
```

33.4.3. Using the write.xlsx() Function

The related package is **xlsx**. The following codes generate an x variable that contains 100 integers from 1 to 100.

```
>require(xlsx)
>x<-1:100
> write.xlsx(x,"c:/test/test.xlsx")
```

33.4.4. Using the xl.save.file() Function

The related R package is **excel.link**. The following program retrieves the historical data of IBM from Yahoo Finance and saves it as an Excel file called **ibm.xlsx**.

```
> library(excel.link)
> t1<-'http://finance.google.com/finance/historical?q=1
> t2<-paste(t1,'IBMSstartdate=Jun+02,+1970',sep='')
> x<-read.csv(paste(t2,'&enddate=Jun+16,+1,'2017&output=csv',sep=''))
> xl.save.file(x,"c:/temp/ibm.xlsx")
```

33.4.5. Using the Write.XLS() Function

The first example shows how to save a vector to an Excel file. The key program is the **WriteXLS()** function. The simplest example is shown below. The function takes two input variables: a variable representing a data set and the name of the Excel file.

```
>library(WriteXLS)
>x<-1:10
>y<-data.frame(x)
>WriteXLS("y","c:/test/test.xls")
>library(WriteXLS)
>x<-1:10
>y<-data.frame(x)
>WriteXLS("y","c:/test/test.xls")
```

Note that the first variable should be a data frame or a list. If we define x as an integer, we will see an error message.

```
>library(WriteXLS)
>x<-1:10
> WriteXLS("x","c:/test/ibm.xls")
Error in WriteXLS("x","c:/test/ibm.xls") :
One or more of the objects named in 'x' is not a data frame or does not exist
```

The second example shows how to retrieve historical price data from Yahoo Finance for IBM and save the data as an Excel file called **ibm.xls**.

```
library(WriteXLS)
t1<-'http://finance.google.com/finance/historical?q='
t2<-paste(t1,'IBM&startdate=Jun+02,+1970', sep='')
x<-read.csv(paste(t2,'&enddate=Jun+16,+','2017&output=csv',sep''))
WriteXLS(x,"c:/temp/ibm2.xls")
```

Obviously it is a good idea to add a column called ticker if we plan to have a combined data with multiple socks (tickers).

33.4.6. Using the writeNameRegion() Function

The function is included in the **XLConnect** R package. Assume that we want to generate **x** from 1 to 50 and write this variable to an Excel file. Assume further that the name of the Excel file is **aaa.xlsx**, under **c:/ttt**, with the spreadsheet name **ttt**.

```
>library(XLConnect)
>f <- loadWorkbook("c:/ttt/aaa.xlsx",create = TRUE)
>createSheet(f, name = "ttt")
>createName(f, name = "test",formula = "ttt!$C$5")
>x<-1:50
>writeNamedRegion(f, x, name = "test")
>saveWorkbook(f)
```

33.5. Using Demo Files with system.file()

To find out the specific location of those system files, we can use following two-line R codes.

```
> data<-system.file("demoFiles/multiregion.xlsx",package="XLConnect")
[1]"C:/Users/yany/Documents/R/win-library/3.1/XLConnect/demoFiles/
multiregion.xlsx"
```

To use a demo data Excel, we have to know whether we should call it by name or by spreadsheet.

```
> data<-system.file("demoFiles/multiregion.xlsx",package="XLConnect")
> x<-readNamedRegionFromFile(data, name="Iris")
> head(x)
  Sepal.Length Sepal.Width Petal.Length Petal.Width Species
1     5.1     3.5    1.4   0.2   setosa
2     4.9     3.0    1.4   0.2   setosa
3     4.7     3.2    1.3   0.2   barbarica
4     4.6     3.1    1.5   0.2   setosa
5     5.0     3.6    1.4   0.2   setosa
6     5.4     3.9    1.7   0.4   setosa
```

33.6. Getting Data from Excel with readNamedRegionFromFile()

In the following program, we use the demo Excel data set called **Calendar** from the Excel file named **multiregion.xlsx**.

```
> library(XLConnect)
> data<-system.file("demoFiles/multiregion.xlsx",package="XLConnect")
> x<-readNamedRegionFromFile(data, name="Calendar")
> x
Year Days

1 1999 365
2 2000 365
3 2001 365
4 2002 365
5 2003 365
6 2004 366
7 2005 365
```

413

In the following program, we create an Excel file call **test.xlsx**. After that, we create a spreadsheet called **myData**.

```
> out_file<- loadWorkbook("c:/temp/test.xlsx",create = TRUE)
> createSheet(out_file, name = "myData")
```

In the following program, we download the daily stock price of IBM from Yahoo Finance. Then we create an Excel file called **IBM.xlsx**. After that, we create a spreadsheet called **IBM data**. Finally we save our data to that specific spreadsheet starting from row 2 and column 2.

```
> library(XLConnect)
> x<-read.csv("http://canisius.edu/~yany/data/ibm.csv",header=T)
> out_file<- loadWorkbook("c:/temp/IBM.xlsx",create = TRUE)
> createSheet(out_file, name = "IBM data")
> writeWorksheet(out_file,x,sheet = "IBM data",startRow=2,startCol=2)
> saveWorkbook(out_file)
```

33.7. When the Data Set Is Huge

When using the **writeNamedRegionToFile()** function from the **XLConnect** package to save data to an Excel file, we might have the following error message. The source of the example is http://www.miraisolutions.com/.

```
>writeNamedRegionToFile("huge.xls",data = giant.data.frame, namedRegion =
"LargeRegion",formula = "LotsOfData!A1")
Error: OutOfMemoryError (Java): Java heap space
```

Below is the solution:

```
>options(java.parameters = "-Xmx1024m")
>library(XLConnect)
```

Exercises

33.1. What are the advantages of using R with Excel?

33.2. How do we assign a value in R then save it to Excel?

33.3. From a standard normal distribution, generate 1,000 random numbers then convert the into a 500-by-2 matrix. Save the matrix to Excel. (Hint: the related R function is **rnorm()**.)

33.4. Generate three columns with the following format. The first column is for tickers, and the second column is for year. The last column is for beta, which is based on the daily data for a specific year. Find a way to fill in the third column.

	A	B	C	D	E
1	"V1" "V2" "V3" "V4"	"V5" "V6"	"V7" "V8" "V9"	"V10"	
2	1 1 6 11	16 21 26	31 36 41	46	
3	2 2 7 12	17 22 27	32 37 42	47	
4	3 3 8 13	18 23 28	33 38 43	48	
5	4 4 9 14	19 24 29	34 39 44	49	
6	5 5 10 15	20 25 30	35 40 45	50	
7					

33.5. In R, generate 5,000 random numbers drawn from a uniform distribution. Retrieve them into Excel with different methods. Compare those methods in terms of convenience. (Hint: see chapter 10 about simulation on how to generate random numbers.)

33.6. How do we generate several ratios—such as debt-assets ratio, current ratio, quick ratio, ROE, ROA—in Excel for the last few years from Yahoo Finance? (Hint: see chapter 4: "Ratio Analysis.")

33.7. Write an R program and call it from Excel to estimate the market capitalization for a given stock at the end of the year. The format can be =market_cap("ibm",2000).

33.8. Write an R program and call it from Excel to estimate the total trading volume. The format can be =annualVol("dell", 2010).

33.9. Write an R program and call it from Excel to estimate the monthly illiquidity. The format of the program will be =illiq("ibm", 1990, 2), which means to estimate illiquidity for IBM in February 1990. The formula to estimate illiquidity (Amihud 2002) is given below:

$$ILLIQ = \frac{1}{N} \sum_{t=1}^{N} \frac{|R_t|}{DVOL_t}$$

where N is the number of trading day within one month,
R_t is the daily return, and $DVOL$ is the dollar volume.

33.10. Write an R program to estimate the liquidity measure defined by Pastor and Stambaugh (2003). The Excel format will be =ps_liq("ibm", 2010, 3), which means we estimate the liquidity measure based on Pastor and Stambaugh's (2003) methodology. For more detailed discussion, see chapter 19 ("Liquidity Measures").

33.11. In chapter 18, we discuss how to use Roll's (1984) method to estimate spread (see the following expression—where S is spread, P_t is the closing price at t, and ΔP_t is the price change at t). The following codes estimate the covariance and the spread for IBM by using its daily prices.

$$S = 2\sqrt{-cov(\Delta P_t, \Delta P_{t-1})}$$

Write an R program to test and save the result to Excel.

33.12. Repeat the above question for Corwin and Schultz's (2011) spread based on daily high and low prices.

33.13. How do we list all R programs for all installed R packages? (Hint: start from **path. package('XLConnect', quite=FALSE).**)

CHAPTER 34

Encryption

It is fun to code a simple message. The simplest way is to shift each letter in our message by a fixed letter, such as shifting to the right by one letter. Thus, *love* will become *mpwf.* To shift to the right by two letters, *apple* will become *crrng.* This is a very simple coding scheme. Below, we offer an R program to implement it. Usually we ignore blanks (i.e., delete blanks in any messages). Thus, "our company's net income this year is $234,124" will become "ourcompanysnetincomethisyearis234124." The major reason is that after we add blanks among those words, it becomes quite easy to break the codes. The following two lines illustrate how to use a coding scheme called shift scheme.

```
>source("http://canisius.edu/~yany/codeyan")
>encodeShift("I love you",1)
[1] "jmpwfzpv"
```

To post students' grades online and protect their privacies, we can code their grades. Obviously the first parameter is the grade while the second one is the key or password.

```
> encode5("eighty","great")
[1] "FZFZXZFZGYYY"
```

To decode it, we simply call the **decode()** function. The first parameter is the coded message while the second one is the key or password. We should use the same key as we code our message.

```
> decode5('FZFZXZFZGYYY','great')
[1] "eighty"
```

34.1. Blanks Are Kept

When blanks are present, it is much easier to decode a secret sentence. However, for fun, we try to keep all the blanks. In other words, we deliberately make it easier to decode. Removing blanks is trivial (see the following codes).

```
> newText<-gsub(' ', '',text)
```

34.2. R Program for the Shift Scheme

The R program we can use to shift letters of our message is given below:

```
encode_1<-function(text,shift){
  #text<-gsub(' ','',text)
  ciphertxt<-''
  for(i in 1:nchar(text)){
      for(j in 1:26){
        if(tolower(substr(text,i,i))==letters[j]){
          k<-(j+shift)%%26
          if(k==0)k=26
          ciphertxt<-paste(ciphertxt,letters[k],sep='');break
        }
      }
    }
  return(ciphertxt)
}
```

The logic of the program is that we have two loops: first one is from 1 to n, where n is the number of characters of our plain text. The second loop is from 1 to 26 (i.e., from a to z for each letter). For example, for letter c, which corresponds to **k=3**, the corresponding letter will be **letter[k+shift]**. Assume that the variable of shift is 4. Then letter c (**letter[3]**) will be replaced by letter g (**letters[3+4]**).

34.3. Simple Letter Substitution

The scheme will work this way: the twenty-six letters from a to z will be replaced by twenty-six letters in a different order. We know that for the reserved variable called **letters** (see below).

```
> letters[1]
[1] "a"
> letters[26]
[1] "z"
```

Thus, we can view the shift scheme: the numbers from 1 to 26 are replaced with those twenty-six numbers in a different order. Recall chapter 9: "Monte Carlo Simulation." We know that we can use the **runif()** function to generate uniformly distributed random numbers. The following codes generate one hundred random numbers distributed between 1 and 26. Since we need just twenty-six numbers, we choose their unique values. The first letter is 13, which corresponds to l. Thus, we use l to substitute a in our original message.

```
> unique(as.integer(runif(100,1,27)))
 [1] 13 23 20 26 3 22 12 15 25 8 2 24 4 16
[15] 14 10 1 11 18 5 7 6 21 17 19 9
```

To make sure that we indeed have twenty-six integers with the minimum and maximum of 1 and 26, we can use the **summary()** function.

```
> x<-unique(as.integer(runif(100,1,27)))
> summary(x)
  Min. 1st Qu. Median Mean 3rd Qu. Max.
  1.00 7.25 13.50 13.50 19.75 26.00
```

Whenever we run the **runif()** function, we would get a quite different set of random numbers. To fix our set of random numbers, we need to use the **set.seed()** function. Since we set the seed, we would get the same set of twenty-six numbers.

```
> set.seed(12345)
> x<-unique(as.integer(runif(100,1,27)))
> x
 [1]  19 23 20 24 12 5 9 14 26 1 4 11 13 25 17 15 6 21
[19] 18 10 7 2 22 3 16 8
> letters
 [1] "a" "b" "c" "d" "e" "f" "g" "h" "i" "j" "k" "l" "m"
[14] "n" "o" "p" "q" "r" "s" "t" "u" "v" "w" "x" "y" "z"
> letters[x]
 [1] "s" "w" "t" "x" "l" "e" "i" "n" "z" "a" "d" "k" "m"
[14] "y" "q" "o" "f" "u" "r" "j" "g" "b" "v" "c" "p" "h"
```

We have the following function called **code_sub()**.

```
code_sub<-function(message){
set.seed(12345)
x<-unique(as.integer(runif(100,1,27)))
y<-letters[x]
text<-gsub("[^a-z]",'',tolower(message)) # remove non-letter
coded_text<-''
for(i in 1:nchar(text)){
    for(j in 1:26){
      if(letters[j]==substr(text,i,i)){
        coded_text<-paste(coded_text,y[j],'')
        break
      }
    }
  }
  return(gsub(' ','',coded_text))
}
```

To use this function, just type its name with a message. From the above function, we know that all nonalphabetic letters, including blanks, will be removed.

```
> code_sub("I love you")
[1] "zkqblpqg"
```

34.4. Letter Frequency

The letter frequency is quite often used to find the substitution scheme. One of the related sources is http://www.increasebrainpower.com/code-breaking.html.

e-t-a-o-i-n-s-h-r-d-l-c-u-m-w-f-g-y-p-b-v-k-j-x-q-z

34.5. Five Letters to Represent Twenty-Six Letters

As we discussed in section 43.3, code breakers can use the frequency table to guess the letters in our coded message. If we can use a few letters to represent all twenty-six letters, then our coded message will be difficult to break since the frequency table will be less useful. Below, we show how to use five letters—*F, G, X, Y,* and *Z*—to represent all twenty-six letters. First, we can generate a table, as shown below, that includes twenty-five letters (letter *i* and *j* will share the same combination). The design of the table is such that we can use a pair of five letters to represent all twenty-five letters. For example, we use *FY* for *a* and *GG* for *s*. The R program used to generate this table is presented in appendix B.

Table 34.1. Using pairs from five letters to represent all twenty-six letters

	F	G	X	Y	Z
F	r	w	f	a	e
G	h	s	l	z	o
X	m	v	x	c	g
Y	b	u	k	y	d
Z	i	p	q	t	n

For example, the pair *FF* represents letter *r*, and *ZZ* represents letter *n*. Note that the letters *i* and *j* share the some pair. In other words, *ZF* represents both *i* and *j*.

Now, let's use an example to show how to code our message. Assume that we want to code *eighty*. According to table 43.1, the row and column for the letter *e* are the first row and last column (i.e., pair *FZ*). For the second letter *i*, we have *ZF*. Proceeding continuously this way, our final codes message will be **FZZFXZGFZYYY**. The advantage of this scheme is that code breakers will have difficulty using the frequency table to break our coded message.

34.5. Making It More Complex

Based on the above scheme, we can make it more difficult to decode. Again, we use the same original message *eighty*. In addition, our key is *great*. We have the following four steps to code our message.

Step 1. According to table 34.1, we code *eighty* into a new message. Let's call it code1:
    FZZFXZGFZYYY.

Step 2. Arrange code1 according to the length of the password. Since there are five letters, we have five columns.

Column	1	2	3	4	5
Password	G	R	E	A	T
Coded message	F	Z	Z	F	X
	Z	G	F	Z	Y
	Y	Y			

Step 3. Rearrange the columns according to the alphabetical order of the password (i.e., from GREAT to AEGRT.

In alphabetical order	A	E	G	R	T
Coded message	F	Z	F	Z	X
	Z	F	Z	G	Y
			Y	Y	

Step 4. Collecting all letters, we will have our final coded message "**FZFZXZFZGYYY**".

```
> encode("eighty","great")
[1] "FZFZXZFZGYYY"
> encode("eighty","vector")
[1] "ZZXZFFZFYYYG"

> encode("nightyfive","vector")
[1] "ZZXZFZZFYYYGZXXGFFZF"
```

34.6. Using Six Letters to Represent A to Z and 0 to 9

Obviously we can use just a pair of six letters to represent twenty-six letters plus ten digits of 0, 1, 2, to 9.

Exercises

34.1. What is the shift scheme?

34.2. How do we use the shift scheme to code our message?

34.3. Why should we remove all blanks in our message before we code it?

34.4. How do we use five letters to represent all twenty-six letters?

34.5. How do we use six letters to represent all twenty-six letters plus ten numerical numbers?

34.6. Please code the following message: "Our biding price is $10.234 m."

34.7. What is the use of key or password in our coding scheme?

34.8. Code all class's scores.

34.9. What is the use of a frequency table for breaking the codes to the use of letter in English?

34.10. Copy a few pages from the Bible located at http://patriot.net/~bmcgin/kjv12.txt then write an R program to generate a letter-frequency table (http://www.stat.pitt.edu/stoffer/tsa2/textRcode.htm).

CHAPTER 35

Reading a Zip File from R

Nowadays, it is the norm that we have to process a huge amount of data, especially finance-related data. It is a common practice that we zip/compress our data sets to save space. It is also very convenient to communicate with others by sending or e-mailing our zipped files instead of many small files. From the data library at the Federal Reserve Bank of St. Louis, we can download bond-related data (http://research.stlouisfed.org/fred2/categories/32348). After clicking **Download Data,** we chose a zip file called **CORPBNDS_csv_2.zip,** which contains one hundred small data sets plus two index files. Alternatively, you can download the file at http://canisius.edu/~yany/data/CORPBNDS_csv_2.zip. The following oneline R codes are used to view the contents, where *l* is a lowercase letter of *L*. We assume the directory contains the zip file called **c:/temp/.**

```
> system("c:/progra~1/7-Zip/7z l c:/temp/CORPBNDS_csv_2.zip")
```

A few lines are given below.

```
7-Zip 4.57 Copyright (c) 1999-2007 Igor Pavlov 2007-12-06
Listing archive: c:\tt\CORPBNDS_csv_2.zip
```

Date	Time	Attr	Size	Compressed	Name
2011-12-19	11:08:10	D....	0	0	CORPBNDS_csv_2
2011-12-19	11:08:10	.....	15635	1790	CORPBNDS_csv_2\README_TITLE_SORT.txt
2011-12-19	11:08:10	D....	0	0	CORPBNDS_csv_2\data
2011-12-19	10:33:30	.....	35451	8 009	CORPBNDS_csv_2\data\BAMLEMHGHGLCRPIUSEY.csv
2011-12-19	10:37:56	.....	58612	13632	CORPBNDS_csv_2\data\BAMLEMFSFCRPIEY.csv
2011-12-19	10:35:38	.....	35683	8357	CORPBNDS_csv_2\data\BAMLEM3RBBLCRPIUSEY.csv

35.1. Downloading a Zip Software

In this chapter, we use 7-zip, and it can be downloaded from http://www.7-zip.org/. Other similar softwares should work the same way.

35.2. Finding the Location of Our 7-Zip Software

Since we will call an executable file called 7z.exe from R, we need know its location.

```
# c: - -> programs File - -> 7Zip - - > 7z.exe
# c:\progra~1\7-Zip\7z.exe
```

35.3. How to Use 7-zip

Since many users are not sure about 7-zip related commands, the following R command offers all related features.

```
> system("c:/progra~1/7-Zip/7z")
```

The results based on the above codes are shown below. Pay attention to a and x options under **<Commands>**.

```
7-Zip 4.57 Copyright (c) 1999-2007 Igor Pavlov 2007-12-06
Usage: 7z <command> [<switches>…] <archive_name> [<file_names>…]
  [<@listfiles…>]
<Commands>
a: Add files to archive
b: Benchmark
d: Delete files from archive
e: Extract files from archive (without using directory names)
l: List contents of archive
t: Test integrity of archive
u: Update files to archive
x: eXtract files with full paths
<Switches>
-ai[r[-|0]]{@listfile|!wildcard}: Include archives
-ax[r[-|0]]{@listfile|!wildcard}: eXclude archives
-bd: Disable percentage indicator
-i[r[-|0]]{@listfile|!wildcard}: Include filenames
-m{Parameters}: set compression Method
-o{Directory}: set Output directory
-p{Password}: set Password
-r[-|0]: Recurse subdirectories
-scs{UTF-8 | WIN | DOS}: set charset for list files
-sfx[{name}]: Create SFX archive
-si[{name}]: read data from stdin
-slt: show technical information for l (List) command
-so: write data to stdout
-ssc[-]: set sensitive case mode
-ssw: compress shared files
-t{Type}: Set type of archive
-v{Size}[b|k|m|g]: Create volumes
-u[-][p#][q#][r#][x#][y#][z#][!newArchiveName]: Update options
-w[{path}]: assign Work directory. Empty
path means a temporary directory
-x[r[-|0]]]{@listfile|!wildcard}: eXclude filenames
-y: assume Yes on all queries
```

On the other hand, if 7-zip is not available, we will see the following results:

```
> system("c:/progra~1/7-Zip/7z")
Warning message:
running command 'c:/progra~1/7-Zip/7z' had status 127
```

35.4. Generating a Zip File

In the following codes, we download the daily price data for IBM from Yahoo Finance and save it to an output file called **ibm.txt**.

```
tickers<-c("ibm","dell","c","f","msft")
t<-"http://canisius.edu/~yany/data/"
dir<-'c:/temp/'
```

The first several lines of the text file called ibm.txt are given below. Then we zip it to a file called **test.zip** under another directory, **c:/temp/**.

Date Open High Low Close Volume Adj.Close
2011-12-20 185.5 187.33 184.76 187.24 4740100 187.24
2011-12-19 184.51 184.69 182.25 182.89 5039900 182.89
2011-12-16 188.01 188.01 181.91 183.57 11849400 183.57
2011-12-15 190.48 191.2 186.89 187.48 4474500 187.48
2011-12-14 189.84 190.28 188 188.72 5057700 188.72
2011-12-13 193.46 194.3 190.64 191.15 5008400 191.15
2011-12-12 193.64 193.9 191.22 192.18 3796100 192.18

To make our example a bit more complex, we need a zip file containing several files. With the following codes, we generate those small files first.

```
tickers<-c("ibm","dell","c","f","msft")
t<-"http://chart.yahoo.com/table.csv?s="
dir<-'c:/temp/'

for(i in 1:length(tickers)){
    web<-paste(t,tickers[i],seq='')
    web<-gsub(" ","",web) # remove blanks
    x<-read.csv(web,header=T)
    tt<-paste(dir,tickers[i],seq='')
    outfile<-paste(tt,'.txt',seq='')
    outfile<-gsub(" ","",outfile) # remove blanks
    write.table(x,file=outfile,quote=F,row.names=F)
}
```

The following codes will choose which files to save to a joint zip file. More specifically in the program, we exclude the stock of IBM (see the variable called **tickers**).

```
dir<-'c:/temp/'
zipfile<-"c:/temp/test" # desired zip file
tickers<-c("dell","c","f","msft") # stocks needed


for(i in 1:length(tickers)){
    t<-paste(dir,tickers[i],seq='')
    infile<-paste(t,'.txt',seq='')
    infile<-gsub(" ","",infile) # remove blanks
    z<-"c:/progra~1/7-Zip/7z a" # files to achieve
    z2<-paste(z, zipfile, seq="")
    system(paste(z2,infile,seq=""))# activate 7z.exe
}
```

35.5. Viewing the Contents of a Zip File

Since we know the location and the name of our zip file, **c:/tt/test.7z,** we can issue the following one-line R codes to view the contents of the zip file. Again, the letter *l* in the middle of the codes is a lowercase letter of *L*, which means "list."

```
> system("c:/progra~1/7-Zip/7z l c:/temp/test.7z")
```

The output is given below. It shows that we have four data files contained in this zip file.

```
7-Zip 4.57 Copyright (c) 1999-2007 Igor Pavlov 2007-12-06
Listing archive: c:\tt\test.7z
Method = LZMA
Solid = -
Blocks = 4
   Date Time Attr Size Compressed Name
------------ ---- ----- ---------- ---- ------ ------
2011-12-21 15:06:59 ....A 287567 70548 dell.txt
2011-12-21 15:07:05 ....A 416390 97351 c.txt
2011-12-21 15:07:11 ....A 416007 96485 f.txt
2011-12-21 15:07:15 ....A 319519 80457 msft.txt
------------ ---- ----- ---------- ---- ------ ------
   1439483 344841 4 files, 0 folders
```

35.6. Reading from a Zip File

In the following codes, the focus will be the number of lines skipped (which is 11 in this case) and number of input lines (which is 4 since we know that we only have 4 potential data files). Later in the chapter, we will show how to find the number of data files by using an R program instead of a manual count.

```
> x<- read.table(pipe("c:/progra~1/7-Zip/7z l c:/temp/test.7z"),skip=13,nrow=4)
> x
  V1 V2 V3 V4 V5 V6
1 2011-12-21 15:06:59 ….A 287567 70548 dell.txt
2 2011-12-21 15:07:15 ….A 319519 80457 msft.txt
3 2011-12-21 15:07:05 ….A 416390 97351 c.txt
4 2011-12-21 15:07:11 ….A 416007 96485 f.txt
```

The following R codes are more readable or relevant since we need, in the future, to modify the first line that contains the name of a zip file as our input file. From the above output, we realize that only the last volume (**V6**) is needed.

```
> infile<-"c:/temp/test.7z"
> t<-paste("c:/progra~1/7-Zip/7z l ",infile,seq="")
> x<-read.table(pipe(t),as.is =T,skip=13,nrow=4)
> x$V6
[1] "dell.txt" "c.txt" "f.txt" "ibm.txt"
```

35.7. Retrieving Data from a Zip File

Let's start from the simplest one. Since we know that **dell.txt** is one of the files included in **test7.z,** we have the following two lines. The input file for the second line is saved under the current working directory. This is the reason that we can use the relative method in the **readLines()** function.

```
>system("c:/progra~1/7-Zip/7z x c:/temp/test.7z dell.txt")
>x<-read.table("dell.txt",header=T)
> head(x)
  Date Open High Low Close Volume Adj.Close
1 2011-12-20 14.95 15.34 14.92 15.15 14839000 15.15
2 2011-12-19 15.03 15.19 14.64 14.68 14961600 14.68
3 2011-12-16 15.10 15.36 15.00 15.03 21286900 15.03
4 2011-12-15 15.21 15.29 14.95 15.05 19056900 15.05
5 2011-12-14 15.20 15.23 14.95 15.05 19268700 15.05
6 2011-12-13 15.56 15.67 15.10 15.19 20616900 15.19
```

When we unzip a specific file and it exists at our designated location (the current working directory in this case), we can overwrite it by adding y, which means "yes."

```
> system("c:/progra~1/7-Zip/7z x -y c:/temp/test.7z dell.txt")
```

After we retrieve data from **dell.txt,** we can remove it by using the function **file.remove()**, as seen below.

```
> file.remove("dell.txt")
```

Now let's combine them together.

```
infile<-"c:/temp/test.7z"
t<-paste("c:/progra~1/7-Zip/7z l",infile,seq="")
x<-read.table(pipe(t),as.is =T,skip=13,nrow=4)
n<-length(x$V6)
for(i in 1:n){
  file.name<-x$V6[i]
  t<-paste("c:/progra~1/7-Zip/7z x -y ",infile,seq="")
  t1<-paste(t,file.name,seq="")
  ticker<-gsub(".txt","",file.name)
  print(ticker)
  system(t1)
  x2<-read.table(file.name,header=T)
  #print(head(x2))
  file.remove(file.name)
  d<-data.frame(ticker,as.Date(x2[,1]),x2[,2:7])
  colnames(d)<-c("ticker","date","open","high","low","close","volume","adj.
  close")
  print(head(d,2))
}
```

If we want to combine those four files together, we can add a few lines.

```
infile<-"c:/temp/test.7z"
t<-paste("c:/progra~1/7-Zip/7z l ",infile,seq="")
x<-read.table(pipe(t),as.is =T,skip=13,nrow=4)
n<-length(x$V6)
final<-NA

for(i in 1:n){
file.name<-x$V6[i]
t<-paste("c:/progra~1/7-Zip/7z x -y ",infile,seq="")
t1<-paste(t,file.name,seq="")
ticker<-gsub(".txt","",file.name)
system(t1)
x2<-read.table(file.name,header=T)
file.remove(file.name)
d<-data.frame(ticker,as.Date(x2[,1]),x2[,2:7])
colnames(d)<-c("ticker","date","open","high","low","close","volume","adj.
close")
final<-rbind(final,d)
}
```

We can view a few lines from the final data set.

```
> dim(final)
[1] 30040 8
> head(final)
  ticker date open high low close volume adj.close
1 <NA> <NA> NA NA NA NA NA NA
2 dell 2011-12-20 14.95 15.34 14.92 15.15 14839000 15.15
3 dell 2011-12-19 15.03 15.19 14.64 14.68 14961600 14.68
4 dell 2011-12-16 15.10 15.36 15.00 15.03 21286900 15.03
5 dell 2011-12-15 15.21 15.29 14.95 15.05 19056900 15.05
6 dell 2011-12-14 15.20 15.23 14.95 15.05 19268700 15.05
> tail(final)
  ticker date open high low close volume adj.close
30035 f 1977-01-10 60.13 60.63 60.13 60.63 1334000 0.50
30036 f 1977-01-07 59.75 60.50 59.63 60.13 940400 0.49
30037 f 1977-01-06 59.00 60.38 59.00 59.75 1670300 0.49
30038 f 1977-01-05 59.50 59.88 58.50 58.75 1481600 0.48
30039 f 1977-01-04 61.25 61.25 59.00 59.50 1504600 0.49
30040 f 1977-01-03 61.00 61.63 61.00 61.25 896300 0.50
```

To remove the first row, which contains many NA, we issue the following codes:

```
> final2<-subset(final, !is.na(final[,1]))
> dim(final2)
[1] 30039 8
> head(final2)
  ticker date open high low close volume adj.close
2 dell 2011-12-20 14.95 15.34 14.92 15.15 14839000 15.15
3 dell 2011-12-19 15.03 15.19 14.64 14.68 14961600 14.68
4 dell 2011-12-16 15.10 15.36 15.00 15.03 21286900 15.03
5 dell 2011-12-15 15.21 15.29 14.95 15.05 19056900 15.05
6 dell 2011-12-14 15.20 15.23 14.95 15.05 19268700 15.05
7 dell 2011-12-13 15.56 15.67 15.10 15.19 20616900 15.19
```

35.8. Example of Corporate Bond Rate Zip File (from the Federal Reserve Bank Data Library)

Assume that we have downloaded and saved the zip data under directory **c:\tt**. Again, the Web page is http://research.stlouisfed.org/fred2/categories/32348. Click **Download Data** and choose **CORPBNDS_csv_2.zip**. After we open a DOS window and maneuver to the appropriate directory (the directory is **c:\tt** in this case), we issue the following command to generate a list of contents of the zip file.

```
# c:\progra~1\7-Zip\7z l CORPBNDS_csv_2.zip >list.txt
```

Alternatively we can issue the following R codes to retrieve just ten lines of contents.

```
x<- read.table(pipe("c:/progra~1/7-Zip/7z l c:/temp/corpbnds_
csv_2.zip"),skip=13,nrows=10)
>x

        V1      V2   V3   V4   V5                              V6
1 2015-05-22 09:21:54 ..... 50570 10850 CORPBNDS_csv_2\\data\\
BAMLEMALLCRPIASIAUSOAS.csv
2 2015-05-22 09:19:18 ..... 50796 11560 CORPBNDS_csv_2\\data\\
BAMLEMPVPRIVSLCRPIUSSYTW.csv
3 2015-05-22 09:21:38 ..... 50570 11050 CORPBNDS_csv_2\\data\\
BAMLEM1RAAA2ALCRPIUSEY.csv
4 2015-05-22 09:19:30 ..... 50741 11475 CORPBNDS_csv_2\\data\\
BAMLEMNFNFLCRPIUSSYTW.csv
5 2015-05-22 09:19:14 ..... 74057 16688 CORPBNDS_csv_2\\data\\
BAMLEMRLCRPILAEY.csv
6 2015-05-22 09:21:18 ..... 81595 18410 CORPBNDS_csv_2\\data\\
BAMLC2A0C35YSYTW.csv
7 2015-05-22 09:21:10 ..... 81595 18114 CORPBNDS_csv_2\\data\\
BAMLC0A1CAAASYTW.csv
8 2015-05-22 09:21:56 ..... 72920 16484 CORPBNDS_csv_2\\data\\
BAMLEMCBPIOAS.csv
9 2015-05-22 09:21:16 ..... 81595 15534 CORPBNDS_csv_2\\data\\
BAMLC1A0C13Y.csv
10 2015-05-22 09:19:20 ..... 50796 11551 CORPBNDS_csv_2\\data\\
BAMLEMPVPRIVSLCRPIUSEY.csv
```

By adding **as.is=T**, we avoid making strings as factors.

```
> x<- read.table(pipe("c:/progra~1/7-Zip/7z l c:/temp/
corpbnds_csv_2.zip"),as.is=T,skip=11,nrows=10)
> x$V6
[1] "CORPBNDS_csv_2\\data\\BAMLEMLLLCRPILAUSEY.
csv"    "CORPBNDS_csv_2\\data\\BAMLC1A0C13YSYTW.csv"
[3] "CORPBNDS_csv_2\\data\\BAMLEMALLCRPIASIAUSOAS.csv"
"CORPBNDS_csv_2\\data\\BAMLEMPVPRIVSLCRPIUSSYTW.csv"
[5] "CORPBNDS_csv_2\\data\\BAMLEM1RAAA2ALCRPIUSEY.
csv" "CORPBNDS_csv_2\\data\\BAMLEMNFNFLCRPIUSSYTW.csv"
[7] "CORPBNDS_csv_2\\data\\BAMLEMRLCRPILAEY.
csv"    "CORPBNDS_csv_2\\data\\BAMLC2A0C35YSYTW.csv"
[9] "CORPBNDS_csv_2\\data\\BAMLC0A1CAAASYTW.
csv"    "CORPBNDS_csv_2\\data\\BAMLEMCBPIOAS.csv"
```

If we intend to retrieve the first ten files and combine them together, we have the following codes:

```
infile<-"c:/temp/CORPBNDS_csv_2.zip"
t<-paste("c:/progra~1/7-Zip/7z l ",infile,seq="")
x<-read.table(pipe(t),as.is =T,skip=11,nrow=100)
n<-length(x$V6)
f<-NA
for(i in 1:n){
  file.name<-x$V6[i]
  t<-paste("c:/progra~1/7-Zip/7z x -y ",infile,seq="")
  t1<-paste(t,file.name,seq="")
  ticker<-gsub(".txt","",file.name)
  print(ticker)
  system(t1)
  x2<-read.csv(file.name,header=T)
  name<-gsub("[CORPBNDS_csv_2,data,.csv,\\\\]","",file.name)
  print(name)
  #print(head(x2),2)
  file.remove(file.name)
  d<-data.frame(name, as.Date(x2[,1]),x2[,2])
  colnames(d)<-c("ID","date","value")
  print(head(d,2))
  f<-rbind(f,d)
}

bond<-subset(f, !is.na(f[,1]))
```

We can save our final data set as an R data set.

```
> save(bond,file="bond.RData")
```

To double check the number of files, we can issue the following codes:

```
> x2<-unique(bond[,1])
> length(x2)
[1] 96
```

35.9. Finding the Number of Files

In the above example, we manually count the number of data files. It is one hundred in this case. It is tedious to do so, and it is prone to errors. Now, we look at **CORPBNDS_csv_2.zip** file to determine the number of data files contained in it. We know that those data files have a common extension of **.csv**. In the following codes, we use this feature. Note that when the **greap()** is **FALSE**, its length will be 0.

```
infile<-"c:/temp/CORPBNDS_csv_2.zip"
t<-paste("c:/progra~1/7-Zip/7z l ",infile,seq="")
x<-readLines(pipe(t))
n<-length(x)
out<-NA
for(i in 1:n){
    if(length(grep("\\.csv",x[i]))!=0)out<-rbind(out,x[i])
    }
out2<-subset(out,!is.na(out[,1]))
length(out2)
  [1] 100
```

35.10. Downloading a Zip File from R Using download.file()

Usually we download a zip file manually. If we can download it with our R program, it will save time. First, let's find the physical location of our intended zip file called USFD_csv_2.zip.

1. Go to http://research.stlouisfed.org/fred2/.
2. Click **Financial Indicator** under Federal Reserve Economic Data.
3. Click **Download Data**.
4. You will see a **USFD_csv_2.zip**.

Alternatively we have the following Web page to access the data set: http://research.stlouisfed.org/fred2/categories/46/downloaddata/USFD_csv_2.zip.

We can use the **download.file()** function to download the zip file (see the two-line codes below).

```
> web<-"http://research.stlouisfed.org/fred2/categories/46/
downloaddata/USFD_csv_2.zip"
> download.file(web,"c:/temp/test.zip")
```

Exercises

35.1. Why do we care about retrieving data from a zip file in R?

35.2. What is the difference between retrieving data from unzipped files and from a zip file?

35.3. It seems straightforward to retrieve data from an unzipped file or files. Why should we pay attention to the method of retrieving data from a zipped file?

35.4. Write an R program to download the daily price data of ten stocks from Yahoo Finance and save them into ten individual output files. Zip them into a file called stock10.zip.

35.5. Write an R program to retrieve data from the above zipped file and combine them together. Save it as an R data set called stock10.RData.

35.6. Go to Professor French's data library and download a zip file called F-F_Research_Data_Factors. Write an R program to retrieve the data.
His Web page is http://mba.tuck.dartmouth.edu/pages/faculty/ken.french/data_library.html.

35.7. Download the 5_industry_portfolios.zip from Professor French's data library. Write an R program to process it.

CHAPTER 36

Small-Program-Oriented Programming

Nowadays most program languages are concerned with an important concept: object-oriented programming. In this chapter, we discuss a similar concept but with a different name: small-program-oriented or smallfunction-oriented programming. There are many advantages of writing small functions and calling them repeatedly. In this chapter, we use many examples to explain this. First, let's look at the following questions. These three questions are part of the final exam in my FI/GB 725 in 2011. We will show how to answer them using many small functions.

Q1. For a given ticker, write an R program to answer following questions:
   a. What is the annualized volatility of the stock?
   b. What is its beta?
   c. What is the total trading volume last year?
   d. What is value of the total assets last year?
   e. What is its debt-equity ratio?

Q2. Assume that you have 100 shares of IBM stocks, 200 shares of DELL, and 300 shares of Walmart. Write an R program to answer the following questions:
   a. What is the value of your portfolio today?
   b. What is your possible maximum loss if your holding period is two weeks (10 trading days) with a 99% confidence level?

Q3. Write an R program to estimate n stocks correlation and answer the following question: What are the correlations among the following stocks—IBM, DELL, C, F, MSFT, and WMT?

36.1. A Small Program (Function) Is Easy to Write

Since we have to use the data downloaded from Yahoo Finance several times, it is a good idea to write a function with just one input variable: ticker. Since there are only five lines, it is quite easy for us to write such a simple program.

```
yahoo_daily<-function(ticker){
    x<-'http://canisius.edu/~yany/data/$S'
    y<-sub('$S',ticker,x,fixed=T)
    z<-paste(y,'Daily.csv',sep='')
    return(read.csv(z,header=T))
}
```

36.2. A Small Program Is Easy to Modify

Since we need to use daily returns, we can generate another program to estimate daily returns. Because we have to merge individual stock returns with market returns, we have to give them different names such as **ret** and **mkt**.

```
ret_f<-function(ticker, name){
# e.g., x<-ret_f('ibm','ret')
 t<-yahoo_daily(ticker)
 n<-nrow(t)
 ret<-data.frame(as.
Date(t[1:(n-1),1]),(t[1:(n-1),7]-t[2:n,7])/t[2:n,7])
 colnames(ret)<-c('date',name);
 return(ret)
}
```

Here is an example of merging IBM's daily returns with S&P 500's.

```
>x<-ret_f('ibm','ret')
>y<-ret_f("^GSPC","mkt")
> final<-merge(x,y)> head(final)
  date ret mkt
1 1962-01-03 0.01167315 0.0023957159
2 1962-01-04 -0.01153846 -0.0068887952
3 1962-01-05 -0.01945525 -0.0138731597
4 1962-01-08 -0.01984127 -0.0077519380
5 1962-01-09 0.01214575 0.0004340278
6 1962-01-10 0.00400000 -0.0027476500
```

36.3. A Small Program Is Easy to Understand

Since the following program has only four lines, it is quite easy to understand. In the program, we load the package called **quantmod** since we need to get a financial statement.

```
get_statement<-function(ticker,type,freq){
  library(quantmod,quietly=TRUE)
  return(viewFin(getFin(ticker,auto.assign=FALSE),type,freq))
}
```

We add certain comments to make the program clearer.

```
get_statement<-function(ticker,type,freq){
" type : 'IS', 'BS' or 'CF'
  freq : 'A' or 'Q'
  e.g.,x<-get_statement('DELL', 'IS', 'A')
  " library(quantmod,quietly=TRUE)
  return(viewFin(getFin(ticker,auto.assign=FALSE),type,freq))
}
```

36.4. Small Programs Save Time Since We Can Reuse Them Many times

In our three exercises, we call Yahoo Finance many times. Thus, it is a good idea to write a function to be used many times in the future.

36.5. It Is Easy to Share a Small Program

When we share a program, one important issue is whether the programmers who receive it can understand. If she/he can understand those programs easily, they would have more confidence to use them in their works.

36.6. It Is Easy to Maintain a Small Program

Since there are only a few lines, it is much easier to update or maintain those small programs. The following codes are used to estimate debt-equity ratio. It is easy to write other ratios by using the same structure.

```
debt_equity_ratio<-function(ticker){
  x<-get_statement(ticker,'bs','a')
  debt<-x[grep('Total Debt',rownames(x)),]
  equity<-x[grep('Total Equity',rownames(x)),]
  return(round(debt/equity,digits=4))
}
```

36.7. Making Our Main Program Easy to Understand

In the following main program, we call several small functions (programs). Thus, the structure of our main program is very clear.

```
Q1<-function(ticker){
 # a) annualized volatility
x<-ret_f("ibm","ret")
 vol<-round(sd(x[1:252*3,2])*sqrt(252),digits=4)
show(paste('Annualized vol for ',ticker,'=',vol))
 # b) get beta
y<-ret_f("^GSPC","mkt")
 d<-merge(x,y)
 d2<-d[1:252*3,]
 beta<-round(coef(lm(d2$ret~d2$mkt))[2],digits=4)
show(paste('Beta for ',ticker,'=',beta))
 # c) one year trading volume
 x<-yahoo_daily(ticker)
 volume<-sum(x[1:252,6])
 show(paste('Volume for ',ticker,'=',volume))
 # d) What is value of the total assets last year?
 x<-get_statement("ibm","bs","a")
 y<-x[grep('Total Assets',rownames(x)),]
```

```
show(paste('Total assets for ',ticker,'=',y[1]))
# e) What is the debt-equity ratio?
x<-debt_equity_ratio(ticker)
show(paste('Debt/equtity for ',ticker, '=',x[1]))
}
```

Exercises

35.1. What are the advantages of writing small programs?

35.2. What might be the disadvantages of writing small programs?

35.3. Write a small program to estimate debt-assets ratio.

35.4. Write a small program to download daily price and estimate daily return for a given pair of beginning date and ending date.

35.5. Write a small function to download monthly data from Yahoo Finance.

35.6. Extend the above function of a given time period. The input variables could be ticker, begdate, and enddate.

35.7. Extend Q1 (question 1) in the chapter to include extra three ratios: quick ratio, acid ratio, and debtto-assets ratio.

CHAPTER 37

Automation Using R

Updating our data sets automatically would save us tons of time. For example, in the previous chapters, we have shown that we can download Fama-French monthly factors to run a three-factor model—market, SMB, and HML—or a four-factor model, those three factors plus a momentum factor. Researchers can download those factors from Professor French's data library. Since Professor French periodically updates such a data set, how do we write an R program to update our own data sets? Another example is related to teaching. When I was teaching options and futures, I generated a link and gave it to my students.

37.1. Getting the Time Stamp of an Existing File

Let us look at a simple program to retrieve the file information, such as when the file was generated, when it was modified, and when it was used.

```
> file.info("c:/t.txt")
  size isdir mode mtime ctime atime exe
c:/t.txt 1781 FALSE 666 2015-01-21 09:21:51 2014-09-26 07:38:42 2014-
10-08 12:57:44 no
```

The **mtime** in the above code is for "modified time," **ctime** is the time the file was created, and **atime** is the time the file was last executed. To find more information about this function, we could use the **help()** function (see below).

```
>help(file.info)
```

Later in the chapter, we will show how to use this function in more detail.

37.2 Checking Your Schedule Whenever R Is Launched

In this section, I show how to write an R program to search a schedule and report the next n-day's tasks including today.

Step 1. Generate a text file. A sample input file is shown below. Assume this text file is saved under **c:\temp**.

```
#schedule.txt
Date;task
08/25/2014;chapter 1,task A
09/30/2014;(Tuesday) prepare Mid-term for FIN508
10/1/2014; Mid-term for MBA students
10/2/2014; Shopping
10/3/2014; teach FIN311 and FIN508
```

Step 2. The program is shown below. Assume that the program is saved under **c:/temp** as well.

```
schedule<-function(infile='c:/
temp/schedule.txt'){
    library(utils)
    today<-Sys.Date()
  x<-read.table(infile,sk
ip=1,header=T,sep=';')
  d<-data.frame(as.
Date(x[,1],"%m/%d/%Y"),x[,2])
  colnames(d)<-c("date","task")
  diff<-d[,1]-today
  d2<-subset(d,diff>=0 & diff<3)
  print(d2)
}
```

Running the program on September 30, 2014 will lead to the following output:

```
> source("c:/temp/schedule.R")
> schedule()
  date task
2 2014-09-30 (Tuesday) prepare
Mid-term for FIN508
3 2014-10-01 Mid-term for MBA students
4 2014-10-02 Shopping
```

Now, we have to make it so that it automatically checks our schedule whenever we launch R.

Step 3. Find out R's starting directory by using the **getwd()** function.

```
> getwd()
[1] "C:/Users/
yany/Documents"
```

Step 4. Generate (or modify) a file called .Rprofile (there is a dot before Rprofile). First, find your starting directory (subdirectory) by issuing the following R command after launching R.

```
> getwd()
[1] "C:/Users/
yany/Documents"
```

Go to the above starting subdirectory, find the .Rprofile, and add the following R codes:

```
.First <- function(){
    source("c:/
temp/schedule.R")
    schedule()
}
```

Quitting R and relaunching R, you will see the result. Actually, we can make our input files without including year, such as 1/22 instead of 1/22/2015. The input file is shown below.

#schedule.txt keep those first two lines
date;task
1/22; Teaching FIN414,FIN480,FIN841
1/27; Teaching FIN414,FIN480,FIN841
1/29; Teaching FIN414,FIN480,FIN841
2/3; Teaching FIN414,FIN480,FIN841
2/5; Teaching FIN414,FIN480,FIN841
2/10; Teaching FIN414,FIN480,FIN841

The following program is called **schedule.R** with a default input of **schedule.txt**, which is located under **c:/temp**.

```
schedule<-function(infile="c:/
temp/schedule.txt"){
 library(utils)
 today<-Sys.Date()
 x<-read.table(infile,skip=1,header=T,sep=';')
 d<-data.frame(as.Date(x[,1],"%m/%d"),x[,2])
 colnames(d)<-c("date","task")
 diff<-d[,1]-today
 d2<-subset(d,diff>=0 & diff<=2)
 if(nrow(d2)==0){
   cat(" No tasks for the next 2 days\n")
 }else{
   tt<-paste(format(d2[,1],"%m"),f
ormat(d2[,1],"%d"), sep='/')
   ttt<-paste(tt, "(",weekda
ys(d2[,1]),")",sep='')
   d3<-data.frame(ttt,d2[,2])
   colnames(d3)<-c("Date","Tasks")
   print(d3)
 }
}
```

37.3. Automatically Updating a Link

Similarly we might be interested in updating something automatically.

```
x <- file.info("c:/temp/schedule.txt")
y<-as.character(as.matrix((x[4])))
dateModified<-as.
Date(substring(y,1,10),"%Y-%m-%d")
today<-Sys.Date()
if(today==dateModified){
  cat("do nothing \n")
}else{
  cat("Please update\n")
}
```

Exercises

37.1. Write an R program to update a schedule every Monday.

37.2. Write an R program to check the schedule whenever R is launched.

37.3. How do we check the date a file was generated or modified in order to update the contents of that existing file?

REFERENCES

Altman, Edward I. 1968. "Financial Ratios, Discriminant Analysis, and the Prediction of Corporate Bankruptcy." *Journal of Finance*: 189–209.

Amihud, Yakov. 2002. "Illiquidity and Stock Returns: Cross-Section and Time-Series Effects." *Journal of Financial Markets* 5: 31–56.

Boyle, Phelim. 1977. "Options: A Monte Carlo Approach." *Journal of Financial Economics* 4: 323–338.

Carhart, Mark M. 1997. "On Persistence in Mutual Fund Performance." *Journal of Finance* 52 (1): 57–82.

Chung, Kee H. and Hao Zhang. 2010. "A Simple Approximation of Intraday Spreads Using Daily Data." Working paper presented at the CRSP Forum 2010, State University at Buffalo School of Management.

Corwin, Shane A. and Paul Schultz. 2011. "A Simple Way to Estimate Bid-Ask Spreads from Daily High and Low Prices." *Journal of Finance*, forthcoming.

Dimson, Elroy. 1979. "Risk Measurement When Shares Are Subjected to Infrequent Trading." *Journal of Financial Economics* 7 (2): 197–226.

Eidleman, Gregory J.. 1995. "Z Scores—A Guide to Failure Prediction." *CPA Journal*. http://www.cpajournal.com/old/16641866.htm

Easley, David, Soeren Hvidkjaer, and Maureen O'Hara. 2002. "Is Information Risk a Determinant of Asset Returns?" *Journal of Finance* 47: 2185–2221.

———. 2010. "Factoring Information into Returns." *Journal of Financial and Quantitative Analysis* 45: 293–309.

Eddelbuettel, Dirk. 2015. "CRAN Task View: Empirical Finance." Last modified March 29. http://cran.r-project.org/web/views/Finance.html.

Ellis, Katrina, Roni Michaely, and Maureen O'Hara. 2000. "The Accuracy of Trade Classification Rules: Evidence from Nasdaq." Journal of Financial and Quantitative Analysis 35: 529–551.

Encyclopedia of Credit. n.d. "The Altman Z Score and Other Scoring Models." http://www.encyclopediaofcredit.com/Altman-Z-Score

Emerson, John W., and Michael J. Kane, 2012, Towards Terrabytes of TAQ, R in Finance conference, http://www.rinfinance.com/agenda/2012/talk/Emerson+Kane.pdf

Fama, Eugene and Kenneth R. French. 1992. "The Cross-Section of Expected Stock Returns." *Journal of Finance* 47: 427–465.

———. 1993. "Common Risk Factors in the Returns on Stocks and Bonds." *Journal of Financial Economics* 33: 3–56.

———.2003. "The C a.m. Theory and Evidence." Working paper, University of Chicago.

———. 2005. "The Anatomy of Value and Growth Stock Returns." Working paper, University of Chicago.

———. 2006. "Dissecting Anomalies." CRSP Working Paper, University of Chicago. http://papers.ssrn.com/sol3/papers.cfm?abstract_id=911960

———. 2015. "A Five-Factor Asset Pricing Model." *Journal of Financial Economics* 116: 1–22.

Gordy, Michael. "CreditRisk+ Toolbox (MATLAB)." Last modified July 07, 2003. http://mgordy.tripod.com/research.html#software.

Hasbrouck, Joel. 2005. "Inferring Trading Costs from Daily Data: US Equities from 1962 to 2001." Working paper, New York University.

Hertz, David B. 1964. "Risk Analysis in Capital Investment." *Harvard Business Review* (January February).

Hyndman, Rob J. and Achim Zeileis. 2015. "CRAN Task View: Time Series Analysis." Last modified March 30. http://cran.r-project.org/web/views/TimeSeries.html.

Jegadeesh, N. and S. Titman. 1993. "Returns to Buying Winners and Selling Losers: Implications for Stock Market Efficiency." *Journal of Finance* 48: 65–91.

Lee, Charles M. C. and Mark J. Ready. 1991. "Inferring Trade Direction from Intraday Data." *Journal of Finance* 46, 733–746.

Liu, Weimin. 2006. "A Liquidity-Augmented Capital Asset Pricing Model." *Journal of Financial Economics* 82 (3): 631–671.

Madhavan, Ananth, Kewei Ming, Vesna Straser, and Yingchuan Wang. 2002. "How Effective Are Effective Spreads? An Evaluation of Trade Side Classification Algorithms." ITG paper, New York. http://www.itginc.org/news_events/papers/Effective_Spread_Paper.pdf.

Maechler, Martin, CRAN Task View: Robust Statistical Methods, http://cran.r-project.org/web/views/Robust.html

Markowitz, Harry M., Portfolio Selection, second edition, Blackwell (1991).

Merton, R. C., 1974, On the Pricing of Corporate Debt: The Rate Structure of Interest Rates, *Journal of Finance* 29, 2, 449-470

Moody's default Case studies, the related web link is given below http://www.moodyskmv.com/research/default_caseStudies.html

Pastor, L. and R. Stambaugh, 2003, Liquidity risk and expected stock returns. *Journal of Political Economy* 111, 642-685.[3]

Roll, Richard, 1984, A simple implicit measure of the effective bid-ask spread in an efficient market, *Journal of Finance* 39, 1127-1139.

Scholes, Myron and Joseph Williams, 1977, Estimating Betas from Nonsynchronous Data, *Journal of Financial Economics*, Vol 5, 1977 309-327.

Sharpe, William F., 1964 , Capital Asset Prices–A Theory of Market Equilibrium Under Conditions of Risk, *Journal of Finance* 19. 3, 425–442.

TAQ manual, www.morningstarcommodity.com/sites/default/files/taq_db.pdf

Theussl, Stefan, CRAN Task View: Optimization and Mathematical Programming, http://cran.r-project.org/web/views/Optimization.html

---

3   http://ideas.repec.org/p/nbr/nberwo/8462.html and http://papers.ssrn.com/sol3/papers.

cfm?abstract_id=331840

Wuertz, D., Chalabi, Y., ChenW., Ellis A. (2009); Portfolio Optimization with R/Rmetrics,

Yan, Yuxing, 2011, On the consistence between Fama-French daily and monthly factors, working paper, Loyola University Maryland.

Yan, Yuxing, 2012, An internet connected financial calculator, *Journal of Accounting and Finance* 12(5), 59-70.

R Development Core Team, 2010 (Version 2.12.1), R Language Definition http://www.r-project.org.

Venables, W., N. and D. M. Smith, 2010 (version 2.12.1 12/16/2010), Introduction to R, Notes on R: A programming environment on Data Analysis And Graphics, http://www.r-project.org

Vergote, O. (2005). How to match trades and quotes for NYSE stocks? K.U.Leuven working paper. http://topics.nytimes.com/topics/reference/timestopics/subjects/h/high_frequency_algorithmic_trading/index.html

Zeileis, Achim, CRAN Task View: Computational Econometrics, http://cran.r-project.org/web/views/Econometrics.html

INDEX

C

L

M

P

Risk-free yield 191
rm() function 50
rm(list=ls()) 50
rnorm() function 108
ROC() function 261
rolling beta 114
Roll's model to estimate spread 213
round() function 102
runif() function 119, 140

S

S&P500 161
save() function 97, 102
saving, to binary file 365
scalar 57, 287
scan() function 275
sd() function 33, 53
search() function 270, 310, 363
Securities and Exchange Commission, see SEC
SEC 73, 101
seed 108, 383
seller-initiated 238, 217
seq() function 108, 119, 167, 179
sequential access 229
shaded area 349
Shapiro-Wilk normality test 154
Shaprio.test() function 139
Sharpe Ratio 91, 101
Sharpe.Ratio() function 265
Shift scheme 382
SigmaA 200
SigmaE 200
Sign issue 181
sign() function 224
simulation 144
skewness 183, 160
skewness() function 183
skip= 121, 100
Small minus Big, SMB
SMB (Small Minus Big) 120